THE AMERICAN MUSICAL

AND THE FORMATION OF NATIONAL IDENTITY

Contrasting Formations of National Identity

Raymond Knapp

THE AMERICAN MUSICAL

AND THE FORMATION OF NATIONAL IDENTITY

PRINCETON UNIVERSITY PRESS · PRINCETON AND OXFORD

Library of Congress Cataloging-in-Publication Data

Knapp, Raymond.
The American musical and the formation of national identity /
Raymond Knapp.
    p. cm.
Includes bibliographical references and index.
ISBN 0-691-11864-7 (alk. paper)
1. Musicals—United States—History and criticism.   2. National
characteristics, American.   I. Title.

ML1711.K6 2004
782.1'4'0973—dc22   2004041469

British Library Cataloging-in-Publication Data is available

This book has been composed in Sabon Typeface
Printed on acid-free paper. ∞
pup.princeton.edu
Printed in the United States of America

10 9 8 7 6 5 4 3 2 1

To my children

RACHEL, DASHIELL, AND GENEVIEVE

CONTENTS

FIGURES

EXPLANATORY NOTE ABOUT AUDIO EXAMPLES

AUDIO EXAMPLES for this book are available online at http://epub.library.ucla.edu/knapp/americanmusical/. Each example is keyed to its appropriate place in the text, and numbered sequentially within each chapter, using the following marginal notation (this particular indication is for the second audio example for chapter ten):

♫ **10.2**

To hear an example, simply click on the appropriate icon on the website. You must have RealPlayer installed on your computer; a link on the main website will direct you to a source for this program if it is not already installed.

In some cases, you will simply hear the example. In other cases where it might be useful, other visual matter may appear, such as musical notation detailing all or part of the example, or perhaps a picture. These may not appear if the appropriate plug-in is not installed. A link on the main website will direct you to a source for the missing plug-in to allow you to view these images.

PREFACE

THIS BOOK grew out of my experiences planning and teaching a course on the American musical at UCLA. But I always envisaged something more than just a college textbook. From the beginning, I have hoped to reach three somewhat distinct readerships: students (as a textbook), lovers of musicals more generally, and academics.

In conceiving this book as a textbook, I have had in mind the diversity of students who have taken my course, who have varied widely in terms of both their cultural and musical backgrounds. Many of my students have been "insiders," drifting in from John Hall's venerated Musical Theater Workshop in the Music Department, or from the fledgling Ray Bolger Program in the Theater Department; many others were relative neophytes. My students' musical interests and tastes, too, have varied widely, with some more at home in classical traditions and others partaking of a wide spectrum of popular alternatives. Many already had a strong background in American history and culture, but others were relatively new to America and its peculiarities. Some had substantial musical training, but most did not. Among those who were already in love with musicals, tastes differed widely, so that musicals beloved by some were actively detested by others, and vice versa. Given this variety among my own students, I have tried hard to meet a dual challenge: to explain things from the ground up, while at the same time teaching something new to those who are already expert in at least some aspect of the subject.

But I have also had a much wider constituency in mind for this book: those myriads who love musicals, but have been frustrated by the books on the subject currently on offer. For this wider readership, in particular, I have made an indispensable dimension of the classroom readily accessible, by collecting a very large number of brief illustrative audio examples and making them available on line, accessible through a computer web browser and keyed to marginal notations in the book. These examples are most often the very ones that I use in my classroom, but with many augmentations. (For more information, see "Explanatory Note about Audio Examples.")

There are, as it happens, many frustrating alternatives for those who might want to read books about musicals. There are a handful of encyclopedic histories, quite useful but only occasionally engaging, and never what one would want to read straight through. Perhaps even more frustrating are the surveys, which necessarily pass over important musicals or developments with only the briefest comment. Another alternative is the coffee-table book; some of these are spellbindingly gorgeous, but encourage vapid indulgence in those who (like me) have trouble forcing themselves past the pictures to actually read the accompanying text. Several quite readable memoirs are available, written by practitioners whose work we may love but whose perspectives often turn out to be either surprisingly narrow or disturbingly vitriolic. Close cousins to these, and exhibiting similar liabilities, are the fan-based tomes that have tended to surround particular figures, as part of either the glitzy haze of celebrity or the gritty fog of cultdom. And, overlapping with the latter, there are more than a few studies of particular aspects or dimensions of musicals that, however perceptive and erudite, seldom treat the overall enterprise of American musicals particularly well or with the respect it deserves.

The present book falls into none of those categories, but partakes selectively of many of them, and is, I hope, well informed by all. Thus, while I have tried to comprehend the full history of the musical, I have steered very wide of attempting to be encyclopedic. I have included some pictures, but these are meant to enhance the text, not justify it. While taking a broad view, I have kept my focus on details of plotting, action, and music; or, to reverse this emphasis, I have engaged intimately with particular songs and shows so as to illuminate the broader strokes of the historical narratives I delineate.

Even though my manner of engaging with the music in these shows is in the main nontechnical, I have also had in mind, as an important readership for this book, my colleagues in musicology. The book's very lack of musico-technical detail will, I hope, allow me also to address, as a musicologist, my colleagues in other disciplines, whether in English, theater, history, or the wide range of cultural studies that my work touches on. Unabashedly, my model here is my dear colleague (and former teacher) Susan McClary, who has been particularly adept at explaining to a wide spectrum of interested parties just how music works its many wondrous effects, whether for nonmusicians, who know *that* it works such wonders but have often been bewildered by musicologists' attempts to explain *how*; for music students, who sometimes need to be reminded that music has a wondrous side; or for other musicologists, whose technical apparatus has pulled their attention for too long away from what actually matters about music for most people.

What has driven me to try to imitate Susan's achievement in the present instance is twofold. First, if I found, to my disappointment, that there were few books genuinely useful to me as I began to plan the course from which this book grew, then perhaps—or so I have thought—the most effective way to remedy that situation might be to write one such book myself, and to hope that others might follow my example. Second, I fervently believe that the repertory I discuss here is an extremely valuable musical heritage, of tremendous import for American culture more generally. But it has not been well understood. In particular, its neglect by musicologists seems due not only to a long-standing aversion among academics (and especially musicologists) for the genuinely popular as a subject warranting serious discourse, but also to the failure of so many who approach this repertory to engage meaningfully with what is actually valuable about it, as a thing unto itself. American musicals do not lack advocates, but they do lack effective advocacy within the academy, that is, advocacy that will connect meaningfully to how and why musicals have mattered to people, and to American culture generally.

I have often been asked what this project has to do with my other work, which has centered on such figures as Brahms, Haydn, Beethoven, Mahler, Wagner, and Tchaikovsky. While I might hope some day to be asked what these others have to do with my work on the American musical, it seems for now to be a fair question, which I can answer both broadly and personally. In broad terms, I am most interested in music that has mattered to a lot of people over a long period of time, and I have been interested in probing how and why it has mattered. All of the repertories in question—including the American musical—have mattered tremendously to people; they have not only served both foundationally within their home cultural arenas, but have also had a significant impact within other cultures. On a more personal level, I am interested in how music helps people to form a sense of who they are, whether as individuals or in relation to others. The repertories I have worked with most often—symphonies, concertos, musical theater—have all involved large-scale, very public works in which one is nevertheless acutely aware of a variety of individualities, be they the performers, the composer, the audience, the subject matter (implicit or explicit), or articulated viewpoints. Within these repertories, musical and personal identities are constantly being negotiated and renegotiated (a process that involves all concerned, including performers and audience). What has made these repertories particularly rewarding to study has been the fact that none of these negotiations seems either fully conscious or entirely unconscious, and that all of the musical works themselves—including especially American musicals—reveal clear traces of enormous skill and painstaking craft applied to the tasks of managing these negotiations, and of shaping experiences that are both very public and deeply personal.

Acknowledgments

Assigning blame for this book is a fairly complicated matter. For the book itself, of course, I am ultimately to blame, but there were lots of instigators. Perhaps the biggest share of blame, though, should fall to my colleague Mitchell Morris. It was Mitchell who helped me plan the course this book is based on, then left me on my own to teach it when his own schedule was too full. It was Mitchell who fielded my complaints about there not being a usable textbook for the course with a cheerful, "Well, I guess you'll just have to write one yourself, won't you?"—so often that I began to think he might be serious. And it was Mitchell who assured me he would write it with me, and even went around to publishers with me to test the waters, but in the end left me to write it myself while he wrote his own (quite glorious) book on the 1970s. It was Mitchell who made me feel like a school kid who suddenly realizes he's been set up to fight the school bully on his own.

It wasn't just Mitchell, of course. There was that sudden spark of interest I saw in people's eyes when I told them what I was working on—a spark somehow lacking when I said I was working on Haydn, or Mahler, or Beethoven. There was the realization that some of that spark was a reflection of my own enthusiasm for the subject. There were my children, to whom this book is dedicated, however tired they might be of my launching into a patch of "Ya Got Trouble" from *The Music Man* with my friend Jon Hofferman, or randomly dropping quotations from the show into conversation (no easy task when your favorite quotation is "I'm expecting a telegram from Rudy Friml. This could be it.") They were always my best copyeditors and cheerleaders, coming to class when I taught the course one summer, keeping me from getting things too embarrassingly wrong (there and in print), and pushing me to include their favorite bits and performers. There were the excellent questions (and even sometimes excellent answers) from a very bright contingent of UCLA undergraduates. There were my many conversations and collaborations with an amazingly knowledgeable and insightful group of graduate students in musicology: Gordon Haramaki, whose presentation on *Meet Me in St. Louis* even as an undergraduate helped open my eyes to the possibilities; my first teaching associates for the course, Francesca Draughon, who with me was making the improbable leap from Mahler, and Olivia Mather, taking a similarly strange leap into the world of Sholom Aleichem; Yara Sellin, who had already found *H.M.S. Pinafore* to be an eminently suitable object of study in my seminar on nationalism; Jonathan Greenberg, caught like me between two musical worlds; my most recent co-conspirators Eva Sobelevski and Griffin Woodworth, whose very different backgrounds managed to converge beautifully; and Erica Scheinberg, thoughtfully interacting throughout.

There has also been the amazing atmosphere in the department I have been blessed to be part of, whose colleagues have ranged over the years I've been working on this book from Mitchell Morris to Robert Walser, a pioneer in the burgeoning field of popular-music studies who doesn't

think he likes musicals as much as jazz and heavy metal, but has only himself to blame that it's come to this (Rob, you did more damage than you
knew when you insisted we all had to pay attention to Kenny G . . .). To
Robert Fink, who had the necessary enthusiasm and prescient courage to
publish something intelligent on Gilbert and Sullivan back in the dark
ages. To Elisabeth LeGuin, whose engagement with issues of embodied
musical performance has seeped into every corner of my own thoughts on
music. To the late Philip Brett, whose sense of the human in music touched
us all so deeply. To Susan McClary, without whom we wouldn't all be here
doing the things we do (and who actually knows all these tunes and can
sing them back at me!).

More tangible help has come from a variety of places and people. Most
important has been the enthusiastic and detailed advice from Rose Rosengard Subotnik, who helped me tremendously in giving this book its final
shape and in cleaning up its details. Mitchell Morris has given me essential feedback at many stages in the project, and has been the guiding spirit
behind much of it in any case. Early on, he and I were able, through the
generosity of the Office of Instructional Development at UCLA, headed
by Larry Loeher, to acquire a rich trove of videos to support our development of the course. The Academic Senate Council on Research at
UCLA has been a valuable source of research funds for this book, and the
Lloyd Hibberd Publication Endowment Fund of the American Musicological Society has supported the inclusion of this book's illustrations
through a generous subvention. The Music Library and Special Collections at UCLA have been endlessly supportive, and I thank Gordon Theil,
Stephen Davison, David Gilbert, Bridget Risemberg, and Timothy Edwards. The Academy of Motion Picture Arts and Sciences provided effi-
cient help in tracking down many of the book's pictures. Tara Browner,
Jonathan Greenberg, Gordon Haramaki, Jon Hofferman, Mark Martin,
Glenn Pillsbury, Holley Replogle, Dan Sallitt, Erica Scheinberg, Cecilia
Sun, Anneliese Veraldiev, and Griffin Woodworth have all contributed in
various concrete ways. My daughters Rachel and Genevieve have between
them read all or most of the book, and saved me from myself on more
than one occasion, and it was Jenny who first conceived the theme of the
frontispiece (even if she had the ulterior motive of finding a place in the
book for Terrence Mann). Fred Appel at Princeton University Press has
been tremendously supportive and enthusiastic, and above all useful, so
that the book owes a lot to his intelligent guidance. Others at the Press
who have been especially helpful are Mark Bellis, Rena Gross, Dimitri
Karetnikov, and Linda Truilo. And special thanks go to Jon Hofferman
for his tireless work on a preliminary version of the frontispiece.

The roots for this book run much deeper than this list would indicate,
however. My interest in musicals has been fostered for a very long time,

initially by seeing my older siblings in high school productions: Robert in *Little Mary Sunshine* and as Nanki Poo, Ruth (whose enthusiasm for *The Music Man* brought the cast recording into our home at what was a much too impressionable age for me) in *The Mikado* and *Camelot,* and David in *Kiss Me, Kate.* By the time I made it to high school, the Sherwood clan—for whom I am eternally grateful, since they were the guiding spirits behind the tradition for doing high school musicals in Grand Forks, the "town that knew me when"—was in transition, as Dwight passed the mantle to his son Ken (who has since passed it to his own son Brad). It was thus with Ken Sherwood (along with Ken Larson and Doug Fosse) that I finally got to work when—after years of slaving in the pit, the curse of being a violinist—I actually got a part in a show, as the "Knight of the Mirrors" in an only slightly bowdlerized *Man of La Mancha.* Thereafter, in college and for a few subsequent years, I was consigned again to the pit (except for a brief stint as stage manager), where I frequently played under the baton of Gerald Moshell (a delightful presence) in productions of Gilbert and Sullivan. In later years, for better or worse, I have drifted irretrievably outward into the audience.

So, there's much blame to go around, and surely more than I've thought to include here. I am profoundly grateful to everyone mentioned here, and to those I have forgotten to mention, but to no one more than to my wife, Ahuva Braverman, who has had to endure so much.

* * *

Portions of this book were published in the following articles, and are used by permission: "History, *The Sound of Music,* and Us, *American music* 22(2004):133–44; and *Assassins, Oklahoma!,* and the 'Shifting Fringe of Dark around the Campfire,'" *Cambridge Opera Journal* 16(2004):77–101.

About the Frontispiece

The collage presents a quartet of American quartets:

1. the four American presidents carved into Mt. Rushmore in South Dakota: George Washington, Thomas Jefferson, Theodore Roosevelt, and Abraham Lincoln (background);

2. the recently deputized school board from the 1962 film version of *The Music Man* (the "Buffalo Bills": Al Shea, Vern Reed, Wayne Ward, and Bill Spangenberg, in the top "snapshot");

3. the quartet of successful and would-be assassins who sing "The Gun Song" from the original production of *Assassins:* Sara Jane Moore, Charles Guiteau, John Wilkes Booth, and Leon Czolgosz (Debra Monk,

Jonathan Hadary, Victor Garber, and Terrence Mann, in the middle "snapshot"); and

4. the performers of "Can't Help Lovin' Dat Man" from the 1936 film version of *Show Boat:* Joe, Magnolia, Queenie, and Julie (Paul Robeson, Irene Dunne, Hattie McDaniel, and Helen Morgan, in the bottom "snapshot").

(Movie stills courtesy of the Academy of Motion Picture Arts and Sciences. *Assassins* photograph © Martha Swope; used by permission. Collage design by Jonathan Hofferman.)

Part One.....................

INTRODUCTIONS

Contexts and Strategies

THE AMERICAN MUSICAL is one of three distinctively American and widely influential art forms that took shape in the first half of the twentieth century.[1] Like jazz and American film, whose histories intertwine significantly with its own, the American musical has continued to evolve into the present, both accommodating changes in American culture and society and, in turn, helping to shape their development in profound ways. And, like jazz and film, the American musical has developed and maintained a solid core of dedicated and highly specialized practitioners, along with an audience that ranges outward from a nucleus of ardent, knowledgeable devotees to a broader public who partake of its products and byproducts in various ways and to varying degrees. These three art forms have become nearly ubiquitous in the United States, each aspiring to the status of art while remaining thoroughly enmeshed with commerce, each capable of embracing interests and attitudes ranging from the most serious to the most playful, from the most religious to the most secular, and from the most complex to the most reductively simple.

If scarcely anyone in the United States has thus not been influenced by, amused by, inspired by—and, yes, annoyed by, but yet somehow deeply affected by—each of these art forms in turn or in some combination, their practitioners and devotees have nevertheless had to contend with troubling issues of cultural prestige. Can American film and the American musical *truly* be thought of as art forms on the same level as, say, Shakespeare's plays and Mozart's operas? Can jazz *truly* be compared to the achievements of Bach and Beethoven? Still, despite entrenched opposition, the cultural prestige of jazz has grown tremendously in recent decades, while that of American film has grown nearly apace—the latter thanks to both a cadre of French theorists writing in the 1950s and the self-serving efforts of the Academy of Motion Picture Arts and Sciences, the American Film Institute, and similar groups. But if American musicals have also increasingly been taken more seriously in recent years, they have only rarely been seen to transcend a medium and venue that has seemed inherently flawed—even though the specific "flaws" of the American musical are virtually the same as those that jazz and American film have to some extent surmounted on their way to achieving the relative cultural prestige they now enjoy. Thus, to enumerate: the musical is a highly collaborative art form that inevitably dilutes whatever individual genius may contribute to particular creations; it draws heavily on elements of society much lower than its well-educated, more aesthetically minded elite; it appeals broadly to educated and uneducated alike; it responds shamelessly to commercial stimuli; and, worst of all, it has managed to grow largely independent of its European roots, from which it might usefully have absorbed that sense of aesthetic elevation Americans have so often found lacking in their indigenous artworks.

Yet, it may be argued, the sharp rifts that developed in all three of these art forms between American practices and their European-based counterparts (if any) were precisely what enabled them to emerge as specifically American, answering to specifically American demands and shaping American experiences more directly than arts imported from Europe could ever have managed to do. While developments in these art forms have been driven to an extraordinary degree by market demand, this may in itself be seen as quintessentially American, enabling and managing a rapid development that has been highly responsive to commercial realities. Which is to say: all of these art forms succeeded because they—as art forms and as individual creations—provided what audiences wanted. Which is to say: all of these art forms are *connected* in vital ways to their American constituency, with a connection more reinforced than undermined by their collaborative and broadly democratic participatory basis. Arguably, then, questions of artistic stature (or, perhaps, merely prestige) must yield to questions of relevancy. Over the course of the twentieth century in America, jazz, film, and the musical have achieved and maintained relevance to greater proportions of the population than any other performance-based arts, notwithstanding the erosive effects on that relevance, especially in the case of film and jazz, by television and rock-and-roll beginning in the 1950s. (Indeed, the advent of the "lower orders" of television and rock-and-roll have a lot to do with the emergent prestige of film and jazz.)

When we in the United States come to study the histories of these three art forms, there is much more at stake for us than when we study Shakespeare and Mozart, whose supposed universality seems plausible to us only because their works are clearly not about us as Americans, yet can matter tremendously to us as human beings. Claims for the universality of jazz, American film, and American musicals are easier for us to see through, and so we tend, as a culture and as custodians of culture, to devalue these forms according to this criteria; by the same token, however, because these art forms are so much about us, we care tremendously about how their histories are told. Thus, for example, telling the history of jazz has been a singularly fraught venture, as its various communities have attempted to define themselves as the mainstream. The issue of race, in particular, has become especially charged in debates over jazz history, which speaks directly to the importance of jazz to a national culture that has been from its beginnings virtually obsessed with race. We may, perhaps, learn a lesson from these debates: through contemplating the embarrassing legacy of early historians of jazz, who saw its strongest line of development only among whites, we may also come to reject as equally problematic more recent accounts that exclude whites altogether from the narrative on the basis of the supposed purity of an essentialized African-American tradition. The real alternative is not to choose along racial or other divisive lines, but to take greater care to construct nonexclusionary histories.

Race and ethnicity matter tremendously as well in the histories of American films and musicals, not only involving divisions between whites and blacks, but also involving Irish, Jews, Asians, Hispanics, and Native Americans, among others. But if the more basic lesson for us to learn from race-centered jazz narratives, with respect to contemplating the history of the American musical, is that we should take care not to exclude obviously central groups, then we must take due note from the outset of the relatively high proportion of (often closeted) gay men within the central communities of the American musical theater, as creators, performers, and devotees. The highly charged "camp" atmosphere that devolves from this circumstance is and has long been a central component of American musical theater, which is reason enough to make gay sensibilities central to our account.[2] More pressingly, however, we should realize that the strong gay presence in musical theater has had much to do with an entrenched general reluctance to see the art form as contributing centrally to American culture, and thereby to our collective image of ourselves.

The situation has much in common with an earlier reluctance among conservative whites to acknowledge the importance of blacks to the development of jazz and related popular musics. The first impulse in the face of what appears to be an important contribution by a marginalized and maligned group—and this is true for both jazz and musical theater—has been to devalue the product; the second to devalue the specific contribution of the group in question. More broadly, with regard to gays in music, there is a third possibility not plausibly available with regard to blacks in jazz, which is to claim that sexual orientation itself is not relevant, a fact of biography that leaves no trace on the artifacts we study. Taking seriously this time-honored but wholly untenable claim allows us, for example, to note as biographical marginalia the homosexuality of Aaron Copland, while maintaining that his sexual orientation is irrelevant to the legacy of "American" music that he left us. But this is patently impossible in the American musical theater, where we may all too easily witness both the visual and musical presence of gay sensibilities on stage, as well as its responsive presence in the audience. While I will here resist the impulse to tell the history of the American musical as an *exclusively* gay tradition (a perhaps understandable reaction that would result in a more obvious falsification than rendering jazz as an exclusively African American phenomenon), the contributions and perspectives of gays must at the very least occupy a prominent position in the story.

While the principal thrust of this book is to tell a coherent story, there are several reasons why adhering strictly to chronology does not seem to me the best approach to take. To the extent that a case needs to be made that American musicals are worthy of study at all, whether because of their cultural relevance or their aesthetic merit, that case can surely be made best with more recent musicals than with largely irretrievable musicals from earlier in the century. Relevance is more easily shown when it can also be experienced, and memorable shows from the more recent past provide crucial evidence. Aesthetic merit (or interest), for its part, may be most easily established and explored within more specific contexts than a belabored chronology permits; moreover, the case is a more difficult one for many earlier works, to which strict chronology would have to give literal precedence, no matter how harshly we may judge some of those works by later standards. There is, too, the problem of establishing a full sense of a show as a basis for discussion; while filmed versions of stage musicals, whatever merit they may have as films, only imperfectly reproduce the shows on which they are based, they are considerably better than nothing, so that we may much more usefully engage with musicals that were filmed after the adoption of synchronized sound, and still more usefully with musicals (mostly from recent decades) that were filmed or videotaped in their original staging. And, of course, the question of whom this history is *for* affects how we tell it. Since this book is intended to serve as both a course textbook and, more generally, a way for those interested in the American musical to extend their knowledge and explore more fully the musicals they already know, it behooves me to move fairly quickly to musicals that may be seen as central works in the tradition, a strategy in direct conflict with chronological concerns.

But there are more fundamental reasons to forego strict chronology. The specific structural design I have adopted for this history emerged forcefully, first, when I started asking pointed questions about why musicals have mattered and to whom, about what specifically they have given us and how; and second, when I considered anew that this history, like most histories, is not a single story, but rather a set of intertwined stories that a master narrative simply cannot do justice to. I therefore decided early on to present the subject thematically, to be concerned first and foremost with what musicals *do* within culture—that is, how they engage with central issues that concern us as Americans—and to impose this approach

Figure 1.1. The implicit gay subtext of Gilbert and Sullivan's *H.M.S. Pinafore* (1878)—easily the most influential work for the early development of the American musical—was splendidly brought out in *Pinafore!*, Mark Savage's adaptation of the show staged in 2001 by the Celebration Theater in Los Angeles. Here, a supposedly "straight" Dick Dockstrap (Christopher Hall) sings "The Nightingale," while being admired by the rest of the crew (Seán Snow, Neal Allen Hyde, John Brantley Cole, Jr., and Jason Boegh). (Photograph by Johnny Nicoloro. Used by permission.)

hierarchically by considering them within specific thematic tropes and traditions. Clearly, individual musicals do many things, serially and at once, and discussions must be flexible enough to accommodate that circumstance. But by organizing the discussions here primarily by themes, I hope not only to enable more focused discussions of those themes and the specific ways in which individual musicals articulate them, but also to establish a structured focus to the discussions of individual musicals even as I consider other aspects of them. (Incidentally, the latter consideration dictates that I treat musicals holistically, rather than discuss them piecemeal, according to the many separate themes each may be seen to take up.)

The four themes I explore in this book all center around political considerations, of how musicals have helped us envision ourselves as a nation of disparate peoples, functioning within a world of even more extreme differences. I start my consideration of these themes with "Part II: Defining America," which is, arguably, *the* central theme in American musicals, to which the other themes relate in both obvious and subtle ways. It is surely no accident that many accounts of the history of the American musical begin with *The Black Crook,* which was first presented the year following the end of the Civil War, and was much revived in the following decades. The specific task of reunification in the recently re-United States, along with Western expansion, the approaching Centennial celebration, and the rise of nationalist ideologies in Europe during the second half of the nineteenth century—all served to heighten the need to define and *re-*fine what precisely it meant to be American. Musicals eventually proved to be a particularly effective place to do that, since what happened on stage not only brought a specific audience together within a constructed community, but also sent that audience out into a larger community armed with songs to be shared, providing at least some basis for achieving a sense of unity among the increasingly varied peoples of a country expanding rampantly both geographically and through immigration. Nor was it an accident that Gilbert and Sullivan's *H.M.S. Pinafore,* appearing just after the Centennial celebrations, provided a particularly strong push in this direction, since *Pinafore* both demonstrated the capacity of musical comedy to express a national identity and provided Americans of a later generation with the opportunity to indulge their own smug belief, as they laughed both *at* and *with* the show's presentation of British foibles and preoccupations, that they had outgrown their principal European "parent."

From these starting points, well before the turn of the century that would give birth to jazz and the film industry, the American musical had a jump start in acquiring the specific capacity and implicit charge of projecting a mainstream sense of "America"—of what America was, what it was not, and what it might become. And since, in many ways, questions of *what* America was and should become involve, as a fundamental question, *who* America was and should become, I begin specifically with that question in a preliminary form (chapter 5, "Whose [Who's] America?") and return to it after considering, in their chronological development on the musical stage, "American Mythologies" and "Counter-mythologies" (chapters 6 and 7). Thus, "Race and Ethnicity" become central preoccupations in musicals early on; almost necessarily, then, this will be the second of the larger themes we take up (chapter 8), as the first part of considering how America has worked around the difficult issue of who might not so easily belong to its much ballyhooed "melting pot" (Part III "Managing America's Others"). The final two themes reconsider the first two within a broader context; thus, chapters 9 and 10, "Dealing with the Second World War" and "Exoticism"—the latter especially as it emerges after the war—are obviously natural extensions of chapters 5 through 8, taking the more local issues of nationalism and ethnic identity to a larger stage.

More immediately than they explore broader issues such as these, however, musicals routinely occupy themselves with the formation of difficult romantic relationships. Whatever larger problems may be posed in a particular show, their working out will frequently involve an interpersonal conflict among or between the lead characters, so that the success or failure of their personal relationship(s) may be seen as an emblem for larger possibilities, as a marker for the resolution or continuation of conflicts between larger antagonistic forces. In this way, relationships provide a readily adaptable dramatic "surface" for musicals, with the shining possibility of marriage standing allegorically for the resolution of seemingly incompatible peoples—or families, classes, races, ideas, ideologies, or whatever—into a stabilized partnership. The trajectory of a successful if rocky courtship provides a sturdy narrative backbone, and offers standardized modes of expression along the way, for the optimistic comedies that are the mainstay of the American musical, and it does so most powerfully when the rocky courtship being related may be seen to embody or symbolize larger issues. Time and again, within a structure we might usefully term the "marriage trope," we will find couples whose individual issues mirror or embody larger ones that turn out to be what the musical in question is "really" about.[3] (For now, I will put off discussing the other side of the "marriage trope" to a second volume, where I will consider how musicals deal more directly with projecting the individual identities and relationships we actually see on stage; see chapter 11, "Afterword.")

To set the stage properly for these separate thematic surveys, I will consider, in chapters 2 and 3, important antecedents from the late nineteenth century. In considering both imported and domestic varieties, I will bring the focus more quickly to particulars than is typical in historical surveys of this kind, and indulge rather more in probing how these antecedents worked as musical shows. Thus, "Nineteenth-Century European Roots: Models and Topics" considers in some detail how and why *The Black Crook* and *Pinafore* appealed so strongly to American audiences, and how their success helped shape later developments. In chapter 3, "Early American Developments: Minstrelsy, Extravaganza, Pantomime, Burlesque, Vaudeville," I have endeavored (without spending more time than is warranted on these more peripheral types) to explain why these antecedents, so embarrassing to the aesthetic ambitions of the American musical "proper" (especially minstrelsy), must be embraced more fully than historical accounts have tended to in the past, as something more than mere oddities but nevertheless already qualitatively different than the American musical as it was already beginning to develop. In chapter 4, "American Song through Tin Pan Alley," I return to what will be the dominant

mode of the book, to consider how the tunes actually work, in some detail but without requiring a particularly high technical knowledge of
music. Of special interest here will be the rapid maturation of the genre
of song that came to dominate the musical stage in America between the
two world wars.

American musicals represent a large slice of our national life and heritage and, as such, include much that we today find dated and, worse,
often obnoxiously so, embodying attitudes and traditions of representation that we have grown to detest. Perhaps the most difficult dimension
of this heritage as it manifests itself in musicals is the tradition of blackface minstrelsy, which has stained the history of musical theater in America with the seemingly indelible imprint of burned cork, grotesquely
painted smiles, and whitely protruding eyes. Even in films and musicals
that seem to embody values we might want to preserve and identify with
as part of our collective past, racist attitudes appear with unsettling fre-
quency. Especially resonant with blackface minstrelsy is the continued
stereotyping behavior and appearance of African American character actors on stage and screen. Spike Lee's film *Bamboozled* (2000) brings the
full destructive force of this tradition to the fore by imagining a contemporary resurrection of the minstrel show and demonstrating vividly a line
of representation that stretches unbroken from whites and blacks in blackface, to contemporary black sitcoms on television.[4]

If we ask, however, why this vestige of the minstrel tradition persisted
with such tenacity in twentieth-century America, we cannot simply conclude that it was a malicious plot to defame blacks as a race, although it
surely did that. Among the cultural needs it served in the late nineteenth
century and well into the twentieth, blackface minstrelsy—with its personae as rigidly established and predictable in behavior as any from the
tradition of commedia dell'arte—served to reassure white audiences that
the social order in America was just, and that blacks on the whole did not
deserve better than they had. But it answered more fundamental needs, as
well. Through its carnivalesque comedy of inversion, it also gave them or
their stand-ins a potentially subversive voice, through which figures of authority and established order could be ridiculed and undermined with im-
punity. Under the protection of a scurrilous, primitivist persona, and in
the guise of humor at that persona's expense, an actor could do or say—
or sing—virtually anything. If the repugnant images associated with the
tradition now seem to us paramount—for images are, after all, the easi-
est for us to recapture—we must remember that these images were in large
part a mask that was put on so that the performers could say inappropriate things, perform objectionable music, and generally misbehave,
which together provided the real point of it all for audiences. The mask
of blackface was thus a particularly effective enabling device, allowing au-

Figure 1.2. A very young Al Jolson getting into blackface. Jolson (ca. 1886–1950) appeared in blackface from 1906 on, most famously in the first commercially successful sound film, *The Jazz Singer* (1927); his 1928 *The Singing Fool* (with one blackface number) is believed to be the top grossing film in America before *Gone With the Wind* (1939). (Culver Pictures. Used by permission.)

diences to take pleasure in kinds of humor and music to which loftier sensibilities had otherwise denied them access.

The mechanism involved in blackface is one of deflection, and it is undoubtedly pernicious, as it seeks out the most vulnerable targets available, makes them ridiculous and even more vulnerable through exaggeration, and then uses them as a conduit for whatever might be seen as culturally dangerous. Perniciousness aside, however, this mechanism played a vital role in popular entertainment beyond its twisted expropriation of African-American identities, and did so by building on two of the cornerstones that would come to support the American musical, as well: the multivalent nature of theatrical and musical representation, and the liberating potentialities of theatrical exaggeration, particularly when combined with music.

The effect of adding music to a dramatic scene that might otherwise play naturalistically serves to exaggerate its content, adding a dimension of artificiality at the same time that it often also strives to tap into a deeper kind of reality, one accessible only through music. Because the addition of music seems to pull in these two opposing directions, the musical as an art form engages routinely in a kind of stratified presentation in which we, the audience, pay attention to both the emotional realities that music seems to body forth and the performance of that music by the actor-singers on stage. Indeed, we are almost forced into this mode of dual attention, since music notoriously does not unfold in "real time," but rather imposes a kind of suspended animation so as to intensify selected emotional moments, and through this dramatic hiatus directs us all the more urgently to see behind the mask/makeup/costume of the performer—even as he or she embodies the role being played even more fully through the enactment of song. And, as our perceptions flip between these strata, additional layers may also open up to us in the expanded fermata of interpolated song: perhaps music, which is always more than a mere vehicle, will impose its own imperatives; perhaps we will become more aware of larger themes prefigured in the expanded moment, or of different authorial "voices," ranging from historical reality and its known associations, to the writers, to the characters, to the actual performers in front of us—each of which may impose a perspective and thus come to occupy a significant stratum in the dramatic texture.

The addition of music to staged, spoken drama thus does not simply heighten emotions; rather, it also imposes, through its obvious and conventional artificiality, a kind of mask that both conceals and calls attention to the performer behind the persona. And, just as in blackface, exaggeration and a ritualized transgression against "naturalness" prove to be liberating; in musicals, however, this plays out differently, as we in the audience pretend through the convention of "suspending disbelief" not to notice how artificially the emotional level has suddenly shifted into a higher gear—all the while relishing the performance as such, as an event unto itself.

It is this expressive double image, of a heightened sense of reality enacted through the brazenly artificial, that makes the musical an ideal arena for camp. Camp, understood broadly, always involves exaggeration and an expressive lack of proportion, either through investing enormous expressive energy in the trivial or by trivializing the most serious of subjects; this is true whether or not we view camp through the particular lens of gay subculture. To some extent, the musical becomes camp the moment it actually becomes *musical,* for the first notes that sound under the dialogue are like a knowing wink to the audience, a set of arched eyebrows that serves as quotation marks around whatever is ostensibly being expressed, whether musically or dramatically. The element of camp in a musical thus shifts sudden attention to the performed nature of the drama, and in particular to the actual performer, thereby providing a more direct channel of communication between the performer and whoever in the audience may note and relish the artificiality. But if camp thus calls into question the specific content of what is being performed through this use of expressive quotation marks, it is also capable of standing back to reveal that those quotation marks themselves are set off in quotation marks, allowing us to reconnect with the content, but at a much higher emotional pitch than could have been achieved otherwise. In this way, camp can revert to a more normally accepted mode of performance, in which it serves primarily as a vehicle, a realization and embodiment of specific aesthetic content. And, again as in blackface, the manipulation of the mask gives us in the audience access and permission: access to a heightened emotionality and permission either to feel the moment more deeply or to laugh at it—or, somehow, to do both at once, in which case we are also laughing at and with ourselves and, perhaps, more fully embracing our humanity.

Within the traditions and conventions of the American musical, the potentialities of camp are often invisible to large segments of the audience, who have no difficulty accepting, as background, the convention of actors bursting into song at a moment's notice and, indeed, will wait with some degree of impatience if this does not happen fairly regularly. Moreover, so as to encourage this acceptance, the writers, director, and actors often go to great and imaginative lengths to make the transition to singing seem as natural as possible, to weld inevitable exaggeration to its dramatic moment as securely as they can—and thus, seemingly, to move as far away from camp as possible. Yet the mechanisms of camp are always present. No one thinks for a moment that singing happens, fundamentally, for any reason other than that, in musicals, people sing as well as talk; the resulting artificiality may be generic, but that does not make it natural. And, however more "natural" the result would be, few who attend musicals would prefer *not* to have song when it is called for, even if sometimes a good effect can be achieved through delaying (but never altogether withholding) the inevitable song. In a curious way, audiences not only relish the heightened dramatic effect that song can create, but also seem to need the comforting artificiality that comes with it. Through precisely the same mechanisms that operate in camp, the inherent exaggeration of interpolated song allows audiences to experience more deeply the dramatic situation and characters on stage because music, singing, and often dancing decisively remove that situation from anything even remotely like the real world; artificiality thus provides essential protection from the dangerous, potentially destructive effect of emotions felt too deeply.

What separates this transaction from camp has mainly to do with our degree of awareness of the processes whereby we are taken to these levels of involvement, with how aware we are of the manufactured nature of musically driven emotion. This is why, within a single audience, there may often be wide discrepancies in reception, so that a particular musical number might be taken by some as high camp and by others as highly pitched but authentic emotion. More to the point, perhaps, this is why, at certain musical moments, audiences may routinely cry but seldom the performers on stage, who may even have to suppress laughter as they provide the exaggerated representation of feeling their audience needs. And it is surely a mistake to see something wrong in this discrepancy, taken in itself— even if depriving an audience, without prior warning, of their feeling of "authenticity" at such a moment, by laughing or otherwise allowing the element of camp to emerge too overtly, may be reckoned one of only a handful of truly unforgivable theatrical crimes.

While focusing on particular themes, then, we will consider most centrally how the element of exaggeration, specifically musical exaggeration, is brought to bear on those themes. The advent of recording has, of course, served to highlight even more the contribution of music to the American musical, for this is what has been preserved most diligently and directly (although, of course, there are important differences between what one hears in a studio-produced "original cast" recording and what one would have heard in the performance it purports to document). Focusing on the music may thus seem to bend, perhaps too easily, to the imperatives of familiarity and convenience: we know the songs best, and so will spend the most time on them. Yet this kind of focus is as necessary as it is convenient. Specifically *because* the songs have been effectively sprung from their original contexts, through being presented separately from the drama and quite often through their reuse in much different contexts, it is necessary here to reintegrate them, to show how they work both as songs and within the shows they belong to. Secondarily, it is also important either to begin with or to arrive at what is most familiar in a decisively central way, in order to chart a path toward a deeper, more grounded understanding of what is already (partially) known. And, of course, it is above all else its treatment of music that defines the American musical; thus, if this book is to serve as a textbook, it will most likely be for a course given in music history. And, finally, showing how and why the music and songs do what they do in musicals, and showing this in a way accessible and valuable to both the nontechnically grounded and the trained musician alike, is what I can most usefully contribute to the larger project of understanding this important American genre.

But what, precisely, *is* the American musical? At the beginning of this chapter I compared the American musical to jazz and American film, art forms with a similar trajectory and intertwined histories. It should be acknowledged, though, that these art forms are also profoundly different from each other, first of all because they refer, respectively, to a genre, a style, and a medium. These categories have significant overlap, since style and medium are important aspects of genre, and, more specifically, since much about the history of jazz and American film suggests that they quite often behave like genres as well. Yet they are scarcely equivalent. In particular, defining a genre, even as opposed to a medium or style, is a notoriously difficult task, and usually involves a complex dance around those aspects that the definer is most interested in; not surprisingly, most attempts to define genres tell us more about the concerns of the definer than about the genre itself.

I am here most interested in the tradition of theatrical presentation that evolves by the third decade of the twentieth century into the semblance of an original, integrated art work intended for a specifically American audience, involving both naturalistic spoken drama and some combination of singing and dancing. Various other staged musical entertainments seem largely irrelevant to this line of development, although they exist side by side: revues, vaudeville, burlesque, and European opera and light opera traditions. While the themes I have chosen dictate that I focus on certain, specifically American, lines of development within more narrative-based traditions, taking too purist a position on what we will consider as a "genuine" American musical may also lead us to be too exclusionary. A more general consideration of the genre would have to give at least token representation, for example, to the several shows that originated outside the United States that have subsequently succeeded alongside indigenous shows. And a more general history of the genre would have to consider—and, I believe, reject—the line now often heard, that the genre has run its course, and that what is now fully entrenched on Broadway is fundamentally different from (and, of course, inferior to) the tradition we are studying, having become too much the product of corporate America. Nevertheless, now that foreign shows have begun to make significant inroads and now that, indeed, large corporations have secured a commanding presence on Broadway, it is clearly a historical moment for taking stock, of considering the trajectory and possible paths, of continuation for the genre. While I am not directly addressing the very last of these—I do not pretend to be a prophet—I am hoping to bring into sharper focus what is at stake in the history of the American musical: what has been, still is, and might become valuable within this genre and its development, and to whom and for what ends.

But there are good reasons for concern about developments in the last decade or so; both importation and recent fairly successful attempts to move from film to stage do erode the immediacy of the musical for American audiences. The stakes have, in a sense, been raised—in part literally, as it has become increasingly expensive to attend a show, and since "hot" tickets are so hard to come by—so that audiences now feel entitled to *both* the excitement of a live performance and the dependable sameness of a finished film. But raising stakes in this manner is problematic, as it does not adequately account for the fact that these two demands are basically opposed to each other. The immediacy of live performance—an essential component of staged musicals and jazz, but not of film and other recorded media—is not truly compatible with the level of dependability more easily attained in film and recordings and now demanded as well by live audiences.

On the other hand, since musicals have never before been shy about trying to achieve great effects from mechanical spectacle—a legacy, perhaps, of the countless "transformation" effects popular in the nineteenth century—they form a natural partnership with the film industry.[5] Despite a strong, healthy tradition of amateur performances of American musicals—ranging from more modest road productions of elaborate Broadways stagings, to community theater, to college and high school productions—there has always been, as well, the sense that the "real thing" takes place with real stars, flawless stage machinery, elaborate sets and costumes, professional musicians and dancers—and, of course, on Broadway. Why, then, should mechanical spectacle not be pursued aggressively, especially since the results can so obviously serve a fundamental task of the musical stage, which is to create illusion, or more precisely, to give a sense of overwhelming reality to what is clearly not real?

A similar tension, between the immediate and transitory on the one hand and the more permanent and standardized on the other, is endemic to this study—as, indeed, it is to some extent endemic to the historical study of any performing art with a written tradition. There are many and various traces that individual American musicals leave us, most of which will be useful here; these typically include a preserved paper record of the "work" in the form of the written music and book, and various preserved visual and audio traces of particular performances of the full work or some of its components, ranging from films and videos of whole shows or adaptations, to "original cast" or "soundtrack" recordings, to still photographs, to similar traces of later performances and revivals, to anecdotal accounts of the show in preparation or performance, to arrangements and recordings made separately of songs from a show. (Quite often, as well, these shows or their revivals have been experienced live by the author.) No one component in this mix is necessarily privileged over the others, for no musical truly lives except within the context of necessarily nondefinitive performance, and no performance is possible without the stability of a book and score as a starting point. For us, most centrally, we thus have the "definitive" artifacts of score and show-based audio and video recording, each authoritative in some way, but representing either side of the work-performance divide. Even here, our experience of the show through its recorded artifacts, however immediately felt, is heavily mediated by the mechanical aspects of camera and microphone placement, by the montage/mixing of the results, and more fundamentally by the sensibilities of those who are more-or-less self-consciously "documenting" the work or trying to compensate for media-based shortcomings by adding explanatory words and sound effects (in sound recording) or by cutting to focus on significant detail or to introduce perspectives not available to a live audience (in film or videotape). More fundamentally, these artifacts *do not change* (except to deteriorate); the more we hear or see them, the less they are *a performance* and the more they become *the work* with which we are concerned.

We must, of course, depend heavily on those things we can study—book, score, films, recordings, etc.[6]—not only to avoid relying too heavily on sometimes faulty memory (if indeed, there are direct memories that are relevant), but also to communicate points effectively. These are the most immediately available materials for classroom presentation, and in teaching it is natural to rely heavily on playing out parts of the score, screening films and videos, and playing audio recordings. (Occasionally, more elaborate enactments might be available, but not reliably.) For this study, I am also effectively limited, in discussions of individual musicals, to referring to the written record and to readily available documented performances. And, since I wish not to exclude those who might not read music, I must be fairly circumspect in my references even to the score, and will most often give descriptive accounts that may be verified through listening, while occasionally providing a clarifying excerpt from the score for those readers who do read music. But it will sometimes be pressingly important to bring into play the relative status of my examples to preserve at least a sense of the fluidity of a genre whose decisive "artifacts," which determine to a large extent the success of a particular show, are no true artifacts at all, but rather the constantly evolving staged performances of the first Broadway run—which, while depending on a score and book as starting points, and while sometimes leaving important recorded traces in its early phases, is an entirely different thing from either. Our dependence on the concrete as a basis for discussing something much more fluid and ephemeral must be acknowledged up front and reaffirmed constantly as we go along; principally, this will involve as full a citation as possible of the basis in scores and recorded performances for the points we make, which will also, I hope, facilitate and encourage as frequent recourse as is practical to those scores and recorded performances.[7]

Finally, it is important to underscore one of the basic strategies in my presentation, which is to provide a rather fuller slate of musicals as exemplars of our themes than might be practical to teach in a single course, particularly if that course deals with more than the four themes included here. In this, I am mindful of many contexts and needs, as well as a pitfall or two. For the instructor, I wish to include a fair range of choice regarding which musicals to focus on, and to leave some room for further elaboration; I expect that only some of the musicals I have selected will actually be studied in any given course, and hope that I have included most of those that a given instructor might find essential to a course on specifically Americanist themes in the American musical. For the student, I wish both to provide some discussion of musicals that she or he might wish to study beyond what a particular course can usefully include, and to indicate how the various themes being studied are worked out in musicals other than those taught in that course. For the independent reader, I wish simply to provide as full and wide-ranging an account as is practical in this format. And, to all, I apologize for leaving out many a favorite musical or song, and for focusing more obsessively on what I consider central issues at the expense of what might well be the life-blood of the tradition for particular readers and approaches, such as the intriguing lives and individual achievements of its many colorful practitioners. But regarding the latter, I may say with some assurance that those readers who care deeply about those aspects do not probably need me to tell them more (but, in case they do, I have provided an extensive bibliography); moreover, it is these readers who may potentially benefit most from this attempt to provide a richer context for what they already know.

Nineteenth-Century European Roots

Models and Topics

THE AMERICAN MUSICAL developed out of the intermingling of a number of musical-theatrical traditions of the late nineteenth century. In this chapter, we will consider the European-derived component of this development, particularly as reflected in *The Black Crook* and in the American reception of *H.M.S. Pinafore*.

The light- and comic-opera traditions of Paris, London, and Vienna ("operetta") were especially important in the development of American musical theater for a number of reasons and in two principal ways. Each of these traditions was at a point of full development in the second half of the nineteenth century, achieving some degree of aesthetic sophistication and commercial success just when its influence on American developments might be most strongly felt. At the same time, each had come to play a significant part in the cultural life of its native city, so that, even when adapted to the American stage, it remained enduringly linked to its city of origin. As each of these types achieved some success in America, it was much imitated, rapidly making the transition from exemplar to model. More subtly, these types offered visions of European life that eventually became important touchstones for American representation. In other words, they served not only as models but also as a source of *topics*, that is, as a source of musical and dramatic conventions and archetypes that could be used to evoke referentially some dimension or attribute of the source from which they were derived. Danced feminine display and bawdy humor, for example, became the knowing, worldly wink of Paris; verbal wit and sly political satire transmuted into that sense of unearned superiority with which Americans project the effete "Brit"; and Viennese waltz came to evoke the special grace of tactful innuendo, sexual intrigue, and "sophistication" associated with eastern Europe, whose sensibilities, at least from American perspectives, were so long dominated by the imperial city of Vienna. Although Vienna's influence was heavily felt in nineteenth-century America, however, this was more through the vehicle of the waltz than through the operettas of Strauss. For this reason, and since Viennese operetta wielded a separate, twentieth-century influence over American musical theater, we will here concentrate primarily on the other two.

Operetta traditions were the principal European sources for models and topics as the American musical took shape. A certain Germanic influence may also be traced, although too early to support fully the parallel structures of model and topic, blending rather into an earnest seriousness and a fascination for the ancient magic of the deep woods, both of which might as reasonably be traced to the Puritans and Salem (or, later, the Scottish highlands) as to *Der Freischütz, Oberon,* and *Der Vampyr.* Italian traditions were, for Americans, irretrievably bound up in "serious" opera, along with Wagnerian *Musikdrama* and French Grand Opera (and this was true even for Italian comic opera—*opera buffa*—which in any case became progressively less important across the nineteenth century); all of these thus provided, collectively, a largely second-hand basis for parody, as Americans followed light-operatic models in mocking the pretensions of loftier traditions. Perhaps, as well, an American fondness for elaborate costumes and stage effects may have developed in part from serious opera, although that fondness may as easily be explained, as it traditionally has been with French Grand Opera, as gratifying a taste for ostentatious display borne of newly acquired wealth within an increasingly moneyed upper-middle class.

Unquestionably, the most successful European imports in the nineteenth century were the comic operas of Gilbert and Sullivan, especially *H.M.S. Pinafore.* But an earlier (mostly) native product was modeled directly on two separate European traditions, and achieved a success even greater than *Pinafore*'s. Despite a substantial dose of improbability, *The Black Crook* has tenaciously held on to its oft-claimed historical position as the "first American musical," even if its spectacular run of revivals did not, like Gilbert and Sullivan's best work, overlap the more mature form of the American genre that developed in the twentieth century.

Paris
(and Berlin)

The Black Crook (1866) was originally conceived as a *melodrama*—a type of theatrical entertainment with musical accompaniment, spoken dialogue, and pantomime, but little or no singing—and was inspired by a performance of Carl Maria von Weber's *Der Freischütz,* which its author Charles Barras had seen performed in Cincinnati in 1857. *Der Freischütz* ("The Free Shot") is the most celebrated of Weber's romantically charged *Singspiele* (German operatic works with spoken dialogue), and had become a fairly popular commodity on the international operatic stage since its 1821 premiere in Berlin. With its story of Christian redemption for a hero who has become ensnared by satanic forces, saved through the love of a pure woman, *Der Freischütz* remains even today a staple of the Christmas season in Germany. In particular, the famous "Wolf-Glen" scene, an extended melodrama within *Der Freischütz* that depicts the casting of seven magic bullets through diabolical means, would have struck a chord with Americans, who also had reason to view the forest with a mixture of fear and awe, and who would presumably have identified with the rather high premium the opera places on good marksmanship. Notwithstanding their alignment with American preoccupations, however, both *Der Freischütz* and Barras's imitation presented themselves to Americans as exotically European, in the latter case through a myth-enshrouded Germanic setting, evocative names—Hertzog (the "Crook"), Rodolphe (the hero), Amina (the heroine), and Count Wolfenstein—dungeons, intimations of depraved nobility and supernatural forces tied to specific geography, and ballroom scenes of imagined bygone splendor.

As fate would have it, however, *The Black Crook* was never performed as a simple melodrama, neither by the English troupe that had performed *Der Freischütz,* whom Barras originally tried to sell it to, nor by Niblo's Garden in New York, whose producer William Wheatley had contracted to stage it immediately following the Civil War. Along the way to its presentation at the latter venue, *The Black Crook* absorbed and integrated a ballet troupe assembled in Europe for the purpose of mounting the Parisian success *La Biche au Bois* (Hervé, 1865) in New York, but which had been blocked by a disastrous fire to their theater, the Academy of Music. *The Black Crook* was thereby able to draw on the dual advantages of offering magic-inspired stage effects and equally elaborate feminine display, and managed to integrate them to some extent through aligning balletic dance with both enchantment and the festive ballroom. Thus, the highlights of the show, which in this form most resembled the contemporary genre of *extravaganza* (see chapter 3), included a "Pas de Fleurs," an adaptation of *Der Freischütz*'s "Wolf Glen" scene (now a "Serpent's Glen," replete with stage effects and feminine "ghosts"),[1] a "Pas de Demons" in the "Grotto of Golden Stalactites" that featured, center-stage, four young women wearing tights and not much else, a grand "Bal Masque" with a series of characteristic dances by the principal dancers, an elaborate "Dance de Amazon," and a concluding "transformation scene" in which stage machinery and chemicals converted the deep forest into "The Palace of Dew Drops" inhabited by "Nymphs of the Golden Realm."

If the frequent displays of young women in revealing costumes in *The Black Crook* could be triply excused through their appearing at climactic moments within the drama, their projections of supernatural power, and their representing a more decadent European sensibility, they were nonetheless also deemed scandalous for what they represented more obviously: shameless pandering to the desire of mostly male audiences to see provocative presentations of attractive teenaged girls in revealing costumes (none of the women in the European troupe was over twenty years of age, although they were greatly augmented by considerably less virtuosic dancers recruited in America). Among many who saw the original production of *The Black Crook* and commented on it was Mark Twain, who described its "endless ballets and splendid tableaux, with seventy beauties arrayed in dazzling half-costumes . . . displaying all possible compromises between nakedness and decency," and wrote that its dancers

> dressed with a meagreness that would make a parasol blush . . . in most princely attire I grant you, but always with more tights in view than anything else. They change their clothes every fifteen minutes for four hours, and their dresses become more beautiful and more rascally all the time.[2]

Public outcry against the show included editorials in the *New York Herald:*

> Nothing in any Christian country, or in modern times, has approached the indecent . . . exhibition at Wheatley's . . . Almost nude females . . . are brought out boldly before the public's gaze. . . . If [readers of the *Herald*] are determined to gaze on the indecent and dazzling brilliancy of *The Black Crook,* they should provide themselves with a piece of smoked glass.[3]

Condemnation was also voiced in a public sermon by Rev. Charles B. Smyth, published in the *Herald* as "The Nuisances of New York, Particularly the Naked Truth," who complained about

> the immodest dress of the girls; the short skirts and undergarments of thin, gauze-like material, allowing the form of the figure to be discernible through it; . . . the flesh colored tights, imitating nature so well that the illusion is complete; . . . exceedingly short drawers, almost tight fitting; . . . arms and back apparently bare, and bodice so cut and fitted as to show off every inch and outline of the body above the waist."[4]

Since descriptive accounts like this only increased the size of the audience being pandered to, it is not surprising to learn that these and other items like them—amounting to thinly disguised ads for the show—were mere stratagems to get around a theatrical boycott of *The New York Herald* that kept Wheatley from placing paid advertisements there.[5] As Twain noted, "The great *Herald* newspaper pitched into it, and a sensation parson preached a sermon against it; this was sufficient to advertise it all over the continent, and so the proprietor's fortune was made."[6] Moreover, although respectable women often resorted to veils to conceal their identity while attending the show, the number of women in the audience reportedly came to at least equal that of men. Twain, who saw the show five months into its run, noted that its visual delights were not intended only for men: "The scenic effects—the waterfalls, cascades, fountains, oceans, fairies, devils, hells, heavens, angels—are gorgeous beyond anything ever witnessed in America, perhaps, and these things attract the women and girls."[7]

The seeming improbabilities of *The Black Crook,* both in its origins and as an artifact, have made it serve durably as a fairy-tale account of the birth of the American musical, satisfying in large part because it does precious little to dispel the mystery shrouding the origins of the genre as we know it. In one fictionalized retelling, the story of the show's origins becomes a fairly hokey musical-comedy plot featuring a double "marriage trope," in which the stars and the management of the seemingly incompatible melodrama and ballet become romantically involved, in the process launching the new genre (Sigmund Romberg's modestly successful *The Girl in Pink Tights,* 1954). Yet, however embarrassed we may now be by the eagerness with which nineteenth-century American audiences accepted Barras's badly executed imitation of Germanic melodrama as suitable dramatic motivation for its multiple tableaux of "Parisiennes" in form-fitting costumes—whose stars, however, were mainly Italian and Dutch—and however much the obfuscations of time and circumstance have obscured the details of the actual adaptation, some aspects of the *Black Crook* phenomenon warrant a closer look. First and foremost—especially considering the importance of commerce to the future history of the American musical—its signal achievement was what we would now call its "bottom line": its unquestioned and lasting commercial success. *The Black Crook* went on to enjoy a then-phenomenal run of 474 performances, and thus became a shining emblem of the potential for commercial success in American musical theater, widely imitated and often revived in the following decades (indeed, there were a dozen successful mountings at Niblo's alone between 1866 and 1887).

But there are three additional aspects of the show that also require comment: its European derivation, the dual source of this derivation—thus, its Germanic father and French mother, figuratively speaking—and the American entrepreneurial midwifery that successfully merged its parents' seemingly incompatible gene-pools. The general favor that America has always bestowed on virtually anything of European origin is especially pronounced regarding those things meant to appeal to the most elevated and, paradoxically, the most lowly sensibilities; in respect to not only arts and letters, but also the decadent and the titillating, Americans looked to Europe first. And so it was with *The Black Crook,* which combines an earnest, "elevated" story of redemption and the prestige of Parisian ballet, with the frank gratification of more plebeian tastes in the visual accoutrement of both traditions: elaborate stage effects and copious feminine display. As the contemporary actress Olive Logan explained it in 1868,

> When *The Black Crook* first presented its nude woman to the gaze of a
> crowded auditory, she was met with a gasp of astonishment . . . but it
> passed; and, in view of the fact that these women were French ballet-dancers
> after all, they were tolerated . . . they represented in their nudity imps and
> demons. In silence they whirled about the stage; in silence they trooped off.
> Some faint odor of ideality and poetry rested over them.[8]

In this way, *The Black Crook* successfully balanced a high degree of
pandering against an enhanced pretension to loftier concerns, implicitly
justifying both ends of the spectrum through an adherence to European
sensibilities.

As would have been dictated by practicality, many of the dance routines
for the show came fairly directly from those already planned or existing
for *La Biche au Bois,* which included extensive ballet sequences closely
matching those of *The Black Crook*—specifically, balletic dances for
"flowers," for sea creatures set in an underwater grotto, for masked
dancers in a fairy-tale ballroom, and for various supernatural beings who
alternately threaten and rescue the central romantic couple. Moreover,
since *La Biche au Bois* ("The Hind in the Forest") was a "fairy-tale" ballet set in the deep woods (like *The Black Crook*) and involving scenes of
magic transformation (like *The Black Crook*), integration of the two
would have been remarkably easy. And, although for the second revival
at Niblo's in 1871 the score was rewritten by Giuseppe Operti, who then
published excerpts from the show, it seems safe to assume that the music
for the premiere, like the balletic sequences themselves, was adapted as
much as possible from the Parisian ballet, especially since it was not then
well protected by international copyright.[9]

Accordingly, the ballet component of the show was most likely based
on the original score by Hervé (Louis Auguste Joseph Florimond Ronger,
1825–1892), a composer, manager, writer, and star performer who is
often regarded as the true father of the French *operette* (rather than Offenbach, who was of course better known internationally). Hervé produced, wrote, and performed in pioneering works in the genre from 1848
on (that is, following directly on the Paris Revolution of that year), and
appeared as the (feminine!) lead in Offenbach's early *Oyayaie* (1855),
which helped launch the latter composer's impressive run of successes in
the still relatively new genre, and which was mounted at Hervé's theatre,
Folies-Nouvelles.[10] *La Biche au Bois* helped launch a comeback of sorts
for Hervé himself after a hiatus in his Parisian career, as he followed it
with a series of *operette* successes beginning in 1866, the same year that
produced not only *The Black Crook* in America, but also Offenbach's *La
Vie Parisienne,* a central work of the Parisian genre. Considering that
Hervé was one of the most adept and beloved practitioners within the

Figure 2.1. Early sheet-music publications of music from *The Black Crook*. In the 1867 publication of "The Black Crook Lancers" (left), credit is given to unnamed "European Authors." The popular "March of the Amazons" was published in many versions, here with a particularly gaudy cover that hints rather broadly at the extravagance of the production itself; the illustration depicts the battle scene in which Stalacta's Amazons rescue Rodolphe. (Reproductions courtesy of UCLA Music Library Special Collections.)

then-burgeoning *operette* tradition, we may reasonably conclude that Niblo's was, in acquiring the dance company, equally fortunate in acquiring an ideally suited musical score to accompany it.

Specific connections between the plot-lines of the ballet and the melodrama would have made adaptation relatively easy. Madame D'Aulnoy's beloved fairy tale *La Biche au Bois* follows a "bad fairy" scenario redolent of *The Sleeping Beauty*, in which the princess heroine, Désirée, is turned by evil magic into a white hind (a female deer), in which form she is shot with an arrow in her leg/arm by the love-besotted Prince Guerrier, whose jilted fiancée, the unnamed "princesse Noire" (a vindictive "éthiopienne"), has joined forces with the bad fairy; the latter are thwarted in the end by the power of love and the intervention of a collective of good fairies named after flowers. In Barras's *The Black Crook*, there is likewise a "black" human conspirator who trades in evil magic: the "Black Crook" himself, the hunchbacked apothecary/alchemist/scientist Hertzog, who contracts with the devil-like Zamiel to prolong his life by seducing good souls to evil (a situational premise taken over intact from *Der Freischütz*). In *The Black Crook*, the benevolent fairies are "Amazons" named after precious gems, whose leader is turned by evil magic into a white dove, in which form she is saved from a snake (an agent of Zamiel) by the love-besotted painter Rodolphe. Besides providing an easy match of specific scenes of animal transformation, of enchantment both good and bad, and of supernatural intervention to ensure the triumph of love, the two scenarios intersect in their ready mapping of white and black to good and evil (white hind/white dove vs. Black Princess/Black Crook), although the racist component of this mapping is blurred somewhat in *The Black Crook*, where Hertzog is only ambiguously marked as Jewish.

There are, however, important differences to be noted, as well, and it is here that we might begin to see a specifically American dimension to the show. Whereas in *Der Freischütz* the rather weak hero is seduced into evil and redeemed only through the (potentially) sacrificial love of a pure woman; and whereas in *La Biche au Bois*, the fates of hero and heroine are similarly charted almost entirely through the intervention of supernatural forces whose alliances are determined (as in *Sleeping Beauty*) by the actions of the older generation; in *The Black Crook*, the hero and heroine are both given considerable agency, and rescue is set in motion not only by Rodolphe's instinctive goodness, which leads him to rescue the dove, but also by Amina's ardor, which in later versions of the play leads her (in feudal Germany!) to send a letter on Rodolphe's behalf to a rich American art collector. The last bit of fanciful nonsense is by no means irrelevant, as the 1866 version of *The Black Crook* is already duly critical of the feudal system whereby Count Wolfenstein wields his despotic power, even though neither *Der Freischütz* nor *La Biche au Bois* finds anything particularly wrong in the birthright privileges of wealth and power underlying its social order; clearly, the possibilities represented by America are implicit in Barras's original melodrama. And the political point is made through the threat of sexual violence to a betrothed woman from under cover of aristocratic privilege; notably, no such threat imperils the heroines of *Der Freischütz* and *La Biche au Bois*. In these ways and others, *The Black Crook* spreads an American parable of self-reliance and political equality over its European sources—and does so, we may note, by pandering to the nineteenth-century taste for damsel-in-distress melodrama.

But the figurative marriage of Germanic "Crook" to French "*Biche*" has a more basic consequence, to which the later interpolation of Amina's letter-writing bears witness. Barras's principal models were, at least on their theatrical surfaces, deadly serious in their evocation of evil magic and the dual possibilities of Kantian resistance and Christian redemption. In the wake of the Paris revolution of 1848, however, the *operette* tradition founded by Hervé took special delight in undermining such earnest regard for the myths and legends of the past. And principal among their devices for stripping away the façade of seriousness from such subjects was to expose their characters to the down-to-earth practicalities of daily life and, often enough, of its ignoble, all-too-recognizably human impulses. Humorous anachronisms, sometimes "inadvertent" puns, and the placement within the drama of characters who seem occasionally to be more up-to-date and street-wise than historically accurate were all key parts of this device, as each located within the stage drama a perspective that allowed audiences to laugh at the pretensions of the drama while also taking it seriously. If these devices seem to us somewhat labored, this is in part because they, like more recent camp, were deliberately dealing in aesthetic "quotation marks," and to some of the same expressive ends. In the contemporary Parisian success *La Belle Hélène* (by Offenbach, with libretto by Henri Mellhac and Ludovic Halévy, 1864), for example, Orestes (a "pants" or "trousers" role, in which the part of a young man is played by a woman) undermines the whole apparatus of lofty love and divine intervention by noting with mirth how often Hélène usefully excuses her sexual indiscretions by evoking the agency of "Fate," and, lower down on the scale of anachronistic debunking (and probably a later interpolation), a feather from a messenger dove is saved for a niece who "saves stamps." In *The Black Crook,* the "Serpent's Glen" is suitably scary, and this dimension is taken seriously, but at the same time we are also invited to laugh at Hertzog's assistant, whose comic misunderstandings (in interpolated "business" and inadvertent puns not included in Barras's original) tend to deflect attention toward the contrivances, both in the story and on stage, by which the scariness is brought about.

Such intermittent references to the here-and-now in *The Black Crook* find significant echoes in more substantial interpolations, natural accretions to a show that was created by interlarding ballet into hackneyed melodrama, and supported by over-lavish, state-of-the-art stage machinery. As noted in chapter 1, this kind of aesthetic imbalance creates the possibility of layered perspectives while allowing full simultaneous access to all layers. If *The Black Crook* exposed a broad population to the special beauties of classical ballet, it did so by crassly presenting its nearly nude dancers as objects of public display. Similarly, if *The Black Crook* presented a serious story that many would, indeed, care to take seriously, it did so with a rather broad wink, undermining its "serious" content with comic business and distracting balletic episodes and elaborate special effects, for which the story itself was all too clearly a mere vehicle. But if these aspects were *generally* important for permitting a layered enjoyment of the show, topical references introduced through comic business and musical interpolations located the show in very specific terms for its American audiences, allowing them a privileged perspective from which to contemplate its various offerings, whether pitched high or low.

The subordinate nature of the story and its characters became increasingly clear with remountings and competing versions, all of which were of course called *The Black Crook,* however different they might have been in many important respects. The first successful interpolation, "You Naughty, Naughty Men" (T. Kennick and G. Bicknell), was already present at the opening: an English music hall number in the soubrette tradition in which the heroine's maid scolds men generally—those in the show, but implicitly those in the audience as well.[11] But later interpolations were more distinctively American. The 1871 revival at Niblo's introduced "The Afternoon Crawl," with lyrics by Philip Stoner, which brazenly violates whatever semblance of Aristotelian unities that might have remained in the drama by describing directly activities from contemporary Manhattan, drawing comic parallels among the behaviors that typify its most characteristic locales. The musical profile is also more distinctively late-nineteenth-century American, with a rapidly delivered, melodically non-descript, duple-meter verse yielding to a shorter, more leisurely chorus in the style of a waltz. As is typical for the waltz song (see chapter 4, pp. 71–73), each revisiting of the chorus adds an interpretive layer, not just in the parallels these returns offer, but in their contrasts as well, as the meaning of "crawl" shifts from the "strut" on Broadway, to the literal crawl of the overmatched brawler in the Bowery (a rough, more lawless area in southern Manhattan), to the parade of the dandy on Fifth Avenue (the song's full title is "The Broadway, Opera and Bowery Crawl"):

> The afternoon crawl, the afternoon crawl, For quizzing the
> darlings or making a call.
> The afternoon crawl, the afternoon crawl, I'll show you the
> Broadway afternoon crawl.
>
> The afternoon crawl, the afternoon crawl, For smoking or
> drinking or raising a brawl,
> The afternoon crawl, the afternoon crawl, I'll show you the
> Bowery afternoon crawl.
>
> The afternoon crawl, the afternoon crawl, Escorting the
> ladies to party or ball.
> The afternoon crawl, the afternoon crawl, I'll show the Fifth
> Avenue afternoon crawl.[12]

♫ 2.1

It is easy to see why such a song would "sell," both to native New Yorkers and to the tourists who attended this famous show and were thereby granted instant "insider" status. Moreover, the song places the show on the "cutting edge" of American popular music, for the waltz song had just emerged as a type, and would reach its heyday only a decade or so later. But it is hard to reconcile the obvious disrespect such an interpolation shows for the story being told (and there were many such interpolations, large and small) with the continued popularity of the show, especially as compared to imitations—some of which, surely, had more dramatically viable stories. One is almost led to conclude that Americans responded specifically to its very badness, and that this was a species of nineteenth-century low camp. But determining what, specifically, was being mocked in the transaction is no easy task. Was it the serious European (specifically, German) source for the story? The American presumption to imitate European seriousness, carried off so badly? Seriousness itself? We must note, however, that both the show and the audience's appreciation of it would have depended finally on the successful resolution to the story; to some extent, the drama did in the end have to be taken seriously, however much it might be ridiculed along the way. And, since the mockery is in this way always and ultimately withdrawn with the denouement, its specific objects may, indeed, be as varied as indicated.

What makes *The Black Crook* a viable candidate for the honor that has been duly if mockingly accorded it, as the rather unlikely "first American musical," has as much to do with its adroit balancing act between seriousness and frank frivolity as with its specific blend of music, dance, drama, and spectacle. By the same token, however, the latter specifics turn out to matter tremendously to future developments, which might easily be traced to the show: a dramatic line presumed to be central, but which is eminently capable of serving as no more than a convenient vehicle (and will only rarely be esteemed as literature); music in the popular style of the day, elevated perhaps through its association with a specific dramatic situation; dance that includes not only important solo work, but also a synchronized chorus whose female contingent is dressed in either extremely elaborate or extremely revealing costumes (or both); and elaborate stage machinery, seen by many to marry technology to art, and often seen as well to be both a measure of relative importance and fundamental to any expectation for commercial success.

London: W. S. Gilbert (1836–1911) and Arthur Sullivan (1842–1900)

England's light opera tradition for a time became the central foreign model for American musical theater, especially and specifically after the team of Gilbert and Sullivan had demonstrated its potential in a series of collaborations that was (for Americans, at least) headed by *H.M.S. Pinafore* (1878), *The Pirates of Penzance* (1879), *Patience* (1881), and *The Mikado* (1885). In all of these, political satire or some other form of cultural critique is wedded to an ostentatiously improbable plot sustaining songs with consistently clever lyrics set deftly by a master musical craftsman to memorable, even extraordinary, music. There has been much speculation regarding how the "chemistry" between these two very different creative personalities could produce a series of (mostly) hits, in America as well as in London, such as would remain an unrivaled achievement until a similar phenomenon occurred some seventy years later on Broadway (with the string of successful collaborations between Rodgers and Hammerstein, beginning with *Oklahoma!* in 1943). This speculation divides readily into two interrelated questions, regarding not only how their words and music, together, achieve a result far surpassing (in its broad, sustained appeal, at least) anything either man would produce on his own, but also how two men who did not particularly like each other managed nevertheless to continue to work together over an increasingly fraught period of some twenty years. While the latter question has received much useful attention (most vividly in the 1999 Mike Leigh film, *Topsy-Turvy*), always with due emphasis on the impresario Richard D'Oyly Carte and his Savoy Theatre, it is the former question that must concern us here.

While both Gilbert and Sullivan had serious ambitions, as dramatist and operatic composer respectively, neither believed that musical comedy was the best place to achieve his larger goals; nevertheless, their principal legacy of valued *works* is wholly within the realm of musical comedy. A version of this paradox, involving a discrepancy between ambition and the perceived limits of genre, haunts the later history of the American musical as well, where it is typically seen to result from a conflict between art and commerce. In the case of Gilbert and Sullivan, venue and medium, backed by commercial considerations, dictated a topical *now*ness that stood squarely behind the immediate success of their best collaborations, but has over time given their work an air of quaintness at odds with our notion of the timelessness of great art. Thus, despite the Savoy Theatre's preservationist energies, interest in the shows has worn thin in recent decades.[13] While there are undoubtedly many reasons for this decline, the principal cause is surely the steady shift over the past century or so in general perceptions of and attitudes toward the age of fading cultural imperialism in which the shows are grounded, from *prideful* national legacy to *shameful* national legacy, sliding gradually along the way from pleasant myth to wistful nostalgia, and from nostalgia to a species of camp. No doubt, some combination of all of these is present in most audiences today, but the pall of collective guilt, especially concerning the most celebrated of the shows, *The Mikado* (see chapter 10, pp. 250–60), casts an increasingly ominous shadow over the future of the shows insofar as they might be indulged as unsullied light diversion. Yet, timeless or not, they have survived well enough to become a central part of America's inheritance, to an extent unmatched by any other European music after Beethoven, both as works and through their impact on American popular music (and most specifically, of course, on the American musical). How is it, though, that a commercially driven body of work devalued by its own creators could have had this lasting an effect?

What has not always been well understood about how art and commerce interact here and in later similar circumstances, is that, for elaborate musical theater generally, commerce enables and sustains art rather than the reverse, and that this is, arguably, far more often for better than for worse. Commerce places the audience squarely at the center of what must matter for artists involved with what is by its nature a collaborative art, so that an audience's continued support ensures both that a given work can be fine-tuned even after it is ostensibly complete, and that its collaborators will be given further opportunities to collaborate, often with more reliable means at their disposal. As the careers of Gilbert and Sullivan demonstrate, this framework, which might as easily (and of course often does) degenerate into pandering, can uniquely and in the best circumstances provide serious artists—providing they are also highly skilled, specialized craftsmen of some facility—a fecund arena to produce work of lasting value that can survive, specifically, as *works* of lasting value.

Nevertheless, the success of Gilbert and Sullivan as a creative team has often seemed surprising, since the collaborative mix in this case is a decidedly peculiar one. The cleverness and pointedness of Gilbert's contribution bespeak his lawyer's training, which bred in him, paradoxically but usefully, both a fondness and a contempt for specious argument—for the ways in which verbal cleverness can seem to create its own reality and imperatives—and provided a context in which he could explore the rich possibilities for making telling points through humor and exaggeration. The sharply calculated aspect of Gilbert's construction of situation and lyrics, which may be seen to result from this background and from his own preoccupations (abnormal psychology and various social/political issues), provides a stark contrast to the warmth and tuneful expression of Sullivan's music. This very discrepancy is often seen as valuable, lending bite to Sullivan's sentimentality and making Gilbert's sometimes bitterly caustic machinations seem surprisingly warm and human. But their collaboration was not simply a "happy accident," for the collaborative component of their art was firmly under the control of Sullivan, who had Gilbert's words in hand before he began to compose, and who was not only immensely talented, but also superbly trained, a former prodigy who had learned his craft well at the Leipzig Conservatory, the premier institution of its kind.

Like Mozart, Sullivan wrote well and quickly because he knew and practiced composition as a craft he had mastered through diligence and application. Like Mozart, he knew through training and study how best to create and manage a whole range of musical *effects,* and thus he wrote with a finely calculating knowingness—a knowingness such as is too often assumed to be at odds with natural warmth and feeling. Above all, however, he knew how to create the central effect of *naturalness.* We must underscore here the nontrivial fact that music is never "natural" in any traditionally meaningful way; naturalness in music is always an *effect,* and a particularly difficult one to achieve for a composer who, like Sullivan, tried hard to transcend the commonplace, who, as a crucial starting point in setting a text, tried "to get as much originality as possible in the rhythm."[14] And, when all is said and done, it is above all the effect of naturalness in Sullivan's musical settings that gave Gilbert's verbal sophistries their persuasive plausibility and won Sullivan instant and lasting success with audiences.

The success of Gilbert and Sullivan's shows in America stems in part from what made them succeed in England: relevance and a consistently high degree of inspiration and craft. In all these dimensions their work enjoyed a supreme advantage over continental offerings. Simply by being in English, the shows were more easily understood in America and, in particular, both Gilbert's wit and Sullivan's musical response to his wit were able to speak more immediately. Additionally, since many Americans continued in the late nineteenth century to locate their cultural roots in England, their quick and positive response to the Savoy operas involved at least some degree of communal pride; in learning the songs and singing them with relish, they strengthened anew their bond to the country from whence the songs came. But the Savoy operas were also, and from the beginning, a somewhat different thing for Americans than they were for the English. Pronunciation had already diverged sufficiently for at least some of Gilbert's rhymes to seem affected to Americans (although in truth much of the affectation was Gilbert's)—which is to say, they seemed foreign. The political basis for Gilbert's humor created not only a sense of recognition in America, but also an awareness of difference, for political structures and issues, too, had diverged dramatically. And the music itself was distinctly more European than American, with little or none of the diverse African-American inflections, already then present to some extent in American music (in minstrelsy and spirituals), that would eventually develop into the idioms of jazz and blues. These subtle shades of difference helped Americans to recognize and appreciate the ways in which their own development had diverged from that of their English counterparts; in conjunction with Gilbert's often pointed critique of English mores, these easily perceived differences encouraged Americans to see themselves in a more favorable light.

In one other respect, the Savoy operas were especially palatable to American audiences, for they managed to provide an extraordinary amount of sometimes wicked fun without transgressing the then-current bounds of respectability. This was no accident, as the team's rise in general popularity in England corresponded precisely with their concerted effort to purge their work of elements that might offend this respectability. Their first collaboration (*Thespis*, 1871—coincidentally the same year Sullivan composed his most famous hymn, "Onward, Christian Soldiers") included a prominent "pants" role, in which a woman plays a young male; in other ways, as well, *Thespis* fit easily into the music-hall sensibilities prevalent in the burlesques, travesties, and extravaganzas of the time. Although reasonably successful, *Thespis* was trapped somewhat within this world (which is probably the main reason it was neither revived nor published), and both collaborators resolved thereafter, as Gilbert would later put it,

> that our plots, however, ridiculous, should be coherent; that our dialogue should be void of offence; that, on artistic principles, no man should play a woman's part and no woman a man's. Finally, we agreed that no lady in the company should be required to wear a dress that she could not wear with absolute propriety at a private fancy-dress ball.[15]

Respectability and propriety became increasingly important as they continued to collaborate. The one-act *Trial by Jury* (1875), which came next, was conceived as an afterpiece to Offenbach's somewhat daring *La Périchole*; this may explain both its occasional "improprieties" and, in particular, its prominent references to being "tipsy," a condition that audiences would have seen enacted on stage by the heroine earlier in the evening. In their next show, *The Sorcerer* (1876), they flirt with the possibility of scandal by introducing a love potion and involving a clergyman in a leading role, but they comically avert offense through reassurances that the love potion cannot work on married people, and conclude with a parodic *bacchanalia* that takes the form of a quite respectable tea party. Significantly, these comic "rescues" not only adhere to the prevailing standards of respectability, they also critique them, so that audiences could as readily take them either way. In this way, as with the imposition of the Hays code on Hollywood films in 1930, the push toward respectability opens up an often witty discourse in which audiences become increasingly alert to the possibility of double meanings, so that respectable surfaces are routinely seen to disguise (or emphasize!) a quite different reality beneath. This potential duality would underlie much of the humor in Gilbert and Sullivan's later shows, as when British sailors appear in the main happy and contented (*Pinafore*) less than a century after the realities of seafaring life were brought under public scrutiny by the mutiny of *H.M.S. Bounty*,[16] and kind-hearted pirates seek only the respectability of marriage (*Pirates of Penzance*). But the team's prudish concern for propriety seems nevertheless quite genuine, and aligns well with their shared aspiration to achieve work of greater artistic merit.

It may well seem ironic, then, that their impulse to move toward respectability, especially in references to sexuality, resulted fairly directly in their opening interpretive avenues to otherwise culturally dangerous alternatives. In cleaning up the sailors in *Pinafore,* for example, dressing them in cute sailor outfits and having them function as a singing and dancing chorus, they provided an important vehicle not only for camp, but also for its homosexual inflections. And in making the rivalry of clergymen in *Patience* less likely to provoke censure by turning the rivals instead into poets, and then proceeding to model one of them directly on Oscar Wilde (albeit well before his ruinous trial for homosexuality), they manage to reinforce not only the strong association of poetic refinement and effeminacy (read homosexuality) in nineteenth-century England, but also—if inadvertently—the growing tendency for Americans to equate both of these, as well as general foppery, with Britishness itself (the latter understood to be a subset of a more general European descent into decadence).[17] Such ironies aside, however, Gilbert and Sullivan's reassuring respectability paved their way to wide acceptance in an America faced with the paradox of feeling hopelessly inferior to Europe in the realm of arts and letters, yet fearing the decadent excess that seemed endemic to European high culture. Many Americans found in Gilbert and Sullivan, and in English culture generally, a middle-ground sensibility, refined in taste and temperament, yet reliably respectable in outlook.

H.M.S. Pinafore; or, The Lass That Loved a Sailor (1878), although Gilbert and Sullivan's fourth collaboration, was only the second to respond to a public that had begun to embrace their work enthusiastically. Its timing for American audiences was especially propitious, coming immediately on the heels of the Centennial celebrations, and referring climactically if comically to one of that event's most celebrated technological unveilings, the telephone.[18] *Pinafore*'s comic engagement with English society's hierarchies and its oblique references to notorious naval abuses would have been comforting to Americans, not only through its suggesting, however satirically, that such abuses were a thing of the past, but also because its characters were, after all, English—*referentially*

English, as historical abusers of personal freedom, and *representationally* English, as regimented, contented mannequins in sailor suits. And *Pinafore*'s self-deprecating portrayal of English seamanship—an important locus of both English patriotic pride and contentious American engagement in the nineteenth century—was all the more enticing in that there were no royalties to pay, since no effective international copyrights existed then.

Particularly memorable and endlessly quoted was the conclusion of the first musical exchange between the Captain and his crew (in bold):

[*recitative*]

CAPTAIN: My gallant crew, good morning!

CREW: Sir, good morning!

CAPTAIN: I hope you're quite well.

CREW: Quite well, and you, sir?

CAPTAIN: I am in reasonable health, and happy to meet you all once more.

CREW: You do us proud, sir!

[*song*]

CAPTAIN: I am the captain of the *Pinafore*!

CREW: And a right good captain, too!

CAPTAIN: You're very, very good, And, be it understood,
I command a right good crew.

CREW: We're very, very good, And, be it understood,
He commands a right good crew.

CAPTAIN: Though related to a peer, I can hand, reef, and steer,
Or ship a selvagee;
I am never known to quail At the fury of a gale,
And I'm never, never sick at sea!

CREW: **What, never?**

CAPTAIN: **No, never!**

CREW: **What, *never*?**

CAPTAIN: **Hardly ever!**

CREW: **He's hardly ever sick at sea!**
Then give three cheers, and one cheer more,
For the hardy captain of the *Pinafore*!
Then give three cheers, and one cheer more,
For the captain of the *Pinafore*!
♪ **2.2**

It is not easy to explain adequately the immediate and enduring popularity of the "What, never?" . . . "Hardly ever!" exchange—not because it is unworthy of this popularity, but because there are so many things to point to by way of explanation. There is, first of all, the conceit of ren-

Figure 2.2. Many of Gilbert's operetta librettos derive from his *Bab Ballads,* originally published in *Fun* magazine and accompanied by his own drawings, signed "Bab." In two of his illustrations for "Captain Reece" (1868), the partial basis for *H.M.S. Pinafore,* we find the good captain of the *Mantelpiece* handing out "cream ices" to his crew and dancing for them "like mad" . . . "If ever they were dull or sad" (top left and right). Gilbert later reversed the process, basing his *Songs of a Savoyard* (for which he again provided drawings) on his Sullivan collaborations; in his drawing for "The Englishman" (bottom), we find Ralph, "in spite of all temptations / To belong to other nations," staunchly remaining an Englishman.

dering dialogue exchanges between Captain and crew as polite, genteel conversation. Supporting that conceit is Sullivan's deft musical setting, the outlines of which are already implicit in Gilbert's lyric, which divides naturally into a *recitative* (a speech-like style of singing used for dialogue in opera) followed by the song proper. This musical construct comically apes the traditional recitative-aria structure of opera, with an effect especially funny in this case because, surprisingly, the lower-class sailors adroitly assume control of an "elevated" musical discourse obviously alien to their lowly station. Beyond tweaking the artificiality of opera, this device thus also has political ramifications, both because it imposes a "leveling of ranks" (on which, more later) and because the crew actually controls and directs the exchange that the Captain ostensibly leads.

The rationale for the crew's dominance is partly musical, derived from the concerto on the one hand and grand opera on the other, wherein the larger musical force (the chorus in opera, the orchestra in the concerto) represents power and stability, giving the soloist the choice of either opposing its authority or forming an alliance with it, the latter either through persuasion or through being persuaded. Since this precisely inverts the autocratic dynamic that normally operates on board a ship (and, implicitly, within a monarchy), we do well to consider that Gilbert and Sullivan might have contrived a more fully supportive role for the chorus—as, indeed, they had just minutes before. In the preceding number, Ralph Rackstraw (traditionally referred to as "Rafe" and described as the "smartest lad in all the fleet") comically acknowledges the echoing support of his "messmates" in order, it would seem, to highlight their punning misconstrual of the final phrase of his lament:

[*recitative*]
RALPH: I know the value of a kindly chorus,
                  But choruses yield little consolation
             When we have pain, and sorrow, too, before us!
                  I love—and love, alas, above my station!
BUTTERCUP: He loves, and loves a lass above his station.
CHORUS: Yes, yes, the lass is much above his station.   ♪ 2.3

But in calling attention to the supportive aspect of the solo-group dynamic here, there is more riding in the balance than the rather tired pun of the final line before Ralph's ballad (which follows immediately), for the scene is also pointedly establishing a model that the Captain's recitative and song in the next number can seem at first to follow, but ultimately deny. In the recitative that introduces *his* song, the Captain begins each phrase but leaves it for the crew to complete, which they do with exaggerated force, reaching a melodic peak in the characteristic concluding phrase. Within the song itself, this principle of exchange develops further, as the crew interrupts and completes the Captain's opening musical phrase, and thus seems to impel, as tribute, the Captain's extensive compliment to them that follows, which they repeat with obvious satisfaction. The second half of the song seems at first to depart from this model of exchange, as the Captain now sings his own praises with a "heroic" melody that climbs steadily up a complete scale and ends in obvious self-satisfaction. But his expansive boast proves, not surprisingly, to be a setup for the deflation to follow. By rights, as in the first half, the crew should at this point echo approvingly what the Captain has sung, but they instead question his veracity, forcing him to compromise his forthright claims, and only then providing a much-abridged supporting echo. Thus re-established as the stronger force, they conclude with a chorus of faintly ironic cheers for their emasculated "leader."

Sullivan's skillful manipulation of musical convention makes this outcome seem "right," however far it may be from the realities of sailors and their captains. The *Pinafore*'s Captain needs the crew's cooperation, not merely to run the ship (which is scarcely an issue in the show), but to complete his song; their first "What, never?" seems at first to give him an opportunity to reaffirm his authority, but their more insistent repetition of the question over a less settled harmony, along with the brief wait that follows it, make it clear that he must accede to them in some way, which he does by reversing the melodic direction of his response (rising instead of falling, following the direction indicated by their query), and by substituting "Hardly ever" for "No, never." Yet, the crew's "cheers" that follow seem genuinely approving, despite a tinge of irony; perhaps they acknowledge that the Captain has performed his negotiation well, yielding gracefully, but only slightly, and with scarcely a musical beat missed.

But has he given in only slightly? Despite the Captain's verbal cleverness, the logic of his "compromise," well conceived by Gilbert (the former lawyer) and quickly caught by practical-minded American audiences, says otherwise. "Hardly ever" means that, in fact, the Captain *has* been sick at sea, and that he *is* (in the next verse) prone to lapses in his refined demeanor. Backing away even slightly from absolute statements is to deny their absoluteness absolutely, and the implications regarding where true authority lies on board the *Pinafore*—and, by an extension audiences were sure to register, within the British monarchical system—was abundantly clear. Moreover, the crew is exercising a power of judgment that the Captain himself has implicitly accorded them, since his claim to personal distinction is defined entirely in relation to them: he is himself a good sailor (first verse), and he treats them with respect (second verse; specifically, "Bad language or abuse, / I never, never, use, / Whatever the emergency; / Though 'bother it' I may / Occasionally say, / I never use a big, big D—").

♫ 2.4

The special affection nineteenth-century Americans had for this exchange probably has multiple bases, all dependent in some way on those verbal and musical elements noted here, but also somewhat independent of them. Within the show, the exchange points to problematic changes in hierarchical social structures (implicitly, in England's class system more broadly), which the show manages to critique from both sides with relatively equal force, not only satirizing the presumption of political equality and its implementation, which is shown to breed disorder on board ship (and implicitly in the country at large), but also thoroughly undermining the institution of unearned authority, whether achieved through birth or through granted privilege. It is to the latter, of course, that Americans would naturally have responded whole-heartedly, but in their reading of the former, for which the "What, never?" exchange is the linchpin, their sympathies would have been strongly egalitarian, leading them to delight, if naïvely, in the crew's cheeky challenge to the Captain's authority. No doubt, from an English perspective, a richer reading is called for, in which one would note that in being "elevated" to a semblance of equality with their Captain, the crew has also become significantly less manly; however bravely they may challenge their Captain in this song, one can scarcely imagine this crew having the collective backbone either for genuine mutiny or to do their duty in battle as "England expects" them to do. Such, after all, is the point of their ship's name, *Pinafore*, taken from a frilly feminine garment. Quite naturally, however, this heightened effeminacy would have been somewhat invisible to Americans, for whom it would merge into the more general parody of English manners.

But equally important to the popularity of "What, never?" in America is its transposability to virtually *any* assertion of certainty, its ability to undermine *any* authority, independent of its specific application in *H.M.S. Pinafore*. The exchange thus came to represent, in America, an emblem of optimistic belief in progress, a device for stripping away the staid, tired, older ways and imagining something new; it became, in essence, a genteel but robust way of saying "Oh, yeah?" to established order and smug certainties. But in so construing this verbal exchange and making it their own, nineteenth-century Americans were implicitly misreading the show; indeed, their reception of this passage points to their more general tendency to broaden the show's critique of class-based hierarchies, and to see that critique as its central, overriding theme. This, in turn, allowed them to put aside *Pinafore*'s incisive engagement on the other side of the issue, and to see its satirical treatment of class as Americans themselves might have presented it—with the result that Americans would, as with the "What, never?" exchange, sometimes invert the point of Gilbert's satire, here embracing with approbation a moment of rebellion against authority that was probably meant instead to point out the dangers and limits of egalitarian attitudes when they are pushed too far.

The plot of *Pinafore* is ostentatiously simple-minded: Captain Corcoran's daughter Josephine inappropriately loves Ralph Rackstraw, a "common sailor," but is to be married off to Sir Joseph Porter, K.C.B., the "ruler of the Queen's Navee," himself under the thumb of his female relations.[19] Taking seriously Sir Joseph's assertion that "Love levels all ranks," Ralph and Josephine declare their mutual love and attempt with the help of the crew to elope, but are caught and about to be punished, when Little Buttercup, a "bumboat woman" (a port-based peddler woman) secretly admired by and in love with the Captain, confesses that she switched Captain Corcoran and Ralph when they were babies entrusted to her care. In the denouement, the two men resume their "rightful" places, Ralph is able to marry Josephine (now too plebeian for Sir Joseph, who is claimed by cousin Hebe), and the former Captain proposes to Buttercup. While the wrap-up has always managed to baffle the literal-minded, who want to know (among other things) how the ages of the principals can possibly be reconciled within the switched-babies gambit—which has the former Captain content to marry his daughter off to someone literally old enough to have been her father, and proposing marriage to the perpetrator of a major crime, a woman who had been his own nursemaid "A many years ago"—yet, such bafflement folds easily into the show's surreal charm.

Within this world, definitively described at the time as "topsy-turvydom," it is not clear if we are to note as more important *Pinafore*'s implicit assertion that social order is utterly arbitrary—or its not-so-subtle hints to the contrary, portraying Ralph throughout as a person of considerably higher sensibilities than the Captain and Josephine, and pointing up the great harm that may befall when someone maliciously tampers, as does Buttercup, with the established institutions of social order. Similarly, it is not clear whether we are to note, most centrally, Sir Joseph's ability to manipulate the system or his ultimate failure to do so (at least, domestically). And we may well wonder whether this early example of a scamp (Sir Joseph) being punished in the end by falling prey to a domineering woman (Hebe) reflects Gilbert's family situation, as many have claimed; obliquely addresses, during the height of Queen Victoria's reign, the peculiar English penchant for enjoying its periods of greatest glory while being presided over by queens rather than kings; explores the paradoxical situation of sometimes powerful women whose power, however, derives from the men they control or manipulate; or merely critiques with bemused equanimity an on-going view of male-female relations as a battleground fraught with sudden reversals.

H.M.S. Pinafore, like many of Gilbert and Sullivan's shows, opens with a fair span of continuous music, in this case linking its first two staged numbers, which introduce the sailors and Buttercup, respectively. As a result, the joke of having the most lowly characters sing in recitative is established early on, with Buttercup's entrance; moreover, the general strategy of working up the social ladder is highlighted, as dialogue then sets off, in the order in which they make their first appearances, Ralph, followed by the Captain and Josephine in succession without punctuating dialogue, followed by Sir Joseph's female relations and Sir Joseph, also in succession without punctuating dialogue. Within this clearly mapped structure, individual song-types demarcate with some precision each of the groups and principals and the interactive dynamic between and among them. The opening number for the sailors, "We sail the ocean blue," rollicks effectively, and establishes immediately their livelihood as the locus for patriotic pride. Buttercup, after announcing herself with what amounts to a musical salute to the brave sailors, sings a simple waltz-song, "I'm Called Little Buttercup," a type of song already marked by 1878 as somewhat lower-class through its popularity in the music halls and other performance venues catering to a less refined population (although a more lilting version of the waltz, following its heritage as a couple-dance and its continued association with Vienna, continues long after to be associated with romance). ♪ **2.5** ♪ **2.6**

Significant as well, the music for both the sailors and Buttercup virtually requires accompanying dance, which helps underscore the effeminacy already established for the sailors through the very name of their ship. Ralph, however, sings more elevated music in slower tempos, betokening his more refined sensibility. He enters singing a madrigal ("The Nightingale"), a type of part-song associated with high musical culture in England even though it was originally an Italian import.[20] From the somewhat archaic language of this and his ensuing ballad ("A Maiden Fair to See"), and from his archly poetic and musical styles, we might easily recognize Ralph even at this stage as well-born, if only in aspiration. Moreover, in the Captain's more matter-of-fact verbal and musical styles (in his "Recitative and Song" already discussed), we might recognize that he is a "man of the people," although, again, that may be only by aspiration. For her part, Josephine also sings a ballad ("Sorry Her Lot"), a musical assonance with Ralph that underscores their as-yet unspoken bond.

With the entrance of Sir Joseph's female relatives, music plays an increasingly subtle role in defining position and establishing relationships. ♪ **2.7** Initially, the women sing a lilting barcarolle, "Over the Bright Blue Sea," a genteel kind of *salon* music meant to depict the motion of a boat in a calm sea (a musical type associated originally with Venice); that this is a rather too-dainty counterpart to the sailor's opening number is made clear enough through the odd profile presented by the climactic line, "Bang-bang, the loud ninepounders go!" as set against the unchanging, rolling pulse of the 9/8 barcarolle. Immediately following, however, the women meet the musical challenge of the sailor's reprise of their opening number by singing a more sprightly song, "Gaily Tripping, Lightly Skipping," that will, in fact, combine well with the sailor's tune as they sing together. This pattern, of singing two songs separately and then together, which is sometimes understood as a subspecies of the older "quodlibet" but which may more simply be referred to as a "combination-song," will become a mainstay of the Broadway stage, not only because of its innate charm, but also because it has proven both effective and versatile in establishing relationships ranging from genuine compatibility—as here—to the strikingly incompatible. Demonstrably, then, the women can stoop easily to the sailor's level—and, indeed, their easy adaptation allows them to serve throughout, musically, as the sailor's feminine (and implicitly feminizing) counterparts. Yet, they can also assert themselves as more than equals to Sir Joseph, as will be clear shortly.

Sir Joseph is given throughout a particularly bland melodic profile, which may have been partly a response to the rather modest vocal capabilities of the original singer-actor (George Grossmith), but which is used nevertheless to telling dramatic effect by Sullivan. In his first song, "I Am the Monarch of the Sea," he sings three phrases to the same boring repeated-note melody before Hebe and the other women take it over, first investing it with more rhythmic energy and eventually carrying it to both a new melodic level and a new key; Sir Joseph can then do no more than accept the new level, whereupon they repeat the process, returning to the home key. In this way, his female relatives usurp all musical control— rhythmic, melodic, harmonic, and dynamic—and reveal Sir Joseph to be impotent to resist their will.[21] In Sir Joseph's following song, "When I Was a Lad," however, his seeming impotence is shown to be his ace in the hole. "When I Was a Lad" recounts, through six verses punctuated by the full chorus of sailors and female relatives, Sir Joseph's rise from "office boy," through junior clerk, articled clerk, junior partner, member of parliament, all the way to his present lofty position as "ruler of the Queen's Navee." Remarkably, each verse individually traces that rise in musical terms, including its bland basis and its nautical goal. The opening phrase begins with a monotonously methodic melodic descent that seems unable to break free from the same four notes of the scale Sir Joseph had been stuck on throughout the previous song, yet it ends with a figure faintly suggestive of the "sailor's hornpipe." While the hornpipe is by origin neither English nor associated with the sea, being rather a traditional country dance similar to the jig and native to Wales and Scotland, its identification with English sailors became fixed by the late nineteenth century, largely through familiarity with this tune (published in 1855–59 as part of W. Chappell's *Popular Music of the Olden Time;* later audiences will recognize it as the instrumental coda to "Popeye, the Sailor Man"). As shown by the brackets in example 2.1, the faint resemblance at the conclusion of the first phrase grows more pronounced across the song in gradual stages, with the conclusion of each successive phrase, until the resemblance to the famous tune is unmistakable.

If Sir Joseph thus musically demonstrates his own trajectory from boring lackey to "Monarch of the Seas," we hear a slightly different trajectory to a similarly seaworthy endpoint in the "glee" that he gives the sailors to learn during the ensuing action (the glee tradition developed

Example 2.1

"Sailor's Hornpipe"

W.S. Gilbert and Arthur Sullivan, "When I Was A Lad" (vocal melody)

When I was a lad I served a term As of-fice boy to an at-tor-ney's firm, I cleaned the win-dows and I swept the floor, And I po-lished up the han-dle of the big front door. He po-lished up the han-dle of the big front door. I po-lished up that han-dle so care-ful-lee, That now I am the ru-ler of the Queen's Na-vee! He po-lished up that han-dle so care-ful-lee, That now he is the ru-ler of the Queen's Na-vee!

during a revival of the English madrigal in the eighteenth century, as an originally all-male alternative). Sung a capella (that is, without instrumental accompaniment), "A British Tar" moves, as the glee tradition dictates, from a homophonic opening to a more intricate contrapuntal section in which the voices become more independent of each other. This results in a patch of thorny counterpoint, which seems to be designed to sound as awkward as possible while staying within the bounds of correct part-writing, but which is deftly put aside in the final section, as the sailors, now with the support of the orchestra, convert its melodic fragments into another hornpipe. Here again the prevailing topsy-turvydom makes interpretation difficult, as we move from the odd starting-point of a ludicrously high level of musical literacy—with the ex-office-boy Sir Joseph giving common sailors a complicated part-song of his own devising, which they then sight-read—to a resolution within the song that reduces those complications to a straightforward hornpipe. Does this process ennoble the hornpipe, by grounding it in both hymn-styles and counterpoint? Or does it do the reverse, by resorting to the hornpipe as a trivialization that rescues the sailors from their failure to execute a difficult style? Does it ridicule the "cultivated" glee tradition through exaggeration? (Here, the presence of an unwilling audience in the person of the much-reviled and grotesquely ugly Dick Deadeye provides some evidence that this is indeed part of the point, since his plain speaking has already offered a needed perspective on the affected pretensions of those around him.) Are the awkward passages a failure of Sir Joseph's compositional abilities or of the sailors' singing abilities—or are they, perhaps, an indictment of the glee tradition itself, in which musically incompetent men aspire to difficulties they cannot master? Any and all of these are de-

♪ 2.14 fensible interpretations, easily suggested and reinforced in performance.

The musical climax of the second and final act amounts to a presentation in Ralph's defense by the boatswain acting for the moment as a makeshift defending barrister, and caps Sullivan's deft manipulation of English musical tropes. Specifically, in "He Is an Englishman!" Sullivan evokes Handel at his most overblown and pompous to set a tautological text that implicitly mocks the core of nationalist ideology, with a dollop of provincialism thrown in for good measure (provided courtesy of Gilbert's exaggerated mispronunciations):

> For he might have been a Roosian,
>   A French, or Turk, or Proosian,
>   Or perhaps I-tal-i-an!
> But in spite of all temptations
>   To belong to other nations,
> He remains an Englishman!
> He remains an Englishman!

♪ 2.15   [as sung: "He remai-ains a-an He-he-he-he-he-he-he-he-he-Henglishman!"]

Choosing Handel as his model is a sophisticated masterstroke on Sullivan's part, not only because the style suits the moment perfectly, but also because Handel, the quintessential English composer, was himself just about everything but English, being "Proosian" by birth and "Eye-tal-eye-an" by training (indeed, putting aside the initial moves from "Roosian" through "French, or Turk," the song amounts to a brief biography of England's most esteemed composer before Sullivan). In fact, Sullivan seems here to culminate a thoroughgoing and quite erudite mockery of English nationalism that he has carefully woven into the show through his music, in which, as noted, the Welsh/Scottish-derived hornpipe defines the English sailor, the Italian-derived madrigal the exalted sensibilities of Ralph, and its offshoot—the glee—the aspiration of the sailors to a greater refinement. (We may wish to recall in this regard that Sullivan, who often seemed to prefer continental Europe to England, was himself of mixed Irish-Italian descent, with possibly also some Jewish heritage.) Despite its late appearance, "He Is an Englishman!" is twice reprised, and actually returns to close the show; remarkably, especially in repetition, the number seems to celebrate, or at least to indulge, the very thing it mocks—a frequently encountered feature of high camp.

More than any other work, *H.M.S. Pinafore* established the tradition of treating England comically, albeit with great affection, in American musicals (cf. *Anything Goes,* chapter 4). As a model, it also suggested the possibilities inherent in musical comedy for demonstrating and encouraging nationalist sentiment, since *Pinafore,* as just observed, celebrated Englishness as much as it mocked it. The great success of *Pinafore* in America was undoubtedly aided enormously by the fact that there were then no effective international copyright laws—a situation Gilbert and Sullivan addressed in the title and subject matter of their next outing (*The Pirates of Penzance*), and by premiering the new work in New York to protect their rights in America. But for better or worse, *Pinafore* was in its early years rarely heard in America in the form that Gilbert and Sullivan intended. This probably facilitated its acceptance by audiences, who would have been more reassured than dismayed at interpolations that made the show seem even more relevant to Americans, and who, as with *The Black Crook,* might return to a new production in part because it would be both familiar and yet different in some of its details from what they would have heard and seen previously.

Pinafore had a distinct advantage over *The Black Crook,* in that it could serve nearly as easily as a vehicle for topical accretion and yet was also in itself a splendidly crafted musico-dramatic piece. The consequences of this disparity are stark indeed. What ultimately is left standing as the legacy of *The Black Crook* is an enviable bottom-line that fostered a taste for the exotic coupled with an indulgence in effect and display. The legacy of *Pinafore,* however, is of a different order, for it was the first such work, pitched within an emergent popular culture, to attain the status of an enduring "classic," in the two senses that it continues to be performed as it was originally written, and that latter-day productions tend to be judged in part for how well they are perceived to capture the spirit of the original. In this sense, the two shows serve as useful bookends, pointing to two different but enduring standards of value for American musical theater, which between them embrace the full history of the genre to date.

For Further Consideration

Offenbach: *La Belle Hélène* (1864) and *La Vie Parisienne* (1866); Strauss: *Die Fledermaus* (1874); Gilbert and Sullivan: *The Pirates of Penzance; or, The Slave of Duty* (1879), *Patience; or Bunthorne's Bride* (1881), and *The Mikado; or, The Town of Titipu* (1885); Lehár: *The Merry Widow* (1905)

See Also

For a good overview of the French operetta tradition, see chapters 1–2 in Andrew Lamb's *150 Years of Popular Musical Theatre;* see also Kurt Gänzl's good, if brief, account in the chapter on "Opéra-Bouffe" in his *The Musical: A Concise History.* Lamb also provides a good account of the American reception of European imports (chapter 8).

Regarding *The Black Crook,* see Gerald Mast's discussion in *Can't Help Singin'* (pp. 7–15), the "Intermission" of Julian Mates's *America's Musical Stage,* chapter 2 of Cecil Smith and Glenn Litton's *Musical Comedy in America,* and Kristina Gintautiene's "The Black Crook: Ballet in the Gilded Age (1866–1876)"; see also pp. 351–53 in David Ewen's *Complete Book of the American Musical.*

Regarding *Pinafore,* chapter 6 of Gayden Wren's *A Most Ingenious Paradox* offers a thoughtful analysis. Regarding the influence of *Pinafore* on the next generation in America, see chapters 2–3 in Gerald Bordman's *American Operetta.*

Early American Developments:

Minstrelsy, Extravaganza, Pantomime, Burlesque, Vaudeville

THE AMERICAN MUSICAL developed, apart from following European models, out of a handful of specifically American types. Before the importation, adaptation, and imitation of European shows changed the direction of American developments, the most popular forms of staged American musical entertainments in the nineteenth century catered to an eclectic and often raucous mix of styles and conceits, never quite left behind even though many of them became quite offensive to later sensibilities (especially minstrelsy, whose legacy is particularly complex and troubling). For a very long time, many of these types remained viable even while what we now consider the mainstream became established, and they continued to wield their various influences. Part of the reason for this tenacity lay in the common dependency of all these types on song, which the more eclectic venues exploited particularly well; this shared basis will be explored more fully in the following chapter.

By the late nineteenth century, America was audience to a wide variety of staged entertainments involving some combination of costumed singing, dancing, instrumental music, humor, and drama. The model of evolution has often been called into play to explain how these various types "evolved" into the American musical, and the model has enough to offer that we might pursue it here. As an explanation for the existence of a "higher form" (thus, *homo sapiens;* or the American musical) that relates more or less directly to earlier "lower forms" from which it may be shown to have derived (thus, from earlier primates, mammals, etc.; or, from minstrelsy, extravaganza, etc.), evolution is at once satisfying and troubling. When we consider these earlier musical traditions, we are reassured that the evolving American musical has welded the good that they have to offer into something more enduring and valuable; evolution thus provides us with a compelling narrative of aesthetic *progress,* and allows us to feel a condescending affection for at least some of the more "primitive" types from which the American musical "evolved." But this narrative of evolutionary progress fails to account adequately for a great deal, since the American musical does not simply displace earlier types, nor foreswear the later acquisition of "inferior" or "regressive" features, nor even evolve appreciably beyond many aspects of earlier types that we are apt to object to, be they persistent racist attitudes, a pronounced tendency to pander, or merely a stubborn resistance to further "evolutionary" refinement. While nearly all of these failures to "progress" satisfactorily can be explained in terms of market forces—the "bottom-line" arbiter of survival in the business of making musicals—such explanations will scarcely matter to those who care deeply about the aspirational dimension of the American musical's developmental history.

If many in the nineteenth century rejected (as do many still today) the idea that traces of the monkey and apes might be found in humanity, so then are many of those involved in American musical theater—including professionals, amateurs, audience, and critics—unhappy with the image of the American musical emerging out of the swamp of minstrelsy and farce of the nineteenth century. Many would rather see the genre in terms of its potential to become the American equivalent of European opera. But here there are important differences between the history of the musical and the controversies centered around evolutionary theory. While the notion that humanity was created in God's image may hinge first of all on disputes regarding God's very existence, there are no such disputes regarding the existence of opera (although its elevated status may perhaps be contested). Even if some would find opera an inappropriate ideal for the American musical to aspire to, there is no doubt that opera has throughout provided an important model both from "above" and "below," that is, both as a standard to aspire to and as a genre whose traces and influence may be found in virtually all of the nineteenth-century "entertainments" from which the musical developed (especially operetta). We have already seen how European ballet played a direct role in the early development of the musical, through the immense popularity of *The Black Crook* (1866), whose success was much imitated. Similarly, musical entertainments of various types often found it useful to draw directly on opera for inspiration; here, too, *The Black Crook* is a prime example, with its direct modeling on Weber's *Der Freischütz*. While this dependence on opera might often take the form of satire, as when elements of the "high style" appear in incongruous circumstances (e.g., the recitatives in *H.M.S. Pinafore*), operatic styles and genres, operatic singers, and actual arias excerpted from operas afforded opportunities to extend the expressive and aesthetic range of an entertainment, offering even the most pandering of them the redemptive patina of higher sensibilities. In short, the American musical both ascended from the "lower" forms we will consider here, and descended from the "higher" forms of opera and ballet, losing sight of neither the market base of the former nor the aesthetic aspirations of the latter. With the American musical, then, it won't do either to take a simple evolutionary approach or to insist on some form of operatically directed Creationism.

That being said, there is little point in recounting here the history of opera in the late nineteenth century, which has been a frequent subject of historical surveys in its own right. Importantly, American veneration of European high culture in the late nineteenth century supported the importation of European opera, especially in New York City, so that the operatic music of Mozart, Bellini, Wagner, and Verdi, among others, was readily accessible as both model and satirical object.[1] Moreover, operatic airs, often in simplified versions and in translation, had long since become the mainstay of both private and public music-making in the United States, and formed the basis for the sentimental parlor style that had emerged by mid-century. While there were valiant attempts—mainly unsuccessful—to produce outright an American version of European-style opera (for example, George Bristow's *Rip Van Winkle,* produced in 1855 at Niblo's Garden), these fared no better than a handful of imported English operas on which they were mostly modeled, and played little part in the later emergence of operatic ambitions within the American musical. Our more pressing task here will be to set out some of the less well-known (because less prestigious) types that contributed to the early history of the American musical.

For somewhat different reasons, we will also forego discussions here of the eighteenth-century genre known as "ballad opera" and of other similar genres from the nineteenth century, despite their striking similarity to many shows that might be counted within the broad rubric of the "American musical" as outlined in chapter 1.[2] Since before the American Revolution, and corresponding to English traditions and early German *Singspiele,* plays with interpolated songs have been common in America. But recounting the history of this general type—of which the ballad opera is the earliest important instance—would be beside the point here, since what counts for the American musical as it emerged in the twentieth century is not the full history of partially sung plays, but the coupling of that general type with the demands and opportunities of commercial success on a large scale. It is the latter consideration that compels us to consider the specific alternative types of minstrelsy, extravaganza, pantomime, burlesque, and vaudeville, with particular emphasis on the first of these.[3]

Minstrelsy

Minstrelsy took hold in New York City beginning in 1843, when Dan Emmett's Virginia Minstrels put together a full evening's entertainment from the kind of blackface specialty acts that had developed over the previous decades (at least as early as 1815).[4] The minstrel show maintained its popularity there until after the Civil War, when it became increasingly marked as a more provincial entertainment. The minstrel show remained popular considerably longer in other parts of America, however, and achieved substantial success in England, as well as in continental Europe. Thus, Gilbert and Sullivan refer to minstrelsy in *The Mikado* (1885) and include a parody of a minstrel number in *Utopia Limited* (1893; see discussion later in this chapter). Among the earliest of its various standard offerings, the minstrel show purported to re-create plantation life and presented in its early stages an idealized, genteel version of American slavery that was partly undercut in some of the humorous exchanges between the central interlocutor and the percussion-playing endmen of the classic minstrel-show lineup.

Minstrelsy had many specific antecedents across the early decades of the nineteenth century, including performing troupes of blacks (with few if any whites in attendance) and an early prototype introduced in England in 1822, but it was really with the growing popularity of Thomas D. Rice's "Jim Crow Jump" specialty number across the 1830s that the marketing potential of whites imitating blacks, as a staged entertainment for whites, became clear. The Jim Crow Jump itself was a shuffling, clownish dance with a reversing leap, done in blackface and supposedly based on direct observation of blacks; like the general type of representation it helped spawn, it traded on and helped develop many stereotypes of black males as uneducated, lazy, cowardly, and ungainly, yet innately musical and capable of a certain knowingness and a slyly undermining humor. While this set of traits might easily indicate a passive-aggressive response to slavery and other prevailing societal hierarchies, and was surely based in part on observed behavior of actual blacks (whether on stage or in life), it quickly became frozen into a set of stereotyped characters that were widely believed to be reasonably authentic, based on actual *racial* characteristics. The way that this came about is tinged with irony: minstrelsy's passive-aggressive attitudes, undermining humor, and music succeeded in the first place because they appealed strongly to working-class white men, who identified with these characters to a significant extent, yet were gratified by the implicit reassurances of their own superiority. The central device of the minstrel show was the juxtaposition of various racially demeaning stereotypes, comically rendered with crude verbal humor and in dialect, and the quite diverse music these shows offered, which could move easily between the catchy, upbeat rhythmic number and the sentimental, closely harmonized song, the latter taking on a musical profile that often anticipates the somewhat later vogues for "negro spirituals" and for the barbershop-quartet, which would itself become emblematic of amateur (white) American music-making.[5]

The instruments used in minstrel shows included, most commonly, the banjo, fiddle, tambourine, and bones (later shows might substitute the accordion or piano for the fiddle, or other castanet-like percussion instruments for bones); while these derive from actual plantation practice, the music mostly did not. Rather, the music of blackface minstrelsy included as its backbone a wide range of European-derived music, and even in its more clearly marked "plantation" numbers offered versions of European or Anglo-American music-making, including most prominently either derivatives of folk song and sentimental parlor song, or lively dances deriving from those of Scotland or Ireland. "Dixie," for example, written by prominent minstrel performer Dan Emmett, bears a striking resemblance to Scottish folk dance. Once blacks began themselves to appear as minstrel performers (mainly after the Civil War)—blackened with burnt cork and made up like their white counterparts so that it was hard to tell the difference between them—we might imagine a gradual transformation of the style to something more "authentic," but, as with the spirituals that had their basis in European hymnody, the result was no less an inflected version of European-derived music. Thus, what later came to be called ragtime, jazz, and blues had important roots in blacks performing in styles and/or venues originated by whites.

Tap dance, too, which has been touted as one of the most distinctive African-American performance styles to emerge in the twentieth century, derives directly from the Irish Jig, as danced in the decades before the Civil War by both free-born blacks and slaves who were subsequently imitated by (mainly) Irish Jig-dancers appearing in blackface. The latter line of development underscores one of the central processes of transformative interactions between blacks and whites, which came about through the kinds of embodiment blackface minstrelsy facilitated, wherein whites strove to represent blacks (who were often themselves already imitating whites), and blacks took over stereotypes created by whites and somehow made them into something of their own. However much this also meant a kind of self-inflicted racial defamation—especially in the decades following the Civil War but extending throughout the twentieth century—there were counter-developments, as well. Thus, specifically regarding nineteenth-century antecedents to tap dance, William Lane ("Master Juba"; 1825–52), a freeborn black, distinguished himself while still a teenager as a dancer without peer, successfully touring Europe and appearing—uniquely so, since he was black—with featured billing on the minstrel circuit throughout the 1840s. Factoring into this, as well, is the apparent ethnic-based motivation for many of those involved in minstrelsy, particularly those of Irish and Scottish origin; by blacking up and dancing in an exaggerated version of their own heritage, these performers from traditionally maligned ethnic groups were to some extent both exploiting and celebrating a connection to a people they (especially the Irish) often lived among after they immigrated to America in the nineteenth century, while at the same time helping to redefine their own place in the cultural hierarchy of mid- and late-nineteenth-century America, which in and through this venue gradually came into firmer alignment with the Anglo-American mainstream.[6] Eventually, from the perspective of black-white relations, complex "negotiations" of this kind led in the twentieth century to modes of specifically black "coolness" that are rooted in stereotypes developed and reinforced through nineteenth-century minstrelsy—involving the projection of a certain mellowed-out detachment descending from minstrelsy's shiftless black male, an unschooled knowingness, a potentially violent passive-aggressive resistance to authority, and assumed high levels of sexual prowess and rhythmic musicality—a combination that would prove alluring enough in its turn to be taken over by whites at different stages of its evolution.

One of the little-remarked but arguably central aspects of blackface minstrelsy was the specific indulgence it permitted for white males to engage in otherwise tainted activities, activities that might be seen, without the mask of burnt-cork makeup, as effeminizing and less than manly according to Anglo-American societal norms. Even more basic in this regard than minstrelsy's frequent reliance on cross-dressing was its presentation of music to audiences predisposed to see music as feminine. Since music-making and dance were supposedly second nature to blacks, however, white men in blackface were virtually compelled to sing, play, and dance, abandoning themselves fully to that dimension of the personae they had adopted. In this way, blackface provided an environment acceptable to middle- and lower-class white men for music-making and dance that was, if not fully masculine, nevertheless capable of being embodied only by men. Blackface thus provided a convenient sidestep to homophobic and incipiently homophobic attitudes based in stereotypes of appropriate (heterosexual) white-male behavior that were no less restrictive in their way than those created for and/or maintained through blackface minstrelsy. Oddly, then, the conventions of blackface performance provided an American parallel to Beethoven, whose unassailably masculine music provided Europe (and the later American composer Charles Ives) with a model for how music and music-making might circumvent the growing uneasiness, borne of attitudes rooted in the still-emergent concept of "respectability," that music was essentially a feminine domain.[7] That the American musical would come to displace this dimension of minstrelsy, in providing an even more respectable arena for men to sing and dance, gradually less (or at least less obviously) tainted by the racist attitudes and stereotypes endemic to minstrelsy, is one of the genre's signal achievements. (A parallel to this process of white males borrowing aspects of perceived blackness as a way to masculinize music-making may be traced in the emergence of rock-and-roll in the 1950s, which was facilitated greatly by the mythology of black-male sexual potency.)

Within the various multi-part schemes of mid-nineteenth-century min-

strelsy—there was no standardized format for these shows, despite reductive claims that there were[8]—the most familiar setup is one that Edwin
Christy would take credit for,[9] calling for a lineup of musicians centered
around "Mr. Interlocutor" and extending to the "End Men," "Mr. Bones,"
and "Mr. Tambo," who would constantly interrupt and undermine their
ostensible leader during comic verbal exchanges. This setup both evolves
from and devolves into the numerous comic pairings of earlier burlesque
and later vaudeville, as well as of the latter's countless radio, television,
and filmic offspring, which, while often reducing the number of performers to two, retain both the reciprocal functions of stuffy authority (Inter-
locutor/Straight Man) and its anarchic nemesis, and the (usually polished)
musical numbers that emerge as the surprising blend of the two. Perhaps,
as well, its musical component survives in the singing-dancing chorus line
that supports a central "star," a standard feature of more elaborate musical numbers in later musicals and other related entertainments that has
numerous antecedents in other genres, including grand opera.

The typical minstrel show had many other components, however,
within its flexible, multi-part structure. It might include a kind of "variety show" (later called an "olio") with a succession of skits and other nov-
elty acts, often involving song and/or dance, and sometimes showing the
blackface performers without their burnt-cork makeup. Part of the function of the latter device was to reassure audiences (and enforcers of restrictive laws against mixed-race performances in many venues) that the
performers were white; additionally, it made clear that the blackface characters were roles being played, which functioned as standardized masks
behind which performers and writers could avoid the censure their outrageous conduct might otherwise provoke. One part of the show might
purport to depict various aspects of plantation life, or that of northern
blacks, in either case with "characteristic" singing, dancing, and instrumental music. As a standard and popular feature of the shows, the "chal-
lenge-dance" or "trial-dance" attempted to reproduce the kind of acro-
batic dancing that both white men in blackface and black men—for
example, Rice's "Jumpin' Jim Crow" and William Lane's "Master Juba,"
respectively—had popularized in the 1830s and early 1840s. Similarly
conceived instrumental sections, in which performers would try to outdo
each other, might also be included. A part of the show might be given over
to parodies of well-known "high art" (and usually European) performers,
such as Jenny Lind (the "Swedish Nightingale") or Ole Bull (the famous
Norwegian virtuoso violinist); similarly conceived parodies might include
"lectures" on phrenology, women's rights, or other subjects, "sermons"
or "eulogies," and "readings" from Shakespeare. Generally, the climax of
a show would consist of an extended skit or burlesque with song and
dance—often, in essence, a one-act musical—built around a set of stock

Figure 3.1. Paintings by William Sidney mount (1807–68) of the most distinctive "plantation" musicians, *The Banjo Player* (right, 1855) and *The Bone Player* (1856). The accomplished and confident demeanor of the performers in these depictions, however idealized they might be, belie the common perception that this kind of music-making was basically a burlesque. (*The Banjo Player:* oil on canvas, The Long Island Museum of American Art, History & Carriages, Gift of Mr. and Mrs. Ward Melville, 1955. *The Bone Player:* oil on canvas, 36⅛″ by 29⅛″, Museum of Fine Arts, Boston, bequest of Martha C. Karolik for the M. and M. Karolik Collection of American Paintings, 1815–65, 48.461; photograph © 2003 Museum of Fine Arts, Boston, used by permission.)

characters and situations, which might, for example, involve the interactions of city and country black stereotypes (e.g., the slick "Zip Coon" and the naïve "Jim Crow," respectively), and include "wench" scenes in which men cross-dressed for comic effect. An early favorite for such a finale was a narrative enactment of the various fancies of "Miss Lucy Long" (a role created by George Christy), a popular minstrel song to be considered in chapter 4 (pp. 68–69).

Whether or not audiences recognized minstrelsy's borrowings from opera as such, they would have recognized well enough that the blackface characters were "putting on airs," that despite the latter's lack of "culture," they were blithely performing musical numbers drawn from what would have been heard as an elevated style. Once again, as in later camp,

Figure 3.2. Blackface performers Tony Hart (in wedding drag), Willis Sweatman, and Emil Ames, ca. 1870. Hart was widely regarded as the best "wench" performer of his day. (Culver Pictures. Used by permission.)

audiences could have it either way—or both ways at once—by taking such numbers as comic parodies of something regarded as pretentious, or as pleasing semblances of what was after all esteemed for its beauties despite its pretensions. Minstrelsy thereby gave its audience an appealing perspective on upper-class entertainments—especially those imported from Europe, whether operatic or instrumental—staking an implicit claim to at least some of the attractions of the "high style" without falling prey to its pretentiousness. In so doing, minstrelsy honored and validated its audience, flattering their sensibilities and suggesting that their perspective, as lower-to-middle-class white Americans, was after all the most privileged.[10] In a broad sense, this dimension of minstrel shows allowed them to function as the "endmen" of society, undermining from its fringes the high-cultural pretensions of an imagined upper-class "interlocutor," through deft musical mimicry and crude verbal wit. Thus, a blackface burlesque given in 1845 New York by the Ethiopian Opera Company (including Edwin Christy) was given the title *Som-am-bull-ole,* alluding at once to Bellini's popular opera *La sonnambula* and Ole Bull, two favorite subjects for blackface burlesque.

Two aspects of the minstrel traditions are especially relevant to the later emergence of the American musical as an identifiable genre, apart from various specific incorporations of blackface and minstrelsy into its story lines. First, like the later genre, minstrelsy established and maintained an important generative link between the theatrical stage and music that was genuinely popular in America (in part because that music was distinctively American). And second, much of its music was presented first and foremost in coordination with either narrative aims or choreographed movement (or both).

One of the richest troves of music that has survived from nineteenth-century America—arguably *the* richest trove—comes directly from minstrelsy, as did countless other tunes that were popular in their time but are now forgotten. In generating a genuinely popular repertory of stage-based songs, minstrelsy anticipates more than any other venue the American musical, which by the first decades of the twentieth century had come largely to displace this dimension of minstrelsy. Stephen Foster (1826–64), who came of age with the advent of the minstrel show and quickly emerged through the popularity of his songs on the minstrel stage as the premiere songwriter of his generation, was as close an equivalent to the Tin-Pan-Alley phenomenon as may be found in his time. Although Foster himself died dirt-poor, his songs achieved immense popularity, largely because minstrelsy put them before the public persuasively; reciprocally, many credit him with bringing a humanizing dignity to the stereotyped world of minstrelsy. As Foster's case underscores, however, the commerce of minstrelsy did not, at least in its early phase, support the professional songwriter very well; Foster himself, for example, received virtually nothing from performance rights (ASCAP, the principal guardian for those rights today, was formed exactly fifty years after Foster's death).

Typically, as well, popular minstrel songs moved easily from stage into daily life, particularly since so many of the prejudices and attitudes they fostered, even though presented on-stage in blackface, had wider application. Indeed, many of these songs became an important part of what might be termed male "junk-bonding" (to adapt a phrase from modern psychological parlance), specifically targeting various groups and attitudes that might be effectively ridiculed from the middle-to-lower-class white-male perspective that provided the audience base of minstrelsy. Thus, misogynist songs on the order of "Lucy Long" were fairly common, as were songs such as "Dandy Jim of Caroline," which ridiculed the pretensions of the urban dandy more generally in its depiction of a Southern black putting on airs. But there was also often a fair measure of self-mockery involved. One of the most popular of early minstrel songs, and still a staple in American songbooks for children, Dan Emmett's "Old Dan Tucker" (1843) recalls within its blackface stereotype a number of other male stereotypes, as well, including the comical exaggerations of Irish braggadocio; the barbarous but indomitable American backwoodsman, at once dangerous and a figure of fun; and the outsider or newcomer of mysterious origin, whose notoriety adds a legendary dimension to his recounted exploits. What all of these songs shared is a quality of adaptability and a capacity for extension and paraphrase; they thus became in many respects a species of folk song, existing in many versions.

Particularly subtle is the case of "Blue Tail Fly" (1846, with versions credited to F. D. Benteen, C. H. Keith, and Dan Emmett), in which a slave describes the death of his "Ole Massa" when the latter's pony is bitten by a fly. On the most obvious level, the song's appeal stems from its carnivalesque inversion, through which the mightiest might be overthrown by the lowliest, a parable of egalitarian justice appealing to anyone who might resent the authority, power, or pretensions of someone in a more privileged position. Curiously, however, as the song has evolved into its enduring form, the perspective of the singer has lost clarity. Thus, the original chorus's repeated phrase "Jim crack corn / I don't care" has degenerated over time into "Jimmy cracked corn, but I don't care" (occasionally, "Jimmy crack corn"): while the former seems quite reasonably to take delight in the fact that it no longer matters if the corn is of lower quality (the original meaning of "gimcrack" corn) since "Ole Massa gone away," the latter is usually taken to be no more than irrelevant nonsense. As the degeneration of this featured line would seem to indicate, even if early audiences probably tended not to understand the line, they liked it anyway, either in spite of its obscurity or partly because of it. Indeed,

spouting apparent nonsense in response to the "sad" events recounted in
the verses of the song fits the nose-thumbing attitude of the song even better than the original lyric's reference to work left unattended.

♩ **3.1**

Still more subtle, however, is the song's engagement with the trope of
nostalgia for the "good old days" of plantation life, for times that, like
the song's "Ole Massa," are "gone away." As the song is often sung today,
it expresses at least a tinge of sadness over the "tragic" events it recounts
and, implicitly, for the times they recall. It is easy enough to imagine a similar tendency in the later nineteenth century to perform the song in a plain-
tive manner—with, however, some degree of doubt being cast as to
whether its projected tears were meant to be taken seriously. Within the
trope of (possibly feigned) grief, "Jimmy cracked corn, but I don't care"
serves as a marker for abstracted grief, and represents a withdrawal from
the cares of everyday life. If the final version of the line is the one that has
best "worked" for audiences, surely it is because its confusions have
helped to open up the possibility of tracking the song in different ways,
in a way that is emblematic of minstrelsy's layered and masked engagement with the real world of its audience.

What this song and so many other minstrel songs (at least those of the
nonsentimental variety) invite most saliently is physical movement, either
to act out the events they relate or to dance to their catchy rhythms, as reinforced by "Mr. Tambo" and "Mr. Bones." They are, in a phrase, first
and foremost stage-songs, and in this they are clearly akin to contemporaneous music-hall songs in England, with which they undoubtedly share
ancestry. But the fact that performers in minstrelsy were traditionally all
men, performing for presumptively male audiences, adds a significant dimension to this aspect of the songs, for both dance and enactment would
quite often require men to cross-dress, to assume the roles of women.
"Lucy Long," for example, occasioned a tradition of enactment in which
the masculinity of the actor playing "Lucy" might be betrayed to comic
effect—say, through revealing his large feet—but only after a considerable effort to make the portrayal as convincing as possible.

"Buffalo Gals" (variously, "Bowery Gals" and "Mobile Gals"; ca.
1844, attr. John Hodges), like "Lucy Long," virtually demanded an interactive scenario that likewise could provide a vehicle for misogynist parody. What remains particularly remarkable about "Buffalo Gals," however, is that it attained, through sheer popularity, the status of classic
respectability (thus, its benign appearance in the 1946 Frank Capra film
It's a Wonderful Life) even though its lyrics point clearly to its origins as
a disparaging song through which men could project a fantasy engagement with women of questionable virtue. Similarly, many another minstrel song, such as Foster's "Old Folks at Home" (1852) and "My Old
Kentucky Home" (1853), or "Carry Me Back to Old Virginny" (com-

posed in 1878 by African American James Bland and still not fully retired as Virginia's state song despite its embarrassing references to "darkeys" and "Massa"), are too often still today taken as simply sentimental and nostalgic, without appreciable concern for the deplorable institution they originally served to idealize.

Perhaps the most important bequest of minstrelsy to the American musical is the atmosphere of carnival it engendered, its quasi-ritualistic escape through elaborate and grotesque costuming and makeup into a fantasy world that permitted full, if transient, redress for the perceived wrongs of the real world. As with the American musical, the music of minstrelsy provided an important vehicle both for its escapist, fantastical side, and for its connection to the real world—the latter since its music either already was, or was rapidly becoming, the vernacular music of its age.

Extravaganza

The relevant connections of many of the other nineteenth-century antecedents to the twentieth-century musical are more easily traced, and are mostly less controversial; it is these others that best support the "evolution" model of development. *Extravaganza*, for example, was applied rather loosely to a number of shows whose main attraction was implicit in its earlier designation, "spectacle." A show of this type might have included acrobats or other circus-like spectacle in addition to scenic or dramatic spectacle, but would in any case always include a substantial offering of music, especially singing and dancing. Central to this tradition was William Niblo, who in 1829 completed a highly successful entertainment complex on Broadway (Niblo's Garden), which he rebuilt after a fire in 1846 and then again in 1866 to make it a suitable first venue for *The Black Crook*. There were ample antecedents at Niblo's for the latter's singular success in such shows as *The Naiad Queen* (1841) and *Faustus; or, The Demon of the Dragonfels* (1851). As late as 1860, the terms used to describe these shows did not tend, however, to include "extravaganza." Thus, *The Seven Sisters* of that year—which, like *The Black Crook*, was based on an earlier "diabolical" German source and ended with a "transformation scene"—was marketed as a "Grand Operatic, Spectacular, Musical, Terpsichorean, Diabolical, Farcical Burletta" (Terpsichore was the one of the nine Muses who presided over dance; "Terpsichorean" thus refers here to the inclusion of balletic dancing). Indeed, the term "extravaganza" came into common usage to identify this kind of show only slightly before the type began to evolve as well into a semblance of the later American musical—that is, around the time of *The Black Crook*—as many extravaganzas began to rely on at least some semblance of an embracing narrative as a means to sustain its parade of song, dance, procession, and scenic "special effects."

Later highly successful and influential extravaganzas included the initially unsuccessful *Evangeline* (1874; score and lyrics by Edward E. Rice; a burlesque of Longfellow's poem) and *The Brook* (1879; no definitive score; plotted loosely around a picnic outing in which a food-basket is found to contain theatrical costumes and props). In different ways, each represents an important beginning: the former because it came with an enduring (if not timeless) score by a single composer/songwriter and was the first to which the phrase "musical comedy" was applied, the latter because it created a vogue for what was known as "farce-comedy," in which the flimsiest of plot-devices provides a narrative gloss for what would otherwise be better identified as variety or vaudeville. Significantly, each of these shows deals with distinctively American topics and/or characters, combines music with often topical comedy in a way that could be easily adapted to current events, and involves a fairly free mix of other theatrical types in a wholly typical hybridization of both genre and designation. Most prominent among the types used by these shows and others like them were burlesque and variety (vaudeville), which, in addition to pantomime, round out the most important developments in the later nineteenth century that may be seen to have had an important and singular influence on the American musical.

Pantomime

If all of these categories mix fairly freely with the others, *pantomime* remains especially in need of being framed by other diverse entertainments, since it offers an absence of dialogue or song where all others provide at least one or the other of these, and generally some range and variety of each. Since pantomime would most often be accompanied by music, it bears some resemblance to both melodrama (dramatic action against a musical background) and ballet, except that its tone was more generally comic and it typically worked with a set of stereotyped characters imported from French traditions. Pantomime does not leave a very obvious trace on the American musical, apart from such latter-day clown-stars as Harpo Marx and Red Skelton, who derive rather less directly from nineteenth-century traditions than from on-going circus traditions and a handful of silent-movie comics, especially those—Charlie Chaplin, Buster Keaton, Stan Laurel, etc.—who retained their largely silent personae into the sound era. The signal success of pantomime in the nineteenth century was George L. Fox's performance in the extravaganza *Humpty Dumpty* (1868, with a run slightly exceeding that of *The Black Crook*), which also included ballet and circus acts involving, variously, roller-skating, ice-skating, and bicycles. Fox's penchant for silent comedy apparently anticipated the likes of Buster Keaton, deriving from a mostly passive enduring of whatever came his way. But pantomime also drew upon older traditions of both mime and puppetry, most prominently the Italian-Parisian commedia dell'arte and its British music-hall extensions, whose stock characters—Harlequin, Columbine, the Doctor, Pantaloon, Pierrot, Pulcinella (in England corrupted to "Punch and Judy"), etc.—would have been easily recognized by American audiences. In the general sense of dealing with stock characters, pantomime's influence on the development of the American musical may be more substantial than is outwardly apparent.

Burlesque

Burlesque, along with vaudeville, was closely related to minstrelsy in the types of entertainment it had to offer, and lines of influence both to and from minstrelsy are fairly easy to draw. In the twentieth century, "vaudeville" was seen to degenerate into "burlesque," but in the nineteenth century the terms referred to quite different, if sometimes overlapping, traditions. Burlesque (or travesty), in general terms, presented a variety of parodistic versions of other, generally more serious entertainments, and the term continues to carry this meaning even in recent times; *Little Mary Sunshine* (1959), for example, is a burlesque of operetta and its American traditions, and the term may also be used when individual numbers in shows re-create standard types with comic exaggeration (thus, "Wunderbar" in the 1948 *Kiss Me, Kate* burlesques the Viennese waltz trope of American operetta). Burlesque could also refer more specifically to the device of having young women in tights play men's parts, as in Lydia Thompson *Ixion* (Wood's Museum, 1868) and *The Forty Thieves* (Niblo's Garden, 1869), through which she and her troupe of mostly bleached blondes achieved brief notoriety.

John Brougham's *Pocahontas* (1855) was the first successful burlesque on an American topic, although Brougham was himself Dublin-born and previously a successful actor/playwright in London. *Pocahontas* in many respects anticipated Rice's more elaborate *Evangeline,* an extravaganza that was also a burlesque in both senses of the word, with its absurdly comical fleshing out of its literary basis and its inclusion of a prominent "pants" role. Rice's later burlesque-extravaganza *Adonis* (1884, Bijou Opera House), which ran for a record 603 performances, well exemplified most of the tendencies of this type, but its success ultimately derived not from a cross-dressed woman playing the hero, but from its male star, Henry E. Dixey, whose blend of dancing, comedic, and singing skills anticipated the later model for success on Broadway. Besides indulging tastes for comic exaggeration, mockery of high culture, and cross-dressing (in whatever direction), burlesque resembled minstrelsy in its obsessive use of puns, malapropisms, and other comic wordplay, and in its reliance on topical humor. Nevertheless, its most elaborate shows, typically called burlesque-extravaganzas, broke cleanly away from both minstrelsy and vaudeville, in being sustained however slightly by a single overarching narrative (which did little to prevent the continual accretion of interpolated topical humor). In this respect, they superficially resembled the "farce-comedy," which had enjoyed a brief vogue in the wake of *The Brook*, but the latter tended to complete the circle back to vaudeville, with attractions that were often identical in kind even while they were redirected toward respectability.

Vaudeville

Especially in its earlier incarnation as "variety," *Vaudeville*, was once considerably less reputable than minstrelsy, housed, as it often was, within drinking emporia that functioned essentially like upscale brothels. Even as it evolved into relative respectability, vaudeville continued, with its glorified presentation of attractive young women, to provide a more genteel version of the latter function, to the extent at least that "dating" between performers and audience members continued to be common. Vaudeville may be understood, perhaps, as the fusion of this earlier mode of feminine presentation (requiring only a modicum of singing and dancing talent) and the earlier extravaganza (or spectacle), especially as the latter was set adrift in the wake of *The Black Crook* and the ensuing growth-industry of extended narrative-driven entertainments. Perhaps more importantly, the rise of this type in New York coincided, in the mid-1870s, with the decline of minstrelsy. Clearly, as the latter fell slowly out of fashion, its somewhat more respectable (and certainly less overtly racist) cousin took its place, and usefully so for the development of the incipient American musical. The earlier long run of *Humpty Dumpty* (1868) and its later offshoots (which continued nearly to the end of the century, long after Fox had died insane in 1877) had already by then established the more upscale variety show as a viable type, but it had considerable competition into the early 1880s from farce-comedy, which could impart a semblance of thematic consistency to its various offerings.

Central to the emergence of variety as both respectable and successful was Tony Pastor, who had even before *The Black Crook* eliminated drinking from his venue and encouraged the presence of women in the audience. Pastor's career intersected with those of his chief competition and sometime collaborators, Ned Harrigan and Tony Hart, whose Mulligan Guard shows at the Theatre Comique were a perennial success. The continued success of these and other venues, while rarely extending to the critical success and prestige of more narrative-driven entertainments, nonetheless contributed importantly to the richness of the musical-comedy offerings of the day. Perhaps most importantly for our present concerns, they provided an important breeding ground for performers and helped to keep song, dance, and spectacular presentation at the center of more "legit" musical theater. Independent of this function, of course, shows of this kind—elevated, as "revues," after George W. Lederer's *The Passing Show* of 1894 (the first in a series that continued until 1924)—continued to be highly successful through the 1920s, and included, besides the famous series of "Follies" presented by Florence Ziegfeld, more-or-less annual series in a variety of venues, including the Hippodrome "Extravaganzas," the Music Box "Revues," the "Grand Street Follies," the "Greenwich Village Follies," the "Garrick Gaieties," "Artists and Models," Earl Carroll's "Vanities," and George White's "Scandals," among others. Although the Great Depression dealt a death blow to vaudeville, some of these series survived into the 1930s and even beyond, producing clear echoes in Hollywood, especially with Busby Berkeley's "Gold Digger" films (1933–37), the "Big Broadcast" and "Broadway Melody" films (1936–40), *The Goldwyn Follies* (1938), and, in television, the many "variety" shows in the 1960s.

A Gilbert and Sullivan Postscript on American Minstrelsy

In 1893, eight years after *The Mikado*, Gilbert and Sullivan attempted to revive their troubled partnership with *Utopia Limited; or, The Flowers of Progress,* in which the direction of Gilbert's political satire is so befuddled that one may read the piece equally well as a celebration of Englishness, as seen against the backdrop of a South Sea island that attempts to model its politics and cultural institutions on those of England; or as a scathing critique of those institutions, and of the smug English penchant for cultural imperialism (or both). One number in particular brings this duality to the fore, and it is especially worth considering here because it seems to be returning the compliment America had long been paying to Gilbert and Sullivan, by adapting a distinctly American idiom—that of blackface minstrelsy—and, indeed, paying direct homage to one of its better-known tunes.

Early in the second act, the King of Utopia lines up with the "flowers of progress"—six English societal leaders imported for the express purpose of "anglicizing" Utopia—to perform in the manner of what Londoners knew as the "Christy Minstrel" style, with King Paramount at the center, unwittingly playing the part of Mr. Interlocutor. As the King elaborates on Utopia's success at emulating and even surpassing England, commentary from either side underscores pointedly how each of Utopia's idealistically "English" achievements is matched by a very real shortcoming in England itself. On one level, then, the song is a harsh condemnation of England, listing many specific failures, accentuating its hypocrisy, and putting the lie to its smug belief that its ways are the best ways.

The staging and musical profile of the number, however, say something quite different. In the dialogue just preceding the song, just after the "minstrels" line up in their positions, we are fully alerted as to what to expect:

KING: You are not making fun of us? This is in accordance with the practice at the Court of St. James's?

LORD DRAMALEIGH: Well, it is in accordance with the practice at the Court of St. James's Hall [one of the principal venues for the Christy Minstrels].

Moreover, the song culminates in a fast "banjo-chorus" setting, in close harmony, of a typical Gilbertian patter:

> It really is surprising
> What a thorough Anglicizing
> We have brought about—Utopia's quite another land;
> In her enterprising movements,
> She is England—with improvements,
> Which we dutifully offer to our mother-land!

♩ 3.2

As George Bernard Shaw noted immediately (and approvingly), Sullivan's tune is an adaptation of "Johnny, Get Your Gun," an "Ethiopian" "fiddle tune" most familiar through its inclusion as the dance-postlude to Monroe H. Rosenfeld's song of the same name (publ. 1886; see example 3.1).[11] Both the setup for Gilbert and Sullivan's song and its concluding chorus thus point directly to the minstrel tradition; since the conceit was quite obviously Gilbert's, however beautifully realized by Sullivan, we might reasonably expect there to be a barb beneath the jest. Why, then, does Gilbert call for a minstrel number, and why here?

Part of the "charm" of minstrelsy for late-nineteenth-century audiences, perhaps particularly for European audiences, derived from its recreation of the plantation spectacle of blacks, who were believed to be culturally and even biologically inferior to whites, nevertheless performing music with consummate skill, whether in a catchy dance number or in a style akin to the sentimental parlor songs of the time. In the dynamic of minstrelsy, "primitives" produce art of surpassing beauty; when layered onto the plot-situation of *Utopia Limited*, this dynamic deftly calls attention to parallels between the two: in both cases, humor derives from a situation akin to that of a child mimicking the words and inflections of an adult with uncanny accuracy, but without fully understanding the words being mimicked. At the very least, then, the song places the South Sea "natives" of *Utopia Limited* in a position analogous to American slaves and

Example 3.1

W.S. Gilbert and Arthur Sullivan, "It Really is Surprising"

Monroe H. Rosenfeld, "Johnny Get Your Gun" (dance episode)

former slaves, as simple-minded inferiors who ape their betters. More-over, Lord Dramaleigh's introductory witticism makes it clear that the En-glish imports are fully aware of this parallel, even delighting in it as they manipulate King Paramount into playing the part of Mr. Interlocutor. As the song unfolds, their interpolations resemble the undercutting inter-changes typical of the minstrel lineup, and their concluding chorus com-bines the rich harmonic blends of minstrelsy's all-male choirs with the snappy dance conclusion to a classic minstrel song.

If the joke turns simultaneously back against the English, since the Utopians in their innocence have managed to implement the English sys-tem without divorce lawyers, unearned privilege, poverty and hunger, pandering, or commercialism—all explicitly recalled in Gilbert's lyric—it merely shows itself as the typically Gilbertian humor of topsy-turvydom, biting viciously in both directions at once. But there is enough here and elsewhere to suggest a third target for Gilbert's satire, that the show was meant to satirize the United States, as well, both in its naïve anglicizing tendencies and its combination of sometimes laughable innocence and corrupting commerce. In any case, *Utopia Limited* shows that Gilbert, and possibly Sullivan, understood better than most Americans not only what minstrelsy was all about, but also how much (and how much to their discredit) Americans and English shared a societal bigotry—a pill sufficiently bitter, on both sides of the Atlantic, that we shouldn't wonder that neither side chose to swallow it. Thus, while reviews of *Utopia Limited* were positive, it achieved only a moderate run of 245 performances, and was not revived until 1975.

See Also

Regarding nineteenth-century antecedents and developments generally, see chapter 2 of Gerald Mast's *Can't Help Singin'*, chapters 1–3 of Gerald Bordman's *American Musical Theatre*, part 1 of Cecil Smith and Glenn Litton's *Musical Comedy in America,* chapters 3–6 in Richard Kislan's *The Musical,* and Katherine Preston's "American Musical Theatre Before the Twentieth Century." Regarding many of the themes developed in the songs of this period, see Jon W. Finson's *The Voices That Are Gone.*

Regarding minstrelsy, Robert Toll's *Blacking Up* remains an important but somewhat out-of-date source, William Mahar's *Behind the Burnt Cork Mask* provides a revisionist account of pre–Civil War practice, Eric Lott's *Love and Theft* considers the social history of the practice with some insight and depth, W. T. Lhamon, Jr.'s *Raising Cain* probes the boundaries of the traditional historical narrative of minstrelsy in an astute and well-researched exploration of how the practice mattered before 1843 and still continues to matter, David Cockrell's *Demons of Disorder* grounds minstrelsy in carnivalesque traditions generally, John Graziano's "Images of African Americans" considers the strange evolution from minstrelsy to African-American musical theater, Charles Hamm considers the (literal!) persistence of the tradition of blackface minstrelsy in "The Last Minstrel Show?" (chapter 17 in *Putting Popular Music in Its Place*), and Alan Jay Lerner, in the opening pages of his provocatively titled "The Land of the Free" (in *The Musical Theatre: A Celebration*), underscores many ironies involving race and music in America; see also chapter 6 of Charles Hamm's *Yesterdays,* chapter 2 of Richard Kislan's *The Musical,* "Scene 2" of Julian Mates's *America's Musical Stage,* and chapters 5–6 in Jon W. Finson's *The Voices That Are Gone.*

American Song through Tin Pan Alley

THE AMERICAN MUSICAL, as noted, developed out of the intermingling of a number of musical-theatrical traditions of the late nineteenth century that achieved commercial success and shared the practice of staging popular song. In this chapter we will consider more closely the development of song itself, beginning with nineteenth-century minstrelsy and continuing through the classic "Tin Pan Alley" type, which emerged in the 1920s and '30s with the generation of song-writers headed by Irving Berlin, Jerome Kern, George Gershwin, Richard Rodgers, and Cole Porter. I am using here a broad understanding of "Tin Pan Alley," extending beyond the period when the production of American popular song was almost wholly centered in lower Manhattan, to include the entire period dominated by the type of song fostered by that centralization.[1]

A detailed history of American song before the full emergence of the standard song forms of classic Tin Pan Alley is beyond the scope of this study. I will instead focus on, from these decades, a handful of song types whose American profile is particularly striking, and which enjoyed genuine and extended popularity both on stage and off. Such a list might well include, in addition to the waltz song, a variety of other dances or marches, but the waltz was in its era by far the most common basis for genuinely popular song, giving way only to ragtime (overlapping with "coon" songs), in an idiom that combines elements of dance and march. Many other types left off this list are more obviously derivative of European models, whether from English music-hall traditions, art song, ballad, operetta, other light-opera traditions, or opera itself.

My approach in this chapter will be to look in detail at specific examples of some of the most important types, rather than to attempt a comprehensive survey. Because musicals produced during the 1920s and '30s have tended not to survive in the repertory as well as many of their songs, I will end with a discussion of *Anything Goes* (1934), everyone's favorite example of great songs wedded to a mediocre book.

Minstrel Songs

Songs for the minstrel stage, while most often deriving from European types, were specifically American in their themes and preoccupations. The fact that they were sung within an environment that explicitly looked down on a segment of the American population made them to some extent about those Americans being represented (black, female, or both); to a much larger extent, however, they were for and implicitly about the audience itself, defined both narrowly and broadly. Thus, these songs were vehicles for establishing community not only within the mostly white-male audiences who went to the shows, but also within the general population; Stephen Foster's songs became (or already were) parlor songs, and dance music for the stage became dance music for the home and for public occasions. In this respect, these songs functioned as a kind of urban folk music, and tended to take on forms common to folk music, with verses that could be rewritten and adapted to various occasions and changing times, and with highly profiled (if quite often relatively short) refrains or choruses. We will here consider a representative song from two basic types of minstrel song, one lively and humorous, the other sentimental.

"Lucy Long"

Among the most popular of the early minstrel songs, "Lucy Long" (1842, with many later versions) became the basis for a tradition of minstrel-show finale that involved cross-dressing, dancing, and play-acting. The name Lucy, through this and the related song "Lucy Neal" (not to mention burlesques on Donizetti's *Lucia di Lammermoor*, such as the 1848 "Lucy-Did-Sham-Amour") became synonymous with a certain black female stereotype: sexy, demanding, somewhat grotesque, and of suspect virtue. The lively banjo tune of "Lucy Long" was eminently suitable for instrumental elaboration, and thus for dancing and play-acting interludes. Furthermore, since the song's refrain—

> Oh! Take your time Miss Lucy, / Take your time Miss Lucy Long!
> Oh! Take your time Miss Lucy, / Take your time Miss Lucy Long!

—uses virtually the same music as the verse, performances could vary greatly the order and succession of verses, refrain, and interludes. Part of the appeal of the song derives from the shifting meanings that the seemingly innocuous refrain could assume according to the verses it follows. Thus, following the verse—

> I axed her for to marry, / Myself de toder day;
> She said she'd rather tarry, / So I let her habe her way.

—in which Lucy is depicted as a sexual aggressor who prefers "tarrying" (casual sex, we may infer) to marrying, the refrain signals the more-than-willing acquiescence of the singer, who not only encourages Lucy to "habe her way," but insists that she "take her time" while doing so. Yet, as is typical of this kind of risqué wordplay on the American stage, such insinuations might well pass unnoticed by someone not "in the know," who would thus hear "tarry" literally, and the refrain as simply formulaic.   ♩ 4.1

"Old Uncle Ned"

Stephen Foster's "*Old Uncle Ned*" (1848; in some later versions simply "Uncle Ned") well exemplifies the sentimental "parlor-song" idiom, often applied, as here, to a sentimentalizing view of plantation life. Everything in the song contributes to this idealizing attitude. Verbally, the song implicitly asserts that the slave Ned was "like family" (thus, "Uncle" Ned), and that his master wept when he died. But the sense of the song is conveyed above all through music, through the slow, direct, sentimental style with few "European-style" ornaments, of which Foster was master, and the extended a capella chorus (that is, without instruments), set originally for three parts but in later versions (published in the nineteenth century, but after Foster's death) made more conventionally a quartet. While we may see the expansion of the chorus as an emblem of things to come in American popular song (especially in the era of classic Tin Pan Alley), what seems particularly striking in "Old Uncle Ned" is how deliberately this expansion is set up by the unaccompanied bass descent on the line "Den lay down de shubble and de hoe-o-o." The choir's response, "And hang up de fiddle and de bow," not only directs the performance in the most literal sense, but also makes a direct connection between why "Uncle Ned" is valued (for his hard work) and how he is to be memorialized (in song), while serving as well as an emblem of respect, marking a figurative moment of silence in its instruction to "lay down the fiddle." While not written directly for the minstrel stage, as were many of Foster's later songs, "Old Uncle Ned" obviously derives from minstrelsy's "plantation" idiom, with its characteristic transformation of buffoon-like stereotypes into harmonious singers of uncommon and innate warmth, so that the song quickly found a receptive venue on stage as well as in the parlor.   ♩ 4.2

Robert Winans's intriguing attempt to reproduce these and other minstrel songs according to the "performance practices" of the mid-century minstrel show (*The Early Minstrel Show*, annotated and directed by Robert Winans, New York: New World Records CD 80338–2, 1985 [re-released 1998]) produces an audibly awkward effect, perhaps unavoidably so, given the nature of the project. As Winans's liner notes for the album tell us, the recording maintains the "correct" instrumental support (a warmer, nineteenth-century banjo, etc.), vocal styles (less vibrato), and verbal idiom (dialect), while attempting to project what he terms "whites trying to imitate blacks," but which is, more precisely, modern whites trying with carefully modulated enthusiasm to imitate nineteenth-century whites, whose own blackface impersonations would have had considerably more verve.[2] Not surprisingly, the recording fails to project true enjoyment in "Lucy Long"; curiously, it also maintains an a capella texture *throughout* "Old Uncle Ned," thereby depriving the song of its dramatic textural shift from mixed (instruments and voice) to a purely vocal texture, as described in the lyric. In this way, the performances do not document nineteenth-century practices so much as late-twentieth-century discomfort with those practices. Such discomfort is perfectly understandable, since performances that more obviously relished the "fun" of "Lucy Long" (that is, its racist and sexist attitudes) or seemed more engaged in the sentimentalizing of slavery in "Old Uncle Ned," would surely be even more disquieting than performances that, like these, emotionally distance themselves from such involvement for fear of taint, even if the results are too often unconvincing.

Emblematic of the discomfort that these songs provoke is the blending in this recording of different versions of "Old Uncle Ned," that is, Foster's original publication and later versions, which tended toward a simplification of both lyrics and music. Thus, in later publications, Foster's original—

> On a cold frosty morning poor Uncle Ned died
> Masters tears down his cheeks ran like rain

—became:

> When Old Ned die Massa take it mighty hard
> De tears run down like de rain.

Moreover, his cadences were rendered more conventional (eliminating Foster's characteristic 2-3-1 escape-tone cadence, with its poignant major-seventh dissonance)[3] and, most significantly, the last line was changed from "He's gone whar de good niggas go" to "He's gone whar de good darkeys go" (even if the latter is now considered only slightly less offensive than the former). Consistently, this recording retains the music Foster wrote (thus, with an a capella trio rather than quartet, and with Foster's original cadences) while using the later lyrics—a strategy that silently documents the unsolvable dilemma inherent in the larger project of preserving Foster's music while suppressing its tainted context.

The Early Tin Pan Alley Era

As Charles Hamm succinctly puts it, "For the entire lifespan of the era known as Tin Pan Alley, popular song in the United States was dominated by New York City and by the musical stage"—the latter institution, of course, having long since also established its center, at least for America, within New York City.[4] The term "Tin Pan Alley," coined by Monroe H. Rosenfeld, referred specifically to the high concentration of music publishers on 28th Street in the 1890s, where showrooms filled the street with the din of upright pianos banging out their offerings. As with the derogatory "Yankee Doodle" of over a century earlier, the intended insult became a badge of honor, and the term "Tin Pan Alley" came to stand for the ostentatiously "popular" genre of American song that emerged in the final decade of the nineteenth century and held sway throughout the first half of the twentieth (that is, before the advent of rock and roll). Most narrowly, the term applies only to the extended era when the sheet music industry continued to be centered around 28th Street, but the term is more commonly applied to the much longer era in which New York City's high concentration of music publishers, and the generalized styles that they favored, dominated the market. In this application, "Tin Pan Alley" shifts its location twice, from an earlier concentration on East 14th Street near Union Square in the 1880s (the heart of what was then the theater district) and, much later, to the relocated theater district—specifically, to the Brill Building, completed in 1931 on Broadway between 49th and 50th streets, and increasingly populated by music publishers during the 1930s. Significantly, then, in each of these other locations the connection between Tin Pan Alley and staged song was reinforced geographically as well as generically.

Waltz Songs

As Hamm notes with some irony, the genre that established white America's musical voice throughout this era, but especially in its central and later decades, was dominated by newly arrived or second-generation immigrants (mainly Irish and Jewish), whose idiom derived in large part from African-American styles (particularly ragtime and jazz).[5] But before the latter stage of development came the hugely popular waltz song, in which the chorus (and usually the verse) adopts a waltz style, in triple meter with a strong downbeat and lilting double-upbeat on the second and third beats. Although the tempo for the waltz song could range from fairly slow to moderately fast, its association with the dance itself, which mattered both practically and referentially, would have been severely undermined if the tempo were either too slow or too fast to permit actual dancing. As noted in chapter 2, this type had already begun to establish itself in America by the early 1870s, when the interpolation of "The Afternoon Crawl" into *The Black Crook* achieved much success (see pp. 28–29). Even at this early stage, the waltz song had been fully naturalized, relocating from its native Vienna to New York (probably by way of the English music hall), capable of capturing in musical terms the sometimes licentious energy of its adopted city.[6] So firmly was this shift accomplished that it would take the American successes of Lehár's Viennese operettas to restore fully the Viennese association as a viable alternative (his *The Merry Widow* premiered in New York City in 1907, igniting a merchandizing craze for "Merry Widow hats" and other related items). Even in "The Afternoon Crawl," where the waltz idiom is relatively sedate, the capacity of the waltz song to represent "New-Yorkness" sustains its transplantation to such diverse areas as Broadway, Park Avenue, and the Bowery. It is scarcely surprising, then, that the waltz song reached its apex of popularity with the full-scale migration of the song-writing industry to New York City in the late 1890s.

One of the many successful songs of *A Trip to Chinatown* (Peter Gaunt and Charles H. Hoyt, 1891), whose run set a record for musicals that would stand for nearly thirty years (657 performances, eclipsing *Adonis*, the first to break 500), was the last-minute addition "The Bowery," which through its perennial popularity helped establish more securely the New York-based, comic waltz-song as a type distinct from the more sentimental waltz song. The conceit of the song embodies one of the themes of the show as a whole, even as it transplants us for its duration from San Francisco (the setting for the musical) to a remembered New York: the contrast between the knowing sophistication of "the city" and its more naïve visitors/victims. The song's self-containedness, especially on a narrative level, was virtually a requirement of interpolated songs that have to "explain themselves," but this is also one of the typical features of the waltz song that tends to distinguish it formally from later Tin Pan Alley songs. Like "The Afternoon Crawl," "The Bowery" delineates a series of fairly lengthy comic verses, each capped with a refrain that is musically much more memorable—although here the meaning for the refrain does not shift as it might in more subtle examples of the type. The humor in "The Bowery," which stems mainly from verbal misunderstandings, is entirely contained in the verses, so that the song may easily be presented either in part (with some verses perhaps reserved for encores) or with additional verses written for the occasion.

♪ 4.3

Charles K. Harris's "After the Ball" was added the following year for a touring version of *A Trip to Chinatown* after Harris bribed the singer with $500. An immediate success even though it had earlier failed as a vaudeville number, it was the first American "megahit," often claimed to be the first to sell five million copies, and doing a lot of that business in very short order.[7] "After the Ball" follows the same basic structure as "The Bowery," with a fairly lengthy narrative verse leading to a shorter chorus (which functions as the "hook" of the song). But the overall shape is quite different, as we are not let in on the full significance of the chorus until the third and final verse, when we learn that the recounted story of a lost love is not one of blame, but of regret tinged with self-reproach;

there can be no question here of adding or withholding verses. Parodies were always possible, however, as Harris himself demonstrated with "After the Fair," written in 1893 specifically for the minstrel stage, in which difficult economic times were predicted for Chicago after the closing of the 1893 Columbian Exposition (where "After the Ball" achieved its first great success).[8]

The success of a sentimental waltz song of this kind, at least over time, depends on how well and subtly the chorus embodies the overall meaning of the narrative verses, since for listeners who will scarcely remember the specific words or music of the verse, the chorus must inevitably stand for the whole song. In the chorus of "After the Ball," the many lilting repetitions of the word "After," recurring across a sequential climb that takes us briefly into a minor-mode key, cast the basically cheerful idiom of the waltz as a memory, rendered sad for being irretrievable. Nearly as important are the "feminine" line-endings on significantly charged words—"over," "leaving," "aching," and "vanished"—linked musically through being set to an expressive swoop downward, which both balances and partly negates the lilting ascents on "After" that set up and maintain the basic rhythmic gesture of the waltz. (The one exception from this series—"leaving"—is set no less expressively, with a chromatic leading-tone that confirms arrival in the minor mode.):

> After the ball is over,
>   After the break of morn,
> After the dancers leaving,
>   After the stars are gone;
> Many a heart is aching,
>   If you could read them all;
> Many the hopes that have vanished
>   After the ball.

♪ 4.4

The coordination of words and musical gesture here is deftly conceived and realized. Overall, the music presents a sonic image of the ball, which serves as a metaphor for the long-gone promise of married bliss, while, overall, the words inflect that image with pastness and regret; in return, specific musical gestures shape, highlight, and inflect with considerable nuance precisely those words that carry this charge most poignantly ("after," "over," etc.).

Coon Songs and
Ragtime Songs

Although they had been around since the early 1880s as an adjunct of the minstrel stage, "coon songs" enjoyed their greatest vogue when they merged with ragtime near the turn of the century, the latter type a derivative of the cakewalk and its ancestor, the clowning blackface dance of the minstrel stage. Since the word "coon" was already then a racial slur (and was to become even more virulently so), these songs have often been referred to, less offensively, as "ragtime songs." But the latter category was a broad one, of which coon songs formed only one subset, however important in the early stages. Ragtime songs, as a broad category—that is, exploiting the characteristic syncopated rhythms of ragtime but often without the overtly racist content of coon songs—remained for some time a staple of Broadway, if only referentially or for the rhythmic energy those syncopations could impart to the staged musical number.

The most distinctive rhythmic charge of a ragtime song stems from syncopation or snap-like figures on various rhythmic levels, layered or in succession; but simple dotted figures were also prominent, probably derived from the quickstep march. While these features carry over into the early jazz era and beyond, the rhythmic feeling of the latter, with its more subtle laying off of the beat (that is, slightly anticipating or delaying melodic arrivals so as to avoid hitting the beat directly), would lend an even more distinctive rhythmic profile to both American song and its performance on the musical stage. While the rhythmic energy of staged song thus became more and more decisively removed from the older-style minstrel stage, it was, initially and through the persistence of blackface, no less an imitation of blacks by whites.

Whether coincidentally or not, the peak in popularity of the coon song occurred in tandem with two other historical developments: the increased importance of the recording medium as both a market and publicity tool (although scarcely the force it would become two decades later),[9] and the venturing of blacks into more viable competition with whites not only in staging minstrel shows, but also in offering black equivalents of more mainstream white shows. Partly because of the limiting requirements of recording—and partly, as well, because of the lessening importance of narrative within a song (see later in this chapter)—the number of verses in a typical song shrunk to two, although, as with "After the Ball," these often carried a narrative that could potentially inflect the meaning or interpretation of the chorus on repetition. The signal event in the development of black alternatives to the white mainstream was *A Trip to Coontown* (1898, Bob Cole and Billy Johnson), the first major show in New York written, produced, and acted solely by blacks. While unsuccessful, this show marked the beginning of a separate, legitimate, all-black musical theatrical tradition in New York, and was soon followed by two more successful shows by Paul Laurence Dunbar and Will Marion Cook, *The Origin of the Cake Walk or, Clorindy* (also in 1898) and *In Dahomey* (1903), which was the first all-black show to open on Broadway. Because these shows lacked full mainstream acceptance, however, the larger popularity of songs in a ragtime idiom at the time of their greatest vogue was largely separate from their possible presence on all-black stages; indeed, although many blacks also contributed to this repertory, most of the popular coon songs were written and/or sung by whites (most often in blackface), who had considerably better access to mainstream markets.

"Bill Bailey, Won't You Please Come Home?" (Hughie Cannon, 1902), like many coon songs, was written for the minstrel stage, and marketed with a sheet-music cover that called direct attention to those roots, in this case showing stereotypical caricatures of a weeping, apparently heavyset woman (a man in drag?) and a grinning man, both in blackface. The song was designed to be almost a mirror reflection of a coon song that had achieved some popularity a year earlier, cast in virtually the same mold: "Ain't Dat a Shame" (by Walter Wilson and John Queen). As a "sequel" to the latter, "Bill Bailey" refers fairly directly to the central events of the earlier song, in which Bill leaves his "ladyfriend," returns at night—hungry, cold, and dripping wet—to make up with her (in the chorus), only to find out (in the second verse) that another man has moved in. In "Bill Bailey," the roles and nearly everything else are reversed: the ladyfriend's new beau has left, and she is left to sing (while hanging clothes out to dry in the sun) "Bill Bailey, Won't You Please Come Home?" vowing that she will "do the cooking" if he does come home—which sets up his grinning reappearance in the second verse, during which, from the vantage point of his "automobile [with its] great big diamond, coach- and footman," he observes with satisfaction how the tables have turned. Although there is no specific musical relationship between the two songs, "Bill Bailey" joins the two song-titles together, textually, at the close of the chorus, referring as well to the inverted situation from the earlier song, in which Bill admitted, "I know that I've done wrong" (here, of course, it is his "lady love" who sings; note also that the insertion of the phrase "ain't dat a shame?" makes full sense *only* as a reference to the earlier song):

> I knows I'se to blame; well, ain't dat a shame?
> Bill Bailey, won't you please come home?   ♪ 4.5

Two things go a long way toward explaining why "Bill Bailey" but not "Ain't Dat a Shame" has enjoyed a kind of immortality. First, of course, there is the reversed situation, tapping more gratifyingly into misogynist male fantasies, which coupled with its mocking ragtime idiom and double punchline (not only does she now need him; he now *doesn't* need her), simply provides more pleasure for its audience than the tired story of the cuckolded male offered by "Ain't Dat a Shame." But, second, there is the distinctive musical moan that occurs in both verse and chorus of "Bill Bailey," the only figure that breaks away from a simple syllabic presentation of the lyric, by requiring the singer to droop down a fifth or more on a

Figure 4.1. Sheet music covers for "Bill Bailey, Won't You Please Come Home?" (right) and its less famous predecessor, "Ain't Dat a Shame," both published by Howley, Haviland & Dresser. Like the songs themselves, both covers trade in offensive racial stereotypes. The custom of advertising songs through their performers, and thus targeting specific markets, is also evident on both covers; thus, different print runs of "Bill Bailey" used the same cover but with different inserts in the lower left corner. (Reproductions courtesy of UCLA Music Library Special Collections.)

single syllable. Repetitions of this exaggerated expressive gesture define the trajectory of the song, from (marginally) sympathetic presentation of the woman's pathos to open mockery of it (justified, supposedly, by the conceit that "she had it coming"), as may be seen by excerpting the lines that end with this formulaic self-pitying groan:

> 1ST VERSE: . . . in her back ya-rd, and weeping ha-rd; . . .
> And to dat cro-wd, / She yelled out lo-ud: . . .
> CHORUS: . . . She moans de whole day lo-ng . . .
> I knows I've done you wro-ng; . . .
> 2ND VERSE: . . . "He's all alo-ne," I heard her gro-an; . . .
> Bill winked his ey-e / As he heard her cry-y: . . .

Obnoxious and ham-handed as the song undoubtedly is, it plays its audience astutely and with more than passing competence.[10]

Classic
Tin Pan Alley

In the second half of the Tin Pan Alley era, when the Tin Pan Alley style developed an even closer connection to the Broadway stage while remaining the source of America's most popular music (roughly from the 1920s through the mid-1950s), a number of factors combined to shift the form and expressive strategies of the basic song-type, thereby creating a new paradigm for Broadway songs that would continue to dominate the musical stage even beyond the point when the latter no longer dominated American popular music. As in the earlier decades of Tin Pan Alley, but to a much greater extent, technology and other considerations imposed stringent demands on the length of a song during this period. Of these, recording was initially the most restrictive in its demands, but the newly important venue of radio—and later, sound film—also wielded some corollary influence.[11] More subtly, the fecundity of the genre as a basis for jazz improvisations and arrangements, as well as for extended dance sequences, tended to dictate a standard formal structure of modest length—analogous in some ways to the binary forms that became standard in the eighteenth century both because they worked well as a basis for variation and because the form was in and of itself satisfying. The most basic change, however, involved the narrative and dramatic role of song; by the early stages of this emergent type, songs had moved away from the self-contained narratives they tended to present in the first decades of Tin Pan Alley to a type of song whose basic task was to articulate expressively a moment within the greater narrative of a show. And, just as in the earlier era, when songs tended to adhere to a standardized approach that worked well in the context of interpolation, later Tin Pan Alley songs also tended toward a standardized approach, albeit one that pointed in the opposite direction, since, within the new paradigm, each song had to fit as precisely as possible into its dramatic moment.

The new paradigm also had consequences for the performance of songs in other venues. Although the emergent type of song—which over time became synonymously identified with the very phrase "Tin Pan Alley"—continued usually to include clarifying and situating verses, these most often were much shorter, sometimes served as little more than introductions, and occasionally simply were not provided even for their original presentation on stage. In short, the song became, in most cases and for most purposes, coextensive with the chorus, but this would scarcely have happened as decisively as it did without considerations for the wider market. As was quickly learned within the time-restrictive environment of recording in the 1920s, the new Tin-Pan-Alley song, uprooted from the stage, worked best without its verses, as a fragment of expressivity whose specific context remained somewhat fluid, presenting an unspecified combination of the song's original stage setting (if it had one), the singer's personae or projected self, and some vaguely universalized feeling shared by performers and audience alike. As this kind of fluidity became the ideal, a specific narrative *within* a song was not only mostly beside the point, but also a potential source of interference. Indeed, when the emergent Tin Pan Alley song was performed separately, the verse (especially if it were of any length) often became little more than a curiosity, which—putting aside many notable exceptions—tended to distract from the emotional immediacy of the song even as it clarified its situational dynamic. Moreover, were the verse to be included in nonstaged settings, it would often be sung only *after* the chorus, which was thus allowed to make the first and most important connection with the audience. By the 1930s, as noted, many songs, including some that were written for the stage, did not include verses at all; many others included multiple sets of lyrics for the chorus (such as many of Cole Porter's comic numbers), making the latter function much like verses had in the past.[12]

While the designation "thirty-two-bar song form" has been used to describe the standard form of the later Tin Pan Alley song's chorus, composers showed considerable flexibility in how they filled those thirty-two bars, and indeed in whether they kept within the prescribed length. More important to the form than its precise length and structural configuration were a strong feeling of periodicity (often experienced as inevitability or simple naturalness) and the repetition of key phrases, which would both "sell" the song commercially and establish the centrality of a central emotional "truth" for a given song. The repeated "hook"—which was often and most usefully simply the sung title of the song—thus served both expressively and as a kind of built-in "jingle" through which a song advertised itself. Apart from occasional exceptions, the "thirty-two-bar form" reduces usefully to one of a handful of types, based on a typical phrase-length of eight bars. The most canonical version of the form would repeat the first of these eight-bar phrases twice, sometimes with slight variants, with a contrasting phrase separating the two repetitions, variously called the "bridge," the "release," or the "middle eight"; such a formal plan may be most easily represented as AABA (or AABC, if the final phrase is substantially different from the first two). But a song could also be scaled somewhat more broadly, as two extended phrases that begin similarly, each composed of an antecedent-consequent pairing; thus, ABAB or ABAC. While this degree of standardization (which in fact many perfectly "normal"-sounding Tin Pan Alley songs did not adhere to) would seem to be inherently rigid, these forms proved in practice to be extremely supple, admitting of a seemingly endless variety of ways their musical and verbal elements could function relative to each other. But the standardization itself had an important payoff, since the resulting forms—all of them easily grasped variants of a simple strophic approach—provided the secure and natural-sounding basic framework required if a song were to be perceived, however complicated it might actually be, as a straightforward and simple expression "from the heart."

For the following brief survey of songs from this era, I have chosen well-known songs written by the most important composers working at the time, unconnected with shows treated separately in later chapters of this or a planned second volume, and taken from the earlier decades of this period (the 1920s and '30s). While considerable credit must be given to George M. Cohan for helping to establish the new type of song, at least insofar as it is dramatically grounded within what was rapidly becoming in his hands something recognizable as the "American musical," his popularity had waned by the decades in question; we will thus consider him in the following chapter, but not here. Those whose songs we will consider—Irving Berlin, Jerome Kern, George Gershwin, Richard Rodgers, and Cole Porter—flourished on and off Broadway for many if not all of the decades in question; together, they virtually define the era. Of these, Irving Berlin was especially central, due in part to how prolific and adaptable he was, and in part to his early start and relatively long career; already by 1911, with "Alexander's Ragtime Band," his songs were selling in the millions. The others, each in his way, brought some combination of artistic aspiration and training, as well as consummate craft, to the medium. Thus, Jerome Kern and Richard Rodgers (who virtually worshiped Kern in his youth, and had written a substantial amount of music before his formal training at Columbia and the Institute of Musical Art) combined a musical sophistication deriving from practices familiar to them from the European classical tradition, with a directness of expression and a sure hand with various musical vernaculars. Cole Porter was probably the best schooled of the lot, having studied music at Yale, Harvard, and the Schola Cantorum (in Paris), and brought a scintillating verbal wit to the enterprise (he, like Berlin and Noel Coward—the latter working mainly in London—wrote both the words and the music for their songs). And George Gershwin, who most successfully approached the prestige of the concert and operatic stages, was also most intimately grounded in the jazz-based musical sensibility of his time (he died young, in 1937; except for Kern, who died in 1945, the others lived and worked productively through the 1950s).

"Always"

Irving Berlin's "Always" was dropped from *The Cocoanuts* (1925; film version 1929) during the process of turning the show into a vehicle for the Marx Brothers; Berlin subsequently presented it (along with what would prove to be substantial royalties) as a wedding present to his new bride, Ellin Mackay, and for the occasion probably added the second verse, which moves on from the first verse's description of awakening love to contemplate the prospect of a life together. With its oft-repeated one-word title, the song (that is, its chorus) well fits the paradigm described above of a song selling itself through "name recognition," and it seems also to adhere closely to a thirty-two-bar, frankly simple structure. But this impression of directness and simplicity is both hard won and somewhat misleading, for the song's complications are many and, as we will see, quite pointed: it modulates freely, flirts with all of the formal patterns described above without fully adhering to any of them, and sets up a somewhat uninspired rhyme scheme—"things you've planned" / "helping hand" / "understand"—only to discard it in favor of unrhymed blank verse in the final phrase (see below). But even apart from these complications, the song's repetitions of the word "always" are not simply formulaic, for they also in and of themselves express the meaning

♩ 4.6   of the word, portending an abiding, unshakeable presence.

The complementarities in the first eight-bar phrase of "Always" set up patterns that the rest of the song will inflect: two rising phrases in a waltz idiom offer slightly overbalancing declarations of love, and each is stabilized in its turn by a slower, falling-third figure on the word "always." The falling third that Berlin uses for the title word is a well-known calling-figure (e.g., "yoo-hoo," or the call of the cuckoo), which helps create here an effect of distance, across which and from above we are soothed by repetitions of that word's sanguine assurances; significantly, Berlin leaves ample room in the fourth and eighth bars of the eight-bar phrase for answering instrumental or vocal echoes of both iterations of the word. Figuratively, in this first phrase, "love" opens up a potentially disruptive trajectory that is then reassuringly closed, as the second "always" connects with the first and carries it safely home to the tonic, so that, together, they fully outline the tonic triad (the chord of the home key).

The second phrase begins as a musically literal repetition of the first—setting up an expectation of AABA or AABC as the governing formal scheme—but extends the rising figure through three rhymed repetitions; without the expected "always" to balance and close down this gesture, it spirals upward and careens into a remote key area, as the words describe the possibility of things going wrong. Again, the word "always" is used to span and close the effect of distance, as created by these gestures and through modulation: at the end of the phrase, two repetitions of the word dispel the tension in two echo-like steps, the first stabilizing the new key, the second bringing us safely back to the original key with reassuring ease, just in time to begin again.

At this point, our expectations for the form have shifted from AABA (or AABC) to the more broadly scaled ABAB (or ABAC). While the latter is what indeed happens verbally and rhythmically, the third phrase, which begins like the first two, takes us to yet another remote key, this time minor-mode ("Days may not be fair"). The final phrase is the payoff. Verbally, Berlin eschews rhyme for the directness of prose-like parallelisms:

> Not for just an hour,
> Not for just a day,
> Not for just a year,
> But always.

Musically, he retains the repeated waltz rhythms of the second phrase, but reconfigures the rising gestures as feather-like swoops that sequence downward to an inevitable close on the tonic for the final repetition of "always." The larger gesture—of a rising sequence taking us *to* a remote key in the second phrase of the song, answered by a falling sequence bringing us back *from* a remote key in the fourth—thus follows the trajectory of the first phrase, whose close it echoes at the end.[13]

"Smoke Gets in Your Eyes"

Jerome Kern's "Smoke Gets in Your Eyes" (from *Roberta*, 1933; lyrics by Otto Harbach) uses a similar device of balanced sequences, but within a single phrase. Since these balancing sequences make up the "A" phrase in a conventional AABA chorus (there is no verse), they might presumably come to seem redundant, but they take on a new significance with each repetition. Moreover, the pat phrase-structure of neatly balanced oppositions (which derives from an earlier, march-like version of the tune that had not been used for its original purpose) subtly sets up the inevitable disillusionment recounted later in the song by providing an effective vehicle for the opening phrase's charged question (sharply rising sequence) and much-too-complacent response (falling cadential sequence):

> They asked me how I knew
> My true love was true.
> > I of course replied,
> > "Something here inside,
> > Cannot be denied."

The reply, too clichéd to hold up and rendered even more contrived and complacent by the musical structure, is rejected in the second phrase, in which "They" offer in its place, as a warning, the central metaphor of the song:

> When your heart's on fire,
> You must realize
> Smoke gets in your eyes.

The "bridge" (the third phrase) is a harmonic "escape" to the remote key of the flat-sixth—a natural choice for the classically trained Kern, since this harmonic move had long served within that tradition as a "release" key that could seem decisively "other" but could also be pulled easily back to the home key. The device works well here for all the traditional reasons, projecting a feeling of escape that nevertheless rings slightly false; indeed, if Harbach's verbal inspiration seems to fail here somewhat ("So I chaffed / Them and I gaily laughed"), this may perhaps be explained as his attempt to reinforce the falseness of the singer's confidence.

The inevitable return in the fourth phrase, and the singer's equally inevitable acknowledgment that he or she, too, is human, gives the concluding descending sequence, and the title phrase itself, a sense of inescapable fate. But something unexpected accompanies the return, which prohibits the descending sequence from unfolding with full regularity. With a subtle twist, Harbach adds another layer to the song's central metaphor and calls attention to this addition through a disruptive extra syllable. Since this awkwardness could have been avoided without much trouble, we must suppose the effect to be deliberate, contrived so that the memory of the "lovely flame," with its extra syllable, might be gently emphasized through being set off as a triplet:

> So I smile and say,
> "When a lovely flame dies,
> Smoke gets in your eyes."

♪ 4.7

And, indeed, without this slight emphasis, the added layer to the metaphor might easily be missed: it is not the flame but its dying that produces the blinding smoke. Implicitly, as well, the blinding comes more from the resulting tears than from the smoke itself, yet neither touches the preserved loveliness of the remembered flame. The great economy of the Tin Pan Alley formula is well exemplified by this barely perceptible maneuver, through which we learn that the singer, though surely disillusioned, remains untouched by cynicism, quietly insisting on the extra syllable that the word "lovely" exacts from the fate-driven sequence.

"I Got Rhythm"

George Gershwin's "I Got Rhythm" (from *Girl Crazy*, 1930; lyrics by his brother Ira Gershwin) comes from a show that boasts many other song hits, including "Bidin' My Time," "Embraceable You," and "But Not For Me." While its catchy rhythm marks it as up-to-date for its time—and in this regard, it had the good fortune of being introduced by Ethel Merman in her first Broadway role—it also hearkens back to the ragtime song in its eminently danceable syncopations and verbal conceits just this side of dialect ("I got" and "Old Man Trouble"), and in-

Example 4.1

George and Ira Gershwin, "I Got Rhythm," beginnings of verse and chorus (vocal melody)

deed, it is designed to be a large-scale dance number, and to show off as well the high-powered pit band, which included Jimmy Dorsey, Benny Goodman, and Glenn Miller at early stages of their careers. The song's chorus pushes its basic rhythmic device hard (see the second segment of example 4.1), as every two-bar unit but the clinching "Who could ask for anything more?" (and its repetitions) employs the same driving syncopated figure, most often setting the verbal formula "I got . . . [in order: rhythm, music, my man, daisies, starlight, sweet dreams]." Moreover, the first three two-bar units present a daisy chain of inversions (or retrogrades), as the second plays back the first in reverse order, which, when reversed again for the third, unavoidably reproduces the first.

Indeed, the song shows many such blends of the "primitive" (or, better, music meant to represent or embody the primitive) and the sophisticated, in a combination typical for Gershwin. Evoking the "primitive" here accomplishes many things besides facilitating dance: a connection to African American traditions, a musical resonance for the lyric's celebration of simple things, and a sense of folk-derived "authenticity," which, as in the final phrase of "Always," gives up the affectation of clever internal rhymes.[14] Except for its setting of a particular lyric and its popular performance idiom, the materials for the song might have thus been right at home in Dvořák's *New World* Symphony (1893), particularly given the latter's deliberate basis in African American styles, its sharply defined rhythmic dimension, its many constructed melodic symmetries, and its focused use of melodies using a "gapped" scale (a "primitive" scale that does not include half-steps; also called "pentatonic" since such scales generally consist of five notes rather than the seven notes of the diatonic scale)—all of which use primitivist idioms to produce something to be taken as particularly American. (Significantly, an important concert piece composed just after *Girl Crazy* opened on Broadway quotes both the song and Dvořák's symphony in turn: the final two movements of William Grant Still's Afro-American Symphony, based on a blues tune, quotes "I Got Rhythm" in the banjo scherzo, and the scherzo of the "New World" at the climax of the finale.)[15]

Even apart from its symmetrical unfolding, the four-note basic figure that opens the chorus is itself symmetrical, both in its rhythm and in the arrangement of its intervals (which is why inverting it is equivalent to playing it backwards); thus, it unfolds as even dotted-quarters (each 1½ beats long), and outlines intervals of a whole-tone, a minor third, and a whole-tone, with a down-beat occurring precisely at the midpoint of the symmetrical pattern. The alignment of the pattern with the "I got . . ." verbal device thus also draws emphasis to the key words of each four-syllable pattern—not only "rhythm," "music," etc., but also "Trouble" in the phrase "Old Man Trouble" (in the bridge). This emphasis, in turn, virtually demands an additional rhythmic nuance: the "laying off of the beat" that is characteristic of the jazz idiom (thus, avoiding a too precise articulation of the beat through anticipation or delaying the arrival). Apart from these nuances, the simple symmetrical pattern, especially in repetition, creates an effect of elemental simplicity, stemming in part from how resolutely the pattern preserves itself across a conflicting metrical structure. But this is just one way in which we may see its simplicity as carefully and pointedly constructed. Thus, Gershwin's gapped scale does not include the seventh degree of the scale (the "leading-tone," or E in the original version in F), nor does that important note appear even in the "ungapped" parts of the chorus's melody; oddly enough, though, the missing E serves as the tonic key for the verse, which makes much of the chromatic movement to its fifth degree (moving incrementally to A, B♭,

♩ 4.8   and B♮; see first segment of example 4.1).

This somewhat odd configuration of the verse—which stems in part from the clichéd device of adding "juice" to a musical event through a sudden modulation up a half-step—provides the impetus for Gershwin's shaping of the primitivist material of the chorus, and thus for the song as a whole, beyond its straightforward adherence to a standard Tin Pan Alley pattern (AABA). Specifically, Gershwin will take up the chromatically ascending melodic structure of the verse, transpose it a half-step higher, and use it to shape the song as a whole, along the gradually emerging rising line B♭ - B♮ - C. The first step in this shaping process is to give weight to the B♭, which is fairly easy to accomplish, since B♭, a half-step above the third in F major, is one of the two pitches from the full scale that would typically be left out to create a "gapped" effect; here, the phrase "Who can ask for anything more?" at the end of the "A" phrase begins with this note, syncopated and presented as a melodic peak, but resolves it in a conventionally descending, ungapped, unsyncopated cadence. With the sudden modulation to a minor-mode key that launches the bridge ("Old Man Trouble"), B♮ emerges, again presented as a syncopated melodic peak ("Trou-**ble**"), and again carried safely to a descending resolution, this time through the most conventional of harmonic sequences. Significantly, this digression also serves as a surrogate verse should the actual verse (with its similar pointing to the note B♮) not be included in performance, in that it "explains" the context for the song, the "negative energy" that the song seeks to displace. The payoff for Gershwin's shaping process occurs in the final phrase, the only place where he departs from the regularities of the thirty-two-bar format: he diverts the cadence upward to point more force-fully to the concluding word "more," which coincides with a dissonant arrival on C, on a full downbeat and as the melodic peak for the song as a whole. Since this occurs at precisely the moment the song should end, it generates a two-bar extension to close off the song, with enough leftover energy generated by the diverted cadence to launch the dance sequence that follows.

♩ 4.9

The importance of this song should not be underestimated, not only as an indispensable jazz standard (virtually every seasoned jazz performer knows the "Rhythm" changes, that is, the song's harmonic structure, to be used as a basis for improvisation), but also as an embodiment of a new sensibility that places music and specifically rhythm (and even more specifically jazz rhythm) at the center of what matters in American life—as the "simple" and "natural" even though, as here, the embodying struc-ture may be carefully planned and executed.[16] Moreover, "I Got Rhythm" stands as part of the generative core of one of the central American move-ments of the 1930s—the balletic/athletic tradition in Broadway's dance sequences—which aspired, largely through rhythmically inflected dance idioms carried onto the "legitimate" ballet stage, to define America in more classically oriented terms. William Grant Still's use of the tune in the most successful movement of his Afro-American Symphony (the banjo scherzo, which was often encored or played separately) becomes in this context even more significant. In the four-note opening figure and its ma-nipulation, Gershwin produced an emblem of elemental American energy powerful enough to serve as a generative motive within the classical tra-dition, functionally related in this regard to the four notes that open Beethoven's Fifth Symphony. Both Still and Gershwin worked hard and with some success to demonstrate the potential for this process to bridge the growing gap between popular music and classical music, and their work became both a bridgehead and a cornerstone for the later similarly conceived successes of such figures as Aaron Copland. That this genera-tive potential should be so effectively embodied within so conventional a Tin Pan Alley song as "I Got Rhythm" provides some measure of how central the genre had become for American music, and for American mu-sical sensibilities.

"My Funny Valentine"

Richard Rodgers's "My Funny Valentine" (1937; lyrics by Lorenz Hart) comes from Babes in Arms, a show that was the first to be fully written by the highly successful team (that is, including the book), and which was also arguably their best, and certainly among the richest in other hits, which include "Where or When," "The Lady Is a Tramp," and "Johnny One Note" (in fact, "My Funny Valentine" had to wait about fifteen years before it really caught on, courtesy of Frank Sinatra's 1953 recording).[17] Particularly striking about "My Funny Valentine" are the contrast between its playfully insulting lyric and haunting music, and its migration into American traditions associated with Valentine's Day—natural enough, given the name, but oddly disjunct from its setting in the show, where it was sung by one teenager to another, who had to be renamed Valentine (Val) to make a place for the song. Both of these aspects may be traced to a set of carefully balanced ambiguities in the song, embodied both verbally and musically.

As a team, Rodgers and Hart typically worked by adding lyrics to music already written (the exact reversal of the procedure Rodgers would follow later with his other major collaborator, Oscar Hammerstein II), and it is hard to imagine how this song could have resulted in any other way. Musically, the song presents within the AABA structure of the chorus what theorists of modernist tonality might call a "double-tonic," hovering uncertainly between C♯ minor and E major. Thus, Rodgers starts firmly in C♯ minor, moves decisively (but in stages) to E major to set up the bridge, and returns to C♯ minor for the final "A" phrase—which, however, collapses the trajectory of the first two statements and, with a final "extra" three bars added to the end, returns once again to E, an arrival that is then dissipated through a series of ambiguous chords that continue to hover between the two keys. In one sense, Rodgers is simply taking advantage of an ambiguity that had long been present in American popular music, engendered by the habitual addition of the sixth scale-degree to concluding tonic chords; in this case, given an ending tonic of E, the addition of the sixth (C♯) effectively presents a "double image" of the two tonic chords. But the hovering between the two keys is also a shaped consequence of Rodgers's subtle play with the opening musical figure. As in "I Got Rhythm," the basic rhythmic idea of the opening two bars pervades the whole (in this case, helping to create and enforce the haunting effect of the song's melody), with the end of each "A" phrase representing a departure from the pattern with an important melodic peak ("You make me **smile** with my heart"), a peak that becomes more elevated with each repetition ("Yet, you're my **fav-'rite** work of art"; "Stay, little valentine, **stay!**").

Because of the tight ambit of the basic motive, comprising only the first three notes of the scale, Rodgers's moving the entire melodic complex up a third for the second "A" phrase suggests, but does not enforce, a corresponding modulation (since the result can still be easily harmonized in

C♯ minor), even though the melodic peak note of the previous phrase (B, on "smile") also points strongly to E. The second phrase thus has a built-in tension between the persistent C♯-minor harmonies and the melodic pull toward E, with the latter finally winning out by the end, just in time for the bridge (which, of course, reverses the process). For the final "A," Rodgers telescopes what had happened in the first two phrases: after only two bars of unequivocal C♯ minor, the melody moves up (as it had for the second "A"), this time continuing upward to close on a high E, the melodic peak of the song; although the harmonic cadence is at first res-olutely to C♯, the held E seems to force a reconsideration, and the har-monies soften toward E, setting up the ending already described.   ♩ 4.10

What Hart does with this harmonically ambivalent structure is to cre-ate a lyric that hovers with similar ambivalence between mockery and adoration for Val, who is described just before the chorus as "Thou noble, upright, truthful, sincere and slightly dopey gent." While, conventionally, the minor-mode alternative would be reckoned the sadder possibility, here it functions as the warmer, with the brighter sounds of E major serving as the carrier for a kind of (possibly) playful mockery. (The move toward E is vocally brighter, as well, less throaty for a singer than the low-lying opening phrase.) Thus, in the first phrase, the words "funny" and "comic" seemingly provoke the first hint of E major in the word "smile," but the line then softens, returning to C♯ minor via the word "heart":

> You're my funny valentine,
> Sweet comic valentine,
> You make me smile with my heart.

The most insulting words emerge during the E-major bridge, but the in-sult is canceled with the return to C♯ minor:

> Is your figure less than Greek?
> Is your mouth a little weak?
> When you open it to speak, are you smart?
>
> But don't change a hair for me . . .

Hart thus finds, in Rodgers's musical structure, the analog for an affec-tionately teasing but ultimately genuine love.

The adoption of this song as an emblem of Valentines Day, explicitly set up by the concluding line of the song, "Each day is Valentine's day," resonates well with traditions associated with that particular holiday as celebrated in America, when declarations of love are traditionally couched in playful terms, ready to be withdrawn or downgraded on a moment's notice, but most often wistfully hoping to be encouraged. The song even evokes fairly readily the extreme versions of this "taking back," whether

in the form of the recurring vogue for vicious anti-Valentines or the famous "St. Valentine's Day massacre" (in which seven bootleggers in Chicago were slaughtered in 1929, in an ambush engineered by Al Capone).
But it fits even more comfortably within the American sentimental tradition, which is often made palatable through a tinge of self-mockery.
Implicitly here, the mockery directed toward Val is also absorbed by the
singer, whose rueful tone acknowledges that if the object of her love is less
than perfect, that fact does not necessarily reflect well on her (although
the song may also be taken to underscore quite specifically the failings of
adolescent awkwardness, which might be outgrown). More broadly, the
ambiguities of the song touch deep currents in American popular culture,
which maintains similar balances between authenticity and mockery, creating a dynamic that plays itself out not only in minstrelsy and camp, as
noted, but also within the mix of exaggerated sentiment and wise-guy sophistication endemic to the American musical as a genre.[18]

Anything Goes (1934)[19] seems, on the face of it, one of
the happiest of accidents, a show that somehow "works" even though its
composer (Cole Porter) was in effect the third choice (after Kern and
Gershwin), and even though its original story and book (by Guy Bolton
and P. G. Wodehouse) had to be almost completely rewritten by newcomer Russell Crouse in collaboration with director Howard Lindsay. But
this was an "accident" driven by a powerful motor—seasoned producer
Vinton Freedley—and fueled by a slate of stars including the comic team
of William Gaxton and Victor Moore, and the relatively new star Ethel
Merman. In some ways the show marks a kind of "changing of the guard"
for mid-1930s Broadway. Its original writers were near the end of their
successful Broadway careers—Bolton, in particular, had been a frequent
collaborator with Kern—while the team of Lindsay and Crouse would
achieve a number of successes over the following decades, culminating
with *The Sound of Music* (1959). Kern's Broadway career had all but
ended (although he continued to contribute successfully to Hollywood
musicals), as had Gershwin's, with only *Porgy and Bess* (1935) to come,
followed by a short stint in Hollywood and his tragic death in 1937.
Porter's Broadway star, on the other hand, was still very much in the as-
cendant. Thus, *Anything Goes*, whose title song articulates a cultural/so-
cietal "sea change," is itself a manifestation of that change—at the center of which are a collection of quintessential Cole Porter songs: verbally
clever (and quite often risqué), musically suave and sophisticated, each
comprising an utterly memorable unity of words and music.

There does indeed seem to be something haphazard about *Anything
Goes*, quite as if its title had been adopted as the credo of its various creative teams. With its substantially reworked plot, its song substitutions

driven partly by the foibles of its stars, and the vocal and dramatic imbalances deriving from the fact that one of the "romantic" leads (Sir Evelyn Oakleigh) doesn't have his own song even though his eventual mate has several, the show seems to exemplify the pre-*Oklahoma!*, pre-"integrated" era of the American musical, a show in which the various ingredients matter—songs, dances, comedy, star turns—but somehow not the totality. Yet, while a full defense of the show would be beside the point here, the case can and should be made that its songs are anything but haphazard, that quite apart from the independent success that a great many of them achieved (having broken away from their specific dramatic context), they are carefully situated within the show, often carrying important dramatic and thematic weight, and consistently setting out the characters' sensibilities and relationships in vivid, yet subtle, fashion. We will address a number of those songs here, in order to consider how adaptable the Tin Pan Alley style was to the dramatic exigencies of the musical stage on the one hand, and, on the other, how the songs in a song-driven show such as *Anything Goes* actually do the driving with which they are credited.

The story in its final form involves a set of relationships centering around Billy Crocker (Gaxton), a stowaway on a cruise ship bound from New York to London, where his beloved Hope Harcourt is to marry Sir Evelyn Oakleigh to secure her family's jeopardized financial position. Also on board are Billy's old flame Reno Sweeney (Merman), an evangelist turned nightclub singer who is still smitten with him, and the hapless Moon Face Martin (Moore), a gangster on the run disguised as "Reverend Moon," who aspires to rise from Public Enemy No. 13 to No. 1. In the end, the Harcourt family emerges financially sound without Sir Evelyn's help (enabling Hope and Billy to marry), Reno attaches herself to Sir Evelyn, and Moon Face is decreed harmless and released. Thematically, the show would thus seem to advance the notion that mid-1930s America could solve its own Depression-era problems without Europe, and would be better served by doing so. Also thematic is its casual interweaving of various divergent "celebrity" elements (nightclub star, evangelist, gangster, and British aristocrat) around the fringes of a wholesome American center (Billy and Hope), marking all of the former functionally interchangeable, and equally suspect (if also appealing).

The oddest feature of the plot is the resolution of the love triangle, with the sexy Reno pairing off with the effete and nonsinging Sir Evelyn. This is odd on another level, as well, since there is no remotely comparable star paired with Reno—except, of course, Billy, who from the beginning is more importantly paired with two others: with Hope, of course, as his romantic interest, but more centrally with Moon Face, his fellow stowaway and (from a marquee standpoint) comic partner. Some have felt this plot-star misalignment to be a sign that, notwithstanding the implications of the show's title, someone with a profession as tainted as Reno's cannot end up marrying the hero on Broadway in 1934 (even if she is allowed to marry into British nobility!). If this seems unlikely, there is perhaps a more daring possibility, that through a network of associations that would have been less than transparent to those not "in the know," Porter might have been trying to establish a semi-closeted homosexual dimension for the show, one that could plausibly support the Reno-Evelyn pairing. Thus, we may note the presence of such "inflected" elements as a men's chorus-line dressed in cute sailor suits (cf. the "Queen's Navee" of *H.M.S. Pinafore*), who sing a "Sea Chantey" in close barbershop-quartet harmony through which they commiserate with each other over the lack of feminine companionship while at sea; significantly, Billy himself launches his series of amusing disguises by appearing first in a sailor suit and next as a woman. Equally intriguing is the markedly effeminate song, "Be Like the Bluebird," the "old Australian 'bush' [!] song" that Moon Face sings to his cellmate Billy, which adds a musical dimension to the clear implication, played for laughs here and throughout, that Moon Face isn't really mean enough (read "man enough") to be a public enemy.

If an audience wishes to see it, there is thus plenty in the show to suggest that Sir Evelyn's effeteness and British mannerisms—not to mention the odd combination of "Sir" with "Evelyn," since the latter would have registered with Americans as decidedly a woman's name—might indicate a homosexual orientation, and that a marriage for him could possibly have been a cover (as it largely was for the homosexual Cole Porter himself); hence Sir Evelyn's telling misuse of American slang when he declares to Moon Face that he has "hot pants" for him. While the show, as mounted in 1934, does not reciprocate with a similar suggestion from Reno's side, Porter had originally written a song for her—"Kate the Great"—that would have provided precisely that reciprocation, projecting the possibility of a rather open sexual environment that a marriage to a European aristocrat of suspect orientation might offer her. If nothing else, the song would surely have added something to our understanding of Reno's relationship with the sixteen "Angels" who perform with her. But the suggestion of a homoerotic subtext also goes a long way toward explaining why Sir Evelyn himself gets no song to sing, which he would surely have gotten if we were meant to believe that, in the end, he truly "gets the girl" in the conventional sense.

Although "Kate the Great" plays with Tin Pan Alley conventions, it thrives more on thwarting the expectations of the genre, a strategy that both serves as an analog for the sexual "deviance" the song alludes to, and accentuates the surprisingly explicit turns Porter takes with his central *double entendre* on the verb "to make" (which has many slang applications, including "to have sexual relations with"). The song proceeds with a fairly lengthy verse, more melodic than might be typical and comprising a full ABAB structure, but which gives few overt clues regarding the song's real agenda beyond rhyming "Kate" with "potentate" and "reprobate." A waltz-like "chorus" then ensues (lilting, but not metrically in three as a genuine waltz must be), outlining the first three parts of another ABA(B) structure. Here, still, there is little hint of what is about to happen, even up to the lines that conclude the second "A":

> So drink
> To that jovial jade
> And think of the history she made.

"Made" is, of course, the pivot point, as the song then launches into a free-for-all, a cabaletta-like spinning out of the possibilities:

> Why, she made the Congress,
> She made the Premier,
> She made the clergy,
> And she made 'em cheer.
> She made the butler,
> She made the groom,
> She made the maid who made the room.
> She made the Army,
> She made the Marines,
> Made some of them princes
> And some of them queens, . . .

But this turns out to be no cabaletta (which would normally provide a slower number with a fast conclusion), for the music has begun gradually to recall more explicitly the music of the verse, if at a somewhat faster tempo, which sets up a final return in which new meanings are now attached to the word "potentate," and to Kate's preference for "affairs of the heart" over "affairs of state." Remarkably, as well, the overall form is thereby rationalized as a larger-scale Tin Pan Alley structure, even to the point of the final return being colored by reinterpretive possibilities enabled by the extended "bridge": AB AB (CDCE) AB (with AB corresponding to the AB of the verse, and CDCE to the chorus/cabaletta). And, especially since the song was intended for Reno to sing early on, we may also wish to note that it touches on important "themes" of the show during the cabaletta-like section, including both the curious melding of the religious and the decidedly secular, and the homoerotic: thus, for the former, "She made the clergy, / And she made 'em cheer"; and, for the latter, "She made the maid who made the room"—the line that Merman refused to sing—and Porter's rhyming of "Marines" with "queens," which brings one to speculate about just how Kate transformed members of the imperial armed forces into "princes" and "queens" (surely a matter more of "dress-up" than political appointment?).

♩ 4.11

If "Kate the Great" represents an opportunity missed, in the many memorable songs that were retained in *Anything Goes,* Porter makes the most of his opportunities, particularly in terms of establishing the quality of the relationships they articulate. Early on, "I Get a Kick Out of You" (originally written in 1931, but not used until *Anything Goes*) perfectly expresses Reno's rueful acknowledgment that Billy is no longer interested in her romantically; significantly, she is the only one who sings. (Famously, Porter broke all rules of "decorum" by placing this hit song so early in the show. While anecdote has it that he did this to punish latecomers, the first scene is in fact the only place this song can fit, in terms of the plotted relationships of the show.) "All Through the Night," with its quality of vigil-keeping, describes the abiding love between Billy and Hope, while letting us know that the wait will be a long one. "You're the Top," Billy's later response to Reno, is a couple-song with absolutely no ignitable romantic charge, however flirty it may get; the song clarifies that these former lovers are now comfortable, both with each other and with the pastness of their affair. And "Anything Goes," Reno's big number in Act I, gives a resigned yet sophisticated shrug to the apparent romantic mismatch of Reno and Sir Evelyn. In terms of the show's relationships, the entire story is fully contained in these four hit songs. Moreover, without them the sorting out of the romantic relationships in the show would simply not matter to an audience.

The conceit of "I Get a Kick Out of You" is that in Reno's seemingly carefree life, Billy alone can provide the necessary spark. Falling in a conventional AABA pattern, the song lists three rhyming sources of intoxication—champagne, cocaine,[20] and a plane (one each for the three "A" phrases)—that no longer have their desired effect on her; in the bridge we have explicit confirmation that he does not return her feeling ("You obviously don't adore me"). Much of the nuance of the song comes from the subtle alternation of triplet and nontriplet figures (a distinction many performers either miss or blur); in the main, the triplets set up an off-the-beat jolt, suspended over the bar-line, setting off the word "kick" in the title line at the conclusion of each "A" phrase.[21] Emblematically, the triplets seem a habitual mode for Reno, projecting a routine sexiness (relating, perhaps, to the driving triplets of "bump-and-grind" music), but somehow not as "real" as the simple syncopated jolt of the final line. As well, the triplets provide a vehicle for the registral shaping of the song, as each time they appear the melody reaches slightly higher, much like the melodic trajectories of "I Got Rhythm" and "My Funny Valentine." Here, the opening line of each "A" phrase ascends (by triplets) to the fifth degree (i.e., "I get no kick from cham**pagne**"), with each follow-up line extending the purview of the triplets and reaching a higher peak; thus, in the first phrase, four sets of triplets reach no higher than the fifth degree already reached, five sets in the second phrase reach the sixth degree (in a repetitive pattern to set up the phrase "That would bore me terrific'ly too"), the bridge reaches slightly higher, to the lowered seventh degree, and five more sets of triplets in the final line soar two additional notes higher to the second above the upper tonic ("Flying too high with some guy in the sky"),[22] with a final set of triplets coming in the final line to push the melody upward to the upper tonic on "you." As in "I Got Rhythm" and "My Funny Valentine," the strategy for registral shaping is set up in the verse, whose high points arch upward, but slightly less dramatically and not quite so high as in the arch of the chorus.

♩ 4.12

"All Through the Night" is a song about being apart, and it is significant that Billy and Hope sing it in sequence, each to the other; only at the end do they sing together, during the last phrase of Hope's verse. The song in the main is thus presented, not as a conventional love-duet, but rather as a duet of separateness, and of Billy's and Hope's separate pledges to each other, projecting their union only as a possibility for the future, with no clear path to achieving it. Verbally, the song constructs night as the only realm in which their union seems possible, a realm of dreams and fantasy that is destroyed by the reality that comes with dawn. Within the song's AABA structure, "A" represents this dreamworld of vigil-keeping, interrupted by day (in the bridge). "All Through the Night" was a substitute written to replace "Easy to Love," which Gaxton found hard to sing. Oddly, however, it is in its way much the harder to sing, even if it has fewer romantic leaps and swoops, and a more restrictive range. What makes it difficult is its central device of spinning a melodic line out of an obsessively descending chromatic scale, often maintaining an aching major-seventh or minor-ninth dissonance with the bass as it falls, pulling us downward with it into sleep and dreams, gradually "losing" the reality of the home key along the way—only to recover it, miraculously, at the conclusion of the phrase. In the first phrase, this "miracle" occurs with an upward leap on the words, "You're so close **to me**." In the second phrase, the upward leap comes earlier, on the word "You," and is set up by the previous line:

> All through the night / From a height far above,
> **You** and your love / Bring me ecstasy.

The "miracle" this time is a sudden transportation, on the concluding word "ecstasy," into a remote key (the lowered mediant, related to the "escape" key of the flat sixth discussed earlier in connection with "Smoke Gets in Your Eyes"). The bridge, naturally enough, brings us gradually back to the "reality" of the home key, setting up the final "A" phrase, in which the leap happens still earlier than before so as to accommodate a final concluding leap to an upper-tonic cadence (this also completes an ascending registral shaping across the "A" phrases, which reach individual peaks, in the key of E♭, on B♭, D♭, and E♭).

♩ 4.13

"You're the Top" reportedly had its origins in a bantering exchange of rhymed "compliments" among Cole Porter and various dinner guests, which he collected, expanded on, and eventually set to a snappy syncopated tune that seems to leave time along the way for "thinking up" the next clever line (which also gives an audience time to savor each in turn). Both music and lyric provide a comfortable and distinctly marked emotional distance between the two singers, neither too close nor too far, projecting a secure environment for competitive banter in which, for example, comparing a woman alternately to "the Coliseum" and "the Louvr' Museum" (both landmarks noted above all else for being old and large) will neither be taken amiss nor fall on ears deaf to the lyric's game of cloaking insults in the guise of compliments. It is a game of barbed, yet affectionate give-and-take that neither lovers nor strangers, one must imagine, could play for long and remain so. For "You're the Top" to work as a song, its formulas must repeat, but the lyrics themselves cannot, and so both verse and ABAB' chorus are treated together, textually, as verse rather than refrain, requiring new, increasingly clever, words at each turn. In the version that appears in the original show, Billy sings through a full verse and chorus to Reno, who responds in kind; encores of the chorus alone then admit of freer patterns of give-and-take. Intriguingly, in the mostly inadequate film version of the show released in 1956, the friendly "distance" established in "You're the Top" provides a vehicle for establishing that the two central couples (in its vastly reworked plot) are

♩ 4.14   wrongly paired.

With its supple song-formulas and wise-cracking verbal style perfectly matched by its music, the song has been much parodied, most famously and wickedly by Irving Berlin, whose ostentatiously obscene version purportedly went as follows:

> You're the top! You're Miss Pinkham's tonic.
> You're the top! You're a high colonic.
> You're the burning heat of a bridal suite in use,
>> You're the breasts of Venus,
>> You're King Kong's penis,
>> You're self-abuse.
> You're an arch in the Rome collection.
> You're the starch in a groom's erection.
> I'm a eunuch who has just been through an op,

> But if, Baby, I'm the bottom,
> You're the top.[23]

"Anything Goes" carries the energy of "You're the Top" into a solo number for Reno. Like "You're the Top" and many another Porter hit (e.g., "Let's Do It" from the 1928 *Paris;* "Let's Not Talk About Love" from the 1941 *Let's Face It;* and "Always True to You, Darling, in My Fashion" from the 1948 *Kiss Me, Kate*), "Anything Goes" is based, entirely it would seem, on formula: a formulaic treatment of the Tin Pan Alley form replete with snappy syncopations, a ready-made punch-line and/or launching premise, and a poetic structure that will permit (or, rather, demand) interpolation of clever rhymes and often topical references. With its dramatic placement, as a song to "explain" Reno's mismatched pairing with Sir Evelyn (a marriage, after all, of plot-convenience), it may seem the least motivated of the four "relationship songs" in *Anything Goes,* yet it is a kind of linchpin, coming late in the first act, to rationalize not only the improbable pairing of Reno and Sir Evelyn, but all manner of other improbabilities and improprieties to come as well.

Porter wrote the song quickly, in response to the new title of the show devised by Lindsay and Crouse during their rewrite. While these circumstances may explain why it adheres even more closely than usual to a standard formal type (AABA), its musical detail includes much nuance. Most strikingly, the melodic, rhythmic, and harmonic details of the minor-mode verse underscore its verbal image of a clock being wound: "ticking" rhythms, ascending melodic sequences propelled by a triplet "winding" gesture in the accompaniment, which also serves to ratchet up the chromatically ascending bass and push the harmony upward accordingly. The effect of "overwinding" that this seems to suggest—thus, what is left to govern the "changed times" of "today" is by implication a broken clock— is taken further in the minor-mode bridge, which holds a single repeated note against which accented leaps climbing steadily upward reach a "breaking point." Within the strictly repeating formulas of the "A" phrases, a jaunty, major-mode tune moves up to a dramatic pause to which the only possible answer—verbally and musically—is the pat title-phrase repeated on the tonic; that we know the answer, every time, is of course the point: if "anything goes," there can be no shock to the punchline.[24]

♩ 4.15

Part of what must be allowed to "go" in the second act of *Anything Goes,* beyond sexual license, is its broad parody of religion, centered around the two seeming incongruities of Reno's evangelist past and Moon Face becoming "Reverend Moon." The act opens with "Public Enemy No. 1," a mock-religious paean designed to ridicule the public idolatry then accorded to gangsters (fueled in part by the folk-hero status many of them attained in the 1930s against the dual backdrops of the Great Depression and the final years of Prohibition). But, by creating a visual/musical double-image that merges gangster with preacher, and church-style with Broadway, *Anything Goes* implicitly mocks religion as well. The verse works as a rather too-jolly "call and response," merging tropes common to both religious services and Broadway numbers that feature a singer and supporting chorus; within its secular context, Porter mixes religious references:

> Our gallant Captain has told the staff,   (the staff-o, the staff-o)
> It's time for killing the fatted calf,
> As he's throwing a party on behalf
> Of Public Enemy Number One,   (Public Enemy Number One-o)

The chorus is, clearly, a hymn; unaware of context and oblivious to the lyric, one might almost take it for the real thing, especially if it is sung, as indicated, in unaccompanied four-part harmony. (Its form, nevertheless, derives from Tin Pan Alley: ABAC, albeit in sixteen slow-pace bars rather than the conventional thirty-two.)

♩4.16

"Public Enemy" was a late addition to the show, written as an opening to Act II that would also serve to set up the following number, "Blow, Gabriel, Blow," a revivalist-*cum*-nightclub number led by Reno. Again, the parody cuts both ways, as "Gabriel's horn" is represented by the phallic imagery of a jazz trumpet playing aggressively ascending licks, cheered on by the group within another call-response structure—here more reminiscent of the religious revival, especially as practiced by African Americans (the responses are cut in many performances, perhaps because they use dialect; see later discussion). The dramatic verse serves to introduce the song proper, which, although in a full AABA structure (again, however, only sixteen bars long), in repetition functions as a verse for a rousing hymn, a framework for the "testifying" that occurs in the faster-paced bridge sections:

> I've been a sinner, I've been a scamp,
> But now I'm willin' to trim my lamp, . . .
> But now since I have seen the light
> I'm good by day and I'm good by night, . . .

The "double-image" effect here is striking, for the final three syllables in each bridge have decidedly saucy interpretive possibilities (well in line, of course, with the similar possibilities of the title itself).[25] As the song builds, these two early verses, musically identical, mutate dramatically, with each sixteen-bar verse functioning as a single phrase within a larger AABC structure, culminating in a final return to the original (thus, AABCA in eighty bars, more than doubling the traditional length of thirty-two bars).

♩4.17

With all its daring engagement with sexual innuendo and religious tropes, *Anything Goes* shows a much too accepting attitude about a number of issues other shows of its era were taking up seriously. Particularly troubling are the scenes in which Billy, Reno, and Moon Face disguise themselves as Chinese, quite as if this did not "count" as racist in the same way as blackface. It was, indeed, common enough in the 1930s to see this kind of complacency—even unapologetic blackface—alongside substantial efforts to deal directly with America's entrenched racism, as well represented, for example, in Kern and Hammerstein's 1927 *Show Boat* and Heyward and the Gershwins' 1935 *Porgy and Bess,* the latter then in preparation. Nor is the Chinese shtick (a Gaxton specialty) an isolated instance of these entrenched attitudes. A later encore of "Anything Goes," suppressed in revivals, concludes with the lines:

> When ladies fair who seek affection
> Prefer coons of dark complexion as Romeos,
> Anything goes.

Also central to concerns taken up in later chapters of this book is the projection in *Anything Goes* of what "America" is, and why that is worth preserving (one of the most common themes of American musicals, treated here in chapters 5 through 7). Markers for this theme are many and easy to spot. The cruise ship that serves as the setting for most of the show is called the "American," headed for England and an uncertain future. Along the way, European alternatives are raised (French in "Bon Voyage"; English with the figure of Sir Evelyn) and mainly rejected, while American misfits, with all their self-contradictions, are treated with endless indulgence. Billy, of course, is the quintessential American, always in trouble, but always landing on his feet. Hope is what's at stake, allegorically and literally, in a manner consistent with the pattern in the show of women representing potential trouble; thus, it is the women who insist on the French pronunciation in "Bon Voyage" (thus, "Vo*yage*" instead of the men's "*Voy*age"), Hope who looks to England for help, her mother who consistently tries to block Billy's way to Hope, Sweeney who ultimately falls for Sir Evelyn. Given this thematic structure, it is of course absolutely necessary that the show's gangster (representing one of America's more prominent—and discomfiting—claims to fame in the 1930s) be rendered harmless in the end, and that the Harcourt's financial troubles be solved without foreign help.

For Further Consideration

Girl Crazy (1930), *Babes in Arms* (1937)

Figure 4.2. Ethel Merman (Reno Sweeney) and Bing Crosby (Billy Crocker) in the 1936 film version of *Anything Goes*. Billy is here using one of his many "disguises," in this case coordinating with Reno's more elaborate "Chinese" costume. (Courtesy of the Academy of Motion Picture Arts and Sciences.)

See Also

Regarding Stephen Foster's impact on American song, see William W. Austin's *"Susanna," "Jeanie," and "The Old Folks at Home": The Songs of Stephen C. Foster from His Time to Ours,* and chapter 9 of Charles Hamm's *Music in the New World.* Regarding the songs of minstrelsy and their performance, see Robert Winans's "Early Minstrel Show Music, 1843–1852."

Regarding Tin Pan Alley generally, Charles Hamm's "The Music of Tin Pan Alley" in his *Music in the New World* remains ever valuable, especially when read alongside chapters 13–14 of his earlier *Yesterdays;* Jon Finson's *The Voices That Are Gone* offers considerable insight into the early stages; David A. Jasen's *Tin Pan Alley* provides a reliable chronicle; Kenneth Kanter's *The Jews of Tin Pan Alley* considers the era from a particular cultural perspective; and Philip Furia provides often brilliant analyses of the subtleties of Tin Pan Alley lyricists in *The Poets of Tin Pan Alley.* See also Nicholas E. Tawa's useful *The Way to Tin Pan Alley.*

Regarding the composers discussed at greatest length in this chapter, Gerald Mast devotes a separate chapter to each in *Can't Help Singin'* (chapters 4–6 and 10–11; see in particular pp. 44–45 on "Always" and pp. 194–196 on *Anything Goes*). Chapters 2–6 in Alec Wilder's *American Popular Song* also offer useful extended discussions of their careers and individual songs—in particular, "Smoke Gets in Your Eyes" (71–72), "My Funny Valentine" (205–7), and individual songs from *Anything Goes* (235–39). Will Friedwald's idiosyncratic *Stardust Melodies: A Biography of Twelve of America's Most Popular Songs* includes separate chapters on "I Got Rhythm" and "My Funny Valentine." Allen Forte takes a musico-technical approach to the songs in *The American Popular Ballad of the Golden Era* and *Listening to Classic American Popular Songs;* see especially, in the former, his discussions of "Smoke Gets in Your Eyes" (64–67) and "My Funny Valentine" (196–202).

Regarding *Anything Goes,* Geoffrey Block provides the best extended treatment, in chapter 3 of *Enchanted Evenings.*

Part Two

DEFINING AMERICA

Whose (Who's) America?

THE AMERICAN MUSICAL is almost always concerned, on some level, with constructions of America. Sometimes this is merely implicit; sometimes, seemingly, a matter of habit. Fundamentally, though, this stems from the simple fact that American musicals play to American audiences, who will be acutely aware of anything that challenges their notions of what or who America is or stands for, or of its place in the world. If Americans see representatives of other lands and cultures on the musical stage, they will see them in relation to some sense of who *they* are as Americans. If they see various constituent groups of Americans, whether in the present or in a re-imagined past, they will be aware of how congruent (or not) those representations seem to be with their own received notions of such groups and their history. Those responsible for creating a musical will probably be consciously aware of this dynamic and will present their assemblage of diverse characters, locales, and events expecting such a context of reception. If they are not consciously aware, they will either *behave* as if they are aware—through a quasi-instinctual sense for this dynamic or because they will observe pragmatically that some things work and others don't—or they will fail to connect with their audiences in the expected way, so that, consequently, what they stage will to that extent cease to function as an *American* musical.

Since American musicals have also played, throughout their history, to immigrants and early-generation Americans, they may function importantly for such groups as more-or-less reliable sources of cultural information, not so much regarding the realities of Americans and American history, but rather of how these are generally understood, of what they are taken to be by Americans. Even for mainstream, heritage Americans, this kind of function is often well served by musicals. How else except through such representations does the New Yorker who has not left the city acquire a multi-dimensional sense for an America geographically removed from Manhattan? And how better might the visitor to Manhattan gain a sense for New York's "sophistication" than in a Broadway theater? In these senses, American musicals become, in part and in some form, an enacted demonstration of Americanism, and often take on a formative, defining role in the construction of a collective sense of "America."

My larger concern in part II of this book is with musicals that pursue fairly aggressive agendas of defining America, often sharply divergent from each other in what they choose to project, selected from a very large number of eminently qualifying shows. I have found it useful to consider these shows within three broad stages of development, both within the tradition itself and against the backdrop of historical circumstance. In the first stage, "Whose (Who's) America?"—explored briefly through two relatively early shows separated as much by the sensibilities of their creators as by the three decades of generic and historical development between them—the defining issue is who counts as American, and how that matters. For the two musicals considered in this chapter, the interlocking questions "Whose America?" and "Who Is America?" take on slightly different casts. For *Little Johnny Jones,* it is the latter form of the question that matters most, with a resoundingly affirmative and (for its time) inclusive response, emerging within an environment of entrenched and somewhat smug conservatism. *The Cradle Will Rock,* written during the troubled era of the Great Depression, when the twin specters of European fascism and communism loomed as frightening prospects for America, aggressively asks both questions and thereby takes sides—on the left—in an emergent internal conflict, a conflict whose resolution a half-decade later in post–Pearl Harbor patriotism would prove, however emotionally and politically effective, neither lasting nor definitive.

Little Johnny Jones (1904) was George M. Cohan's first hit on Broadway, and his first collaboration with Sam H. Harris, who would produce nearly all of his later successes, with Cohan, as here, assuming the triple role of writer, composer, and performer. After their breakup in 1919 in the wake of Cohan's bitter opposition to Actors Equity (a labor union founded in 1913), Cohan became rapidly outmoded, enjoying but few successes thereafter as a performer and virtually none as a writer. *Little Johnny Jones* took as its starting point the career of Tod Sloan, a brash, womanizing American jockey who had revolutionized racing both in America and in England by introducing the crouched, over-the-neck position that has since become standard, but whose career eventually fell apart through his gambling and knack for making enemies. In Cohan's appropriation of Sloan's persona and story, the jockey is disgraced but later vindicated (through the prearranged signal of a skyrocket fired from a ship far out at sea, witnessed by the abandoned jockey on the pier).

Cohan introduces a nose-thumbing patriotism early on through his big number, "The Yankee Doodle Boy," built around the tune and jeering epithet, "Yankee Doodle Dandy." As is well known, American colonialists had endured hearing this tune from the British, which carried a variety of offensive texts, in the decades before 1776 and during the early stages of the Revolutionary War. The colonialists, however, began playing it back at their former taunters to humiliate them as the tide turned, by some accounts playing it even during the surrender of British General Charles Cornwallis at Yorktown in 1781. The surface rationale for Cohan's borrowing stems from the traditional lyric:

> Yankee Doodle went to town
> A-riding on a pony,
> Stuck a feather in his cap
> And called it macaroni.[1]

—which Cohan converted to the following for the end of his chorus, borrowing the "Yankee Doodle" tune itself for the first two lines:

> Yankee Doodle came to London
> Just to ride the ponies;
> I am the Yankee Doodle Boy.

But the deeper rationale is the inverted chauvinism of the song's heritage, to which Cohan, as an *Irish* American, would have been especially sympathetic.

As noted in chapter 3 (pp. 51–52), the Irish in the nineteenth century were victims of racial prejudice in both Europe and America. Their involvement in American blackface minstrelsy stemmed largely from that circumstance, fueled dually by their close association with American blacks, with whom they were thrown together in Northern slums before the Civil War, and by their implicit attempt to identify with the Anglo-American "white" community through a kind of double negative, by blacking up (thus, becoming obvious *imitations* of blacks), and so to escape, by degrees, the low social position they continued to occupy in America at a time when signs reading "No Irish Need Apply" were common currency.[2] By Cohan's time, the Irish had moved up the ladder of respectability from minstrelsy to a secure place in the vaudeville circuit, especially following the successes of Ned Harrigan (in his "Mulligan Guard" series and elsewhere) and others from the late 1870s on. As with other disadvantaged groups at various points in American history (such as Jews, Italians, and African Americans), show business provided the Irish with an avenue toward wider acceptance, most visibly as performers, but also as writers and composers. But the Irish were by no means fully accepted as *Americans* at the turn of the century, since they were outside the Anglo-American cultural mainstream that continued to dominate; moreover, they had scarcely even begun to shake their low societal standing from an English perspective. Under these circumstances, Cohan's character in *Little Johnny Jones* had a rather aggressive point to make. Cohan, who had performed in vaudeville from an early age with his parents and sister (the Four Cohans), made no bones about his Irish heritage, and few would have missed the double significance of his "Johnny Jones," so obviously *Irish,* thumbing his nose at the English as a proudly patriotic *American*—another double negative, perhaps, but this time inverted in precisely the manner of the original "Yankee Doodle."

Little Johnny Jones asserts its vision of America at every turn. As a show, it managed in the face of critical dismissal to begin to displace what had become standard fare for Broadway—that is, a species of musical comedy deriving from the English music hall and the operettas of Gilbert and Sullivan, and given to flowery sentimentality and stilted dialogue— offering instead a dramatically serious story engaged with current events, employing a brashly vernacular verbal idiom based directly on current American usage. Thus, for example, "The Yankee Doodle Boy" begins with the then slangy "I'm the kid that's all the candy" and proceeds in short order to rhyme "Doodle" with "boodle" (i.e., fortune). Importantly, the show's two biggest numbers lay out a map of what America then was, geographically. "Give My Regards to Broadway" recites its quick tour of Central Manhattan (Broadway, Herald Square, Forty-Second Street) to a relaxed but snappy syncopated melody over sentimentalized harmonies. For its part, "The Yankee Doodle Boy" refers in various ways to New England (the original "Yankee," supported by many musical recollections of "Yankee Doodle Dandy"), the South ("I love to listen to the Dixie strain," recalling the tune for "Dixie" at that point and elsewhere), the West ("I long to see the girl I left behind me"—whose name is Goldie Gates, a "Yankee" from San Francisco), and the whole package ("Oh say can you see," set to the opening phrase of the "Star-Spangled Banner," the official American anthem whose verses were written during another Anglo-America conflict, the War of 1812). Implicit, as well, is the Irishness of the whole enterprise, with Cohan's brogue supporting the stereotypical locu-

♩ 5.1   tion of Irish braggadocio, set to its musical correlative: a devil-may-care amalgam of strung-together allusions and quotations.

One might infer from this that the Irish have merely *appropriated* an American identity, assembled like the rags of tunes in "Yankee Doodle Boy" to hide a poverty of native substance. But the sheer aggressiveness in Cohan's presentation—and here, Cohan's spectacularly athletic dance style comes into play—nevertheless carries great conviction, arguing, im-plicitly, that such posturing is basic to what it means to be American, which is something one may be born to ("born on the Fourth of July"), but more importantly what one aspires to become, in part through patri-otic posing. The strategy of "Give My Regards to Broadway," on the other hand, is to efface through nostalgia the "Johnny-come-lately" aspect of the American persona, so vividly projected in "The Yankee Doodle Boy." Thus, nostalgia (also evident in "Good Old California" and elsewhere in the show) evokes the sense both of a valuable past and a deeper interiority, as part of the American experience and psyche. In "Give My Regards to Broadway," the indulgence in close, chromatic harmony, especially in the supporting voices when the song is performed (as it fairly begs to be) as a barbershop-style quartet, gives a musical presence to the sentimental support of friends united in common feeling, while at the same time indulging a musical genre, deriving from the minstrel stage and black spirituals, that was becoming emblematic of America.   ♩ 5.2

Other songs provide additional nuances, regarding both America's relationship to England and its own demographic makeup. "Nesting in a New York Tree" tells the parable-like story of an English sparrow who stows away on a ship to find a new home in America, thereby offering a less-than-subtle rationalization for the Anglo-American mainstream as somehow grounded in "nature." "Captain of the Ten Day Boat" (a boat available for hire), a direct parody of *H.M.S. Pinafore*'s "When I Was a Lad," begins in a way similar to its model:

> And I polished up the handle such a shine, make note,
> That now I am the Captain of a ten day boat.

Yet it soon lays out an alternative route to captaincy, decidedly less upwardly mobile than for Gilbert's "Ruler of the Queen's Navee"—

> As good as gold, no lies I told
> And I never drank a drop 'till I was ten years old.
> Then I started in a-drinking 'till a ship I'd float,
> And now I am the Captain of a ten day boat.

—in essence giving the lie to the genteel fictions of *H.M.S. Pinafore* (and, perhaps, somewhat missing the pointed satire of its model). Most sympathetic to the "Old World" is "'Op in Me 'Ansom Cab," through which a group of cockney cabbies gently mock their American fares. America's own profile, apart from its treatment in the two big numbers discussed above, is given additional definition in "Good Old California," establishing a sentimental tone through its already slightly old-fashioned waltz idiom and occasional chromatic harmonies, and in "They're All My Friends," which refuses, democratically, to choose between "Bowery kid in ragged kilts / [and] people like the Vanderbilts," or (with a touch of cynical wit) between "the maker of protections / And the leader of elections."

Perhaps most intriguing, though, are those songs that *exclude,* whether explicitly or implicitly. Fundamentally, Cohan's America aggressively asserts its difference from the Old World rather explicitly. Thus, in response to the question, "What makes Americans so proud of their country?" an American in the show replies, "Other countries."[3] But somewhat more interesting in this regard is the odd "If Mr. Boston Lawson Has His Way," which harangues against the writings of Thomas W. Lawson, whose series of articles (later to be published as *Frenzied Finance*) were then appearing. This song signals Cohan's true sympathies, whatever the democratic platitudes of "They're All My Friends." Lawson, a former stockbroker, was a scaremonger and would-be reformer who advocated insurance reforms (which were acted upon) and stock-market reforms (which were not) that many saw as threats to basic American freedoms. More offensive—although understandable in terms of Cohan's background and the current vogue for such fare—is the racially obnoxious "ethnic" song "Foong Toong Fee," whose title refers to "a little bit of China bric-a-brac" who is being propositioned by the singer. The proximate excuse for the song is the situation, borrowed from "A Trip to Chinatown" of over a decade earlier, which takes us to San Francisco in the second act, where Johnny searches for Goldie Gates and her abductor (played respectively by Cohan's wife and his father, Ethel Levey and Jerry Cohan).

But there is a less obvious rationale, based again on Cohan's Irish heritage, and on an impulse similar to what had animated an earlier generation of Irish blackface minstrels. Between 1863 and 1869, in their competitive attempt to build (and thus to own) as much as they could of the first transcontinental railroad, the California-based Central Pacific Railroad and the Union Pacific (starting from Omaha) employed cheap labor in huge numbers, who worked long hours under a variety of life-threatening conditions. This labor consisted mainly of Chinese and Irish immigrants, respectively, who were pitted against each other as bitter rivals during the later stages of their employers' "race" to complete the longest segment of track. The alignment and opposition of these specific disadvantaged groups at such a relatively late date in the century underscores how rapidly the Irish had risen by century's end, at least in comparison to their Asian counterparts. "Foong Toong Fee" may easily be read as a minstrel-like dance on the back of those whom the Irish had by then managed to rise above, although, to be sure, its obnoxious "fun" was utterly conventional for its time. In any case, it is clear enough that Cohan's vision of America, newly re-centered around Irishness, continued to consign Chinese Americans to the margins.

The seriousness of Cohan's vision of an American sensibility is best represented, musically, by "Life's a Funny Proposition, After All," sung at the height of Johnny's despairing search for Goldie late in the second act. In a later version of this song (retitled "I'm Mighty Glad I'm Living and That's All" and with a completely rewritten lyric, but with a similarly "philosophical" substance and a similar point to make), Cohan refers explicitly to Shakespeare, and it is clearly to that level of profundity that he aspires here and in similar songs from other shows, however abjectly he fails to achieve such a level. Cohan himself recorded his later version, virtually ignoring the melodic line in favor of declaiming the lyric in what might be described as a "Hamlet's soliloquy" style (a mode of delivery that James Cagney reproduces, along with Cohan's stiff-legged, staccato dance style, throughout the 1942 Bio-Pic of Cohan, *Yankee Doodle Dandy*). The somewhat maudlin attempt in this song to contextualize human existence within the "greater scheme of things," and thus to project a sense of deep interiority onto Cohan's brash exterior persona, may well illustrate a central problematic of the American musical's ongoing quest to achieve a refined sensibility and lofty substance while at the same time validating mainstream America's insistence on the directly simple, the vernacular, and the unabashedly popular.[4]

♩ 5.3

Figure 5.1. James Cagney as George M. Cohan in *Yankee Doodle Dandy* (1942), here portraying Johnny in an extended sequence from *Little Johnny Jones*. Defeated, disgraced, and snubbed by his former companions, he will remain behind on the dock, awaiting vindication. (Courtesy of the Academy of Motion Picture Arts and Sciences.)

The Cradle Will Rock (1938) has managed to acquire a history as a theatrical property that resonates remarkably well with its own themes and plot concerns, adding a sense of both depth and reality to its allegorical, sometimes stick-board approach to character and situation. The show was conceived at a time when America's alignment of big business and big government, especially as viewed against the backdrop of the Great Depression and the widespread hunger and poverty among the 1930s' American working class, seemed to the American left to be bringing America close to the fascistic regimes that had established themselves in Spain, Italy, and Germany. This was especially true just after mid-decade, when the union question—with its patterns of strikes, strike-breaking, and retaliatory measures taken on both sides—began to heat up in earnest, and brought the dread spectacle of spiraling factional violence to the American workplace. From both ends of the political spectrum, it was disturbing to see how closely the struggles to establish unions, and through them to force management to negotiate with the increasingly disenfranchised worker, paralleled the struggles of communist factions in Europe against the various brands of fascism then emergent. To be pro-union in 1930s America was probably to *be* communist (or at least sympathetic to communism), and it certainly meant to be *branded* as such, and therefore to be marked from a conservative perspective as dangerously un-American. In being pro-union, then, *The Cradle Will Rock* was swimming in politically treacherous waters, even if those on the corresponding "other side" in Europe—the fascists and Nazis—were soon to become America's official enemies in World War Two.[5]

The show's strategy is, in part, to achieve a sense of reality and gritty truth by rejecting the escapism then rife on Broadway (cf. *Anything Goes,* discussed in chapter 4, pp. 88–98) and attacking emblems of established power within an idiom derived from the socially conscious, often hard-nosed *Zeitopern* ("operas of the time," which is to say, *relevant* operas) by Kurt Weill and Bertolt Brecht of a decade earlier. Arguably, the show might have developed into a better show, more worthy of the stage on its own terms, had it not itself become a player in a larger drama, a circumstance that virtually demanded that it be frozen into a semblance of its shoestring first performance in order to serve as an icon of survival in the face of attempted political repression. Indeed, its occasional dramatic and musical inadequacies—not least of which has been the tradition of performing it with little more than piano accompaniment—serve to mark its "authenticity," both historically and as a product of artists preserving their integrity by working outside the corporate mainstream of Broadway. In any case, by the time attempts were made—in the late 1940s and early 1960s, for example—to revive the show in the more lavish form originally planned, its sharply drawn allegorical stereotypes, so resonant and

Figure 5.2. Cary Elwes, Hank Azaria, and Angus MacFadyen, in the 1999 film *Cradle Will Rock,* portraying John Houseman, Marc Blitzstein, and Orson Welles as they lead the way down Broadway to the Venice Theater, after being barred by the United States government from opening their subversive *The Cradle Will Rock* in its scheduled venue. (Courtesy of the Academy of Motion Picture Arts and Sciences.)

daring in the 1930s, seemed dated and irrelevant, and thus failed to attract audiences.

Marc Blitzstein, with the active encouragement of Bertolt Brecht, was the sole creator of the book, music, and lyrics for *The Cradle Will Rock,* which takes the form of a morality play with a single main point to make: in the absence of unions to fight the autocratic power of capital and management, people are forced into a kind of prostitution, forced to do whatever they do—teach, preach, edit newspapers, paint, make music, practice medicine, work in factories, etc.—not out of love, but according to the dictates of whoever is paying. The formative idea was Brecht's, who heard Blitzstein's song "The Nickel under Your Foot," intended for a dramatic scene where it would be sung by a prostitute, and suggested he do a show about "all the other prostitutes," all those who "sell out" for money. The scenario for *Cradle* introduces a cast of allegorical characters, whose names tell us not only who they are and what they do, but also that they and their situations stand for larger issues and a farther-reaching conflict: Mister Mister (the "boss" of Steeltown); his wife Mrs. Mister (patroness of the arts); their irresponsible children Junior Mister and Sister Mister; Mister Mister's "Liberty Committee" and others whom he "owns," including Reverend Salvation, Editor Daily, Dr. Specialist, President Prexy and Professors Mamie, Trixie, and Scoot (the latter four from College University); Mrs. Mister's artist protégés Dauber and Yasha; and a set of representative victims of the existing power-structure, including the dramatically central figures of Moll (a prostitute) and Larry Foreman (the rough-and-tumble union organizer, whom Mister Mister will try unsuccessfully to buy off), Gus and Sadie Polock, Harry Druggist, and Ella Hammer (whose partner, Farmer "Sickle," was dropped from the show; together they would have constituted Communism's "Hammer and Sickle").

The Cradle Will Rock thus defines "America," presented allegorically as Steeltown, as a contested place, run by bosses and their lackeys but rightfully belonging to those who have actually built it, continue to work there, and have somehow managed not to sell out. "Who *is* America?" and "Whose America?" are thus precisely the questions being put by the show. According to the sympathies *Cradle* embodies, the existing power-structure separates America from its true standard-bearers, so that a forthright answer to the first question demands a realignment of the second.

Given its subversive premise and content, it may seem remarkable that the show was funded by the Federal Theater Project (FTP), an arm of the Works Progress Administration (WPA) established by President Roosevelt in 1935 to put America back to work. But the FTP, under the direction of Hallie Flanagan, had from the beginning been partial to intellectually and politically challenging projects. Blitzstein's attempts to have the show mounted commercially were unsuccessful, even after promising discussions with Orson Welles and John Houseman, who were then deeply involved in experimental theater. Houseman had directed Virgil Thomson's 1934 surrealist opera *Four Saints in Three Acts,* with a libretto by Gertrude Stein and a cast of African Americans (although race is not a particular issue in either the opera's libretto or its eclectic and congenial musical styles), which had enjoyed much notoriety and considerable success when it was restaged a year later in New York. Welles, who had just mounted Shakespeare's *Macbeth* for the FTP in Harlem with an all-black cast (1936, with Houseman producing), was just becoming famous for his radio voice (e.g., as "The Shadow," which ran from 1937 to 1938), and about to become notorious through his panic-mongering radio performance of H. G. Wells's *War of the Worlds* (the night before Halloween in 1938) and his nearly career-ending film *Citizen Kane* (1941).

Blitzstein performed the show privately in early 1937 for a number of central figures who were either involved in or supportive of the FTP, including Welles and Houseman, and at that point things went forward quickly. Others present included Thomson, who hosted the event, Flanagan, and actor Howard da Silva, who would be blacklisted after his uncooperative appearance before the House Un-American Activities Committee (HUAC) in the early 1950s. Da Silva was a member of Lee Strasberg's left-leaning "Group Theatre," which had produced an earlier play by Blitzstein, and some of whose other members—Clifford Odets and Kurt Weill—were contributing influences for Blitzstein's *Cradle.* Will Geer, who took the role of Mister Mister, was also a member of the Group Theatre and would also find himself, like da Silva, blacklisted in the 1950s. By the end of the evening, it was decided that Flanagan's FTP would sponsor the show, Houseman would produce, Welles would direct, and da Silva would take the pivotal role of Larry Foreman. By June the show was nearly ready to be performed by its scheduled mid-June opening date, with elaborate sets and a full pit orchestra, but growing concern among conservatives in Congress regarding the "communist" subjects favored by the FTP led to massive cutbacks and the abrupt cancellation of the show's opening; it has always been assumed that the timing was no accident, and that *The Cradle Will Rock* was the specific target of these cuts. In the following year, 1938, in which *Cradle* moved to Broadway for a successful run, HUAC would be formed, with the FTP itself as a main target of its investigations. Thus, *The Cradle Will Rock* became a key player in a larger battle over defining America, involving Congress and eventually spilling over from HUAC's investigation of FTP under Martin Dies in 1938 to its major intervention into the Hollywood film industry during the McCarthy era of the late 1940s and early 1950s.

The more immediate resurrection of *The Cradle Will Rock* is now the stuff of legend. While accounts differ somewhat, the basic facts are that an empty theater—the Venice—was found many blocks away; the score was smuggled out of the now-locked and guarded theater that *Cradle* was supposed to have opened in; under a single spotlight, Marc Blitzstein performed the show at the piano alone on the Venice stage to a jammed, enthusiastic house, since, ironically, both the Musicians Union and Actors Equity had forbidden their members to take part. As he began to play, whether by plan or by inspiration, members of the cast joined him, performing their roles from the audience as Blitzstein described each scene and took the parts of those either not present or unwilling to join in. A vestige of this first performance was preserved as the show continued its run (briefly under renewed FTP sponsorship) and moved to a commercial venue on Broadway after a national tour. Thus, even though they still had to pay orchestral musicians according to union rules that governed Broadway productions, *Cradle* continued to be performed with only piano accompaniment (Blitzstein himself, initially) and the staging was kept simple—in part, to be sure, because Welles's complex staging, involving glass wagons to carry the scenery, had never really worked reliably. Leonard Bernstein's involvement with the show over the next decade tended to confirm its peculiarly fetishized niche as a "lean" show without frills, as he mounted the show as an undergraduate at Harvard with great success in 1939 with himself at the piano (playing from memory), yet helped engineer a flop when he tried to take it to Broadway in 1947 in a more lavish version.

"The Nickel under Your Foot," the song that launched the project, mixes occasional lyricism into a style reminiscent of the jarring, almost brutish "cabaret" style characteristic of the late-1920s *Zeitopern* of Bertholt Brecht and Kurt Weill, whose most famous work, *Die Dreigroschenoper* (1928) would be mounted with reasonable success in 1954 as "The Threepenny Opera," in a translation by Marc Blitzstein. Blitzstein, like Weill, was schooled as a modernist composer, and earlier wrote in a more difficult idiom, returning to a "popular" style so as to make his art more meaningful and relevant to a broader audience. Neither composer forgot his training, however, and each found ample opportunity within "popular" idioms to indulge the more innovative harmonic and melodic language typical of modernism. As in much of the Brecht-Weill collaboration, "Nickel" establishes a fairly conventional motor-rhythm in the accompaniment, against which harmonic slippage and dissonance can occur while allowing an audience to retain at least a modicum of musical "comfort." Here, the accompaniment "trudges" in a rhythm suitable for the singer's "street-walking," and the lyrical moments (starting with the song proper, "O, you can live like hearts and flowers . . . ") reveal an inner grace and

humanity. Deliberate crudities in the rhythmic setting of the lyric highlight her lower social status and create a "realistic" effect by approaching
a prose-like style. In the first section of what sounds like the song proper
(but isn't yet), the poetic/rhythmic style is barely poetry:

> Maybe you wonder what it is
> Makes people good or bad,
>> Why some guy, an ace without a doubt,
> Turns out to be a bastard,
>> And the other way about;
> I'll tell you what I feel,
> It's just the nickel under the heel.

The jarring end of the first line ("what it is") is more than matched by the
later parallel moment ("bastard"), which sticks out not only for its rhythmic lack of grace, but also for the abrupt, barely motivated harmonic shift
that comes with it, creating a chilling effect that not only fits the lyric (the
"ace" turning out to be a "bastard"), but also seems to motivate the trun-
cating of what poetic structure there is. In a comparable way, the twenty-
three-bar (!) chorus (which repeats twice with different lyrics) seems awkward, losing its "balance" midway through its most lyrical turn—

> O, you can dream and scheme and happily put and take,
>> Take and put,

—only to right itself, with some resignation and effort, for the final line:

> But first be sure
> The nickel's under your foot.

If the song's message is suitably simple—that without the security of that
nickel, happiness is impossible—it manages a subtly complex presentation that nevertheless reinforces rather than contradicts the sympathetic
persona of the prostitute who sings it.

♪ 5.4

Blitzstein's conversion, to a more populist approach to music, was a rebellion against the "art for art's sake" ideology, which dictated that there
is no (social) meaning in art (a notion that has been particularly prevalent
among many who study music). In many ways, the show seems to run
counter to this populist insistence on relevance, introducing modernist
pretensions whenever possible, and scorning popular song through parody. Yet, the suspect slogan takes it squarely on the chin in the paired
numbers, "Ask Us Again" and "Art for Art's Sake," which portray the
"modern" artist as a kind of prostitute, trading the prestige of "mean-
ingless" art for money. The commodification and resulting trivialization
of art are here symbolized earlier in the scene, between Mrs. Mister and
her two "artist" protégés), through her showing off her new car-horn,

which plays the motto-theme from Beethoven's *Egmont* Overture, a musical work based on the tragedy written by Beethoven's contemporary and fellow "great artist" Goethe: "Tah-Tah-Ti-Tah-Tah-Ti-Tah-Tah—Yoo Hoo!" "Ask Us Again" seems to cheapen this famous "tragic" motive even further through inflecting it with a tango rhythm in the "dance" Dauber and Yasha perform for and with Mrs. Mister. And a recollection of *Egmont* at the end of "Art for Art's Sake" reveals that it, too, with its rhythmic reiterations of a single pitch, has derived from Beethoven:

> And we love
> Art for art's sake.
> It's smart, for art's sake,
> To part, for art's sake,
> With your heart, for art's sake,
> And your mind, for art's sake.
> Be blind, for art's sake,
> And deaf, for art's sake,
> And dumb, for art's sake,
> Until, for art's sake,
> They kill, for art's sake,
> All the art for art's sake.
> (Tah-Tah-Ti-Tah-Tah-Ti-Tah-Tah—Yoo Hoo!)

♫ 5.5
♫ 5.6
♫ 5.7

In Blitzstein's construction of what does *not* count as truly American, not only effete art but also mindless popular styles are seen as indulgent and escapist. It is through this prism that the crooning vocal styles adopted by such figures as Bing Crosby and Rudy Vallee a few years earlier are disparaged in "Croon-Spoon," sung by Junior and Sister Mister, and fairly obviously linked to the escapist, upper-class fantasy represented by Hawaii in "Honolulu" slightly later in the same scene. Crooning was originally regarded as dangerously sexy, especially as it took the form of a disembodied voice "seducing" women in the privacy of their homes, through their radios (in much the same way that Orson Welles's "Shadow" would frighten them a few years later). Yet, however popular, by the late thirties the crooning style had become a mannerism, and so quite an easy thing to ridicule. Blitzstein's parody of the device, in which the crooner slides into arrival pitches from below, results frequently in prolonged dissonances that look, on paper, almost modernist, but sound simply unmusical, as if the crooner can't quite make it up to the correct pitch and thus seems to sing "out of tune." It is as though Blitzstein—and Weill, too, for that matter—though willing to work within accessible styles, nevertheless had to prove their seriousness by refusing simply to pander, and so created richer, more complicated versions of what was outwardly simple (a principle Copland was at almost the same historical moment applying to concert and ballet music aimed at defining a mainstream American style).[6] Although words play an important part in the satire (especially so in the clever "Croon-Spoon"), so also does the music, both with the repeated not-quite-there melodic arrivals of "Croon-Spoon" and with the banal repetitions of a single musical phrase in "Honolulu."

♪ 5.8
♪ 5.9

Satirical humor undermines all the members of the "Liberty Committee," typically by revealing through song either their pomposity or their willingness to bend with the wind (or both). Typical is the treatment given Reverend Salvation, whose ongoing "Sermon" justifies a full range of mutually contradictory behaviors and attitudes associated with "The Great War" (as World War I was then called), presented and adjusted according to the dictates of the shifting realities of "the powers that be," evolving from "Thou shalt not kill" through "No peace without honor," all the way to "Thou shalt . . . Kill all the dirty Huns," sanctimoniously recycling all the appropriate clichés along the way ("Make the world safe for . . . ," "A war to end all war").

Serious as its subject may be, "Sermon" is grimly funny; only with the major numbers for the most sympathetic characters do we hear full seriousness. Thus, "Nickel" is sung directly, without archness, its undermining plainness serving to reinforce its basic "truth." "Joe Worker" is an implacable march, deriving power from its gradual shift, from representing the forced march of a whole population trapped by their circumstances, to representing the potential power of a united army built from such a population; the song achieves this effect largely through its accumulation of ascending chromatic lines energizing the minor-mode march idiom. And the title song, "The Cradle Will Rock," derives its energy from the metaphor of nature threatening the smug structures of security erected by Mister Mister in the form of his "Liberty Committee," whose cradle the "final wind" will rock. Musically, the song pushes for a moment of truth by suggesting alternative harmonic centers, not only in sequence but also, crunchingly, at the same time. In this regard, it is Blitzstein's most "modern" song in the show, yet it is not particularly off-putting, since the clearness of the central metaphor and the strength of its rhythmic drive channel its modernist tendencies and make them tell without losing a sense of accessible naturalness; thus, the song's brutal dissonances and harmonic swerves register as forces of nature, their ugliness a measure of the pain and suffering that the coming storm will avenge.

♪ 5.10
♪ 5.11
♪ 5.12

Ultimately, of course, *Cradle* does not define America so much, or at least so well, as it defines a particularly fraught moment—indeed, a *defining* moment—in its history. America in the 1930s was at a crossroads, waiting to be defined in a way palatable to its larger population. *Cradle,* however much it sought to give voice to the multitude, was not embraced as their anthem. Nor could its creators have envisioned how very different the voice would be that would emerge a mere five years later—with *Oklahoma!*—to speak for that multitude. But by then the storm had broken, and on a much larger scale than Steeltown's Mister Mister or Larry Foreman could have imagined.

For Further Consideration

Rose-Marie (1924), *Show Boat* (1927), *Of Thee I Sing* (1931), *The Phantom President* (film, 1933), *I'd Rather Be Right* (1937), *Pal Joey* (1940)

See Also

Regarding *Little Johnny Jones,* see Stephen M. Vallillo's particularly useful account in "George M. Cohan's *Little Johnny Jones,*" and pp. 78–81 of David Ewen's *Complete Book of the American Musical Theater.*

Regarding *The Cradle Will Rock,* Geoffrey Block provides a good extended discussion in chapter 6 of *Enchanted Evenings,* and Scott Miller gives a provocative director's overview in *Rebels with Applause* (chapter 1). Carol G. Baxter provides useful background information in "The Federal Theatre Project's Musical Productions" (differing slightly from most accounts of *The Cradle Will Rock* and its non-opening).

American Mythologies

THE AMERICAN MUSICAL has long been involved in creating, developing, or in some cases merely exploiting a variety of American mythologies, but this involvement grew especially evident as the United States became an increasingly major player on the world stage during World War II and its aftermath. During this period, several important musicals provided reassuring accounts of who "we" are (that is, who *Americans* are, the presumed "we" of the principal audience for these musicals), and how we have—deservedly, of course—emerged as a secure nation and a model for how a better world might function. Central to the mythologies these musicals project were the ways that many in the United States, in forming a conception of America as a nation, departed substantially from European concepts of nationhood and nationalism, which had been developed with increasing vehemence across the nineteenth century and into the twentieth, when they reached their horrific apex in two world wars, the Holocaust, and other instances of ethnic cleansing.[1]

According to the European model of nationalism, which took root early in the nineteenth century, forming a "nation" would ideally unite an autonomous "people" to their rightful land.[2] The alignments proposed within nationalist ideologies specified who belonged to a particular land and vice versa, and at the same time clarified who did *not* belong. Such ideologies, which thus sought both to *en*franchise and *dis*enfranchise, were grounded importantly in both history and myth, which together created a sense of a valuable past that corroborated a group's right to a land. The growth of such ideologies coincided rather closely with the first century of American independence, presenting to America, with its Anglo-derived mainstream, the peculiar problem in the late nineteenth century that its "people" were understood to have European roots, and thus were living in a land not truly theirs, since the center of their "valuable past" lay in Europe.

This basic problem, which undoubtedly fed America's enduring sense of cultural inferiority, had already in the late nineteenth century led Dvořák to forge an "American" idiom for his Symphony *From the New World* (1893) that drew on a mixture of Indianist, African American (spirituals), and—whether intentionally or not—Eastern European musical styles, coordinated so as to evoke a strong sense of a primitive, rugged landscape. While many found this a rather confused response to the situation, Dvořák's solution was in its way particularly Americanist in aspiration.[3] After all, America's way out of its nationalist quandary, at least politically, was to highlight its inclusionist ideology. In America, "all men were created equal" (however perversely "men" might have been defined at different times in its history), and rights—including property rights— were held by individuals rather than groups. That this ideology was in fact *not* realized in late-nineteenth-century America, unless one excluded Native Americans, blacks, Asians, and women (and, for that matter, the Irish for most of that span) from the category of "men" in this implied global sense, was an essential part of the rationale for Dvořák's musical blend, which sought to give an elevated presence to two of the groups who were then most obviously *dis*enfranchised in America, for whom Dvořák himself, as a Czech under Austrian rule, felt deep empathy.[4] As Dvořák's experiment proved, probably unwittingly, the unrootedness of America's dominant population was thus a double problem, reinforcing a sense of inferiority many felt regarding Europe's sense of a deep past enshrouded in myth and celebrated in high culture, and creating a fair amount of uneasiness about who had the greatest claims to its lands according to history and myth.

Aesthetic representation had from the beginning been a core component of successful nationalisms, for it was by such means that existing mythologies could be reconstituted and brought into the present in a provocative and relevant way, and new ones created as possible and as needed. The most effective model for doing this may be traced to the German lands—the cradle of European nationalism—where Friedrich Schiller (best known today for his poem *An die Freude,* the main text of Beethoven's Ninth Symphony) provided a persuasive model for the cultural role of the poet and, by extension, of the artist more generally. Within Schiller's historical schema, "we" in the urbanized present (by extension, those in *any particular* urbanized present) stand in imperfect relation to a more ideal past—identified variously depending on one's situation and beliefs as "Arcadia," "Sicily," or "Eden"—a past in which the human and the natural were in much closer alignment than now; significant remnants or "echoes" of this lost past may be found among the folk of today's countryside, traditionally the subject of the pastorale as a genre. From the vantage point of an imperfect present, we may look forward to a return to this alignment (Utopia, Elysium, or Heaven), and it is the poet/ artist who articulates our position and attitude. Satire, for example, critiques current reality; the idyll and elegy look nostalgically to the past as a lost ideal; and the pastorale purports to represent vestiges of that past surviving in today's countryside and country life. The supreme task of Schiller's poet/artist is to create hope in the face of realist confirmation that hope is not justified, by projecting as real what can never be achieved; to this end, elements drawn from all of these approaches—satire, idyll, elegy, pastorale—may come into play, with the latter emerging as particularly important since it purports to correspond to at least a part of current reality.[5]

Coupled with the idea of the *Volksgeist* (the spirit of a people), advanced contemporaneously by fellow German Johann Gottfried Herder, Schiller's structure becomes a recipe for the nationalist artist: the idealized past, for the nationalist, is the past of a "people" who survive into the present (i.e., in the *Volk* of the countryside), and the ideal future for which one strives is a "nation" in which that people is restored to its earlier oneness with the land of its past. Images, narratives, and projections that instill belief in a people's valued past—that is, mythologies—thus become a core ingredient of nationalism.

The twentieth-century legacy of European nationalism is a mix of idealism (or at least idealistic posing) and horrific violence, the latter manifest particularly in the Holocaust and other instances of ethnic cleansing, in each case undertaken so as to create a "nation" purified of its (human) elements that did not belong. In many instances, sympathetic nationalist ideals—involving the restoration of past glories, and the correction of presumed wrongs, all easily embraced as "noble"—combined with pseudo-scientific racial theory, derived in part from Charles Darwin's theories of "natural selection," to produce a particularly virulent form of racism, seemingly backed by both noble ideals and science. But even without such overt racism as a driving force, any nationalism based on the European model, demanding a realignment of peoples and land, has to resort at some point to advocating and carrying out either forced migration or mass murder. Seen in this light, and from a moral standpoint, America's failure to conform to the European model should be ranked among its signal successes and, indeed, many of the reasons for this failure have been developed into a theory of American exceptionalism. The latter, besides providing an inscrutable rationalization for many American peculiarities and lapses, specifically sets America apart from Europe in a variety of ways. Thus, people who lost their "place" in Europe could find it in America, and things that didn't work in Europe could be made to work in America. From the context of this mode of theorizing, and apart from feelings of cultural inferiority, which cut against the grain of exceptionalist beliefs, America's differences from Europe have been seen to matter positively, since those differences were the foundation of America's political and humanistic successes. Nevertheless, the idealistic tone of nationalism has proven irresistible to Americans, who tend to see nationalism as a kind of super-charged patriotism, and who have, accordingly, enthusiastically produced and embraced their own mythologies. Indeed, we may note with some irony that this process began in earnest on the musical stage at precisely the historical moment when European nationalism reached its frenzied peak of violent confrontation: when the Germans, who had been at the forefront in articulating and implementing its precepts and strategies, had just begun to engineer the mass subjugation and murder of Europe's Jews, Slavs, and other non-"Aryan" peoples.

American nationalist mythologies tend to adopt some tropes of "authenticity" derived from European models, finding their highest value in simple goodness, most often in rural or small-town settings, rather than in the sophisticated complexities of modern urbanity. Yet they also exhibit a specifically American strain of inclusiveness and reconciliation; not surprisingly, mythologizing musicals frequently use the marriage trope to represent the merger of supposed incompatibilities. Such mergers, and America's capacity to nurture them, provide the implicit foundation of America's peculiar strength as a nation. Thus, the American mythologies of the musical stage tend to invert the structure of European mythologies, advancing the "melting pot" model rather than the "pure strain" demanded of European nationalism. That America's own historical realities sometimes get grossly misrepresented in the process is perhaps the inevitable by-product of mythologizing on the one hand, and an inevitable shortfall between ideals and reality on the other.

In the three musicals we will consider here, we move among three quite different settings: rural (*Oklahoma!*), city (*Guys and Dolls*), and small town (*The Music Man*). Yet in each case the issues raised and resolved have a similar profile, as each show presents a community threatened by something either within or outside the group, which grows wiser and more secure through pursuing an initially resisted approach to community-formation that is more inclusive than exclusive, with the marriage trope placed squarely at the center of the conflict and its resolution. And the settings are in some ways more alike than different, for all three shows are peopled by very white, very mainstream Euro-Americans, whose musical idiom projects a particularly "American" innocence; jazz styles and related musical inflections are thus downplayed, conservatively present but not obtrusive. That race is scarcely an issue in these musicals, which purport to portray a country that has in fact been beset throughout its history by racially motivated violence and discrimination, speaks to a smugness endemic to mythologies created, as these seem to have been, to reassure a nation of its own essential goodness.

Oklahoma! (1943), based on Lynn Riggs's folk-play *Green Grow the Lilacs* (1931), is generally considered one of the major breakthroughs in the development of the American musical, a landmark on the order of *Show Boat* sixteen years earlier (to be discussed in chapter 8). Its huge success ushered in the age of the "integrated musical," in which all the elements involved in a musical—music, drama, song, dance, scenery, costumes, etc.—contribute to a single integrated whole. It also inaugurated the collaborative team of Richard Rodgers and Oscar Hammerstein II, who would go on to write a string of important shows with a consistency of success unparalleled before or after on Broadway, culminating in *The Sound of Music* in 1959. Both men had already had significant careers before *Oklahoma!*, Rodgers mainly with lyricist Lorenz Hart (see my discussion of "My Funny Valentine" in chapter 4, pp. 85–88), and Hammerstein with various composers including Vincent Youmans, Rudolf Friml (*Rose-Marie;* 1924), Sigmund Romberg (*The Desert Song,* 1926, and *The New Moon,* 1928), and, most importantly, Jerome Kern, with whom he wrote *Show Boat* (1927). The formation of their new partnership came at an auspicious moment in each man's career. Many thought Hammerstein's career to be winding down in the wake of Kern's move to Hollywood in 1939, despite a 1941 Academy Award for "The Last Time I Saw Paris" (which they shared); while Hart's alcoholism had made his partnership with Rodgers less and less workable. Ironically, both Hart and Kern would die during *Oklahoma!*'s five-year run. Given that both Rodgers and Hammerstein had independently developed an interest in turning *Green Grow the Lilacs* into a musical (an interest shared by neither Kern nor Hart), the new partnership seemed to have the imprimatur of fate.

But even if *Oklahoma!* had not launched an important chapter in the history of the American musical, it would have been historically important for the role it played in providing America with a strongly embodied sense of a central national myth. We might call this particular strand of American mythology its "frontier brinkmanship": its ability to manage the threshold of its domain, to extend its purview carefully, wisely, and inclusively, and thereby negotiate the transition from wilderness to civilization, from lawless to law-abiding, from frontier to community, from territory to state, from fledgling nation to world power.

The specific site for *Oklahoma!*'s drama of transition was itself one of the focal points for the difficult times America had recently endured, between the stock market crash of 1929 and its entrance into World War II. Oklahoma had been hit hard by the great "Dust Bowl" and "Black Sunday" (1934 and 1935, respectively), part of a series of catastrophic events extending from 1930 to 1936 in which the results of years of mismanaged land-use and prolonged extremities of weather (drought, rains, winds, blizzards, dirt storms, tornados, and even an earthquake) conspired to lay waste to much of the state's rich farmland just when market forces were already beginning to impoverish the region. *Oklahoma!,* with its mix of hopeful and playful songs partly eclipsing America's memory of a devastated landscape and displaced multitudes of people, quickly became a vital component in building and maintaining America's resolve during the height of its involvement in World War II, and in providing it afterward with the confidence and energy to help rebuild a world ravaged by years of war. In *Oklahoma!*—with its vital images of people cheerfully and energetically "making do," overcoming conflicts and adversity, forging an enduring larger community, and offering homespun folk-wisdom in common, direct, everyday language—America saw itself in a microcosm and acquired a vision of what it could offer the rest of the world.

By singing the songs of *Oklahoma!*, and thereby taking on the naïvely attractive personae of the show to a significant extent, Americans found it that much easier to believe in its gratifying visions. Moreover, it has since often seemed that the partnership of Hammerstein with Rodgers offered an ideal creative mix for this kind of self-reflective cultural function, which many of their later musicals would also advance. Thus, Rodgers layered appropriately romantic feeling onto the direct, homespun simplicity of Hammerstein's carefully cultivated vernacular, usefully reversing (with occasional exceptions) Rodgers's previous working relationship with Hart, who generally added his words to Rodgers's already-written music, and whose cynicism so often cut against the grain of Rodgers's music.

Yet it is important to underscore the deep ironies of this particular show appearing at this particular historical moment with this particular mythologizing role to play. *Oklahoma!* looks back to a moment earlier in the twentieth century when the territories that would become Oklahoma, surrounded by long-time states, were themselves finally poised to combine and join the Union as the forty-sixth state (which would occur in 1907; only New Mexico and Arizona in 1912, and Alaska and Hawaii in 1959, were admitted later). What one could never know from the show is *why* Oklahoma was such a late holdout. To understand that, one would have to remember that Oklahoma, a name that in Choctaw means "Red People," carries America's shameful treatment of its indigenous populations as a central part of its legacy, and that Oklahoma represents an expropriation by America in many ways worse than its still-contested theft of the Black Hills. *Oklahoma!*, as a show, colludes in how thoroughly this chapter of American history had been conveniently forgotten at a historical moment—that is, 1943—when America had recently entered into a war against an enemy whose behavior was uncannily resonant with the actual history of Oklahoma.

In a series of provocative land grabs in the late 1930s, Nazi Germany seized military control of the Saar region from France in January 1935, the demilitarized Rhineland in March 1936, Austria in March 1938 (the "Anschluss"), the Sudetenland from Czechoslovakia in October 1938, and the rest of Czechoslovakia (Bohemia and Moravia) in March 1939; in September 1939, they launched World War II by invading Poland, extending their "Reich" to include Denmark, Norway, Belgium, the Netherlands, and France by early Summer 1940. Their watch-cry throughout was "Lebensraum" ("living room"), a term Hitler gave to his expansionist agenda in February 1933.

In 1830, after a series of treaties and forced migrations of American Indians, an act of the United States Congress expelled European Americans from present Oklahoma, then already long known as "Indian Territory," ceding the land to be shared by five nations for their exclusive use in perpetuity. Over the next two decades, further treaties and forced migrations (sometimes of fully settled and assimilated populations of Indians) brought a fragile stability to the region. Starting at about mid-century, however, trails were cut through the territory to facilitate western expansion and, after the Civil War, the territory came under increased white control owing in part to the wartime alliances some tribes made with the Confederacy. Simultaneously, expansionist railroad interests began to encourage illegal encroachment in the form of "Boomers" (illegal settlers), and cattle ranchers expanded into the western territory. Although attempts by whites to settle in the territory were repeatedly repulsed by the U.S. Army, a pressured Congress finally authorized the famous "Land-Run" of 1889, which opened up a segment of the territory to white settlers ("Sooners" was a name given to the many who went in before the official beginning of the land-run). Not long after, in 1891, 1893, and 1895, the entire territory was "opened up" incrementally, setting the stage for Oklahoma's admission to the Union slightly over a decade later. "Manifest destiny," a phrase coined in 1845 to describe America's already-entrenched expansionist sentiment, continued throughout to be America's galvanizing watch-cry, functioning much like Hitler's "Lebensraum" would a few decades later.

To compound the irony of these discomfiting parallels, we may note that Lynn Riggs, the author of *Green Grow the Lilacs*, was himself part Cherokee, and wrote the play as a nostalgic account of a time he had lived through. Yet, despite the fact that in Riggs's play (which takes place, specifically, in Indian Territory, *not* Oklahoma Territory), many of the characters claim Indian heritage and defiantly assert their separateness from the United States, this dimension has been completed effaced in *Oklahoma!,* where there is not a single Indian to be seen, and where joining the Union is joyfully anticipated by all. The extended parallel can only be imagined as part of an alternate history following a projected Nazi victory in World War II: thus, we might imagine, in a fully Germanized Europe some thirty years later, a Pole born around mid-century on a "reservation" somewhere in the former Poland writes a play that re-creates

nostalgically a past era, which is then converted into a musical that celebrates the emergent German community overcoming its petty internal
conflicts and assuming its place as a full-fledged "state" of the German
Reich—to be performed in Berlin or Leipzig for an audience who had
managed to forget that Poland had once belonged to someone else and
that its very name announced that fact.

There are, of course, extremely important differences between Nazi
Germany and nineteenth-century America. On the one hand, however
much they had been provoked, American Indians were often actively wag-
ing war on Euro-America; some of them, at least, posed a genuine threat
to security. And, on the other hand, the case for treating American Indians in the nineteenth century as something less than civilized humans,
however far off the moral scale we would today place that behavior, carried much greater conviction to outsiders than so treating Poles and other
European peoples in the twentieth, for the Indians had considerably less
elaborate urban and governmental infrastructures, and little in the way of
cultural history that Euro-American settlers could at that time relate to
and recognize as valuable. Moreover, however cruel and bloody the consequences often were, America's concerns in their dealings with Indians
tended toward either the elimination of the threat of violence or, much
less honorably, the appropriation of their land—but not to enslave, murder, and otherwise degrade them in the wholesale, government-sponsored
way pursued by Nazi Germany against many whom they conquered (although the wholesale murder of Indians did occur fairly often, and only
ineffectual protests, if any, were mounted against the practice).

But the parallels rehearsed above are nevertheless sobering and warrant
contemplation before we proceed to discuss *Oklahoma!* as a show. Most
directly to our point here, they underscore just how effective myth-mak-
ing in this form can be, for the image America retains most vividly of its
frontier days remains the West portrayed in *Oklahoma!*, which has long
eclipsed widespread concern for the shameful history that lay little more
than a decade behind the events it re-creates.

The issues taken up in *Oklahoma!* recall neither of the two sustained
tragedies of the state's actual history, for there are neither Indians nor dust
storms in its re-imagined landscape. Rather, the show sets up a problem
it can actually solve: reconciling the farmer and the cowman, whose conflict—scarcely even alluded to in Riggs's play—centers mainly on overcoming mutual distrust and ongoing disputes regarding how best to use
their land, and only obliquely concerns itself with the priority of either's
claim to the land. Solving problems in *Oklahoma!* seems largely to be a
matter of "growing up," a process of maturation overseen by a patiently
understanding, folk-based wisdom (provided mainly by Laurey's Aunt
Eller), and which resonates with both the United States' emergent role in

world affairs and the manifest-destiny-driven evolution of its western lands into statehood. The show is thus a kind of morality play about the path to adulthood, both culturally and in terms of its characters. The two romantic leads, Laurey and Curly (farmer's niece and cowhand, respectively), pay a price for their youthful inability to act well on their obvious love for each other, but they learn and mature, and deal as necessary with the consequences of their romantic misfires; as "children" becoming mature "adults," they overcome both shyness and distrust of sexual and cultural otherness. Jud Fry (Jeeter Fry in the play), who is at once the monster within (America's "Id") and an outside intruder, is a dangerous force empowered by Laurey's coquettish capriciousness, but is in the end defeated through heroic action. Jud's death after his attempted murder of Laurey and Curly (he falls on his knife while fighting with the latter) is thus a necessary act of purging that solidifies an emergent community of former antagonists (in the play, the Curly-Jud conflict is considerably more central; see later). Negotiations of affection and alliance permeate the show, most notably in "I Cain't Say No" (sung by Ado Annie, who with Will Parker make up the "comic" couple, a convention of musicals not present in the original play), "People Will Say We're in Love" (sung by Laurey and Curly), "The Farmer and the Cowman" (sung and danced by most of the company, the "community" under construction), and "All Er Nothin'" (sung by Ado Annie and Will).[6]

The first number of the show sets the tone with remarkable deftness, borrowing a "naturalistic" device from the original play, in which Curly enters while singing a cowboy song, "Ta whoop ti aye ay, git along, you little dogies!" Here, Curly responds to the bird-like twitterings of the orchestra with a sentimental waltz-song, "Oh, What a Beautiful Mornin'."[7] As will be noted two numbers later in the show ("Kansas City"), the waltz was by the early twentieth century being displaced by the two-step and ragtime, and its presence here would have thus seemed nostalgic for a simpler time, not only for the audience but also to some extent for the characters within the show. Even its form supports the suggestion that this song is of a simpler type and from a simpler time, as we hear a series of apparent verse-chorus alternations within the song melody, an effect achieved in part by a deliberate contrast between its two halves. The first half begins with a repeated line of text set within a comfortable, limited range—almost as if Curly cannot remember the words, an authenticating imitation of what frequently happens when ordinary folk try to sing the verses of familiar songs. The culmination of the first half is a repeated note held over four bars, from which the "chorus" will launch a more broadly scaled melody with the title line, more expansive harmonically as well as melodically. While the proportion between the two halves is not "authentic," since the "verse" is the same length as the "chorus," the result seems nevertheless a far cry from typical thirty-two-bar Tin Pan Alley forms, even if the repeated verse-chorus combination does happen to be exactly thirty-two bars long.[8] In the 1955 film version of the show, the waltz tempo seems to fit the easy lope of Curly's horse (the loping effect was surely intended even for the stage show), but the style itself indicates that behind Curly's appreciation of nature lies an anticipation of romance ("a little brown mav'rick is winkin' her eye"), an element that finds immediate echo in Laurey's singing the same song on her entrance, again initially without accompaniment. Indeed, in the dream-ballet sequence at the end of Act I, their doubles will dance together to this music. The song uses its one minor departure from simplicity well, with the lowered pitch in "Oh, what a beautiful **morn**-in'" corrected with the rising affirmation at the end of the parallel line, "I got a beautiful **feelin'**." (A very similar effect, of achieving a satisfying arrival by reversing the direction of a previous downward chromatic slide, occurs in their big "couple" number, "People Will Say We're in Love," with the first two repetitions of the title line.)

Optimistic and self-assured as the song is, it nevertheless holds signs of impending trouble: Curly is a shade too self-assured and in any case sees ♫ 6.1   only what he wants to see—

> The breeze is so busy, it don't miss a tree,
> And an ol' weepin' willer is laughin' at me.[9]

—while Laurey's penchant for flirting leads her to dismiss Curly ("Oh, I thought you was somebody!") even as she is in the middle of singing his song. Perhaps most importantly, the song advances two sets of linked claims: Laurey's and Curly's claims on each other's love, and their claims to the landscape they inhabit, implicit in their appreciation of, emotional ties to, and felt oneness with that landscape, as expressed through this song. Thus, implicitly, both cowman and farmer have just claims to this land, and we are made to understand that their shared love of it will end up mattering more than their differences.

"Kansas City," although a comic number sung and danced by secondary characters (Will, the cowboys, and Aunt Eller, who acts as a kind of "chaperone"), is nevertheless pivotal in setting the era of *Oklahoma!* and establishing it as a place that has to "catch up" with the rest of America. Perspective here plays out in two ways: our (that is, 1943's) sophistication relative to this more innocent time, and Oklahoma's territorial provincialism relative to the "urban" Kansas City, where "They've gone about as fur as they c'n go!" Working within a Tin Pan Alley framework (ABAC), but with the final phrase greatly extended as an emblem of unchecked "progress," the song builds up elaborately to its punch line so as to underscore both perspectives (not least through the broadness of its humor), the first time emphasizing building and comfort ("a skyscraper seven stories high," with homes including radiators and indoor plumbing), and the second, licentious display (the "burleeque" where girls "peel"; in this case, the "about as fur" in the punch line seems designed to reassure us—or Aunt Eller—that the dancer did not strip completely, even if "She proved that ev'ry thin' she had was absolutely real"). Actual dance in this song (as opposed to the described dance of the second chorus) is fully integrated into its theme, with Will demonstrating new styles of dance that he tells the others have now replaced the waltz; these include the two-step he dances with Aunt Eller (which proves to be "about as fur as [she] c'n go"), and the ragtime style of dancing (tap) he "seen a couple of colored fellers doin'." The latter is one of the show's few overt references to race, and is as remarkable for what it tells us about 1943 America—when casual references to "colored fellers" carried no special charge—as for what it seems to have said to audiences then about turn-of-the-century Oklahoma, when experience of urban blacks was ostensibly minimal.

♩ 6.2

The "trouble" forecast in the first scene manifests itself when Laurey, to provoke Curly, agrees to go to the box social with the farmhand Jud Fry, a dark, psychotic loner who (*shudder!*) orders pornographic literature from the peddler. At the first crisis point of the show, in the finale to Act I, Laurey then "dreams" an elaborate ballet in which her marriage to Curly is interrupted by Jud knocking Curly unconscious and carrying her off. In this balletic sequence, which famously represents a dimension of the "integrated" nature of *Oklahoma!*, ballet takes on a quasi-naturalistic combination of traditional and "vernacular" movements. The latter, in particular, included a growing vocabulary of exuberantly masculine movement that had emerged through the recently developed "American" ballet styles pioneered by Eugene Loring in Lincoln Kirstein's Ballet Caravan, Agnes de Mille in the Ballet Russe de Monte Carlo, and Martha Graham. Significantly, all of these, who would wield a growing influence over Broadway and Hollywood dance styles, collaborated with Aaron Copland in his influential series of ballets on American subjects: *Billy the Kid* in 1938 with Kirstein and Loring; *Rodeo* in 1942 with de Mille; and *Appalachian Spring* in 1944 with Graham. *Rodeo* and *Oklahoma!* were professional breakthroughs for Agnes de Mille after years of difficult struggle, and launched a Broadway career as a choreographer rivaled only by the later figures of Jerome Robbins, Bob Fosse, and Michael Bennett. De Mille, more than anyone else—and her dream-sequence in *Oklahoma!* in particular—was responsible for the emergence of choreography on Broadway to a position of nearly equal importance with book, lyrics, music, and direction in the decades following World War II.

Ballet here serves to establish a dream-like nonreality; musically, this is accomplished through a seemingly irrational medley of various tunes from the show—which, however, through their familiarity, helps convince us that the dream presents at least one possible narrative outcome. Different styles of dance set character above all: the doubles who substitute for Curly and Laurey dance exuberantly to the wholesome waltz "Oh, What a Beautiful Mornin'"; the basic goodness of the cowboys is conveyed through their child-like miming of riding horses; Curly's dance-hall girls dance provocatively to "I Cain't Say No"; and Jud, the misfit, is forceful but spectacularly ungraceful. If Curly's overconfidence and Laurey's provocation present the initial problem for the show's romantic center, Laurey's fears as revealed in the ballet provide the motivation for a happier resolution in Act II; thus, the ballet is dramatically the pivotal event.

Act II opens with the box social, whose central dance number is also dramatically conceived. Extending the song "The Farmer and the Cowman," the dance also advances its "playful" engagement with the conflict between the two groups, which stands in the way of community building (and statehood). In many respects—though not all—the antagonists are "gendered," not only through the central character pairs of Curley and Laurie, and Will and Ado Annie, but also through some of the lyrics:

D: (AUNT ELLER): The farmer should be sociable with the cowboy,
                  If he rides by and asks for food and water,
E: Don't treat him like a louse,
                       Make him welcome in yer house,
   (CARNES):   But be shore that you lock up yer wife and daughter!

Aunt Eller's later intervention with a handgun when the "play-acting" threatens to turn violent and disrupt the social, evokes the familiar trope of the "shotgun wedding"; overall, the even more basic trope common to many representations of frontier life, which pits masculine lawlessness against feminine civilization and community-building (often symbolized through a church or schoolhouse) is given sufficient reinforcement so that, at least in general terms, the farmer and cowboy are mapped as feminine and masculine, respectively, even if occasionally, as in the short recurring chorus, the balance is partially restored:

C: Territory folks should stick together,
                       Territory folks should all be pals,
                       Cowboys dance with the farmers' daughters,
                       Farmers dance with the ranchers' gals.

As in "Oh, What a Beautiful Mornin'," the song type is a complex variant on a throwback to the turn of the century, when a short distinctive chorus would typically follow a verse that is musically plainer but tex-

tually more interesting. The song begins as a somewhat unusually configured thirty-two-bar form, ABCC, in which C, beginning "Territory
folks," functions as a short, immediately repeated chorus. But the song
then moves into exchanges between the two antagonistic groups in a more
"relaxed" key (the subdominant), within sixteen-bar melodic units (DE,
as in the exchange given above, beginning "The farmer should be sociable"). These exchanges move gradually from quite contentious comments
about fence-building to more playful engagements with laughable stereotypes, and thence lead back to a shortened version of the original (AB-C),
now more closely matching the earlier type of song structure prevalent at
the turn of the century. As the smaller formal units continue to replicate
themselves, the subdominant exchanges take on a limerick-like structure
similar to the first two phrases of the original thirty-two-bar unit—

> A: The farmer and the cowman should be friends,
>   Oh, the farmer and the cowman should be friends.
> B: One man likes to push a plow—
>   The other likes to chase a cow—
>   That's no reason why they cain't be friends.

—using that familiar joke-formula as a vehicle for someone, as in Aunt
Eller's verse above, to interject a concluding punch line that overturns the
apparent reconciling thrust of the verse. After Aunt Eller halts the fight
midway through the song, its structure is reconstituted as a more pleasing whole, AB-DE-DEE-C; here, the subdominant "DE" sections address
two of the show's central themes in turn: Oklahoma becoming a state (but
only when "The farmer and the cowman and the merchant . . . behave
their sel's and act like brothers") and equality ("I don't say I'm no better
than anybody else, / But I'll be damned if I ain't jist as good!").   ♪ 6.3

In this extended number, social dance (either a "square dance" or a
"line dance," but not a "couple dance") serves as a rather obvious metaphor for social order, and its disruption through uncontrolled conflict (itself choreographed, of course) gives both social order and what threatens
it a vividly embodied presence that could happen only through the
medium of dance, which not only controls and mediates the presentation
of both of these dimensions, but also provides the organizational occasion for tableau (the visual presentation of dramatic opposition) and articulating song. In this way, dance serves as the integrating focus for all
elements of the drama. Important, too, is the sexual dimension of social
dance, which provides both motivation for establishing a rapprochement
between the two groups and a civilized, ordered means of doing so; both
aspects are articulated in the "chorus" (C), which is set up, as indicated,
to function as a musical goal, but which is then withheld until those dra-

matic moments when its assertion of cooperation and community can carry conviction.

Significantly, it is at the box social that Curly and Laurey begin their romance in earnest, a romance that both represents the greater union *in nuce* and is enabled by it. Thus, with an almost comic obviousness, when their marriage is celebrated in song, the frame of reference shifts suddenly to that greater union which it symbolizes through the marriage trope, as Curly leads the assembled company in "Oklahoma," a song that attempts to capture, in music and on stage, the spatial expanse of the territory's "wide open spaces." The opening of each of the main phrases of the song's AABA chorus—in which each "A" is double the traditional length of eight bars—creates the signature expansive effect of the song, a single note held for more than three bars on a single syllable, growing to the breaking point. The device adds an audible dimension to the description given in the final words of the preceding verse, which links expansive geography to an interior landscape of endurance and optimism:

> Flowers on the prairie where the June bugs zoom—
> Plen'y of air and plen'y of room—
> Plen'y of room to swing a rope!
> Plen'y of heart and plen'y of hope!

This initial effect of expansiveness is systematically augmented in various ways, and its basis in landscape clarified by the relatively short bridge, according to which Oklahoma is a land that engulfs its people, but cannot be owned by them in the conventional sense (implicitly an argument for manifest destiny, or at least for eminent domain—just in case someone might want to remember the Indians at such a moment):

> We know we belong to the land,
> And the land we belong to is grand!

Thus, although the verse is in D major, Curly sings the first chorus a half step lower, setting up an effect of enhanced excitement through the shift back to D as the full choir enters to repeat the chorus. With the repeat, an effect of expansion occurs not only with the added forces, but also with interpolations between phrases, which in the case of the bridge extend its original eight bars to fourteen. The ending, too, is extended, mainly through repetitions and spellings of the title word. Moreover, as if asserting the readiness of Oklahoma for statehood, the song presents not only the land and its people in perfect alignment, but also its *weather,* with the first lines of the chorus:

> Oklahoma—
> Where the wind comes sweepin' down the plain,

And the wavin' wheat can sure smell sweet,
When the wind comes right behind the rain.

—in brazen defiance, it would seem, of the devastating dust storms to
come in the 1930s.

♪ 6.4

Only one character in *Oklahoma!* is clearly identified as non–Euro-
American (even if the show does not intrinsically rule out using more integrated casts): Ali Hakim, the Persian peddler with designs on the free
spirit Ado Annie. The narrative parallel between the position of this con-
spicuous outsider and that of Jud Fry is striking enough that we might
well wonder if, perhaps, Jud's obvious otherness might also be presumed
to have an ethnic or racial basis. Lynn Riggs's own outsider status, which
extended beyond his being (mixed-blood) Cherokee to his being a closeted homosexual, may well find its analogue here, although the specifics
of Jud's characterization do not support a literal connection. The interpretive possibilities compound when we consider how Riggs elsewhere
characterized the white settlers of Oklahoma, as a whole population of
shunned outsiders:

> a suspect fraternity, as fearful of being recognized by others as they were by
> themselves. Gamblers, traders, vagabonds, adventurers, daredevils, fools.
> Men with a sickness, men with a distemper. Men disdainful of the settled,
> the admired, the regular ways of life. Men on the move. Men fleeing from
> a critical world and their own eyes. Pioneers, eaten people. . . . And so they
> don't speak. Speech reveals one. It is better to say nothing. And so these
> people . . . have been *not quite known*—a shifting fringe of dark around the
> camp-fire, where wolves, perhaps, and unnamable things lurked.
>
> I happened to be born myself just outside the rush of light. And I know
> how it feels, and I think, how those others felt.[10]

Within the very different community projected in *Oklahoma!*, only Jud
seems truly "outside the rush of light," and so in some ways he must stand
in for the larger population of gamblers and vagabonds Riggs recalled.
The overall darker tone of Riggs's *Green Grow the Lilacs* throws a harsh
spotlight on Jud's (Jeeter's) "distemper," most forcefully in a speech by
Curly that comes, in the musical, between his comic "Pore Jud Is Daid"
and Jud's scary "Lonely Room" (brackets indicate text from *Green Grow
the Lilacs* omitted in *Oklahoma!*):

> In this country, they's two things you c'n do if you're a man. Live out of
> doors is one. Live in a hole is the other. I've set by my horse in the bresh
> som'eres and heared a rattlesnake many a time. Rattle, rattle, rattle!—he'd
> go, skeered to death. [Skeered—and *dangerous!*] Somebody comin' close to
> his hole! Somebody gonna step on him! Git his old fangs ready, full of pizen!
> Curl up and wait! . . . How'd you git to be the way you air, anyway—set-

tin' here in this filthy hole—and thinkin' the way you're thinkin'? Why don't you do sumpin healthy onct in a while, 'stid of stayin' shet up here a-crawlin' and festerin'![11]

The ending of the play, in particular, is much darker and more prolonged than that of the musical, including two elements partially restored in the film version: a more extended and disturbing "shivoree" (short for "chari-vari," a raucous post-wedding "serenade" of the new couple as they pre-pare for their wedding night) in which Laurey is manhandled and taunted, and made to climb a haystack in her nightgown with Curly, where they are urged to consummate their marriage; and Jud's attempt, while the shi-voree is in progress, to set fire to the farm, including the couple's haystack. The aftermath is also much extended in the play, encompassing Curly's three-day imprisonment and escape, an assertion of Indian pride, and a somewhat less certain outcome. In the play, this darkness has but one real antidote: a full-bodied acceptance of life, good and bad. In Aunt Eller's words,

> They's things you cain't get rid of—lots of things. Not if you live to be a hundred. You got to learn. You got to look at all the good on one side and all the bad on the other, and say: "Well, all right, then!" to both of 'em.[12]

This speech is cut for the more upbeat musical, which has no need for such a stern pronouncement (although it is partially restored in the film ver-sion—in part, perhaps, to counterbalance the restored haystack scene).

Since the musical barely hints at this more pervasive darkness, Jud re-mains the lone "wolf" in the "shifting fringe of dark around the camp-fire"—the only likely candidate, in fact, for a role that might possibly be understood as Indian (at least from the entrenched whiteness of *Okla-homa!*'s perspective), even if not identified as such. Marked from the be-ginning as a primitive and an outcast who is *among* the people of Okla-homa but not truly *of* them, Jud's misdeeds offer what might almost seem an implicit justification for all those forced marches of America's Indians along one "Trail of Tears" after another, so often leading to Oklahoma.[13] But by the same token he could simply be one of those many "eaten peo-ple" who drifted into Oklahoma, for whom Riggs himself felt both kin-ship and separateness. And, of course, he may be no more than what he seems to be: a somewhat generic, unredeemable enemy whose demise by heroic action enables the innocent to flourish unimpeded—in other words, a mythological archetype, and one particularly relevant to Amer-ica's task at hand in 1943.

Guys and Dolls (1950), with music and lyrics by Frank Loesser and book by Jo Swerling and Abe Borrows, brings a version of

Figure 6.1. The shivoree scene from the 1955 film of *Oklahoma!*, just after Jud has set fire to the haystack that Laurey and Curly (Shirley Jones and Gordon MacRae) have been forced by the wedding party to climb. The haystack sequence, restored in the film after being eliminated from the stage version of *Oklahoma!*, comes from Lynn Riggs's original play (*Green Grow the Lilacs*, 1931), which he at one point planned to call "Shivoree." (Courtesy of the Academy of Motion Picture Arts and Sciences.)

America's mythologized West to the heart of the American City—indeed, to its heart of hearts, for the setting is New York City's Times Square—at the same time that it brings America's West-based literary tradition to the Broadway stage. The central figure of that literary tradition is unquestionably Mark Twain (1835–1910), whose books on American subjects, starting with *Roughing It* (1872) and continuing with *The Adventures of Tom Sawyer* (1876), *Life on the Mississippi* (1883), and *Huckleberry Finn* (1884), established an American "voice" based in the realities of American life and dialect. Twain indulged both a sentimentalizing nostalgia and a particularly American type of humor that undermines both in its laconic delivery and ironic import—a style still much in vogue during the time frame of *Guys and Dolls,* courtesy of Will Rogers. Significantly, Twain's "breakthrough" work was a short story ("The Celebrated Jumping Frog of Calaveras County," 1865)—a genre much revisited by Twain himself, and which became the basis for a particular line of folkish American literary development traceable mainly through Twain and the younger figures of O. Henry (1862–1910), whose books of short stories began to appear in 1904; Ring Lardner (1885–1933), beginning about a decade later; and Damon Runyon (1884–1946), whose 1931 collection of stories, *Guys and Dolls,* provided its later Broadway namesake with a set of characters and situations along with a distinctive manner of expression that is often known as "Runyonese."

Between Twain and O. Henry, the setting moves gradually from the outposts to the centers of American urban civilization—without, however, the inhabitants of those stories changing much from the innocent, essentially good-hearted and naïvely wise folk of an earlier, more primitive landscape. If something is lost along the way of Twain's distinctive manner of expression—a combination, perhaps, of dialect and attitude— Runyon's further development of the form "balances the books," as he populates his cityscape with not only versions of the gangsters, politicians, and other celebrities that he himself rubbed shoulders with, but also, and more centrally, a full array of their lower-profile counterparts. Most distinctively, he gives his characters considerably more wise-guy cynicism (without, paradoxically, their losing much in the way of essential good-heartedness), and virtually invents an urbanized dialect for them, which combines Twain's laconic delivery and irony with a comic pretension to a more elevated (or at least more wordy) locution that seems—perhaps as an emblem of American sensibilities—to know no tenses but the present and future.

Loesser's *Guys and Dolls* is based directly on two stories from Runyon's *Guys and Dolls,* "The Idyll of Miss Sarah Brown" and "Pick the Winner," from which its central characters and situations are drawn. Thus, "The Sky" (Obadiah Masterson), a high-stakes gambler so smitten with Sarah Brown of the Save-a-Soul Mission that he puts his bankroll up against the "souls" of his fellow gamblers, derives directly from "Idyll." Less directly, the unsuccessful gambler Hot Horse Herbie of "Pick the Winner," along with his long-suffering fiancée Miss Cutie Singleton, whom his chronic ill fortune keeps him from marrying, are transmuted into the parallel love-interest of crap-game-running Nathan Detroit (borrowing the name and profession of a minor character in "Idyll") and Adelaide, who has been conveniently transformed into a night-club performer. The language is consistently "Runyonese," perhaps even slightly more so—a locution that had become standard on Broadway as the language of its peculiar breed of comic hoods and gangsters (cf. Porter's *Kiss Me,*

Kate, 1948). The strategy of further exaggerating this verbal mode may be traced in The Sky's recounting of his father's parting advice, which finds its way into the musical more or less intact:

> Son, I am sorry that I am not able to bank-roll you to a very large start, but not having the necessary lettuce to get you rolling, instead I am going to stake you to some very valuable advice. One of these days in your travels, a guy is going to show you a brand-new deck of cards on which the seal is not yet broken. Then this guy is going to offer to bet you that he can make the jack of spades jump out of this brand new deck of cards and squirt cider in your ear. But son, you do not accept this bet, for as sure as you stand there you are going to wind up with an ear full of cider.[14]

Significantly, this exaggerated locution finds an echo in the occasional quotations from the King James Bible (borrowing a device used to great effect in "Idyll"), which The Sky knows backwards and forwards from perusing Gideon Bibles during his many stays in hotel rooms.

Yet, the reconstituted story is considerably softer-centered than either of its principal models, with Runyon's wry cynicism put aside to achieve a straightforwardly sentimental conclusion, a far cry from the series of ironic twists in Runyon's originals. In Runyon's "Idyll," The Sky is on the verge of shooting Brandy Bottle Bates for using loaded dice, but instead gives those same dice to Miss Sarah Brown to roll against his soul, never telling her that the dice are "strictly phony"; then, in a saucy interchange of Bible verses, The Sky responds to Miss Sarah Brown's "You are a fool" by quoting St. Paul, "If any man among you seemeth to be wise in this world, let him become a fool, that he may be wise" (1 Corinthians 3.18), after which she refers him to the second verse of the Song of Solomon (a verse Runyon does not provide, however: "Let him kiss me with the kisses of his mouth, for thy love is better than wine"). And, in "Pick the Winner," Miss Cutie Singleton breaks off her long engagement to Hot Horse Herbie to marry Professor Woodhead, whose erudition leads him to misconstrue Hot Horse Herbie's tip and win big. The principal "Dolls" in the stage show, on the other hand, are far more forgiving, as both Sarah and Adelaide seem in the end reconciled to their future spouses' inadequacies and even willing to become, like them, gamblers ("Marry the Man Today"). For their part, neither Sky nor Nathan seem quite so profligate as they would have others believe, with Sky maintaining a strict code of honor in his dealings with both Sarah and his fellow gamblers, however hardened to the world he might seem, and Nathan genuinely torn between his "calling" and his love for Adelaide.

Like *Oklahoma!, Guys and Dolls* thus loads its dice in favor of reconciling the opposites it presents at the opening, so that, when reconciliation comes, it entails no significant compromise on either side, only accommodation and maturity. The show reproduces one of the basic tropes of the Western, in which a lawless, mostly male society is civilized through religion and marriage and other "feminine" contributions, but with the difference that no one is really forced to change his or her nature in *Guys and Dolls;* they remain, as the title indicates, "Guys" and "Dolls." This outcome is not simply sentimental, although it surely is that, for along the way, and in myriad ways, both sides reveal themselves as closer to the other than they might like to suppose. Particularly striking is how often music provides the medium in which those similarities are revealed, and apparent opposites united.

For *Guys and Dolls* to manage this mythological rapprochement between religion and gangsterism, both the rigidity typical of the former and the extreme violence of the latter have to be significantly softened. While it may seem quite natural for Runyon's The Sky to be on the verge of pulling a gun on Brandy Bottle Bates, such behavior is quite out of bounds for the musical's Sky, although he is perfectly capable of out-toughing the likes of Big Julie from Chicago when the occasion demands. Behind *Guys and Dolls'* rather charitable look at the world of gamblers and gangsters—which we know to be peopled, in reality, by victims and victimizers, the latter ranging from thieves and thugs to habitual murderers—is the "folk hero" status of the American gangster, which grew alongside prohibition in the 1920s and continued apace in the depressed 1930s as a facet of dissatisfaction with the official power structure in America.[15] By 1950, when newspaper headlines detailing mob-related murder and political corruption in American cities had long since given way to the far greater horrors of the Holocaust and the atomic bomb, the way was well-paved for the re-imagined gangster of this more innocent time to became a mythologized version of a familiar all-American male hero: the "maverick," making do by his wits as best he can on the fringes of society.

Also contributing to the persuasive power of *Guys and Dolls's* reconciliation of apparent antagonists is another American mythology reinforced in the aftermath of World War II (at least before the Cold War had a chance to set in). The myth of the American "melting pot," of a society that tolerated ethnic and cultural differences and that had learned to recognize the similarities that existed beneath strongly differentiated exteriors, seemed best represented by America's cities, and in particular by New York City, whose Statue of Liberty set the tone for this spirit of welcoming tolerance. While realities were surely different from this fairy-tale view of the American ethnic blend—and here, it does us well to remember that 1957's *West Side Story,* whose story details ethnic clashes on the streets of New York, was in its initial planning stages before *Guys and Dolls* opened—many believed, and still believe, that the *essential* story of America is precisely that fairy tale, and the hope that it has provided both its own citizens and the world at large. Without making race or ethnicity a particular issue, *Guys and Dolls* builds directly on projecting the energy of New York City as one where opposites of whatever kind rub against each other freely, creating inevitable frictions but leaving no real trace on the capacity of each differentiated group to muddle through without undue interference from the other.

The opening ballet sequence, "Runyonland," originally choreographed by Michael Kidd, depicts precisely this mode of interaction. Accompanied by a somewhat chaotic mélange of tunes and tune-fragments from the show, interspersed with ambient "car horn" effects and the like, a variety of street-wise types and tourists in various stages of naïveté interact in Times Square without causing appreciable harm to each other. Metaphorically, the sequence carries the jostling of the city street to a higher level of abstraction, depicting a version of the American city's "melting pot" in which not much actual melting happens but within which diversity is tolerated according to a broadly conceived "give-and-take" (some of it literally, as with the pickpocket and photo sequences), and with a kind of "knowing wink" that acknowledges all human types to be, at bottom, the same. Yet, while everyone is on to each other, they tend not to be on to themselves, which permits, even in the ballet sequence, the occasional "O. Henry twist" to set matters aright, establishing a dynamic pattern that will play out in the larger plotting of the show as well. Within the hodge-podge of "separate but equal" stereotypes that emerge in the ballet, there is nevertheless one differentiation that truly matters: gender.

In parallel to the central "problem" in *Oklahoma!*, *Guys and Dolls* thus takes on as its central "problem" one that can be fairly easily resolved, especially in a musical: the conflict between its Guys and Dolls. Significantly, if guys are inevitably guys and dolls inevitably dolls, other problems must eventually take a secondary place in the hierarchy. Thus, "gambler" and "gangster" are simply modes of being a "guy," a species whose only real failing (in this resolutely heterosexual fantasy-world) is its susceptibility to dolls. And "religion" and "display"—the two aspects of femininity that define the female leads of Sarah and Adelaide, which together offer a slightly more genteel parallel to the familiar "Madonna/Whore" trope—are both subsets of dollness, which (somehow) connect at a deeper level. Thus, for all her attempts to reform the male "sinners" of Times Square, Sarah shows only sympathy and camaraderie to Adelaide, her ally in arms.

The first two sung numbers of the show—"Fugue for Tinhorns" and "Follow the Fold"—which ostensibly establish the basic conflict as "gamblers vs. religion," establish as well a set of intricately drawn parallels between the two worlds as the basis for their eventual merger. "Fugue for Tinhorns," whose title plays on the expression "tinhorn gambler" (a small-time gambler), is no more a fugue than a tinhorn is a real musical instrument; rather, it is a "tinhorn fugue," a simple canon "putting on airs," in which each singer sings the same tune starting at a different time, as in a nursery round. But the idea of a fugue, in which fairly equal voices vie against each other for prominence within a complex contrapuntal texture, often with a sense of combativeness, is nevertheless well-embodied in the situation, as each gambler sings of his own "hot tip" with utter conviction, oblivious to the opposing and equally fervent views of the other two, "agreeing" (that is, singing in unison) only in the end, and only to the extent of each gambler's individual assertion, "I got the horse right here." During Sarah's sermon after the Mission Band's marching-anthem "Follow the Fold," a similar but nonmusical "fugue" develops between her sermon and a huckster selling "solid gold watches" for a dollar. As in the earlier musical "fugue," there is verbal counterpoint, as each picks up on the other's language and develops it individually. Implicitly, as in the "Fugue for Tinhorns," they are "separate but equal" voices in apparent disagreement but united in general orientation. As the sequence underscores, both are selling their wares on the street, and use similar language in their efforts to instill belief in something that is palpably at odds with the realities familiar to their pickup audience; both are, we may infer, all-American hucksters, with the significant difference that the Mission Brothers and Sisters are more naïvely gullible (Brother Arvide, Sarah's main confidante, actually buys a watch).

♪ 6.5

If religion is thus shown to be first cousin to hucksterism, we are soon enough given a musical representation of the obverse: the seemingly inherent religious sensibilities of the male gamblers, who, like early Christian zealots, are so devoted to their calling that they seek out secret places in which to practice it, away from the prying eyes of the authorities. "The Oldest Established Permanent Floating Crap Game in New York" responds to the prospect that Nathan's ongoing struggle to maintain the traditional game will soon founder because of the "heat" being applied by Lieutenant Brannigan of the New York Police Department. The sometimes religious tone of the song serves in part to parody religion, but more importantly to demonstrate the gamblers' innate affinities for the religious feelings they overtly shun. Thus, the opening verse adopts the style of religious chant over sustained chords as Nathan discusses the situation with his cohorts Nicely Nicely and Benny Southstreet, with each alternative proposal pointing to another remote key, until they are discovered by the "congregation" of gamblers, who begin the chorus in the simplest of keys, C major, in seeming ignorance of Nathan's troubles. In the final section of the chorus's straightforward thirty-two-bar form (ABAC), the title phrase carries a tone of exaggerated reverence, and moves toward an elaborate, four-voiced plagal cadence, the "Amen" cadence familiar from

Protestant hymn-singing. Effectively, the song thus ends by merging the styles of the barbershop-quartet and the church congregation, which are each based on four-part chorale writing. In the film version, the song is actually sung in a barbershop, obliquely underscoring what is in fact a historical connection between barbershop quartet practices (among both whites and blacks) and the close harmonies of the black "plantation" style of singing spirituals, itself partially derived from white hymn-singing.[16] ♪ 6.6

Within the other dimension of the Guy-Doll conflict, as embodied in the fourteen-year engagement of Nathan Detroit and Adelaide, it is the Guy who potentially offers respectability, through marriage, to a Doll who, as a nightclub singer, is otherwise marked as a "sinner." Remarkably, her two "onstage" numbers manage to combine apparent naïveté with what seems to be habitual cynicism, making her seem outwardly oblivious to the sexual innuendos and rampant double entendres that pervade her milieu. Both the name of the nightclub that she performs in (the "Hot Box") and her first number there ("A Bushel and a Peck") wear their verbal play so openly that it can either pass unnoticed or be taken for granted by audiences and characters alike, almost as if it were merely a part of the scenery. In the chorus of her second "Hot Box" number, "Take Back Your Mink," Adelaide sings ruefully in a waltz tempo about returning gifts—all items of apparel or accessories—given to her by a "him" who has (at long last!) asked her to compromise her virtue. As the tempo switches to a fox-trot for an "upbeat" repeat of the chorus as her backup "Dolls" join in, all pretense to virtue is mocked by the ensemble's taking the song's described actions of moral outrage literally, removing fur coat, pearls, gown, and hat in time to the music.

If virtue and display, naïveté and worldliness are thus held in rather precarious balance in these numbers, Adelaide's solo songs that immediately follow them—"Adelaide's Lament" and its second-act reprise—invert the logic of these faux-naïve turns, supporting her catalogue of "psychosomatic symptoms," which she attributes to a parallel catalogue of Nathan Detroit's broken promises, with an exaggerated "bump-and-grind" musical style, the kind of music that conventionally accompanies a striptease. Despite the aggressively repeated triplet buildups to Vegas-style "hip thrusts," which occur in virtually every phrase of the chorus, this aspect of the song most often passes unnoticed under the weight of her complaining lyric, perhaps because the style seems so "natural" and in character for Adelaide. In both her "Lament" and her on-stage numbers, the scandalous musical and textual elements point to a dissolute life-style and help establish a sense of atmospheric "realism," but do not occupy the center of our attention—except perhaps to point out how unwise she, like all the characters in the show, is to herself. Highlighted instead are the rustic innocence of "A Bushel and a Peck," with its pastoral references to ♪ 6.7

farm life (a life-style Adelaide truly craves, however self-delusionally), and the simple equations of maintaining virtue and delivering on promises made, as set out sexually in "Take Back Your Mink" and in terms of married respectability in "Adelaide's Lament." Sarah's parallel song, "If I Were a Bell," which she sings to Sky after her first exposure to Havana and alcohol, also indulges in sexy wordplay ("If I were: . . . a bridge I'd be burning . . . a gate I'd be swinging . . . a salad I know I'd be splashing my dressing")—she, too, has been unwise to herself. But it is in each case the woman's essential "Dollness" that matters most, which moves both ♩6.8 extremes toward a more human center, whether from Sarah's religious ♩6.9 rigidity or from the objectification inherent in Adelaide's profession.

In two pivotal songs late in the second act, which enable the two couples finally to find their way to the marriage altar, religious expression originates from particularly incongruous sources. "Luck Be a Lady" is an out-and-out prayer sung by the gambler's gambler, Sky Masterson, an oddly appropriate gesture even though the setting is a sewer and the context a crap game. The stake in the game is the "souls" of the other gamblers who, if they lose, must attend Sarah's prayer meeting; also at stake is Sky's entire bankroll and his very credibility, since he has promised Sarah to deliver at least a dozen sinners. Although Sky "prays" to Lady Luck—a cheeky substitution for the conventional Virgin Mary—he also charges her to play by the rules and comport herself as a Lady ought to, addressing her as he would any other "Doll" and warning her not to repeat her unladylike habit of "running out." Through saucy wordplay, Sky implicitly equates such projected fickleness with sexual infidelity:

> A lady doesn't wander all over the room
> And blow on some other guy's dice.

True to the show's general strategy of conflating opposites, especially in musical settings, the overtly religious verbal trope is cast against musical type. The music of "Luck Be a Lady" has from the beginning an edgy quality of harmonic uncertainty, constantly wavering between chromatic alternatives and introducing ambiguity in the simplest of chords (the first chord, for example, borrows from the harmonic language of the Russian mystic Scriabin, using a whole-tone version of a simple dominant-seventh chord that includes a pungent augmented triad).[17] This uncertainty, and the excitement it brings, also extends to a broader level, as the chorus— an expanded Tin Pan Alley form of sixty-four bars, AABA—modulates up a half-step with each phrase, from D♭ to D for the repeat of "A," and to E♭ for the bridge, before returning to the original key in the final phrase.

♩6.10   But the clinching "religious" number occurs at the prayer meeting itself, with Nicely Nicely's simulation of religious transport in "Sit Down, You're Rockin' the Boat," a revivalist hymn supported by (former?) gam-

Figure 6.2. Marlon Brando, ready to roll as Sky Masterson, singing "Luck Be a Lady" in the 1955 film version of *Guys and Dolls*. The song is a "prayer" to "Lady Luck," delivered from a sewer. Earlier in the song, we see Sky with hands clasped as if in prayer (around his dice, of course), gazing upward, face aglow. Here, as his fellow gamblers register their impatience, we know from the "halo" above Sky's head that his prayer will be answered. (Courtesy of the Academy of Motion Picture Arts and Sciences.)

blers and Mission dignitaries humming and calling their responses out in five-part harmony. According to the "dream" he recounts, Nicely continues to gamble and drink until, just as he is about to be punished and cast from the lot of the righteous, he wakes up in relief ("Thank the Lord"). Like Sky and Nathan, Nicely has thus managed to accommodate to the demands of religion and respectability without compromising his nature or identity in any significant way. What redeems him and (most of) the other gamblers, from the perspective of religion (at least as represented in *Guys and Dolls*), is an emerging recognition of an already existing common ground. And that—along with a strong show of tolerance—is also what ultimately redeems the religious perspective within a show whose sympathies obviously lie on the side of sin. Although the show provides strong indications that actual change must inevitably happen for things to last, especially in the title song and in Sarah's and Adelaide's duet, "Marry the Man Today (and Change His Ways Tomorrow)," the final curtain allows us to retain a relatively intact image of the well-functioning urban melting pot, with its tolerant accommodation of difference. We see the couples to the altar but are not asked to contemplate (beyond Nathan Detroit's psychosomatic sneeze) the inevitable problems of the marriages themselves.

♪ 6.11

The Music Man (1957), with book, music, and lyrics by Meredith Willson, has seemed to many the most perfect of American musicals—and why not, when every problem it presents is solved specifically *through* music? Even the more general problem that has often troubled many with regard to the musical as a genre—centering on that fraught moment when the spoken word gives way to song—is here absorbed into the process of solving problems through music. Thus, the opening number, "Rock Island," though eminently musical, is neither sung nor accompanied by the orchestra, deriving its rhythms directly from two central features of turn-of-the-century America: the train ride across vast tracts of relatively empty land, and the incessant patter of traveling salesmen. Part of what sets "Professor Harold Hill" apart from these other salesmen is his attraction to music, an attraction that has led him to the unlikely profession (especially for a nonmusician) of selling boys' bands to unsuspecting towns on the prairie. Hill's affinity for music is given a precisely configured, specifically musical presence in the show. Thus, in "Rock Island," music intrudes only to bring the number to a close (with a mildly dissonant "pentatonic" chord consisting of all five notes of that scale), but Hill's first three numbers ("Ya Got Trouble," the introduction to "Seventy-Six Trombones," and "The Sadder but Wiser Girl") all begin with him speaking, only gradually making the transition into song. Already in his opening speech-song, Hill is more musical than the other salesmen in "Rock Island," whose flow of words fall into uneven groupings and virtually never rhyme. But even in "Ya Got Trouble," end-rhymes and a true melody do not occur until midway through, when they emerge simultaneously just after the townspeople have begun to respond musically themselves (sung material in bold):

HILL:	Friends, the idle brain is the devil's playground, trouble!
TOWNSPEOPLE:	**Oh, we got trouble!**
HILL:	Right here in River City!
TOWNSPEOPLE:	**Right here in River City!**

HILL:	With a capital "T" and that rhymes with "P" and that stands for pool.
TOWNSPEOPLE:	**That stands for pool.**
HILL:	We've surely got trouble!
TOWNSPEOPLE:	**We surely got trouble,**
HILL:	Right here in River City!
TOWNSPEOPLE:	**Right here.**
HILL:	Gotta figger out a way to keep the young ones moral after school.
HILL AND TOWNSPEOPLE:	**Our children's children gonna have trouble.**

♪ 6.12

♪ 6.13

In a telling parallel to what is thus shown to be Hill's *developing* musicality, Marian Paroo, the town's librarian and only trained musician, who will eventually fall in love with Hill after initial resistance, begins her first "song" by singing instructions to her piano student Amaryllis, intoning the notes Amaryllis is playing—

> Sol, Do, La, Re, Ti, Mi,
> A little slower, and please keep the fingers curved as nice and high as you possibly can.

—and sings the next number, "Goodnight, My Someone," as a descant to Amaryllis's "cross-hand" piece.

♪ 6.14

♪ 6.15

The catalogue of characters in *The Music Man* who find their redemption through music includes all but the authorities (the mayor and constable of River City) and Charlie Cowell, the anvil salesman who returns to expose Hill as a fraud—none of whom sing. Most basically, as Marian points out in the climactic scene, the town itself is saved from the summer doldrums by the energizing adventures music provides, not only with the projected boys' band, but also with the Ladies' Dance Auxiliary that Hill organizes to gain the support of the mayor's wife, Eulalie MacKecknie Shinn. But there are many specific focal points for this dynamic, as well. The perpetually arguing school board reaches accord as a barbershop quartet, effecting another transition from speech to music, this one directly engineered by Hill, who reassures them that singing is merely "sustained talking"—initially a ruse to distract them from trying to get his credentials. The shy, lisping Winthrop Paroo, Marian's fatherless little brother—the presumed stand-in for Willson himself, who would have just turned ten on July 4, 1912, when the show begins—emerges out of his shell, in his excitement over the arrival of the band instruments, to sing a verse of "The Wells Fargo Wagon" during the finale to Act I. This is the trigger event for Marian, who has been poised to expose Hill as a fraud but in that moment chooses not to. Marian herself, ostracized at the beginning of the show, gains acceptance by playing piano for the dance group and through her association with Hill. Marcellus Washburn, a former traveling salesman who has settled down in River City but who remains on the outskirts of respectability, sings "Shipoopi," bringing popular dance-musical styles (the very "ragtime, shameless music" that Hill railed against in "Ya Got Trouble") to a suddenly more receptive town. Tommy Djilas, the immigrant "wild kid" from the other side of the tracks who is in love with the mayor's daughter Zaneeta (he is identified as "Nithulanian" by the malapropism-prone Mayor Shinn), moves toward respectability as an assistant to Hill, bringing his "gang" into the fold with him. Above all, music solves the problem of Hill himself, the lawless loner who is in the end compelled to join the band (Hill: "For the first time in my life, I got my foot caught in the door"). But if music brings redemption to individuals and groups within the town, that redemption is always configured as acceptance by the larger group. Thus, to have music is to belong, to be a part of the band (Hill: "I always think there's a band, kid."); in *The Music Man,* music serves both as the literal and metaphoric basis of community-building.

Before Hill comes to the mythical all-American Iowa town of River City (built upon Willson's own memories of his childhood in Mason City), it is lethargic, dysfunctional, and isolationist. It is full of separate individuals distrustful of each other and prone to gossip and scape-goating, and it is continually undermined by youthful rebellion, a bickering leadership, the perceived threat of outsiders, and the cynical pandering of its mayor, who owns the billiards parlor. Yet, the town is also essentially innocent. Figuratively, every one of these traits (except possibly the last) had its correlative in the mid-1950s, just after the Korean War and the McCarthy era, and just as a rebellious youth-culture had begun to emerge from both well-off suburbs and troubled inner cities to scare the hell out of the conservative American establishment. The show functions, then, to connect the problems of the 1950s, when America emerged fully as one of two world powers, to the problems America faced just before World War I, just after its main outlines had been officially drawn, when becoming a single nation ready to engage as such with the rest of the world seemed of paramount importance (in other words, very soon after the time frame of *Oklahoma!;* earlier in 1912, Arizona had joined the Union as the forty-eighth state, completing the map of contiguous states). The "community" being built through music in *The Music Man* is thus at once that of River City, of America just after the turn of the century, and of an American-centered "free world" just after mid-century. Within the paradigm discussed above, a nostalgic mythology of emerging community set in the past serves both to reassure a troubled America that its problems are manageable, and to goad it out of its lethargic smugness—its summer doldrums—to recognize the energizing power of community-based feeling and activity.

Hill, in "Ya Got Trouble," takes over and redefines within one persona a number of American stereotypes, including most obviously both the traveling salesman with his huckstering patter, and his close cousin the religious demagogue (recalling the "fugue" in *Guys and Dolls* between Sarah Brown and the watch salesman), but also evoking the temperance sermonizer ("I say, first it's a little medicinal wine from a teaspoon; Then beer from a bottle"), the stumping politician up on his soapbox ("Remember the Maine, Plymouth Rock, and the Golden Rule"), and even, perhaps, the fast-talking auctioneer ("Ya got ONE, TWO, THREE, FOUR, FIVE, SIX pockets in a table!"). Linking all of these is the special fascination Americans have long had for rapid verbal patter, evident from their earlier fondness for Gilbert and Sullivan and their later love-hate relationship to rap. The song itself is delivered as the first half of a one-two punch; only in the reprise later that evening does Hill actually make the pitch for a boys' band, selling the idea hard with the ultra-patriotic "Seventy-Six Trombones," the centerpiece of Act I and the linchpin for the show. The setup is based on the reality that band music had become in the decades around the turn of the century, thanks to the likes of Sousa and Handy (Hill's complete list, recited in reverent tones, reads "Gilmore, Liberatti, Pat Conway, The Great Creatore, W. C. Handy, and John Philip Sousa"), both a hallmark of American music-making and an important source of civic pride. (In this case, of course, calling up the number "seventy-six" on the Fourth of July recalls the year America declared its independence.)

♩ 6.16
♩ 6.17

"Seventy-Six Trombones" balances its allegiances to the Tin Pan Alley song-format (AABA, but with a sixteen-bar A) with traditions associated with the march; thus, honoring the latter, its "B" phrase expands into a "trio" in the relaxed key of the subdominant, extending to thirty-two bars ("There were copper bottom timpani in horse platoons . . ."). More importantly for the musical dynamic within the show, "Seventy-Six Trombones" combines, in distinctive profile, two songs we have already heard at that point. The melody nearly duplicates that of the more lyrical waltz song, "Goodnight, My Someone," sung by Marian in her earlier scene with Amaryllis, a derivation that is made explicit late in Act II when the two songs are combined in alternation; the pairing thus offers a correlative, perhaps, to the convention of deriving "masculine" and "feminine" themes within a symphonic movement from the same thematic basis (Willson, we must remember, also wrote symphonies).[18] This implicit link between Hill and Marian balances an earlier, more subtle linkage between them: as Marian and her mother argue, following the contours of the simple tune Amaryllis plays during her lesson ("Piano Lesson / If You Don't Mind My Saying So"), their combined "song" degenerates into unrhymed patter, in this case forging an explicit connection between the stereotypical fast-talking Irish (the Paroos) and their more generically American counterparts (Hill):

> MRS. PAROO: . . . if you don't mind my sayin' so, there's not a man alive
> Who could hope to measure up to that blend a' Paul Bunyan,
> Saint Pat and Noah Webster you've concocted for yourself
> Out a' your Irish imagination, your Iowa stubbornness, and your libery full a' books!

A less obvious basis for the opening phrase of "Seventy-Six Trombones"—in fact, for the one detail in that phrase which most obviously differentiates it from "Goodnight, My Someone"—is the distinctive triplet launching figure in "Iowa Stubborn," the "anti-welcome" song sung by the townspeople upon Hill's arrival. "Seventy-Six Trombones" begins each phrase in its opening section with the trajectory and precise rhythmic configuration of that figure (as shown in bold):

> "IOWA STUBBORN":   **We can be cold** as our *fall*ing ther***mom***-eter . . .
> "SEVENTY-SIX TROMBONES": **Seventy-six** trombones led the big parade,
> With a **hundred-and-ten** *cornets* close at hand.
> They were **followed by rows** and rows of the finest virtuosos . . .

Indeed, in the second phrase of the latter, "hundred-and-ten cornets" is set to precisely the same notes as "We can be cold . . . fall . . . mom" (as indicated above in bold-italic combination). In its melodic details, then, the march-song not only helps forge the romantic connection between the two leads, but also provides a subtle layer to its more obvious point, which is to provide a marching anthem to galvanize River City into becoming a genuine community. Thus, embedded within this anthem are the musical personalities of the town itself, the ostracized Marian, and, more basically, the outsider Hill.

♪ 6.18

Although it is not made into a central theme of the show, we may infer from the mayor's crack about the "Nithulanian" Tommy Djilas that the Paroo family's Irishness is part of what sets them apart from the community, as not fully integrated even by 1912. To this extent, given the show's inclusionist trajectory, it may also be seen to embrace America's melting-pot ideology, even though some of its central pillars of Americana—the barbershop quartet, the fast-talking city man, and the tendency toward

unconsciously punning malapropisms (Mayor Shinn: "The Sword of
Restitution has cut down Professor Harold Hill")—stem from either
African American traditions or minstrelsy, neither of which is directly represented. But the connection between the two romantic leads has less to
do with ethnic difference than with the intertwined auras of music and
sex, two forces that, while basically healthy, are also potentially dangerous (from "Ya Got Trouble"):

> One fine night they leave the pool hall headin' for the dance at the Arm'ry,
> Libertine men and scarlet women and ragtime, shameless music
> That'll drag your son and your daughter to the arms of a jungle animal instinct
> Mass-steria!

Hill, we are given to understand more than once, is given to using his
sex appeal to seduce women musicians who might otherwise seek to betray him. Late in the show, Marian, who has a wholly undeserved reputation for promiscuity, nevertheless turns the tables when she tries to seduce Charlie Cowell to the strains of Bizet's *Carmen* to keep him from
unmasking Hill, and in the end it is she who becomes the sexual aggressor in her relationship with Hill. The marriage trope in *The Music Man*,
if there is one, is between sex (Hill) and music (Marian), with marriage,
symbolic and deferential to the larger community, making the union of
the two respectable.

At every turn, then, music turns individuals into members of a community. The barbershop quartet (the top "snapshot": in this book's frontispiece) is formed from men who do not get along, but thereby become
inseparable; significantly, their songs tend to be about leaving and returning home, and articulate both verbally and stylistically a sense of belonging. Even their interplay communicates this dynamic: early in their
first number ("Sincere"), at the end of the key line "Where is the good in
goodbye,"[19] the upper voice "strays" but is pulled back into consonance
(a sung effect, called "swiping" in barbershop traditions, that is usually
also staged as "business" among the singers). Their Act II "Lida Rose,"
about a homecoming and anticipated marriage, implicitly welcomes Marian more securely into the community by offering supportive counterpoint
(as part of a combination-song) to her "Will I Ever Tell You," in which
she confesses her growing love for Hill. "Wells Fargo Wagon" stages a
community event, in which nearly everyone seems to take a solo turn;
when the lisping Winthrop does so as well, the community responds in
quasi-religious tones, and Marian herself seems redeemed in our eyes by
how clearly she sees Winthrop's progress as Hill's—and music's—ac-
complishment. Perhaps most significantly, Marian, who has long seen
through Hill's phoniness, in that moment sees beyond that phoniness to

Figure 6.3. Marian, Winthrop, and Harold Hill (Shirley Jones, Ronny Howard, and Robert Preston) in an outtake from the 1962 film *The Music Man*. This grouping occurs twice in the show. At the end of the first act, Winthrop's reaction to receiving his cornet (his lisping rendition of "The Wells Fargo Wagon") prevents Marian from unmasking Hill; at the fadeout, she holds the incriminating page from one of her sacred library books behind her, having just torn it out of the book she has given to Mayor Shinn. Near the end of the second act, just before the outraged townspeople arrive to arrest him, it is Hill's turn to be rendered powerless by an inability to disillusion the boy. When Winthrop asks why he doesn't try to escape, he replies—reversing the usual salesman's cliché—"For the first time in my life, I got my foot caught in the door." (Courtesy of the Academy of Motion Picture Arts and Sciences.)

♪ 6.19
♪ 6.20
♪ 6.21
something more important and vital than reality, something that perhaps could not exist without the grandiose lies that support it (a virtual parable of Broadway, if not America!).

But the central image in *The Music Man* of music bringing people together into a community remains the patriotic march, and that image brings with it the rather terrifying joy of utter conformity and complete regimentation. We ought to know that such conformity is incompatible with what is most appealing about Hill: surely we would completely lose interest in him were he actually to stay in River City and form a band, and just as surely he would be smothered by the love of a woman who sees through him so utterly and loves him all the more for being such a phony. But music solves *our* problems, as well, as we march out of the theater in time to the big tune, "Seventy-Six Trombones." We, too, have willingly joined the band, and the moment of joining, at least, is an exhilarating one.

For Further Consideration

Strike Up the Band (1930), *Anything Goes* (1934), *San Francisco* (film, 1936), *The Wizard of Oz* (film, 1939), *This is the Army* (1942), *Yankee Doodle Dandy* (film, 1942), *Holiday Inn* (film, 1942), *Meet Me in St. Louis* (film, 1944), *Anchors Aweigh* (film, 1945), *Annie Get Your Gun* (1946), *An American in Paris* (film, 1951), *A Star is Born* (film, 1954), *Damn Yankees* (1955), *High Society* (film, 1956), *Li'l Abner* (1956), *The Unsinkable Molly Brown* (1960), *Camelot* (1960), *How to Succeed in Business Without Really Trying* (1961), *1776* (1969), and *Annie* (1977)

See Also

Regarding nationalism generally, the best concise account is in Ernest Gellner's *Nationalism*. Regarding nationalism in music, the best overall discussion is by Richard Taruskin, in his extended "Nationalism" essay in the 2001 *New Grove Dictionary of Music and Musicians*. Regarding America's quest for a musically expressed national identity (within the realm of high culture), see chapter 15 in Charles Hamm's *Music in the New World*. Regarding nationalism on the musical stage (and in film musicals), Ethan Mordden's "Americana" chapter in *Beautiful Mornin'* provides a good account of the 1940s era, and Jennifer Jenkins's "Say It with Firecrackers" considers more narrowly the film musicals made during the World War II years.

Regarding *Oklahoma!*, Max Wilk's *OK!* provides a substantial amount of valuable background material, as does chapter 1 of Frederick Nolan's *The Sound of Their Music;* Ethan Mordden's "Rodgers and Hammerstein" chapter in *Beautiful Mornin'* gives a good account of the beginnings of the partnership; "Second Maturity" in Joseph P. Swain's *The Broadway Musical* considers the show as both innovation and summation; chapter 4 of Graham Wood's "The Development of Song Forms in the Broadway and Hollywood Musicals of Richard Rodgers" offers considerable insight into how the show makes song forms thematic; and part 2 of Geoffrey Block's *Richard Rodgers Reader* provides a variety of perspectives on this show (and others), many from collaborators. See also chapter 13 in Meryle Secrest's *Somewhere for Me*; 201–9 in Gerald Mast's *Can't Help Singin'*; chapter 5 in Abe Laufe's *Broadway's Greatest Musicals*; chapter 3 in Scott Miller's *Rebels with Applause*, pp. 306–14 in Rick Altman's *The American Film Musical*, and the opening pages of Ann Sears's "The Coming of the Musical Play."

Regarding *Guys and Dolls*, see the second chapter of Ethan Mordden's *Coming Up Roses*, and chapter 10 of Geoffrey Block's *Enchanted Evenings*.

Regarding *The Music Man*, Willson's memoir *"But He Doesn't Know the Territory"* is an amusing and sometimes revelatory account, and Scott Miller includes a provocative chapter on the show as the centerpiece of his *Deconstructing Harold Hill* (chapter 5).

Counter-mythologies

THE AMERICAN MUSICAL has never been as monolithic in its development as might be indicated by the huge success of the three "mainstream" shows considered in the previous chapter, although countless other shows have offered similar engagements with America's aspirations and mythologies. Alongside such shows were also many that pointed to quite different aspects of America, overlapping the Rodgers and Hammerstein era and even at times to be found among their own works (e.g., *Carousel*, 1945). Two musicals from the 1950s, for example, each composed by Leonard Bernstein, took shape in part out of a concern for current realities that did not conform to the sanguine reassurances of *Oklahoma, Guys and Dolls*, and *The Music Man*. Thus, *Candide* (1956) drew implicit parallels between the McCarthy era in postwar America and the Spanish Inquisition, while *West Side Story* (1957; see chapter 8) took on the specter of ethnic-based, gang-related violence that had become part of life on the streets of New York and other large American cities. If such shows were a minority in the 1950s, however, the sanguinities of that era did not last. Beginning in the 1960s, alternative visions of America began to emerge forcefully in what I group together here as "counter-mythologies."

The political and musical turmoil of the 1960s precipitated a two-fold crisis for the American musical stage. Politically, central events of the 1960s seemed to cry out for theatrical representation, including the Vietnam War and the protests it engendered among the nation's youth, the civil rights movement and its attendant protests and repressive police actions, women's liberation, ecology, a wave of political assassinations, and increased sexual promiscuity and recreational drug use among the younger generation. Musically, the 1960s saw not only a tremendous surge in the popularity of politicized folk-based music (Bob Dylan, Joan Baez, etc.), but also the development of various genres that remained grounded in regionally based African American performance traditions but that were widely embraced by whites and others across the United States (soul, funk, Motown, gospel, etc.), and the explosive emergence of an increasingly diverse rock music from the waning momentum of the rock-and-roll movement of the 1950s, initially spearheaded by the Beatles and the near hysteria with which they were received in America.[1] In both politics and in music, sharp divisions between the older and younger generations opened and then hardened into something definitive and institutionalized. Music, politics, appearance, and life-style were the central arenas of contention, to such an extent that all four were presumed to be in a fairly reliable alignment, with new departures in all taken to be part of what had become known as the counterculture.

Among the early responses on the American musical stage to this increasingly volatile situation were occasional attempts, such as *Bye, Bye, Birdie* (1960), to acknowledge emergent music and life-styles from the standpoint of prevailing norms—that is, from the parental side of the "generation gap"—but to render them in the end unthreatening and even laughable. But by the mid-1960s, this kind of dismissive response had become untenable. While a significant number of essentially status-quo musicals would appear in these years, such as *It's a Bird—It's a Plane—It's Superman, Mame,* and *I Do! I Do!* (all 1966), *You're a Good Man, Charlie Brown* (1967), and *1776* (1969), the subversive yet spectacularly successful *Hair* (off-Broadway 1967, moving to Broadway in 1968) broke entirely new ground. *Hair* marked a deliberate attempt to create a viable alternative to the musicals of the older generation, grounded in a documentary-like approach to life as it is actually lived, and steeped in the emergent political issues, alternative life-styles, iconoclastic manner of appearances—and, of course, the music—of the younger generation (an approach significantly echoed thirty years later in *Rent*). *Hair* may thus be considered as a propositional redefinition of America, aspiring to establish an alternative mythology to displace those celebrated and elaborated on the American musical stage across the previous two-and-a-half decades. But there was also a revisionist spirit at work on Broadway that sought to expose the realities behind American mythologies, stemming from those, such as Stephen Sondheim and producer-director Harold Prince, whose roots were in the traditional musical but who felt and acted on a strong desire to transform and reform the genre and its conceits from within. Sondheim's *Anyone Can Whistle* (1964), a box-office failure, was an early work of this stripe, as was his bicentennial offering *Pacific Overtures* (1976; see chapter 10). The show that we will consider here in tandem with *Hair,* however, is undoubtedly Sondheim's hardest-hitting work along these lines: *Assassins* (1991).

Hair, The American Tribal Love-Rock Musical (1967–68) grew out of Gerome Ragni's and James Rado's desire to create a musical that would reflect the hippie life-style, and evolved into what would be hailed as the first "rock musical"; its other "firsts" for the legitimate musical stage included most famously an extended nude episode (during the "Be-In" at the end of the first act) and on-stage drug use. Ragni and Rado were both actors who were in part creating a vehicle for themselves, and would assume the pivotal roles of Berger and Claude around which the loosely organized events of the show would revolve. While they aimed in part for a documentary-like truth, conducting ethnographic "research" in Greenwich Village and recruiting cast members from the street, they also aimed quite clearly for commercial success, and so hired Galt Mac-Dermott—a Grammy-award-winning jazz composer with Broadway ambitions but no experience in rock idioms—to write the music. Intertwined with the mythologies elaborated and explored by the show is the mythology of the show itself, particularly regarding its "authentic" evolution and development, and the remarkable way its success manifested itself in a proliferation of simultaneous productions worldwide.

Among the many features designed to set *Hair* apart from standard (that is, "establishment") Broadway shows, besides its subject matter and its reliance on a variety of popular musical styles from the 1960s, were its partial erasure of the boundary between audience and stage, its avoidance of conventional narrative (it was ostentatiously a "non-book" musical), its attempt to achieve a spontaneous feel to the choreography, and its evocation of a group-based culture superseding the star-driven dynamic typical for Broadway[2]—all of which was meant to convey the sense that *Hair* was not a show so much as a "happening." Thus, it had no "cast" in the conventional sense, but rather what its members called a "Tribe," alluding in general to a simple, primitivist, nonhierarchical interactive group dynamic, and in particular to the American Indian, one of many disadvantaged groups in America whose cause was being taken up by the younger generation. Many trace the roots of the "concept" musical to *Hair;* typical of this type is the way the show unfolds as a series of associated vignettes related to a central theme, with the barest hint of a storyline connecting them. But this structure (or lack thereof) also reflects the mellowed-out drifting characteristic of the milieu that *Hair*'s creators sought to reproduce, and seems a logical extension of the tendency among its central population for free association (both mental and sexual), and of the heightening of sensation and "spacing-out" that went along with their experimental drug experiences. Thus, like the short "blackout" sketches and vividly colored decor of the contemporaneous television show, "Rowan and Martin's Laugh-In" (1968–73), the loose structure and other disorienting strategies of *Hair* served to promote a strong association with drug culture and a more casual attitude toward expressed sexuality. The counterculture with which both these and related shows and films sought to align themselves was most importantly a West-coast phenomenon (especially San Francisco), but quickly spread: in part, then, *Hair* may be seen to relocate this movement to New York City at the same time that it asserts its universality.

As an idealizing quasi-documentary, *Hair* was able to give a palpable and focused presence to a number of disparate trends among America's young, creating the sense of a vibrant and extended youth-based commune that had come to exist outside the mainstream establishment, whose members had successfully forged a new way of living in the wake of rejecting the values and structures their parents had tried to impose on them. Within this vision of the counterculture, prejudice, war, and taboos of every kind were replaced by "harmony and understanding, sympathy and trust abounding," as set forth in the opening number, "Aquarius"—a song whose very name seems to offer itself as a substitute for the similarly sounding "America." The hard fact that this was merely a vision, and often quite far from reality (especially regarding the presumed melting-away of racist attitudes), hovered uncomfortably around the edges of the show, most clearly stated in the ways *Hair* catered to its often middle-class audience by presenting token representatives of its various contributing strands (e.g., black, or a still not fully explicit homosexuality), all sharply etched as intriguingly different against a familiar, basically white, middle-class background. Audiences who were not already "converted" might thereby see a version of themselves, freed of inhibitions and joyously forging new relationships and embracing new ideas and behaviors within the security of a "Tribe" that was already dominated by their "own kind," and governed by their own values in a purer form (that is, their aspirational values, however unactualized). This was especially important for those many in the late sixties, on either side of the generation gap, who had been frightened by the rapidity and extremity of change over a mere handful of years, yet who were perhaps ready to embrace a less threatening embodiment of those changes. While trying to preserve to some extent the eclectic chaos of youth culture, *Hair* also tried to enact a vision of that culture as a *community*—what might be described (expanding on the familiar marriage trope) as an extended "group marriage" involving all the disparate disenfranchised elements represented in the show.

And it was, after all, as easy to join this community as it was to join those of *Oklahoma!*'s frontier, *Guys and Dolls*'s savvy yet oddly provincial Times Square, or *The Music Man*'s all-American River City—all you had to do was learn the songs and join in. This, ultimately, was the real point of breaking down the barriers between audience and stage, which found larger expression in the way that the show's songs saturated the country's airwaves, to an extent that had by the mid-sixties become quite rare for a Broadway show. The combination of the show's framing numbers, "Aquarius" and "Let the Sun Shine In" (The 5th Dimension) rose to the top of the 1969 Billboard charts, but other songs from the show also made the charts for 1969, including "Hair" (The Cowsills), "Easy to Be Hard" (Three Dog Night), and "Good Morning Starshine" (Oliver). Not only did this exposure help sell the show as a commodity, but it also gave credence to the notion that the show's "Tribe" actually did represent something like a coherent movement, giving it voice in a literal way and validating the show's claims for the authenticity of its musical offerings.

The most visible members of the Tribe represent key constituencies of the movement *Hair* seeks to embody. Its creators assumed the key roles of the free spirit Berger (Ragni), who is the group's center, and Claude (Rado), who does not burn his draft card and therefore remains to some extent on the periphery; together, these two mark both the boundaries and the core of the "group marriage." Other characters are no less archetypal: Sheila is the college student, upper class but politically active; Woof the androgynous, long-haired goofball of somewhat mysterious sexual orientation (thus, to be understood as homosexual, still somewhat closeted even within the Tribe's vaunted environment of sexual freedom); Hud the token black character; Jeannie the spiritual, mystic, acid-head hippie who is pregnant but unsure of who the father is; Crissy the lost-soul hippie; and Claude's parents the establishment, undermined through camp (his mother was sometimes played by a male in drag).

The first span of the opening number, "Aquarius," presents itself as something between religious chant and incantation, leading to a "magic" effect at the arrival, when the harmony suddenly shifts down a whole step for the words "the age of Aquarius" after the breakthrough "dawning" in C major. The song's central conceit is to project an alignment with a universal power through astrology, and the music makes clear through its paired evocation of magic and religion that a religious merger of sorts, inclusive of pagan ritual and Eastern mysticism, is to be inferred. In the 1979 film version (directed by Milos Forman), this implication is expanded to include evocations of Eastern dancing and to imply control even over the animal kingdom, as two of the Tribe entice the policemen's horses to join the dance—in a playful sequence meant perhaps to recall the vaunted close spiritual affinity many American Indian tribes developed with horses after Europeans introduced them to America. The song's bridge makes clear that the catalyst for achieving this alignment ("Harmony and understanding") is drug-based, offering "Golden living dreams of visions, / Mystic crystal revelation, / And the mind's true liberation." Particularly telling here is the central phrase, whose "crystal" refers both to the perfect nature of the mystic revelation promised in the song and to its source (specifically either methamphetamine or the particularly risky hallucinogen PCP; less probably, they could have meant LSD, which emerges in crystalline form when it is first "cooked"). Stylistically, the lyric exhibits more naïveté than sophistication, however. Indeed, it sometimes borders on incompetence, as in its confused rhyming of "derisions" and "visions," which follows an equally awkward pairing of the pseudo-rhymes "understanding" and "abounding"; in the former case, the "No more" that heads the phrase could in fact be taken to apply not only to the "false-hoods or derisions" that immediately follow, but also to the "Golden living dreams of visions" and "Mystic crystal revelations" that come just after. But this naïveté, too, registers importantly as aligned with the counterculture, offering here (and elsewhere in the show) a mode of discourse attuned more to then-current popular styles than to Broadway's somewhat higher verbal standards.

Musically, the song is based securely in the styles, instruments, and forms of rock, but blends these with traditional theatrical strategies, as well, much like the opening number of *Oklahoma!* reproduced a turn-of-the-century waltz-song's verse-chorus format within the later thirty-two-bar form (see chapter 6, pp. 127–28). The archetypal rock beat, with its characteristic "back beat" emphasizing the second and fourth beats of the bar, is largely absent from the original stage version of the song, which instead emphasizes its mystic-psychedelic dimension (a strategy followed as well in the 1969 version by the 5th Dimension, which adds the back beat

Figure 7.1. *Hair*'s core "Tribe"—Woof, Jeannie, Hud, and Berger—frolicking in their Manhattan playground (Don Dacus, Annie Golden, Dorsey Wright, and Treat Williams in the 1979 film). (Courtesy of the Academy of Motion Picture Arts and Sciences.)

as it segues into "Let the Sunshine In"; for its part, the 1979 film version plays the whole song against an already long-established back beat). But the basic beat nevertheless establishes an unvarying metrical pace—perhaps as an analogue of the eternal—against which the more fluid declamation of the song itself stands in relief.

♪ 7.1
♪ 7.2
♪ 7.3

Both the repeated outer part of the song and the internal "bridge" are based loosely on the twelve-bar blues patterns traditionally used in rock and roll; for both spans, something like the AAB verbal-melodic pattern (traditionally four bars for each phrase, with its concluding phrase often serving as a "punch line") is supported by a harmonic structure that emphasizes tonic and subdominant harmonies in the first two phrases and makes a much stronger harmonic move to mark the third phrase (traditionally to the dominant, though not here). In the first span, the "incantation" style against the steady rock beat creates a sense of suspension over the first two phrases, reinforced by the decentering modal qualities of D-Dorian (D minor, but with raised sixth and lowered seventh), which here helps achieve a sense of "floating," reinforced with great effect by the circling camera movements of the 1979 film. The end of the second phrase—"love will steer the stars"—makes the first harmonic move away from D-Dorian toward the "dawning" in C major, but the final phrase ("This is the dawning") begins with an abrupt fall to B♭, as noted. This startling drop seems to take us farther afield but actually sets up the return to D minor, which gradually reverts to D-Dorian through celebratory expansions on the word "Aquarius." Particularly striking in these expansions is the emphasis given to the charged last syllable of "Aquarius"—a subtle assertion of the preeminence of the collective ("-us")—as the pitch level leaps upward and drifts back down for the final iteration of the title word. Dramatically, the "punch line" basis of the blues pattern is thereby easily converted into a variant of the verse-chorus structure typical for musicals, recalling as well the recitative-aria structures of older opera, in which the aria represents the main event and presents an expansive setting of comparatively few words (note that the only text for the "aria" segment here is "the age of Aquarius," since the antecedent part of the sentence, "This is the dawning of," occurs before the harmonic shift on the first downbeat of the phrase, and is not repeated).

The larger structure also supports the implied connection to earlier operatic types, as the "bridge" behaves much like the middle section of a da capo Aria, moving more quickly through its text and beginning in a more relaxed key that is eventually undermined by enriching harmonies in preparation for a return to the main key. The opening key for the bridge is C major, forging an appropriate connection to the earlier breakthrough phrase, "love will steer the stars," and the harmonic structure is a placid alternation of tonic and subdominant until midway through the second phrase, when the textual allusions to drug use ("dreams," "visions," "crystal revelation") initiate a descending melodic sequence that seems to descend deeper and deeper into the mind, until it achieves "true liberation" on the ascending last syllable of "Aquarius," returning decisively to an "Amen" (plagal) arrival in D minor as "-us" ascends from the depths once more to its high G. Significantly, the descending sequence that enables this liberation is broken apart into overlapping and interrupting voices (in both the stage version and the cover by the 5th Dimension, although not in the film), creating a brief strobe-like effect to color the descent in terms compatible with the verbal suggestion of drug use.

The implied alignment of religious transport with drugs in "Aquarius" is extended to include sex in "Donna," which conveys the urgency of its seeking through a driving rock beat significantly harder than that of the seductive "Aquarius." Verbally, the song rather conventionally conflates the feminine with the religious, through the image of the Madonna (here given ambiguously as "my Donna"), but casts its religious quest in terms of sexual urgings: the "Donna" that Berger searches for transmutes from "a sixteen-year-old virgin," to "San Francisco psychedelic urchin" and "tatooed woman," while his search takes him not only to San Francisco's drug scene, but also to India and yoga (which does not involve drugs), and to South American "Indian smoke." The veiled references to drugs in this song seem to provoke the segue into "Hashish," a "list song" of drugs and sometimes comical stream-of-consciousness extensions—"L.S.D., D.M.T., S.T.P., B.M.T., A and P, I.R.T.," etc.—which serves both to normalize drugs and to distort and elevate the more prosaic additions to the list,[3] especially in this mantra-like setting, with its incessantly repeating rising third. Here again, the lines blur within the trance-like state projected in the song, intertwining sex, religion, and drug use (foreshadowing the "Hare Krishna" refrain of the "Be-In" that ends Act I), while referring to yet another musical style emergent in the sixties: minimalism.

♪ 7.4

The list-songs of Hair—"Hashish," "Sodomy," "Colored Spade," "I'm Black / Ain't Got No," "I Got Life," and parts of "Manchester England," "Air," and "Initials"—have a didactic component that has not worn particularly well. In the sixties, playing to a mixed audience of insiders, outsiders, and wanna-be's, these lists were essential exposition, part of the show's implicit mission to serve as a kind of "teach-in" (thus, all of these occur in the first act). In some cases they provided an "in-your-face" exposure of verbal taboos similar to Lenny Bruce's deliberately offensive use of profanity in his comedy acts (starting about a decade earlier; Bruce died of a drug overdose in 1966); in some cases they made telling points in their montage-like juxtapositions; and in some cases they merely conveyed a certain verbal virtuosity and playfulness. All of this worked reasonably well with early audiences, but has proven problematic with attempted revivals. "Sodomy," for example, initially daring and liberating, now seems dated and a little confused, although its setting, which layers religious feeling onto a fifties-style love-anthem, can still charm. More troubling is "Colored Spade," sung by Hud in a James Brown–derived funk style associated with the black power movement, and consisting mainly of a list of racial epithets that still hold a tremendous charge of residual collective anger; the result carries an explosive potential not really contained by its arch presentation, which in the film version even manifests a leftover trace of blackface minstrelsy in its emphasis on wide, white eyes against dark skin. Here, especially, the disparity between the aspirations and realities of the counterculture are set in such bold relief that the message becomes too strident, with the show's preachiness reminding us that the community it seeks to project is in reality little more than a jumble of disparate elements, which no list-song, or collection of list-songs, can convincingly unify.

♩ 7.5
♩ 7.6

To some extent, these list-songs contribute to a general strategy of generating opportunities to expose and explore both the political issues and the musical styles that lie behind the various strands of the counterculture. Some of these have been noted; others include "Air," which addresses pollution, extending the subject to include pollution of the body; "Initials," which addresses issues of class (LBJ riding the IRT; thus, the President of the United States riding a Manhattan subway line); "Manchester England," which refers musically to the "English Invasion" (specifically, Herman's Hermits) while exploring issues of identity formation. Particularly effective is the pairing of "Black Boys" and "White Boys," which recall the girls' groups of the early sixties; here, similar formulaic verses are set in two different styles, first presenting, with some daring, white girls singing about black boys, then shifting to considerably sexier "black" music for the obverse. The white girls' half falls back on a fifties "bubble-gum" style and Broadway's tradition of double entendre ("Black boys fill me up. / Black boys are so damn yummy, they satisfy my tummy. / I have such a sweet tooth when it comes to love"), whereas the rhythm and blues style of "White Boys," while also faintly nostalgic, carries a much more palpable sexual charge.

♩ 7.7
♩ 7.8
♩ 7.9
♩ 7.10

The most serious issue *Hair* confronts, which takes over its center in the second act, is the Vietnam War, in which Claude will serve and die (although in the 1979 film, it is Berger who goes in Claude's place). Most important here is the pairing of "3-5-0-0" (referring to the number of Marines who landed in Vietnam in March 1965) with "What a Piece of Work Is Man," derived from Shakespeare. Part of the point here is the juxtaposition of statistics with poetry, the one canceling out the other, with neither able to do true justice to the loss of human life in war. More subtly, the gospel style of the refrain in the first song emphasizes the racial aspect of the war ("Prisoners in Niggertown, it's a dirty little war, 3–5–0–0"), reminding us even today that a disproportionate number of those sent to Vietnam were black. Ultimately, the show barely pulls an optimistic conclusion out of its finale, "The Flesh Failures," a grim march forecasting the death of Claude against the backdrop of "a dying nation," set within a blues structure. Yet somehow—courtesy of Timothy Leary, the most prominent advocate of LSD and other consciousness-altering drugs—this death-march transmutes into a loop on the final phrase of its repeating blues formula, as "Let the sunshine in" cycles back and forth between its opening C minor and its concluding "Amen" cadence in E♭ major. By joining this refrain directly to "Aquarius" in their cover of the latter song, the 5th Dimension draws attention to the show's framing device, in which the outer songs look for sustaining power from the heavens (thus, from planets and stars in the opening song, from sunshine in the finale); they thereby also short-circuit the ambiguity of that final refrain, which returns as surely to the minor as it emerges hopefully in the major.

♪ 7.11
♪ 7.12
♪ 7.13

The project of filming *Hair* a decade later presented two large problems: the lack of a live audience and the datedness of its material, both of which undermine the "authenticity" of the show's initial appeal as a "happening." Milos Forman's solutions to these problems seem reasonable, but have engendered controversy because they required substantial tinkering with the original premises of the show. In the film, Claude more fully assumes the perspective of the outsider, being welcomed in but stubbornly resisting assimilation; in this sense, he assumes from the opening sequence the role of the missing live audience, allowing the actual audience for the film to identify either with him or the Tribe, or somewhere in between. More broadly, the film presents itself as a period piece, rendering both sides of the conflict nostalgically, as inhabiting a more innocent time, and lessening significantly the presence of the show's various "lists." The most important thing the film does, though, is to take the show outside, offering comforting visions of rural America in the opening sequence, finding refuge in the open spaces of Central Park for the heart of the film, and in the end venturing again across America as the Tribe follows Claude to his military base (yet another open space, but much less welcoming). Thus, the film does something the stage show could not: it locates its alternative vision within the landscape that is centrally at stake: America itself.

Assassins (1991), like *Hair,* has been called a concept musical, but it has more in common with other concept musicals by Sondheim, such as *Company* (1970), *Follies* (1971), and *Pacific Overtures* (1976; see chapter 10). Whereas *Hair* tries hard to achieve a naturalistic effect, almost in the manner of a documentary, Sondheim's concept musicals all place a strong emphasis on their narratives even if they often favor a more oblique, nonchronological approach, stepping in and out of literal, realistic depiction for dramatic effect. *Assassins* is especially close in kind to *Pacific Overtures,* since in both cases the story is really a selective enactment of (and commentary on) actual historical events. Significantly, the books for both shows were written by John Weidman, and were much revised in consultation with Harold Prince and Stephen Sondheim.

The history that *Assassins* tells is that of America's growth to maturity, roughly the century between Lincoln's and Kennedy's assassinations (1865 and 1963, respectively, although later events figure prominently, as well); thus it, too, deals in part with the tumult of the sixties, seen as a crucial watershed for America. The perspective in *Assassins* runs closely parallel to more conventional narratives detailing the progress of the American dream as the country grew to world prominence, but it focuses on the shadow of that more hopeful narrative line, projecting a dark and sinister spirit hovering disturbingly close to America's main road. *Assassins,* like *Hair,* thus offers a counter-mythology, but in a decidedly different way, focusing not on an emergent ideology but rather on a disturbing presence that has always been there, the "wolves" and "unnamable things"—to borrow Lynn Riggs's language regarding the settlers of Oklahoma—lurking in the "shifting fringe of dark around the camp-fire . . . just outside the rush of light" (see chapter 6, p. 133). Thus, *Assassins* takes up the point of view of what *Oklahoma!* destroys, of what *Guys and Dolls* and *The Music Man* absorb into community, and of what *Hair* converts into an alternative community: it tells the story of Jud, or perhaps of what Sky Masterson and Harold Hill might have become had they not been invited to "join up." In engaging with the well-known history of American assassination, *Assassins* considers how a cohort of such outsiders has—in the popular imagination, at least—formed itself into the semblance of a community, located outside temporality.

America has often been understood as founded on two principles, embodied in the name "United States": union (community) and independent units (states). Thus, America tries to preserve both of these sometimes opposing principles, balancing the strength promised by union against the rights and independence of the smaller units being joined, ranging from states, to minorities defined in various ways, to individuals. Accordingly, America in principle asserts an overall unity but endeavors not to enforce belonging or uniformity, and instead encourages independence. *Assassins* deals explicitly with the problematic between union and independence as so conceived. Thus, early on, in "The Ballad of Booth," the balladeer paraphrases Abraham Lincoln's assassin, John Wilkes Booth, as follows: "Damn you, Lincoln, and damn the day / You threw the 'U' out of U.S.A.!" Here, as throughout *Assassins*, the perpetrators see themselves as adhering to the American dream, whether as its protectors (Booth) or, perhaps, as claimants on a birthright entitlement (see my later discussion of "Ev'rybody's Got the Right").

In an early stage of planning the musical, after its creators had narrowed down the scope of the story to American presidents, they realized, as John Weidman said in an interview,

> "Presidents have never been attacked for purely political or economic reasons," as [political leaders] were in Europe, and no assassin has been black. . . . Men and women who had attempted to kill Presidents believed that everyone had a right to happiness, not just to its pursuit.[4]

In an early review *Assassins* was labeled an "anti-musical about anti-heroes."[5] This view arises from the implicit premise that musicals, by definition, work securely within a mainstream and adhere to a specifically American set of tropes regarding behavior, motivation, and musical expression. Yet, even given this strangely restrictive premise, the characterization is wrong on both counts. The figures presented in *Assassins* are not anti-heroes, exactly, in the way defined by Gary Cooper in *High Noon* or Clint Eastwood in *Dirty Harry,* who renounce their commitment to community. Rather, these are people who desperately want *in* to American society, and will kill to do it. Moreover, as a musical, *Assassins* builds deftly and knowingly on existing traditions. Sondheim's signal achievements in musicals have been his consistent ability to build character into song (after an early embarrassment over "I Feel Pretty" in *West Side Story*), and to do so with consummate verbal skill built solidly on the traditions established from Gilbert through Cole Porter. *Assassins,* far from being an exception to this, plays directly on these strengths and is one of Sondheim's strongest demonstrations of how much can be done while adhering closely to the traditions of the American musical.

The failure of *Assassins* to reach Broadway despite its off-Broadway success has been ascribed in part to its timing, as its opening coincided with a historical moment of intense patriotic feeling in America (the Persian Gulf crisis and the "Desert Storm" military operation in Kuwait and Iraq). *Assassins* is a show easily misunderstood as unpatriotic; in any case, America had a serviceable exterior villain in Iraq's Saddam Hussein, and few had an inclination then to contemplate the monster within. There have since been many successful mountings of the show in repertory, however, and plans were underway to revive the show for Broadway when the attacks occurred on the World Trade Center and the Pentagon, September 11, 2001, scuttling many Broadway shows but most of all this one, as those tragic events brought back the blinkered patriotism of the "Desert Storm" episode in even more intense form. Perhaps *Assassins* will never be a popular show, but it engages with rare intelligence a topic that exhibits no inclination to disappear or become less critical to America's continued health: the violent underside of the American dream.

Part of the problem *Assassins* has had to contend with involves the subtradition it seems closest to, that of Weill and Brecht, and of Blitzstein's *The Cradle Will Rock* (see chapter 5, pp. 110–18), in which characters are primarily understood to represent something else, and where automatic and often unquestioning sympathy is accorded to the disenfranchised.[6] Understood within this tradition, the show's main characters will be seen as glorified, with any indications to the contrary offering only confusion to a message already received and misread. Yet Sondheim departs markedly from the heavily politicized tradition of Brecht (and Blitzstein, as well, by implication):

> One of my objections to Brecht is that it's always politics to the forefront and the characters to the rear, and what I hope we have done with *Assassins* is to put the characters to the forefront and the political and social statements all around.[7]

The principal characters in *Assassins*—that is, the assassins themselves—are indeed placed in the forefront, most of all by virtue of their being actual historical figures (as opposed to, say, "Larry Foreman"), whose circumstances are given a genuine presence in the show, not only through deriving their verbal material whenever possible from their own writings, but also through a careful deployment of musical types. In telling its version of the story of America, *Assassins* uses musical styles to evoke different periods, locating its characters within a recognizable musico-historical landscape at the same time that that landscape is made to seem eerily distressed.

Sondheim's broader reputation comes into play here, as both a musical modernist and a master of Broadway pastiche—the latter manifest in his particularly sure touch for re-creating song genres and subgenres, often imitating the styles of particular composers.[8] Even if these two highly profiled aspects of his style might seem incompatible, since the one brokers innovation and the other imitation, they are ideal for producing, in combination, the slightly askew versions of the normal that define the disturbed outsiders of *Assassins* in musical terms. The general approach of distorting well-known types, serving both as a musical marker for modernism and as a nuanced setting of character and worldview, has a venerated twentieth-century history, with exemplars ranging from Berg's *Wozzeck* and the aforementioned *Dreigroschenoper* and *The Cradle Will Rock*. If Sondheim's technique thus helps reinforce a perceived connection to the Brecht-Blitzstein tradition, however, it also helps distance *Assassins* from the latter, through its even more forcefully stated basis in models, procedures, and themes deriving from the mainstream traditions of the American musical (cf. Jud's "Lonely Room" in *Oklahoma!*). Even with its distortions, the musical fabric of *Assassins* is one we know well, especially on the Broadway stage. Those distortions, in coordination with dramatic context, invite us to look closely at the seams of that fabric, and to notice that those seams are tearing and pulling apart. In bringing these characters face to face with each other, *Assassins* may be understood to create a makeshift fabric consisting of only those strained seams, a grotesque parody of its source material, similar in kind to Sondheim's distorted pastiche, but extended to a larger level.

Assassins begins with an "Opening" rather than an overture,[9] set in the shooting gallery of a carnival midway. The scene thus brings together the carnival and America's gun culture, two mainstream American institutions that are linked in their blending of a specifically American promise of rights and entitlements with something roguish and unsavory. Indeed, the carnival merry-go-round tune that opens the show carries both ingredients of this blend, as its oddly familiar, mechanized waltz idiom seems somehow a cheapening of something much more venerated than what we would normally find in such a setting, even if we don't recognize it immediately. But we will be reminded soon enough of what the waltz is based on, when the "Opening" segues into "Hail to the Chief," the official march tune used to honor the President of the United States—and of which, if we care to notice, the carnival tune is a cheesy variation.[10] Thus, we may infer, the carnival is to serve as a nightmarish metaphor for America, and the shooting gallery as its promise of opportunity. As the huckstering proprietor of the shooting gallery begins to goad his customers, one by one, to "C'mere and kill a President," we meet each of the main characters: Leon Czolgosz (who assassinated McKinley in 1901), John Hinckley (who wounded Reagan, 1981), Charles Guiteau (James Garfield, 1881), Giuseppe Zangara (missed Roosevelt, 1933), Lynette "Squeaky" Fromme and Sara Moore (missed Ford, 1975, in separate attempts), Samuel Byck (failed to kill Nixon, 1974), and John Wilkes Booth (Lincoln, 1865). The choices for this community of the discontented are intriguing ones, drawing only on presidential assassins and would-be assassins, including all three of the successful assassins before Lee Harvey Oswald (Kennedy, 1963) and the most publicized of the unsuccessful attempts. Especially noteworthy is the fact that Oswald is *not* included at this point; his recruitment will come later, as the show's culminating dramatic event. Of those assembled at the opening, Booth becomes the leader almost by default, providing a semi-respectable figurehead for their "movement."

As the proprietor hands out his guns, he also introduces a suave soft-shoe number as part of his sales pitch, based on a reductive version of the

♩ 7.14
♩ 7.15

inalienable rights identified in America's *Declaration of Independence*: "Ev'rybody's got the right to be happy," set as a fox trot. Booth is the first among the assassins to take up the tune, but by the end they are all singing it, having formed a standard Broadway community: the chorus line. The number unfolds continuously, stitching together the carnivalesque variation of "Hail to the Chief," the abrasive huckstering pitch of the shooting-gallery proprietor with his sloganeering soft-shoe, and the concluding chorus line of assassins. In one number, we thus witness the recruitment of the show's community of outsiders, and are shown what they all have in common: a discontent regarding their own share of America's promise of individual fulfillment, and the belief that a gun aimed at the top of America's hierarchy will solve their problems. The number may be seen as a perverse version of Harold Hill's "Ya Got Trouble," and its reprise as an introduction to "Seventy-Six Trombones," recalling as well both the huckstering peddler in *Oklahoma!* and the pairing of huckstering salesmanship and religion in "Guys and Dolls." It is in any case instantly recognizable as part of America's culture of advertising, trading on the peculiarly American sense of individualized "manifest destiny," by offering a slight but devastating variation on what has become the basis of our national religion: the belief in unlimited opportunity for each and every citizen.   ♪ 7.16

The choice of a carnival midway for this scene is a particularly deft one, as large-scale fairs—basically grandiose versions of the traveling carnival, replete with midway and its less respectable attractions—were important tokens of America's emergence after the Civil War as an increasingly important presence in the world. Among the milestones of this tradition were the Centennial Exhibition (Philadelphia, 1876, celebrating American technology, including the newly invented telephone, as noted in chapter 2, p. 34), the World's Columbian Exposition (Chicago, 1893, commemorating Columbus's discovery of America 400 years earlier and used as a backdrop for part of *Show Boat;* see chapter 8), the St. Louis World's Fair ten years later (1904, commemorating the Louisiana Purchase, and the background for the 1944 film musical, *Meet Me in St. Louis*)—and, two years before that, in 1901, the Pan-American Exposition in Buffalo, where President McKinley was assassinated by Leon Czolgosz at point blank range, after he had made his way "To the head of the line" ("The Ballad of Czolgosz"). Thus, the opening strategy in *Assassins,* as with so much in the show, is to highlight how central its catastrophic events were to mainstream American life, in this case taking as emblematic both the carnival-setting for the third presidential assassination, and within that setting, the patient waiting on line that is both the reality of carnivals and part of the mythology of the American dream, which promises every American his or her "turn."

Even though *Assassins* does not chart a strict chronological path, the first assassination it details is in fact the first, so that the assassinations of Lincoln and Kennedy might serve to frame the action of the show. As will be true as well for the two successful assassins in between, the "balladeer" of the show "honors" Booth with a quasi-narrative ballad detailing his exploits, cast in an appropriate musical style and including significant interaction with the assassin himself. In "The Ballad of Booth," the nineteenth century is evoked instrumentally, through the banjo and harmonica. Booth's motivation is also conveyed musically, self-servingly by his own singing in a quasi-hymnic, sometimes inspirational style—"Now the Southland will mend, / Now this bloody war can end . . . Damn my soul if you must, / Let my body turn to dust, / Let it mingle with the ashes of the country." But the insinuating intrusions of the balladeer tell a different story, periodically drifting downward into harmonic uncertainty before throwing an accusation of personal grievance at Booth with a sudden harmonic recovery and a taunting "nyeh-nyeh" melodic gesture (the latter in bold): "Why did you do it, Johnny? . . . Some say it was your voice had gone. / Some say it was booze. / They say you killed a country, John, because of bad re-**view-ews**"; and, later: "Your brother made you jealous, John, / You couldn't fill his shoes. / Was that the reason, tell us, John, / Along with bad re-**view-ews**?"; and, finally, "But traitors just get jeers and boos, / Not visits to their graves, / While Lincoln, who got mixed reviews, / Because of you, John, now gets only **ra-aves**."

♪ 7.17

Part of what "The Ballad of Booth" sets up for the show is the sense of the actors on stage interacting as actors in history, with the posing and artificiality that goes along with that, when one eye is always looking out to see how the audience is responding (thus, the recurring taunt about reviews); again, Sondheim and Weidman take the actual setting of the assassination and use it as a touchstone of mainstream American culture, in this case pointing to its *media* culture. But the song also exemplifies a central musical strategy of *Assassins*, of providing a familiar musical landscape in which something is noticeably wrong: in this case, this is managed through the irregularity of the meter within a folk-like context, which constantly stretches and compresses the diction without obvious necessity. (While strict metricality is by no means a reliable feature of genuine folk-music, the manipulation of meter here is both extreme and chaotic.)[11]

Other assassinations and attempted assassinations are also given appropriate music, although not always strictly period. Thus, Zangara's attempt on Roosevelt ("How I Saved Roosevelt") takes a Sousa march as its starting point ("El Capitan"),[12] in the same meter and tempo as "Seventy-Six Trombones," while Charles Guiteau sings a hymn based on his own poem written while he awaited execution, and exits with a cakewalk / ragtime shuffle, only slightly ahead of its time for 1881 ("The Ballad of Guiteau"). But by far the most telling numbers in this regard are the early "Gun Song," Hinckley and Fromme's "Unworthy of Your Love" midway through, and "Another National Anthem," which serves as the true "Seventy-Six Trombones" of the show, sung by the entire cast of assassins just prior to their recruitment of Oswald. In most cases, specific models for Sondheim's approach may be found within the mainstream tradition; thus, in addition to those already given, we may note that the balladeer's banjo and Guiteau's cakewalk recall the general strategy and period idioms of *Show Boat*.

The "Gun Song" builds gradually from an opening brooding monologue by Czolgosz ("It takes a lot of men to make a gun"), accumulating characters and their divergent perspectives on the guns they hold in their hands. When Booth enters, he moves smoothly into a suave waltz tune redolent of the late nineteenth century, rendered nostalgic and faintly disturbing by a chromatically descending bass, but buoyed by the occasional lilting lift on the second beat: "And all you have to do is / Move your little finger, / Move your little finger and (*Click!*) / You can change the world." The tempo changes as Guiteau enters, singing a flighty paean to guns—"What a wonder is a gun!" Since all three of these sing in a triple-meter waltz idiom, we might expect that the number is being set up as a combination-song, in which the three separate tunes will eventually be sung together. But the obsessive fascination each has with his gun has mainly its scariness to connect it with the other two, so that combining them could only diffuse what are already three chillingly isolated profiles: Czolgosz's moody contemplation of how one gun connects backward to the many lives it consumes in its manufacturing, and forward to the "just one more" it might consume; Booth's fascination with its magnifying power, able to turn the course of the world on a single small gesture; and Guiteau's giddy infatuation with his moment in the spotlight: "First of all, when you've a gun, (sudden silence as he points the gun at the audience) / Ev'rybody pays attention." But Booth's more lyrical waltz song does serve to bring the three assassins together around a point midway between Czolgosz's more brooding contribution and the faster and more lightly European variety of waltz sung by Guiteau. As the three move suavely together in close harmony, they present a parody of another classic trope of musicals, the achievement of community through an enactment of social dance, made creepy here because the visual element is at odds with the musical enactment of community, since each assassin is singing to his own gun with an undercurrent of hymnic reverence. We are suddenly, it would seem, in the smokehouse with Jud and Curly in *Oklahoma!,* when "Pore Jud" similarly projects—and with a similar patina of religious feeling— a false community of individuals of quite disparate perspectives who do not, in reality, harmonize with each other.

♪ 7.18

♪ 7.19

If these three are not exactly the ones we might want to see armed and ready to "change the world," the final addition to the group is even more frightening (if also the funniest): Sara Jane Moore. Spastic, scattered, little more than a bag lady, she sings unrhythmically against an even more energetic waltz tempo (Guiteau's tempo, but with a slightly more agitated rhythmic configuration): "I got this really great gun—*(Fishing in her bag)* / Shit, where is it?" With her addition to the group, one of the most familiar staples of American music-making takes shape, albeit somewhat unconventionally: the barbershop quartet, established in *The Music Man* as having the hypnotic power to bring together the most divergent individuals into close musical and personal harmony. As they all sing Booth's waltz tune together, a capella (that is, without accompaniment), the image becomes a nightmare version of the American ideal, of separate individuals united in common cause. Their narrow focus on the guns they hold, whose menace is unexpectedly reinforced (as in the smokehouse scene in *Oklahoma!,* just after "Pore Jud") by the shock of actual gunfire (Moore: "Shit, I shot it . . ."), comes across as a kind of autism, underscoring their failure to connect even within a musical idiom that connotes connectedness.

♪ 7.20

Both musically and dramatically, the number seems perfectly conceived and shaped, moving through its four sharply drawn individual perspectives arranged so as to produce a steady crescendo of hysteria—from Czolgosz's sullen moodiness and Booth's suave reverence, to the flighty Guiteau and the spastic Moore—each with its own variant of the waltz idiom, but all pulled back to (and controlled within) Booth's contribution, the most distinctively American of the four. Conceptually, the number recalls Ravel's *La Valse* (1920), which presents the crisis of fin-de-siècle Vienna as a steady crescendo across a steadily evolving waltz idiom, in the end whirling out of control and collapsing in brutal exhaustion—emblematically also representing an epochal (but not American) assassination, that of Archduke Franz Ferdinand in 1914. Here, however, the collapse is managed in increments, first resolving Moore's cluttered discourse into the barbershop quartet before fading back all the way to Czolgosz's brooding monologue to set up "The Ballad of Czolgosz," which follows immediately. Not surprisingly, the "Gun Song" has been widely understood as an indictment of the gun lobby and the National Rifle Association, whose collection of (presumably) well-meaning cranks similarly cloak themselves in the garb of fundamental Americanism.

The special appeal of the "Gun Song" stems in part from its very satisfying presentation of the very thing it parodies, so that we can appreciate both the generic appeal of the a capella barbershop style and the perverse discord between that style and its setting. Indeed, the parody works well only because the style itself is so well realized, with the characters themselves unaware of how far they are from the ideal they mean to project.

Something of this double-image, but in an even more intense and disturbing form, is also at work in "Unworthy of Your Love," styled as a late-1970s pop ballad / torch song à la the Carpenters (or perhaps Elton John) sung first by John Hinckley to Jodie Foster (with whom he was infatuated), and then by Lynette "Squeaky" Fromme to Charles Manson. Here, too, an important model may be found in *Oklahoma!*, when Curly and Laurey sing "People Will Say We've in Love," idiomatically a fully realized love song that outwardly denies that love. (The falseness in "Unworthy" is of a different kind, however, although the element of misdirection is similar.)

As in the quartet heard earlier, the musical profile is perfectly realized, generically, replete with one of the standard harmonic effects in such songs, the transporting resolution to the flat sixth ("I would do **anything for you**" . . . "Tell me to **tear my heart in two**"), and taking the typical form of such love ballads, with interactive exchanges following their separate verses, leading to a culminating reprise sung together in parallel harmonies. But here it is even clearer than with the quartet in the "Gun Song" that the singers' separate obsessions isolate them from each other. Thus, musically, Fromme and Hinckley are behaving as a couple joined in song, but they sing to their own separate fantasy loves, each oblivious to the other's presence. Dramatically, it is the youth-culture version of the American dream that links them, but as the familiarity of the song itself vividly projects, that sensibility also links them to nearly everyone else in their generation, whose fantasies are similarly interwoven with the idolatry of celebrity. The nature of such celebrity worship, directed abjectly outward and upward at the object of veneration, is enacted musically through Hinckley's initially hesitant guitar playing and opening vocal line, which moves spasmodically through the first six syllables before the enabling image of Jodie Foster supports a more assured lyricism ("I am . . . nothing. . . . You are . . . wind and water and sky"). As with the barbershop-quartet segment of "Gun Song," "Unworthy of Your Love" is an extremely persuasive example of the very thing it travesties, and succeeds as parody in direct proportion to its capacity to indulge in the formulaic pleasures that the genre provides in and of itself. In both numbers, Sondheim allows us, if not to have our cake and eat it too, at least to savor our cake in full measure while we hold it at arm's distance. ♪ 7.21

The parody of "Another National Anthem" is of a different order, specifically because the assassins are at this point fully aware of the hopelessness of their situation, of their place in the shadows while everyone else celebrates their participation in the American dream (in the figurative language of the song, singing the National Anthem "at the ball park"). It parodies the anthem of unity ubiquitous to the Broadway stage: the title songs of *Oklahoma!* and *Guys and Dolls,* or "Seventy-Six Trombones" in *The Music Man*. The sense of a shadow world existing alongside the main road, as described above, is made most vivid in this number, and not only through the image described by the title. Long before that anthem takes shape, the major mode of the balladeer's reassuring story of how "the mailman won the lottery" is shoved aside by an abrupt shift to the minor, as the assassins give voice to their brutal realization that "Yeah, it's never gonna happen, is it? / Never. / No, we're never gonna get the prize—/ No one listens . . ." Eventually, as the balladeer reappears but is eventually swallowed up and discarded by the assassins—a disturbing echo of the narrator's sacrifice in Sondheim's 1987 *Into the Woods*[13]— the audience is left without his normalizing reassurances, and virtually defenseless against the twisted perspective of the assassins themselves. As the assassins, thus empowered, take over the stage, they assert themselves as a shadow community with their own "National Anthem," and the clichéd, self-serving justifications they offer at the beginning of the song give way to bitter bile. Accordingly, their anthem becomes a grotesque march, and wears its grotesquerie on the surface; as it emerges by degrees, it carries dissonant harmonies against its reassuring oompah beat, much in the manner of Weill (in his work with Brecht) and Blitzstein. We are repelled by the march on all levels: by its bitterness, by its profanity, by its dissonances, by its distorted image of the familiar, which carries the implicit assertion that these monsters somehow represent a version of us. But even though neither the harmonies nor the words they carry are affirmative or palatable, the march nevertheless functions as a patriotic march, uniting its community to purposeful activity, and the momentum it thereby acquires becomes all the more disturbing, especially as it takes place on the stage of a musical, where the generic expectation is that such large-scale "community" numbers will lead to thunderous affirmative applause

♩ 7.22 from the audience.

"Another National Anthem" seques, however, into a country-western tune playing on the radio, and we are suddenly with Lee Harvey Oswald on the sixth floor of the Texas School Book Depository, with Kennedy's motorcade approaching. With a compelling kind of logic, the big event, "November 22, 1963," plays out like a musical number but without music—the one place in the show, in fact, that might justify the contention that *Assassins* is an "anti-musical." The conceit here is that Booth, eventually with the other assassins past and future, convinces a desperate Oswald to pull the trigger. As Rose Rosengard Subotnik puts it, *Assassins* in general, but particularly in this scene, exposes "a landscape that exists inside the heads of every American . . . a landscape that contains both Oswald and John Wilkes Booth."[14] This idea of a landscape imprinted on the American mind—especially as it involves Lincoln—inevitably evokes yet another scene, across a great divide from America's assassins: Mt.

Figure 7.2. The book depository scene in rehearsal at the Knightsbridge Theatre in Los Angeles, 2002, dir. Karesa McElheny. Late in the scene, Booth asks the other assassins and would-be assassins for help persuading Oswald to shoot Kennedy, then steps aside while they circle him, offering him a cult-like intensity of support. Besides Oswald (with the gun; August Vivirito) and Booth (far right; Beau Puckett), those pictured are Byck (far left, in the Santa Claus suit; Jeffrey Cabot Myers), Guiteau (Don Schlossman), Hinckley (David H. Ferguson), Czolgosz (partly obscured; Jay Willick), Zangara (Jamil Chokachi), Moore (Sharonlee Mclean), and Fromme (Thia Stephan). (Photograph courtesy of Robert Craig. Used by permission of the Knightsbridge Theatre and the National American Shakespeare Company.)

Rushmore, a formation that also brings together thematically similar figures who do not belong in the same historical frame, yet are grouped together almost as if in conversation (or, perhaps, as a barbershop quartet posing for a group photograph); see this book's frontispiece, which juxtaposes the "Gun Song" quartet with Mt. Rushmore.

For the most part, *Assassins* does not concern itself with the possible constellation of forces that many believe contributed in some way to Kennedy's assassination—retaliation by the mob, Cuba, or the Soviet Union are the "usual suspects" in such speculations—nor does it care whether Oswald acted alone or even if he was the actual murderer (both of which are simply assumed). Rather, we are encouraged to see how much Oswald, as a disenchanted American, belongs to this community of assassins, and indeed has come to serve as its prototype, its enabling force, and its defining focus. Implicitly, the scene does reference the various conspiracy theories, but reconfigures them: here, the "conspiracy" is fed by Oswald's desperate desire to belong, manipulated by Booth with the help of the others, whose intertwined voices aptly evoke an intricate web of co-conspirators. The particular power of the scene derives from this assonance—our collective sense, even as we may discount conspiracy theorists, that Oswald did not act alone—and our sure knowledge of the outcome, which functions dramatically as a kind of fate (as is often the effect of basing staged drama on historical events).

That there is no music for the first part of the scene will seem particularly appropriate to those in the audience (such as Sondheim himself) who have vivid memories of Kennedy's assassination and the feelings of devastation that followed. But it also resonates with the starting point for the most reassuring of American musicals: the unsung, unrhymed ensemble that opens *The Music Man*—indeed, it has almost the same point to make, that these are people who have no musical voice until their own "music man" (that is, Oswald) gives it to them, yet it is they who first show him that the music is real, and that it comes from community (see chapter 6, pp. 144–45). The drama is one of watching a reluctant Oswald resist and then embrace his fate. At the moment he seems to reject joining the "community" of assassins—as Booth asks the other assassins for their help— the music starts, and their chanting becomes hypnotic and ritualistic, like a mantra, overlapping and alternating in a kind of musical counterpoint as they translate from Zangara's Italian.

♩ 7.23

The initial failure of *Assassins* in America was perhaps inevitable, for it touches too close to home, and so has given Americans too many ways to be disoriented and confused by it. Critics argued that it had no viewpoint, and that it often gave the impression that it actually advocated assassination (as, after all, the assassins themselves do in "Another National Anthem," sung directly to the audience). In London, on the other hand, as one reviewer said, "its viewpoint is as clear as a Presbyterian sermon."[15] But their view was also often reductive. In parallel to the smug reactions of Americans to *Pinafore* over a century earlier, who liked to believe that they had gotten past England's class-based society (see chapter 2, pp. 34–46), the English critics identified *Assassins* as a moral tale exposing the falseness of the American dream, as an assertion that dreams of this kind are dangerous. From such a perspective, the show can only be taken as an indictment of America, much as *Pinafore*'s American audiences had understood that show as an indictment of England. In the end, however, this view of the matter is no more nuanced than the typical American reaction that *Assassins* is unpatriotic.

If the English critics believed they understood the message of *Assassins* better than Americans, however, they had an unfair advantage, because Sondheim had by then added an opening number, "Something Just Broke," which established within the show the perspective he and Weidman had elected to take for granted in their first version. "Something Just Broke" presents the reactions of ordinary Americans to the three assassinations before Kennedy's, overlapping each other much as the assassins' voices do near the end of the book depository scene. While *Assassins* as it was originally presented merely assumed that such a common, easily generalized experience would be its audience's rooted perspective, "Something Just Broke" actually models this experience for us, as if to remind the audience of who they are, and reassuring them that the sensibility behind the show is the same as theirs, and not that of its titular "heroes." It remains to be seen if the show, thus resituated, can succeed on Broadway.

As this book goes to press, *Assassins* is scheduled for a limited Broadway run, beginning April 22, 2004, The unusual strategy of scheduling a limited run seems eminently reasonable, given the nature of the show and the traumatic events that have framed the dozen or so years following its off-Broadway run, which include three separate American wars in the Middle East and the attacks on the World Trade Center and the Pentagon in September 2001.

But "Something Just Broke" may not completely solve the problem *Assassins* presents for American audiences. After all, that the locus of sympathy for *Assassins* lies within its audience, rather than on stage, is a point made explicitly in the parallel moments ending "Everybody's Got the Right" and its final reprise at the end of the show. Thus, in the first instance, the assassins' guns point at presidential targets, but in the end they point at us in the audience, the real target of their rage. And the point did register, albeit not with everyone. In a conversational exchange overheard between a couple leaving the theater during the show's initial off-Broadway run, the man's observation, "'I liked it, but who are you supposed to feel for?'" is answered with wonderful astuteness by his woman companion, "her eyes filled with tears, 'Us. You're supposed to feel for us.'"[16] Yet, when all is said and done, the show fails to accord with an important reality of the Broadway stage, that the American musical is generically built on the dynamic of *approval,* wherein an audience is presented with "something to sing about," and is encouraged to register its approval through applause and, indeed, through sympathetic singing of its songs. One cannot sing the songs of *Assassins,* off stage, without a tinge of queasiness, even though many of its songs are musically quite seductive in this regard, and eminently singable. "Everybody's Got the Right," Booth's contribution to the "Gun Song," and "Unworthy of Your Love" seem particularly so. Yet, how can we sing these songs with any sympathy and remain part of the "us" that the show virtually demands that we "feel for"?

The American musical has tended to differ from other theatrical traditions in a way not generally taken note of, perhaps because the genre is so obviously different from "straight" theater in so many ways that are, in most circumstances, much more salient. But a particular feature of the American musical, consistently present across its century-long evolution, is the ability for its high moments—its songs and sometimes its dances— to transfer readily to life beyond the stage. Certainly, we quote from plays—who doesn't know at least part of Hamlet's soliloquy? But when we quote Hamlet, we adopt his persona to some extent, whereas, when we sing Broadway songs, we sing in large part to affirm something of our own selves. *Assassins,* more than any other show I am aware of, presents the paradox of being on the one hand gripping theater and on the other knowingly responsive to the traditions and often latent possibilities of the American musical—yet managing to position its audience awkwardly between the two. Perhaps inevitably, a musical as true to its inspiration as this one is, whose characters and larger issues seem to overwhelm the performers themselves, will leave much of its devastated audience with the difficult feeling that their applause may be taken as approval of the actual characters, and not just of the performers who have given them life. But even more distressing, perhaps, is the audience's inability to connect to those characters and performers through sharing their songs.

For Further Consideration

Carousel (1945), *Candide* (1956), *Gypsy* (1959), *Bye, Bye, Birdie* (1960), *Anyone Can Whistle* (1964), *Sweet Charity* (1966), *The Producers* (film, 1968), *Grease* (1972), *Chicago* (1975), *The Rocky Horror Picture Show* (film, 1976), *1600 Pennsylvania Avenue* (1976), *Saturday Night Fever* (film, 1977), *Sunset Boulevard* (1993/1994), *Rent* (1996), *South Park: Bigger, Longer & Uncut* (film, 1999), and *Urinetown* (2001)

See Also

Regarding *Hair,* see Barbara Lee Horn's *The Age of* Hair; chapter 14 in Ethan Mordden's *Open a New Window;* chapter 5 of Scott Miller's *Rebels with Applause,* and pp. 231–36 of Scott Warfield's "From *Hair* to *Rent:* Is 'Rock' a Four-Letter Word on Broadway?"

Regarding *Assassins,* Jim Lovensheimer and Timothy Clutter, in separate studies, consider the show a culmination of an extended line of development, in "Stephen Sondheim and the Musical of the Outsider" (especially 189–196) and "Alone: The 'Outsider' in Sondheim's Works," respectively; Steven Swayne details the stylistic sources and rationales for many of the songs of *Assassins* in "'It Started Out Like a Song': Sondheim's *Assassins* and the Power of Popular Music" (pp. 115–58 of his "Hearing Sondheim's Voices"); Scott Miller both offers a director's view of the show (chapter 1 of *From "Assassins" to "West Side Story"*), and a contextual consideration (*"Assassins* and the Concept Musical"); Mark Eden Horowitz interviews the composer in *Sondheim on Music* (57–79); and Meryle Secrest provides a good overview (chapter 19 in *Stephen Sondheim; A Life*), as does, more briefly, Stephen Citron (344–52 in *Sondheim and Lloyd-Webber*).

Part Three ·················

MANAGING AMERICA'S OTHERS

Race and Ethnicity

THE AMERICAN MUSICAL has always been deeply involved in questions of race and ethnicity, with racism and other forms of xenophobia continuing to constitute one of America's most contentious and persevering problems. To be sure, racism has long been a worldwide problem, yet it has seemed an especially grievous one in America, since the country's founding on individual rights and its "melting-pot" ideology are so obviously at odds with its history of race-based injustice, involving slavery, massacres, lynchings, land seizures, wholesale internment, and, more generally, often scurrilous treatment of immigrant populations. But America's racial problems should not be surprising in and of themselves, since discourse on racial difference grew rampantly during the very period in which the American colonies were first established, as a fairly direct result of the European imperialist expansion that followed Columbus's voyages, when Europe's exploration and exploitation of the rest of the world and its peoples were at their height. Inevitably, European attitudes were transplanted intact to America, leading Americans also to find important differences, for example, between English and Irish, or between French and German, or between mainstream populations and Jews (or Gypsies), or between European-based peoples and virtually all others, and to essentialize such differences as racial. But America's most virulent racial issues grew to maturity on American soil. To be sure, the identification of American Indians as a primitive people, sometimes conceived as noble but generally assumed to be inferior, was a European prejudice applied fairly routinely to the peoples it encountered and (for the most part) subdued. But it was Americans who enforced separation from them and consigned them to separate and increasingly unequal portions of the continent. To some extent, as well, the culture of importing and enslaving Africans had important European roots, but it was Americans who failed to abolish this practice and chose early on to condone it on a horrifically large scale, and it has thus been Americans who have had to deal, in later generations, with the bitter aftermath of its inevitable demise.

While the black-white racial axis has been the most contentious, pervasive, and persistent of America's racial problems, it has scarcely been the only one. Moreover, it is rare for such problems to reach satisfactory resolution in America—as when, for example, the adoption of assimilationist practices has led to a significant withering of entrenched racist attitudes (i.e., in the case of the Irish, as discussed in previous chapters). Where obvious differences in skin color have been involved, assimilation has tended not to work, since such obvious physical manifestations of racial difference make it easy to enforce barriers between races, thereby preserving not only the divide between blacks and whites, but also that between Euro-Americans and those who have settled in America from Eastern Asia (until fairly recently grouped together under the category of "Oriental"), from India and Pakistan, from the Middle East, and from the various racial mixtures that formed in Mexico, Central America, the Caribbean, and South America, where interbreeding among European, African, and surviving native populations became standard practice early on. And, of course, there have been many forces within these various groups that have worked against assimilation, with motivations ranging from the level of comfort that might be derived from being among one's "own kind," to a fierce preservationist attitude toward customs and traditions that would inevitably fade within a climate of assimilation.

But the involvement of the American musical in these issues also has a somewhat separate basis. As detailed in chapters 3 and 4, blackface minstrelsy had a profound effect on the late-nineteenth-century development of the musical, and the tradition itself continued more-or-less unbroken until World War II.[1] Brave attempts to integrate blacks and whites in the American musical theater, in terms of both audiences and performers, began well before the turn of the century,[2] but in the early stages tended to produce even more emphatic periods of retrenchment. Yet, throughout, black performance styles, even if in part projected or invented by whites (as in the early minstrel tradition), have held an irresistible appeal for white audiences, who found particular pleasures in a panoply of black musical styles ranging from closely harmonized spirituals to ragtime, blues, and jazz; black dance styles (especially tap); and the kind of subversive comedy that came to be associated with African American experiences (often, however, as an extension of stereotypes created or perpetuated on the minstrel stage). Blacks have been admired as well for their modes of religiosity as expressed musically, ranging from spirituals through gospel and soul, and for the permission these and other performing styles seem to give for the mixture and integration of religious expression and more earthly concerns, especially as the former involves bodily movement or overt sensuality, with, in some cases, a pronounced admixture of sexuality.

But what will concern us most centrally in this chapter is not the still-ongoing effort to enfranchise blacks as creators and performers on the American musical stage, so much as the ways in which some musicals have made race-based politics and dynamics a central theme. Of the four musicals I have chosen, the first two engage with this issue specifically in terms of America's most prominent "color-line"—between black and white—while the later two confront other race-based or ethnic conflicts, and to some extent thereby broaden the issue of racial prejudice for Americans while at the same time remaining clearly grounded in their specific contexts. In different ways, each of these four musicals has been seen as a central breakthrough in the aspirational history of the American musical, for reasons seemingly independent of the societal problems they address. But, surely, this is no coincidence; rather, the seriousness of the issues they engage has tended to impel sensitive treatment, while the kind of socially responsible ambition that conceived and executed these landmark musicals has tended to be matched by a commensurate artistic ambition. Perhaps, as well, the seriousness of the issues involved has simply kept less assured practitioners from either attempting to treat them or succeeding in such attempts. The political and artistic ambitions that fueled these shows are evident in their inspirations, which in each case involved a well-known literary property.

Show Boat (1927), for example, has been widely seen as *the* breakthrough in the history of the American musical, establishing in one show not only the point when the American musical "grows up," but also the advent of the "book musical" with an integrated musical score, and the first secure base for the practice of staging revivals of important musicals from the past. Besides racial politics, the show introduces other troubling issues, such as broken marriages and the destructive effects of gambling and alcoholism. Moreover, its creative team was top drawer. Jerome Kern (music) was the most revered composer then working on Broadway. Oscar Hammerstein II (book and lyrics), already a major force on Broadway, went on to make an even bigger impact in his partnership with Richard Rodgers. The producer Florence Ziegfeld had already undertaken a leadership role in the effort to integrate the Broadway stage racially. And the 1926 book that the show was based on, by Edna Ferber, was then considered a major literary property.

Porgy and Bess (1935) was also based on a well-respected literary property, by DuBose Heyward, which was turned into a highly successful play in the same year that *Show Boat* opened (*Porgy*, 1927). Its composer, George Gershwin, had reluctantly abandoned plans to compose an operatic musical for the Met, and this show reflects that lingering ambition, marking the first serious attempt to "elevate" the American musical all the way to opera.

The literary source for *West Side Story* (1957) was even more venerated, if considerably older and more loosely adapted than the others (Shakespeare's *Romeo and Juliet*). Its creative team included the best talent working on Broadway in the 1950s, including Leonard Bernstein (the most significant "cross-over" composer since Gershwin, whom he would eventually eclipse in many respects), the then-unknown Stephen Sondheim (who took over writing the lyrics from Bernstein, but was given full credit by a generous and prescient Bernstein), Jerome Robbins (director-choreographer; arguably the most important Broadway choreographer ever), and the prolific and prodigious Arthur Laurents (book; working as both writer and director on Broadway, and in Hollywood as a writer). Its dance element is perhaps the most ambitious contribution of *West Side Story;* the degree and subtlety with which dance not only establishes character and situation, but also develops theme and plot, set a new standard for the American musical stage.

Fiddler on the Roof (1964) is in some respects the poor relative in this group. True enough, its (non-English) literary basis is much venerated, but is neither as elevated as Shakespeare nor as obviously relevant for mainstream American audiences as either Ferber or Heyward, drawing directly on Sholom Aleichem's stories, in Yiddish, about Tevye the Dairyman. Nor did the creative team, however talented and prominent their careers, have quite the same star-power as the three other shows, apart from producer Harold Prince and director-choreographer Jerome Robbins; thus, Jerry Bock wrote the music, Sheldon Harnick the lyrics, and Joseph Stein the book. But it yields to none in terms of either its thematic relevance here or its nuanced treatment of racial and ethnic themes.

Predictably, none of these shows is optimistic, since the problems each addresses are still very much with us; arguably (if not technically), they are all tragedies, which alone makes them a statistical aberration on Broadway. Nor were they all popular successes or widely embraced when they first appeared. *Porgy and Bess* went through many transformations across several decades before the effectiveness of the original show became widely recognized. *West Side Story* had a respectable run but lost out to *The Music Man* for all the major awards in 1957,[3] and only gradually came to be regarded as a classic (with help from both its many musical hits and the film version, which took its explosive dance sequences into the street and exposed them to a wider public). *Fiddler on the Roof,* although its long run would establish a new record for the Broadway musical, was initially seen to have only limited appeal, and its early success was for a time ascribed primarily to Zero Mostel's performance as Tevye. Moreover, the first three of these shows have been widely attacked for the presumption of their writers to create language, music, and characters that would truly represent their maligned constituencies (blacks for the first two, Puerto Rican immigrants for *West Side Story*). Black cast members in the first production of *Show Boat* refused to sing the very first word, "Niggers." The dialect of *Porgy and Bess* has been condemned as offensive, and the entire project as exploitative, a kind of high-art blackface minstrelsy. And the allusions to the primitive living conditions of Puerto Rico in *West Side Story* ("wall-to-wall floors in America") have been seen as either ignorant or shamelessly pandering to the presumed prejudices of its American audience. That *Fiddler on the Roof* escapes similar reactions is largely due to the strong Jewish presence on the creative team, and to its careful withholding of judgment on Tevye's hardline anti-assimilationist position. In many ways, despite the copious humor and wonderful music offered by all four of these shows, they are difficult to mount and demanding of both performers and audiences, easily touching off intense reactions in the latter, whether of outraged anger or admiration.

Show Boat (1927), although much venerated and often revived, has long been understood as dramatically weak, lacking an adequate or convincing second act. In broadest terms, this is because the show seems to point generically to a happy ending as it recalls America's hopeful reemergence in the generation after the Civil War, but then sabotages this optimistic trajectory with fairly honest presentations of two fundamental American problems, so that, in the later stages, it must try to snatch the semblance of a happy ending out of the jaws of tragedy. The bittersweet ending quite reasonably seems to acknowledge that some problems cannot be solved, at least not for those whose lives have already been rent asunder. In accepting that condition, however, it has to disconnect with the optimism of the first act, and with the generic expectation that when problems emerge late in the first act of a musical, they will be solved in the second act.

The two "problems" that *Show Boat* confronts are, first, the difficulty of achieving true racial blending in America and, second, America's enchantment with fantasy and make-believe, which impairs its capacity to distinguish between appearance and reality. To some extent, these issues blend within the figures of Julie La Verne, the sultry female star of the *Cotton Blossom* (*Show Boat*'s showboat), who is a fair-skinned black passing for white, and Magnolia Hawks, the show's female lead and Captain Andy's daughter, whose naïveté encourages her to associate freely with blacks, learning their music and free-styled dancing. But the two issues are mostly presented separately within a pair of marriage tropes; in this case, emblematically, both marriages ultimately fail: Julie's to her co-star Steve Baker, a white who suspects her of infidelity, and Magnolia's to Gaylord Ravenal, a handsome gambler incapable of leading a settled life. The symbolic presence of the river serves both themes, as well, offering most vividly an escape into fantasy (via the *Cotton Blossom*); thus, when we move to dry land for the second act, the allure of fantasy seems a less compelling defense against increasingly hard realities, although the Midway of the Columbian Exposition in Chicago offers some compensation in this regard. But the river also separates the blacks from the whites, who have very different relationships to it. For the blacks, the river also offers escape, in its timeless endurance and symbolic promise of release ("Ol' Man River"; see later), but for them it is the reality of hard work that is the real story, the difficulties that must be endured and from which release is fervently sought. Significantly, the river provides a focal point for that hard reality, too, with the very name of the showboat underscoring the opposing perspectives of blacks and whites. Thus, for the blacks—as is made explicit in the opening number—the cotton blossom symbolizes hard work despite its cheerful appearance: "Cotton blossom, cotton blossom, love to see you growin' free. / When dey pack you on de levee / You're a heavy load to me!"

Post–Civil War life along the Mississippi River vividly demonstrated the dismal legacy of American slavery to anyone who cared to see it, especially in the early 1880s, when the first act of *Show Boat* takes place. The Hayes-Tilden Compromise of 1877 effectively ended reconstruction and paved the way for the gradual erosion of the rights blacks had just begun to acquire during the decade immediately following the end of the Civil War. Within a few years, new legislation that sought to grant increasing rights and privileges to blacks was in practice ignored while existing racist laws were fully enforced. Notably, the frank depiction of the stark contrasts between whites and blacks in *Show Boat* ("Niggers all work on de Mississippi, / Niggers all work while de white men play") resonates with another important literary accounting of this period: when Mark Twain returned to the river in 1882 to research *Life on the Mississippi,* he was confronted with the spectacle of large numbers of poor, hard-working blacks, which provided the impetus for him to complete his own great work on America's black-white problem, *Huckleberry Finn* (1884), which had been languishing for several years.

The music in *Show Boat* is itself an intriguing blend of African American and European-derived styles and techniques. Some of this blending is probably inadvertent, stemming from the attempt to represent the two sides of the racial divide separately, but through styles, forms, and techniques that derive to some extent from the opposing side. But some of the show's stylistic blending results from an overt strategy, for it is through music—the ultimate "fantasy" medium—that the show presents and savors the potential for racial blending, which is thereby made to seem both attractive and plausible. Thus, in *Show Boat,* we hear a sometimes quite fluid grouping of spirituals, blues, ragtime, waltz, and standard light Broadway styles, and even pseudo–Middle Eastern music, generally set within standard Tin Pan Alley forms, but often adapted as well to a quasi-leitmotivic technique, in which music associated with a particular char-

acter or mood recurs as underlay, often transformed. ("Leitmotives"—
leading motives—first identified in the operatic work of Richard Wagner,
are short, highly characteristic motives that signal the presence of a character or idea in the drama.) This practice in turn enables music to carry
an integrative burden, making it the principal vehicle for crossing the
color-line, as is established early on with the song "Can't Help Lovin' Dat
Man," which Julie sings to an enraptured Magnolia, but which gives her
away to the other blacks in the show, who recognize it as a "heritage"
black tune. (It is, of course, no such thing, but rather a carefully crafted
blend of a blues idiom and Tin Pan Alley; see pp. 191–92).

The opening sequence lays out the contrast between the hard-working
blacks and the fantasy offered by the approaching showboat in fairly stark
terms. Thus, the banjo underlay for the opening "coloured chorus" reminds us that we are not here far removed from the slave culture of the
plantation; for their part, the whites' inability to maintain clear distinctions between fantasy and reality is emphasized when the "preview" that
the showboat's cast provides ("Cap'n Andy's Bally-Hoo") includes a very
real display of Steve's jealous rage over Julie—itself, as we will be led to
infer, partially driven by his inability fully to trust the love of a woman
who is part black. "Make Believe," which follows on the heels of Ravenal's self-introductory "Who cares if my boat goes up stream," paints this
kind of inability as a virtue, suggesting that make-believe creates its own
reality. First and last words are especially telling here, as Ravenal's opening "Who cares?" is eventually answered by the final words of "Make Believe," which he sings first to Magnolia as a solo: "I do." This answer not
only claims reality for his "make-believe" loving of Magnolia, but also indicates a level of commitment he has only recently shown himself incapable of, and hints rather broadly of marriage vows to come; thus, res-
onating thematically with all three, the music breaks into a brief waltz
tempo with these final words of the chorus,[4] an effect that will be repeated
at the end of their second-act "Why Do I Love You?" Overall, waltz
tempo is used sparingly in *Show Boat;* when it comes in as underlay, as in
these two instances, it is always in association with Ravenal, and nearly
always in association with Magnolia's idealizing view of him. Of the songs
written for the show (thus, excluding the period waltz song, "After the
Ball," which is interpolated in the second act), only their first-act love
song, "You Are Love," is a traditional waltz song, finding an echo in the
first-act finale's "Happy the Day," a festive "valse brillante" that celebrates their union. In this way, the waltz style itself takes on the function
of a quasi-leitmotive, connecting the relationship between Magnolia and   ♪ 8.1
Ravenal as well to the larger issue of fantasy vs. reality.   ♪ 8.2

More generally, *Show Boat* uses other specific dance types (e.g., fox-
trot, polka) and conventional Broadway styles (e.g., the bouncy "Life

upon the Wicked Stage") to establish a substantial presence of white music-making. Even more memorably, however, the show gives a powerful presence to black music-making. Most of the "black" numbers use a pentatonic or gapped scale (a five-note scale without half-steps, a familiar device for representing a variety of folk-based or non-European derived musical styles), but each of these numbers also establishes a more specific style through other means. Most powerful of these numbers is undoubtedly "Ol' Man River," whose general style is based on the spirituals that became widely popular in the late nineteenth century, after the Fisk University Jubilee tours (beginning in 1871). The song seems to be based on one of the most venerated among those spirituals, although now less familiar than it would have been in the 1920s: "Deep River,"[5] which uses a similar set of symbolic associations with the river and, in its best-known versions, follows a similar ternary structure in which the middle part (the bridge) moves well above the profoundly deep tones of the opening and closing sections.[6] In "Deep River," the descent on the word "river" suggests its deepness, and may as well suggest immersion, as in baptism. But the singer moves on from this initial musical image to express a different desire—"I want to cross over into Campground"—which for American slaves in the south had two possible frames of reference: following Biblical references, it could mean crossing the Jordan into paradise (an inverted variant, perhaps, of the River Styx in classical mythology) or, within a specifically American context, crossing the Ohio to freedom along the Underground Railroad.

♫ 8.3

"Ol' Man River," while eventually calling up the first of these meanings explicitly ("Show me dat stream called de River Jordan / Dat's de ol' stream dat I long to cross."), also makes of the river a mute, flowing, eternal, presumably wise but apparently indifferent presence, at once the confidant of the blacks and yet allied with the carefree whites since, like them, it does not "sweat and strain." The form of the song follows Tin Pan Alley conventions, falling into a broad AABA, with each "A" section tracing a higher trajectory than the last. The song thus requires not only a deep *basso* voice for the beginnings of these phrases, but also a voice that can carry the final climax an octave and a sixth above the starting pitch. The song was in fact written for a specific singer, Paul Robeson, already well known as both a singer of spirituals and as an actor, but Robeson didn't take on the role until the London run in 1928 (returning to the role for the 1936 film version) because he was playing Crown in the 1927 play *Porgy* at the time. The song's lyric casts the hard lives of the blacks along the river against the mute, powerful flow of the river. It is with the latter that the song opens and closes, with the fate of "You an' me" set off mainly in the bridge, starting at a higher pitch level and gradually descending. But the contrast is more than a matter of alternation within the

Figure 8.1. Paul Robeson about to sing "Ol' Man River" in the 1936 film *Show Boat*. (Courtesy of the Academy of Motion Picture Arts and Sciences.)

form, as the musical language also changes when the words describe human anguish, filling in the gapped scale with an expressive half-step late in the second phrase (the only non-pentatonic pitch in the three "A" phrases) and hammering repeatedly on that added pitch during the first half of the bridge (see the boldface in the following excerpt; in the second part of the bridge, an additional half-step motion is introduced, as indicated by italics). In this way, the musical line adds bite to the plaint, and in its repetitions conveys as well a sense of the drudgery of continuous back-breaking work:

> He don't plant 'taters, / He don't plant cotton
> An' dem dat plant 'em is soon forgotten, . . .
> **You** an' me we **sweat** an' strain,
> **Body** all achin' an' **racked** wid pain.
> "*Tote* dat *barge*!" "*Lift* dat *bale*!"
> *Git a* little *drunk* an' you'll land in jail.

♩ 8.4

The particular discomfort that sometimes arises when whites represent blacks—even if with the best of intentions, as here—is augmented for many by the appearance of black dialect in written prose, where it can seem simply substandard—"An' dem dat plant 'em is soon forgotten"—representing yet one more way in which blacks are "kept in their place." To some extent, the latter objection rings true—certainly so long as the primary way that blacks are allowed to express themselves is through words written by whites, and even if adherence to reality is an obvious guiding principle when black dialect is so rendered. But we must also acknowledge that more goes into a performance than the words spoken and sung and the ways that those words are pronounced; and in any event, even these are often renegotiated in practice.[7] In embodying a part written by whites, a black performer will ideally re-create the part on his or her own terms, creating something at least incrementally closer to what will seem authentic to an audience. In small ways, this kind of embodied transformation may be easily heard in performances of "Ol' Man River" by blacks, whose substantial divergences from each other and from the written indications of Hammerstein range from their using more extreme instances of dialect (e.g., pronouncing "River" as "Ribber") to their restoration of some elided consonants, so that, for example, "Ol'" becomes "Old." Similar alterations might occur musically, as when, later in the song, Joe sings descant against the chorus; here, not only is the precise rhythm necessarily flexible, but there is also room for additional improvisation, since, as with Hammerstein's indications for dialectal pronunciation, it is the general feeling of informal naturalness that counts.

♫ 8.5

Robeson's own acting and political careers provide additional examples of how the dynamic of embodiment works, of how a performer can create and inflect a character beyond what might be indicated through written words and/or music. Robeson's many performances of Shakespeare's Othello—a part written to be performed by a white man in blackface—for example, convinced many that the part should never again be performed in blackface (although of course it has been), so completely did the part itself seem transformed through his performance of it. Within the context of Robeson's political life, in which he came under severe and prolonged attack as an activist and for his close association with the Soviet Union, he felt impelled to change the text of "Ol' Man River" when he performed the song in concert, substituting, as part of the melodic climax of the song, "I must keep fightin' until I'm dyin'" for the original "Ah'm tired of livin' an' scared of dyin'"—thereby converting the musing, philosophical persona of Joe to one of resistance and defiance (something much closer to himself). Even within the context of the show, the specific meaning of the original line, highly charged both musically and textually, will seem to be grounded in the character as the actor embodies him, which might range from a conventional version of the shiftless black male stereotype ("scared of dyin'") to a passive-aggressive pose adopted as a form of rebellion.

The 1936 film version of *Show Boat,* directed by James Whale (best known for his *Frankenstein* films; he was also the subject of the 1998 film *Gods and Monsters*) provides another intriguing intersection of real life and staged persona in the figure of Hattie McDaniel, a blues singer with two "firsts" to her credit: she was the first black woman to sing on the radio (1915) and the first to win an Academy Award (for Mammy in *Gone With the Wind,* 1939). McDaniel had toured in *Show Boat* as Joe's wife Queenie, and she again played the role in the film; the part fits well within her characteristic screen persona—for which she has often been criticized—of a contented household domestic. But her career as a blues singer is at least as relevant as that persona to *Show Boat,* for she is involved in the pivotal performance of "Can't Help Lovin' Dat Man," the song that gives Julie away as a black even before she is accused of miscegenation (mixed marriage between black and white, which was illegal in many states at that time). The song is a partial fusion of Tin Pan Alley and blues, taking on a larger Tin Pan Alley form (AABA), but creating a semblance of the blues within both the verse and the "A" phrase (which repeats unvaried). Thus, the "A" phrase is laid out as a blues-like form (aab) in which the first two parallel lines are capped by a third explanatory line:

> Fish got to swim and birds got to fly,
> I got to love one man till I die,
>> Can't help lovin' dat man of mine.

The "A" phrase also allows for a typical blues-style instrumental response (after b, but not after the two a's) and indulges in bluesy harmonies that emphasize one of the so-called "blue" notes (here lowering the third degree) on the key phrase "lovin' dat man." Moreover, the bridge ("When he goes away . . .") employs a standard blues device of steadily repeated chords, here creating a trudging effect, which, combined with the rising bass-line, conveys a sense of persevering under duress.[8] And, finally, the verse for the song, which Julie withholds until pressed by Queenie, is even more directly modeled on a blues idiom:

> Oh, listen sister, I love my mister man
> And I can't tell yo' why.
> Dere ain't no reason why I should love dat man.
> It mus' be sumpin' dat de angels done plan.

Here, the phrasing is precisely that of a twelve-bar blues: each four-bar phrase ends on its third bar, a "response" is added to the final two bars of the first phrase (after the rhyme), and, as in the "A" phrase of the chorus, the second phrase recasts the first, with the third acting as explanation. In beginning the song with its chorus, Julie attempts to bypass its most obviously "colored" part, consistent with her attempt to pass more generally as white.

♪ 8.6

Although the song is far from convincing as what it supposedly is—a song passed down from generation to generation, known only to blacks—it is made to stand emblematically for what African Americans offer Euro-American culture, a relationship that is modeled for us in Magnolia's enchantment with it. In the 1936 film version, Magnolia (Irene Dunne) joins in with the blacks swaying to the music in the full-chorus followup, dancing a "shimmy" with rolling eyes—with an effect almost as embarrassing to watch as blackface (see the bottom "snapshot" in this book's frontispiece). While this is presented in the film as though it is to be taken at face value, as a successful crossover participation, what it instead shows audiences today (and probably then as well) is an awkward lack of compatibility, as her contortions seem all the more caricatured when seen against the blacks' more natural movement. Nevertheless, we are led to believe through this number that within the fantasy world of music-making, whites and blacks can indeed "get along." When "Can't Help Lovin' Dat Man" returns in the second act (in Chicago), sung by Magnolia at an audition, the pianist speeds it up, converting it into ragtime, with the clear implication that ragtime is a commercial appropriation, a coarse cheapening of black styles by whites. While this was not precisely the case regarding ragtime (which in any case developed before blues), the imputation reflects another common line of thinking, which contends that whites more generally appropriated black musical styles and made them into something less authentic.

♪ 8.7

The 1936 film offers yet another instance of Magnolia's "crossing over" into what she seems to regard as black performing styles, when she becomes part of the show following Julie's dismissal (because state laws forbade racial integration on stage). Just before her entrance, two "rubes" who have taken the exaggerated melodrama on stage as real—thus providing a primitive form of the "fantasy vs. reality" theme—have forced the show to a standstill, and we cut to see Magnolia (Dunne) applying burnt-cork makeup as Captain Andy stalls the audience. Her subsequent song—"Gallivantin' Aroun'," which is not in the stage version of Show Boat—is a clowning, eye-rolling, verbally unpolished minstrel number, excruciating to watch. Perhaps it is an attempt to provide, in parallel to the later "ragtime" version of "Can't Help Lovin' Dat Man," an even more obvious instance of the appropriation of blackness by whites, with a similarly inauthentic result. Yet, the decision to show us Dunne getting into her makeup was surely in part designed to ensure that any "rubes" in the movie audience would know it was indeed she performing the number.[9] This scene shares a certain narrative awkwardness with the earlier "shimmy" episode, preventing us in both cases from being certain of the attitude of the filmmakers. Thus, we might assume that the point of showing us the blackface number is to highlight the fact that this was acceptable whereas racially mixed performances were not, but this assumption is undercut by the circumstances, since the number involves Magnolia's debut appearance and is approved of by all present.

The Chicago Midway sequence that opens the second act presents the most famous attraction of the Chicago World's Fair, best known as "Little Egypt" but here identified only as "La Belle Fatima," who dances the "couchie-couchie" belly dance in the "Streets of Cairo" exhibit to a familiar orientalist tune (for many, most easily recalled through its *contrafactum* lyric, "There's a place in France . . ."; apocryphally, "Little Egypt" saved the Chicago Fair from being a financial disaster, and helped establish the striptease as a standard attraction in America). But the climax of the Fair sequence is "In Dahomey," which comes after the intervening "Why Do I Love You?" and provides another opportunity to bring the show's two main themes together. "In Dahomey" parallels the "Streets of Cairo" exhibit in purporting to be something it isn't for crowds who willingly believe in its fantasy concoction: an African village whose inhabitants dance and sing wildly and threateningly to primitive music ("Dyunga Doe! Dyunga Doe! / Dyunga Hungy ung gunga, / Hungy ung gunga go!").[10] Once the white audience has been scared away, we learn that the dancers long to return to their home—which is not, however, in Africa, but "Avenue A / Back in old New York." What makes this number so problematic is the very real exploitation and repression that lies behind its thin veneer of humor, in which the only work available to these black dancers is a kind of blackface *in extremis,* implicitly closing the gap between their marginal place in American culture and an imagined African tribal savagery in an exhibit show whose only point would seem to be to reinforce reprehensible prejudices. That the black dancers are given the last laugh, seems hardly enough redress for the ugly and persistent reality the number underscores, although the scene does usefully hint at a dynamic common to such pandering entertainments, in which the performers come to feel contempt for their audience, in parallel to the contempt slaves often have for their masters. ♩ 8.8 ♩ 8.9

Yet there is a disjuncture between the troubling issues raised in such scenes and the show's seeming inability to give those issues dramatic reality. The subsequent shift back to the foreground inhabited by the white characters, who have not themselves been affected measurably by the underlying bleakness of "In Dahomey," consigns the number to a function within *Show Boat* essentially the same as its function on the Chicago Midway: a diversion whose primary purpose is to entertain. Likewise, the larger construction of *Show Boat,* with its bittersweet ending, has a similarly trivializing effect on the racial issues the show deals with, however poignantly, along the way. In the climactic scene (in 1904, a decade after the Chicago Fair), when Magnolia wins over the patrons of the Trocadero with her "retro" performance of Harris's "After the Ball" (discussed in chapter 4, pp. 72–73),[11] the spotlight remains fixed on the white players, and we are led to forget that part of the cost of Magnolia's success is Julie's career-ending self-sacrifice in the previous scene.

If the fundamental reason for the perceived weakness of the ending to *Show Boat* is, arguably, the insolubility of its basic problem, behind this we might see a greater problem inadvertently represented by the show's structural premise. On one level, then, we might reasonably note that there *is* no solution to the race problem in America—not in the 1880s, nor the 1890s, nor the 1900s, nor the 1920s—so that *Show Boat* has no option but to leave its related dramatic problems unresolved. But on another level, we may also note that despite the extended representations of the plight of American blacks in *Show Boat,* the show's dramatic focus remains resolutely on its white population, whose problems are at each turn placed in the foreground. Thus, the context in which there seems to be no solution to America's race problem is already a closed shop, for this is Magnolia's story, not Julie's; while Magnolia may or may not be fully aware of Julie's presence in the shadows of her life, Julie, watching from the shadows, is always and necessarily aware of Magnolia.[12] It is in its bringing the focus more fully to bear on what life in those shadows is like, that *Porgy and Bess* may be seen to take a significant step forward from *Show Boat*'s laudable presentation of a full-bodied—and fully embodied—black presence within the American landscape.

Porgy and Bess (1935) is set within the black community of "Catfish Row," a fictional conflation of locales in Charleston, South Carolina, during the early 1920s. Its protagonist, the crippled beggar Porgy, is in love with the beautiful but sluttish Bess, and takes her in when her man Crown flees after killing a man in a fight. With Porgy, Bess becomes integrated into the community, resisting the advances of Sporting Life (who offers her "happy dust" and high times in New York) and briefly assuming the role of mother to a child orphaned by a hurricane. When Crown returns to reclaim Bess, Porgy kills him with a surprising show of strength, but is then arrested, leaving a desperate Bess with few options but to leave for New York with Sporting Life. Porgy is soon released, however, and at the end sets off to New York in his goat cart to find Bess.

In preparing to write the show, George Gershwin traveled to Charleston and spent time making music with people thought to be similar to those in "Catfish Row," with the aim of achieving the right "feel" for both the music and the people being represented. But the latter "feel" had already been well realized in literary terms by DuBose Heyward, a white native of Charleston, whose 1924 book *Porgy* had placed the inhabitants of Catfish Row before a receptive public, leading almost immediately to Gershwin's initial interest in bringing the book to the musical stage. Meanwhile, however, Heyward's wife Dorothy had fashioned a play based on the book, which was to enjoy a successful Broadway run and keep the dramatic rights to the property out of Gershwin's reach for a number of years. By the time Gershwin was able to take up the project, his mind had already turned in general toward the idea of composing an extended opera based on popular musical styles, as an extension of his concert works from the mid-1920s (e.g., *Rhapsody in Blue,* Concerto in F, *An American in Paris*). Prospects for pursuing this particular project with the Metropolitan Opera seemed remote, however, since at that time no black singers were allowed to sing at the Met.

According to the best evidence, the book for *Porgy and Bess* was substantially Heyward's work and is in any case true to his original novel; many of the song lyrics were also his, although Gershwin's brother Ira was brought in to polish some of Heyward's poetry to produce more singable lyrics, and to write some of the more traditionally "Broadway" lyrics, such as "It Ain't Necessarily So."[13] For a variety of reasons, however, Gershwin has emerged in the public eye as the principal author of *Porgy and Bess,* especially after Heyward's death in 1940, three years after Gershwin's. While this elevation of the composer may be common in the world of opera, it seems decidedly unfair in the case of a property that belongs, commercially if not artistically, within the domain of the Broadway musical. In any event, however much Heyward's contribution has been gradually but emphatically pushed to the margin, it is with his book that we need to begin here.

Porgy was a highly controversial book among American blacks, although it has been widely accepted by whites as an authentic account of life in an urban black community, based on real-life characters. Indeed, its main situation was inspired by a newspaper item concerning the indictment of a crippled beggar in Charleston, "Goat Cart Sam." But the account given in *Porgy* seemed unrealistic to those who knew what life for urban blacks in the South was like at that time. Charleston was, by the 1920s, already integrated to a significant extent, with many blacks among the professional class; this more assimilationist aspect to race relations in Charleston was apparently not, however, the story that Heyward wanted to tell. Rather, well in line with the aims of the Harlem Renaissance then in full swing, which tended to fence off and explore the American black experience as a separate domain, his story involves a set of "archetypes" within a willingly segregated community, sustained by its rooted simplicity and threatened by both a hostile world beyond and a corrupt presence within. In the world of *Porgy*, mobility between this segregated community and the dominant white world of greater Charleston seems not to be an option, although escape to New York City—that cesspool of sin and decadence to the north—is. Thus, in *Porgy*, Heyward hews closely to the formula outlined in chapter 6 for creating a nationalist mythology according to the European model, adhering closely to Schiller's view of the artist's position and function in society, as adapted to the differentiation of peoples into communities and potential nations (see pp. 119–21). In *Porgy*, the sustaining roots for the community are distinctly African, and the embodied threats of the urbanized present are just as distinctly white, ranging from the white police in Charleston to the light-skinned Sporting Life, the latter bent on undermining the "Catfish Row" community by providing easy access to "happy dust" (which is, of course, also white).

Porgy and Bess uses the unusual operatic device of defining its central community in purely musical terms, and this in the most obvious way possible: the blacks sing, almost always, while the whites, when they appear, only speak. Besides drawing a circle around the blacks and defining them as central, this device also emphasizes the particularly potent threat that "Sporting Life" poses, since, in a show in which representatives of the outer menace do not sing (not even the "good white," Mr. Archdale), Sporting Life *does* sing, and often persuasively. Although the whites do figure prominently in the plot—their imminent arrival scares the murdering Crown away early on, and they later arrest Porgy, leaving Bess susceptible to Sporting Life's enticements—in an important sense, they don't *count*. In fact, they are moved to the background, as mere accessories, so that their function is analogous to that of blacks within more conventional stories about whites (i.e., as in *Show Boat*). In yet another sense, however, the whites are the only thing that is truly "real," revealing through their inability even to hear the music of the blacks that the world spun out by the wall-to-wall music of the opera is no more than a romantic projection. Thus, the operatic device of continuous music, through being broken occasionally by the "real-time" speech of the whites, who refuse (or are unable) to expand into the embrace of the orchestral musical fabric, becomes a powerful agent of nostalgia, acquiring great sympathy but at the same time denoting something quite different from the realities of the here and now.

Despite this powerful device, however, of aligning the music of the opera precisely to the discourse of its blacks, *Porgy and Bess* is at bottom a story told *by* whites and *for* whites, since its mythological "archetypes" are often little more than standard racial *stereotypes*: the brutish savage

(Crown), the slick, shiftless "Zip Coon" (Sporting Life), the "Mammy" (Serena Robbins), the mystic Porgy, and the wayward Bess. Among the remainder of the cast are good people that whites can easily accept as the basis of community: they are hard-working parents (Clara and Jake, Serena and Robbins), and they share a strong religious feeling. Perhaps a similar set of characters might emerge independent of these racial stereotypes and projections, but the particular dramatic structure of *Porgy*, with a crippled beggar and a whore at its center, seems an unlikely conception for a show written more from the "inside."

The show has thus proven to be a contentious property, whose worth has been measured according to a variety of attitudes and principles. Two particularly useful discussions (in that they consider multiple perspectives) identify a number of important contexts for assessing the show: Richard Crawford breaks these down in terms of the show's operatic dimension, its value as folklore, its trading in racial stereotypes, and its taint of cultural exploitation; David Horn's similar list additionally considers the contribution of its performers, described in terms similar to the kind of embodiment issues raised earlier in connection with *Show Boat*.[14] Taken individually, these contexts produce radically different assessments. As opera, *Porgy and Bess* has been increasingly admired, although originally seen by many as an eclectic mishmash. As folklore, it accords dignity and poetry to a people caught between two worlds, who have adopted Christianity, the English language, American customs, and European American musical styles, while inflecting each of these with something derived from their African heritage, in the form of African-based mysticism, dialect, communal practices, and jazz-based musical styles. Yet the fact that it was created by whites has made its recourse to stereotypes seem all the more pernicious, so that its strong dose of nostalgia (a necessary ingredient to this kind of mythologizing) recalls too easily the sentimentalizing attitudes of the minstrel stage, bringing the show perilously close to the very thing it tries to displace—blackface minstrelsy—replete with its cultural appropriations and, even at its most benign, a strong dose of insulting condescension.

What can redeem the show, as Horn argues, is its performance by singer-actors who create and embody the characters; thus, not only are these performers given a legitimate and legitimizing place on Broadway, but they also transform the material into a vehicle for what they themselves bring to the show, both as individuals with empathy and skill, who command the rich musical and dramatic material fashioned by Heyward and the Gershwins, and as blacks who will be perceived by audiences as obviously more authentic than whites in blackface ever could be. The show may thus be seen as *potentially* rich in valuable possibilities, even if its history has been a mixed bag. For example, the show has led to significantly more employment opportunities and visibility for black performers—who are often, however, deeply ambivalent about the characters they portray, and who perform to mostly white audiences, whose attitudes about blacks will be both reinforced and challenged through its mix of racial stereotypes on the one hand, and well-developed characters with human aspirations, warmth, and dignity on the other.

With the addition of "Bess" to its title, *Porgy and Bess* underscores the dramatic position of the central romantic couple, who according to the conventions of the musical stage represent in some important sense the stability of the larger community. Here, as is especially typical for musicals, the union of the couple stands fairly directly for that larger community, with the climactic love duet—"Bess, You Is My Woman Now"— serving as the centerpiece for its fullest achievement. This climax occurs about midway through, as the climax to the first half of the second act (*Porgy and Bess* has three acts, as is more typical for opera than Broadway)—precisely in the analogous position to the central love duet in *Tristan und Isolde* (Wagner, 1859). Indeed, the rationale for this placement is similar, since the two stories have a similar structure, involving first the difficult path to the formation of the central couple (Act I), the subsequent confrontation with the woman's "betrothed" (second half of Act II; here, the characters' names—Crown and King Mark—even hint at this connection), and the fragmented aftermath, ending with a projected reunion of the couple in a distant place (Act III). But the real protagonist of *Porgy and Bess,* arguably, is the Catfish Row community whose individual members, like the titular couple, are imperfect in obvious ways yet constitute essential parts of a functioning whole. Indeed, everyone except Sporting Life has something to offer: Clara embodies a conventional Christian goodness; Porgy (the cripple) and Serena (the nagging Mammy) provide important access to a mysticism rooted outside Christianity; Crown (the quintessential bully) is strong and courageous, the only one both willing and able to go out into the storm to try to find Clara (who drowns trying to rescue her husband Jake). But what Bess (the weak sensualist) offers is most important, even if seemingly not a positive quality in itself: the possibilities of aspiration and redemption. By seeking and finding a place within the community, Bess herself provides an important model for redemption, and becomes as well an agent of redemption for the larger community. Thus, while on an obvious level her "healing" demonstrates the sustaining vitality of the community, it is possible only because she has forced the community out of its narrow-minded rejection of her.

In this way, Bess, whose soul is tremendously at risk, represents what is most at stake for this community, and it seems important to note that if she would seem thus to embody, figuratively, the rather fragile soul of the larger community, her character, even as it aspires to redemption and acceptance into a Christian conventionality, lies perilously close to a purely animalistic sensuality. While arguably this construction might be taken to be simply human, it is also securely rooted in the suspect notions that have traditionally supported missionary-based imperialism, which hold that European-derived Christianity is the only route to the salvation of the world's primitive populations, especially those of Africa. Porgy, too, is emblematic; as the community's moral and gravitational center, his character embraces central components of its diverse population: he is good-hearted, is Christian but with access to African-based mysticism, is physically strong enough to kill Crown, and is drawn to sensualist and escapist pleasures (Bess and gambling). But he is cast as a cripple, severely impairing his ability to hold the community together, which at key moments matters crucially. For example, he is unable to go with Bess to the church picnic (when Sporting Life will wield increasing influence and Crown will reappear), he is unable to stand up to Crown (both literally and figuratively) or help Clara during the hurricane, and he is unable to satisfy Bess fully, so that her commitment fades quickly whenever he is absent. And, because he is cast as the moral center of this community, Porgy's brokenness serves emblematically as an *essential* brokenness, a center that cannot hold.

The opening scene as originally written shows a community of unreconciled contrasts, easily disintegrating into violence. In a passage that Gershwin cut (but which is now often restored), the powerfully building orchestral ostinato that opens the show gives way suddenly to an onstage broken-down piano playing the same riff (Jasbo Brown), an act of reduction that suggests strongly that Catfish Row itself stands similarly as a reduced and broken form of something potentially larger and more powerful. Gershwin undoubtedly borrowed this device directly from a similar moment in Berg's modernist opera *Wozzeck* (1923; premiered 1925), which, like *Porgy and Bess,* is grounded in the harsh realities of life within a low stratum of societal privilege; at the climax of the opera, after Wozzeck murders Marie, the orchestra's powerful statement of the "death" rhythm suddenly yields to a honky-tonk version of the same rhythm. In both operas, the reduction in forces provides implicit commentary, juxtaposing a powerful larger force and its trivial echo within a low-life urban setting.

♪ 8.10
♪ 8.11

But this is only one dimension of Catfish Row. A second orchestral buildup takes us back outside, and yields to the show's most comforting image of communality, as Clara sings a lullaby to her infant:

A	a	Summertime an' the livin' is easy,
	b	Fish are jumpin', an' the cotton is high.
B	a	Oh yo' daddy's rich, an' yo' ma is good-lookin',
	c	So hush, little baby, don' yo' cry.

Figure 8.2. Introducing the contrasting worlds, and contrasting couples, of *Porgy and Bess* (from Trevor Nunn's television production with the Glyndebourne Opera, 1993). In the opening sequence, Crown and Bess (Gregg Baker and Cynthia Haymon) dance to Jasbo Brown's honky-tonk riff, just after Bess has taken "happy dust" (left). This brief wordless opening sequence moves directly into Clara singing "Summertime" to her soon-to-be orphaned child, as her hard-working husband Jake looks on (Paula Ingram, sung by Harolyn Blackwell, and Gordon Hawkins).

A	a	One of these mornin's you goin' to rise up singin',
	b	Then you'll spread yo' wings an' you'll take the sky.
B	a	But till that mornin' there's a nothin' can harm you
	c	With Daddy an' Mommy standin' by.

"Summertime" comforts in myriad ways, not least for its being comfortably within the framework of a thirty-two-bar Tin Pan Alley tune (ABAB; alternatively, since both halves are musically nearly identical, the song may be understood as a repeated sixteen-bar form, abac / abac, as shown). Gershwin by this time had had considerable experience blending his strong classicizing inclinations into what seems a fairly straightforward rendering of a jazz-blues idiom, which allows him here to achieve extraordinary harmonic and instrumental effects that sound like the latter but derive from a more "elevated" tradition. To set the sultry heat and the rocking motion needed to support the sense of a lullaby, Gershwin borrows the unsettled harmonic idiom of *Tristan und Isolde;* thus, each "a" phrase rocks gently between two "Tristan" chords a whole step apart, while the second half of "b" cycles repeatedly through the chromatic motive that opens *Tristan*. The concluding cadence ("c") is no less extraordinary, introducing a series of nonfunctional major triads (within B minor: D, E, and G—the latter triad supported in the bass by A, the lowered leading-tone of B minor) that manages to be comforting without being traditional, evoking a "modal" character that betokens an unlearned, folk-like simplicity. Moreover, while the song is clearly a separate "number," it "evolves" from the bluesy "Dooda Owadewa" heard just earlier from the dancers swaying to Jasbo Brown's hypnotic blues riff, and so seems to transmute one escapist idiom, reeking of sexuality and drugs, into another one, equally hypnotic but cleansed of such improprieties, as an opposing dimension of the same musical face.

♪ 8.12
♪ 8.13

As the scene continues to evolve, Clara will sing her lullaby in counterpoint to the men shooting craps, a strange harbinger for the conclusion of the scene, in which Crown kills Robbins and is forced to flee. The murder provides another chance for Gershwin's European-based harmonic sophistication to emerge, as the death blow occurs over a series of rhythmic hammer blows that recall the moment of death in *Wozzeck*, delivering a dissonant seven-note chord that superimposes dominant-seventh chords a tritone apart, with a blues-based chromatic third added (thus, the superimposed chords are on A and E♭, with an added C♮).[15] Gershwin's device of tritone superimposition derives from the "octatonic" practices of Russian and French composers (from Musorgsky in the nineteenth century to Stravinsky, Debussy, and Ravel in the early twentieth); that Gershwin was evoking this tradition with some deliberateness becomes clear when the moment of death arrives, which evokes the opening motto of Beethoven's Fifth Symphony (fate!), with its distinctive three-shorts-and-a-long rhythmic profile, to land emphatically on the remaining pitch of the octatonic collection (F♯).

♪ 8.14

Perhaps the most remarkable dimension of the music in *Porgy and Bess* is its sense of flow, which carries song, arioso, recitative, and multiple layers of melodic and dramatic activity within a continuously unfolding stream, with a sometimes fluid dynamic between these various types of discourse. Forms, too, become fluid, as in "Bess, You Is My Woman Now," which follows the basic contours of an AABA Tin Pan Alley form, but in an expansive, almost prose-like way. Gershwin's musical conception builds in part from a Wagnerian (and Bergian) operatic principle, which sought to blur the lines between dramatic dialogue (recitative) and song (aria), a distinction that had long been central to Italian operatic practice and might have seemed a more natural way to produce an operatic idiom using a Broadway-derived song idiom. Also Wagnerian is Gershwin's manipulation of "leading motives" (leitmotives), which weaves associational music in and out of the ongoing musical flow.[16] Probably, Gershwin's ability to manage this flow stemmed in part from his work with Joseph Schillinger, an influential teacher whose mathematical applications to music were especially useful to Gershwin, geared as they were toward creating a musical logic both to flesh out a musical idea to any desired length, and to allow it to merge with contrasting material.[17] While in Europe in the 1920s, Gershwin had unsuccessfully sought to take composition lessons from prominent composers (Ravel refused him, saying he had nothing to teach him), so that he was especially eager to work with Schillinger, a Russian-trained musician/mathematician who came to America in 1928. (Gershwin was quite profuse in his praise for Schillinger as a teacher and recruited, among others, Glenn Miller and Benny Goodman, who also studied with him; Schillinger also collaborated with Russian physicist Leon Theremin in his innovative work in electronic music.)

One of the most effective numbers in *Porgy and Bess,* curiously, stands at some remove from this fluid kind of discourse, and is often cited as one of the closest in spirit to more standard Broadway fare: Sporting Life's "It Ain't Necessarily So," sung as a sacrilegious "sermon" at the church picnic. The particular danger that Sporting Life poses stems from his ability to "speak" the language of the Catfish Row black community (which is to say: to sing), so that the highly profiled "Broadway" dimension of the song is undoubtedly deliberate, perhaps even meant to place Sporting Life as a New Yorker—or even, more extremely, to evoke minstrelsy, with its important dimension of falsity, especially in this context. But the number is scarcely typical in its formal layout (see the following outline); moreover, it is quite subtle in the way that it foreshadows the main events to come in the show (as a kind of prophecy), and offers a deft parody of the community's religious music that blends that music with tropes of Jewishness, managed both musically and verbally.

A	a 8+1	It ain't necessarily so, . . .
	a 8	L'il David was small . . .
	b 8+1	Wadoo / Zim bam boddleoo . . . (faster tempo)
A	a 8+1	Oh, Jonah, he lived in de whale, . . .
	a 8	Li'l Moses was found in a stream, . . .
	b 8+1	Wadoo / Zim bam boddleoo . . . (faster tempo)
B	a 8	It ain't necessarily so, . . .
	c 8	To get into Hebben . . .
C	a 8+1	Methus'lah lived nine hundred years, . . .
	d 8+1	I'm preachin' dis sermon to show, . . .
	a 8+1	(dance)
	d 5	I'm preachin' dis sermon to show,
		It ain't necessarily . . . (cut off)

The Bible stories that Sporting Life casts in doubt lay out the key elements of the remaining plot of *Porgy and Bess:* the improbable return after an unexplained absence (Jonah and the whale, anticipating Crown's return during the hurricane), the unexplained appearance of a motherless child (Moses's discovery in the stream, anticipating Bess's brief mothering of Clara's orphaned child), the improbable slaying of a strong man by a weaker (David and Goliath, anticipating Porgy's slaying of Crown), and the sad linkage of physical infirmity and sexual inadequacy (Methus'lah, pointing to Porgy's inability to satisfy Bess sexually). As prophecy, it also borrows significant and distinguishing features of black religious music, including call-and-response (nearly every phrase) and speaking in tongues ("Wadoo / Zim bam boddleoo"), but in the service of mockery rather than reverent belief, citing stories that would seem bald-faced lies if they weren't in the Bible, and subtly implying that two of those stories seem designed to cover up sexual indiscretion (the unexplained absence of Jonah and the "finding" of the infant Moses by Pharoah's daughter).

But the song also hints broadly at a Jewish connection. As Geoffrey Block has pointed out, the opening melody blends one of the familiar Jewish-prayer melodies with the chromatic slithering of what he terms Sporting Life's "Happy Dust" theme:[18]

| It ain't ne- | ces-sa-ri- | ly so |
| Boruch | attah | adonoi |

Notably, the specific stories that Sporting Life undermines through innuendo are all "Old Testament" stories, the part of the Bible shared (more or less) by Jews and Christians. And, in particular, the song includes the story of Moses, who led his people out of slavery, a figure who for obvious reasons became emblematically central to black Americans (e.g., "Let My People Go"). Thus, on this broader level, Sporting Life may be understood as urging his "congregation" to discard the Bible along with the other lies they have been fed by whites, including the promise of release from bondage. Significantly, this message is nonetheless cast in terms that imply a linkage between blacks and Jews, who similarly had never fully been released from bondage, as events in Europe at the time were making clear. (This particular linkage would hold at least until the early 1960s, when there was a significant Jewish presence in the civil rights movement, but would eventually erode, especially with the spread of Islam among American blacks.)

♪ 8.15

In important ways, *Porgy and Bess* puts the lie to the American idealist notion of a melting pot by underscoring the separateness of blacks from white America. Yet the implicit platform for this message is the ideal of ethnic preservation as a form of nationalist ideology, which the show seems to violate as an appropriative commercial property written by whites. If this seems an unreconcilable contradiction, we must remember the limited possibilities of the 1930s and concede that *Porgy and Bess* is a bold step forward that redefined the possibilities for integration on Broadway. Thus, it has been an important vehicle for substantial progress, even given the objectionable baggage that has found its way aboard that vehicle. And it continues to provide a useful focal point for renewed consideration of the race problem in America.

West Side Story (1957) would seem to present one of the clearest examples of the marriage trope in the history of the American musical, since it was derived fairly directly from Shakespeare's *Romeo and Juliet,* arguably the prototype for this plot device. Thus, in both *West Side Story* and *Romeo and Juliet,* the two central lovers come from separate groups whose intense conflict provides the principal context for the story; in each, the couple fails to achieve a stable union because of that conflict. But in an important sense, neither story uses the marriage trope according to the way we have defined it here, for the love that binds the two lovers is not truly grounded in the differences that matter in the world around them, but is presented rather as a pure force independent of that world and the opposing factions within it. The situation is thus importantly different even from the mixed marriage of *Show Boat,* since there Julie's blackness manifests itself musically and is an intrinsic part of her romantic appeal, while Steve's jealousy is fueled by the same passionate nature that makes him seem a viable match for Julie; we see in this couple a race-based component to *both* their love and their inability to sustain their relationship. Here, however, the capacity for Romeo / Tony and Juliet / Maria to love each other has almost no effect on anyone's assessment of the larger picture; it is the failure of their union through death, not their love or the union itself, that may perhaps provide a catalyst for lasting change. Before the ending cataclysm, their love ineffectively opposes the hate associated with the ongoing conflict, creating a divided allegiance even within the two lovers (especially within Romeo / Tony). If we are convinced at all by the hope offered up at the end of *West Side Story,* it is not because anyone has been convinced that Tony's and Maria's mutual *love* should be a model for them to follow, but rather because Maria herself has learned to *hate,* and because she has redirected her hatred away from particular individuals and groups, hating instead the very hatred that has divided them and driven them to murder. Hate, not love, is the operative currency in the world of *West Side Story.*

Implicitly, then, race-based hatred is the given core to *West Side Story,* the non-negotiable point of reference for everything that happens. Even the hope for reconciliation advanced at the end, like the love of Maria and Tony, is plausible only within a context removed from the here and now; the most we can say is that it *may* happen, over time. On this level of abstraction, *West Side Story* is no less fate-driven than *Romeo and Juliet,* from which the creators of the musical did their best to purge the "inexplicable fate" dimension of its plotting, including the unexplained basis for its familial conflict and its unconvincing plot twists, undelivered messages, convenient misunderstandings, and implausible philters. Because fate in *West Side Story* takes the specific form of an endemic xenophobic racism, it makes little difference to the musical's plot that Jerome Robbins's original 1949 conception, involving Catholics and Jews (to be called *East Side Story*), was ultimately changed to set an immigrant Puerto Rican gang against a rival gang composed of "melting-pot" Americans—thus, to repeat the epithets used in the show, *West Side Story* sets "Spics" (generically, Spanish Americans) against a composite group who only a short time before would have been regarded as the immigrants, including a "Polack" (Tony) and a mix of "Wops" (Italians) and "Micks" (Irish; intriguingly, although this composite gang has been referred to as WASP— White Anglo-Saxon Protestant—its only identified nationalities would indicate that virtually everyone in both gangs is Catholic and non-Anglo Saxon).

To be sure, there are important differences that result from the switch from Jews to Puerto Ricans, beyond reflecting the headlines of the mid-1950s and determining the specific musical and dance profiles for the show as it would eventually be written, but these differences tend mainly in the direction of making the basis for the conflict more generic and thus better able to stand for ethnic hatred more generally. Presumably, the familiar contours of Jewish persecution would have charted a path both too well worn to seem fresh and too specifically charged to stand for something more universal. Tellingly, at no point did the creators seriously consider placing the show within a white-black context, which would have had a similar profile of being both too familiar and too distinctive. In using as their basis the conflict between Puerto Rican immigrants and longer-established constituencies, as compounded by big-city, gang-related violence, Robbins and Bernstein, along with Laurents (and eventually Sondheim) were paradoxically *not* particularly interested in the life circumstances (or music) of actual Puerto Rican immigrants, but only in their current relevance and comparative facelessness, as the "other" to the mainstream Jets, who (like the Montague family in *Romeo and Juliet* and the whites in *Show Boat*) occupy the dramatically central position in the story.

In creating the musical and dance styles for the rival gangs, Bernstein and Robbins did of course respond powerfully to the redefined situation. Thus, Bernstein used a hard-edged jazz-blues idiom for the Jets (the composite "white" Americans) and a rhythmically charged but generalized "Latin" style for the immigrant Sharks, truer to what Americans would recognize as "South of the Border" or generally Caribbean than to the music specifically native to Puerto Rico. (This strategy was in line with Broadway musical conventions—not to mention those of opera and concert music—of setting ethnicity according to what a projected audience will recognize and accept, without much concern for authenticity.) Similarly, the show generalizes the politics of immigration so as to apply in blanket fashion to Spanish-speaking populations in the New World who moved to cities in the United States, whose motivation might have included, in some combination, extreme poverty, crowded and unhealthful living conditions, limited opportunities for advancement, or frequent outbursts of political violence and revolution.[19] As Anita sings, in "America,"

> Puerto Rico, / You ugly island, / Island of tropic diseases.
> Always the hurricanes blowing,
> Always the population growing, / And the money owing,
> And the babies crying, / And the bullets flying.

But these and other complaints in the song give a sufficiently distorted view of Puerto Rico—which was, after all, a part of the United States and seemed in the late 1950s almost on the verge of statehood—that protests have often been mounted against the show, and in particular against this song. While the song also advances the opposing viewpoint—in similarly universalized terms, presenting Puerto Rico as an "Island of tropical breezes"—its negative stereotyping is far from a trivial matter. Thus, even if we might understand that, for *West Side Story,* Puerto Ricans stand for a larger population of resented immigrants, the show nevertheless purports to depict a specific population and describe a specific place in often derogatory terms. On the face of it, perpetuating this kind of preconception and prejudice would seem to be a decidedly odd way to promote ethnic tolerance.

　　Jerome Robbins's choreography is similarly conceived in terms broader than the specific situation in the show. Particularly striking is the use of vigorous and expressive hand and body gestures to define the Puerto Rican immigrants. While this strategy of representation may be grounded in actual perceived behavior, it also derives from a general tendency in America to perceive many immigrant populations as gesturally more exuberant and colorful, which might be explained in terms of a need to compensate for inadequate English, but which also reflects the contrast this presents against the more restrained gestural vocabulary of a predominantly Anglo-Saxon culture. As for the Jets, their style of movement, no less aggressive, aligns with their jazz-based musical styles, embodying cool detachment and hot-blooded passion in volatile alternation. These styles are first developed across four broadly scaled dance numbers in the first act: the "Prologue," an extended ballet depicting gang interactions on the streets and playgrounds of the Upper West Side of Manhattan; a dance-set ("The Dance at the Gym"), which includes a variety of "American" and "Latin" dances within a "neutral" setting; and two numbers that define the gang-communities separately, "America" and "Cool."

The dance-set is the most explicit in its designations, which helps to clarify how deliberately it is laid out:

Blues riff that is then "rocked"
Paso Doble (a Hispanic line dance, here in duple meter, as typical for Mexico)

> Mambo (originated in Cuba but also extremely popular in the United States; it is during this comparatively "neutral" dance that Tony and Maria first see each other)
>
> Cha-Cha (also Cuban; a more restrained dance type derived from the Mambo, here anticipating the melody of "Maria" and providing an aura of "private" space away from the other dances, in which Maria and Tony can interact undisturbed)

Paso Doble
Jump (a swung blues idiom)

As may be noted, the symmetrical frame contrasts a lively American style with a contrasting "Latin" style (the dignified paso doble), while the middle pair, another lively-quiet pairing, includes Latin dances that were quite popular in America, providing a more relaxed inner section in which the future lovers can meet and interact. In its larger symmetrical shape, the dance-set follows an old tradition of arranging dances within an ABA (ternary) form, with a central "trio" that is more relaxed than the outer dances (as in the minuet or scherzo movements of classical symphonies).

♩ 8.16
♩ 8.17
♩ 8.18
♩ 8.19
♩ 8.20
♩ 8.21

"America" is sung in the stage version by the Puerto Rican women as they argue the relative merits of Manhattan and Puerto Rico, but is converted for the film into a number that pits the Sharks against their girlfriends, with the women on the American side. The opening "seis," which combines a variety of duple and triple metrical configurations, is in this case a particularly appropriate choice, since the seis was indeed quite popular in Puerto Rico, and was often used, as here, for the delivery of sly insults, or for improvising argumentative exchanges (the *seis de controversia*). The main part of "America," however—beginning "I like to be in America!"—adopts a faster, sharply rhythmic style, the "huapango," which originated in Mexico but has close relatives in the folk dances of many cultures in its alternation of 6/8 and 3/4 (two sets of triplets alternating with three slower quarters, with each grouping occupying the same span of time; more broadly, this kind of alternation is called either hemiola or, somewhat archaically, sesquialtera).[20] Bernstein manipulates the highly repetitive patterns of the huapango, in which the harmonic basis typically reduces to a simple alternation of tonic and dominant chords, by keeping to this simple structure in the bass, but imposing increasingly divergent harmonies against it across the second half of the refrain. This creates a brief "bi-tonal" effect and provides a harmonic punch to the verbal punch line, at which point melody and bass return to sudden realignment (against a bass in C):

> Ev'rything free in America   E♭ - B♭
> For a small fee in America!   A♭ - C

In the exchanges that separate the repetitions of this driving refrain (roughly following the manner of the *seis de controversia*), one side mocks the other's claims in taunting parody, with a closing gesture, a kind of musical sneer ("nyah"), that is twice repeated by the orchestra; notably, the figure that carries this musical sneer derives, like the huapango, from Mexico rather than from Puerto Rico (specifically, from the sweet harmonies typical of a mariachi band). Thus, even though the number is mounted in full accordance with Puerto Rican traditions, the music for the main part of the song derives from Mexico, as part of a generically conceived "Latin" sound.[21]

♪ 8.22

The musical style Bernstein uses to set the Jets is best exemplified by "Cool," which uses a "cool jazz" idiom (a subspecies of bebop that took root in the 1940s), but also employs modernist musical techniques that may be traced to the resurgence of high modernism around mid-century, when Anton Webern's highly systematic use of Arnold Schoenberg's "twelve-tone" system (variously called dodecaphonic or serialist) became a much-imitated model. The modernist, twelve-tone component is most obvious in the central fugue, which is built around a subject that uses all twelve pitches exactly once. While this specific device may well pass unnoticed, its effect of abstraction will not, for it perfectly captures the edgy emotional detachment through which the Jets seek to control the volatility of their situation—and is thus quite opposed to the exuberance just heard in "America." In the lyric (i.e., "Breeze it, buzz it, easy does it. / Turn off the juice, boy!"), Sondheim tried to avoid current slang, so as not to date the number, and was thus eager to point out later that "cool" was not yet in widespread use as slang in the mid-1950s, although the implication that *West Side Story* introduced the expression or led directly to its popularity seems a stretch. (In the film version, this number was moved to the second half in an attempt to create a more continuous buildup to the final climax.)

♪ 8.23

Even though Bernstein "borrowed" much of the music in *West Side Story* from music he originally intended for elsewhere, the show maintains a very high degree of musical integration, as many studies have shown in a variety of ways. Except for the two songs borrowed from the nearly contemporaneous *Candide* ("One Hand, One Heart" and a much revised "Gee, Officer Krupke"), most of these borrowings were from the 1940s, including many of the individual dances for the gym scene (originally for an uncompleted ballet on a Cuban theme, around 1941), "Somewhere" (from around 1944), and "Maria" (an early idea for the show, around 1949). The show's oft-remarked motivic integration is somewhat different from the nineteenth-century models it is most often compared to (e.g., Wagner), however, even though it serves a similar dramatic and integrative function; rather, Bernstein's manipulation of two related three-note cells is based to some extent on the practice of Webern and his mid-century disciples. The most important of these cells is the "tritone / half-step" cell that occurs throughout, with the related opening melodic gesture of "Somewhere" (minor-seventh / half-step) figuring somewhat separately, at a deliberate remove from the central conflict:

Example 8.1. Motivic cells in Leonard Bernstein and Stephen Sondheim, West Side Story

(Example 8.1, *continued*)

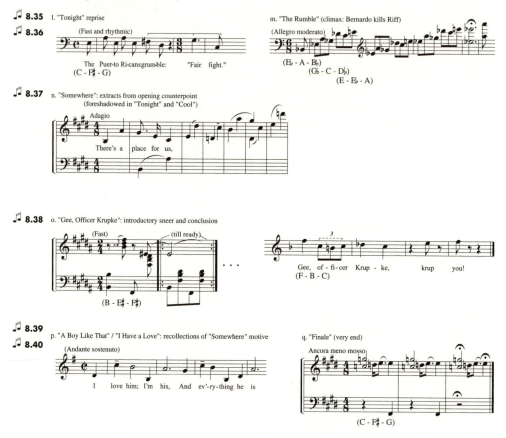

As might be expected, both of these cells figure prominently in the twelve-note fugue subject in "Cool," which subdivides into three four-note cells, each of which evokes and extends one of these two cells:

Example 8.2. Leonard Bernstein, "Cool": 12-note fugue subject, showing relationships to "Somewhere" and "Maria" motives

Laying out the motivic integration of *West Side Story* has become a standard approach to the show, perhaps inevitable for one of the major public successes of a cross-over figure of Bernstein's stature.[22] What is especially important to note here, however, is not the sophistication itself, nor its basis in the high modernist tradition stretching from Wagner through Webern and his disciples, nor even the pointed ways in which what has been termed the "hate" motive (first heard at Bernardo's entrance; see ex. 8.1b) is later transformed into the "love" motive ("Maria"; ex. 8.1i) in a process that recalls Franz Liszt's "thematic transformations" from the nineteenth century. Rather, just as in the musical world that Wagner creates for *Tristan und Isolde* (to choose an important example referred to earlier in connection with *Porgy and Bess*), which is saturated with interwoven and interrelated leitmotives, it is the consistency of the musical fabric that creates the affective logic of the piece, gives the basic premises of the world it creates a tangible shape, and thereby encourages belief—without which support the drama would be considerably less convincing. In this way, as with *Tristan,* the consistency of the musical language in *West Side Story* helps give its events the force of inevitable fate, the sense of "How could it be otherwise?" Nor should we forget, in this regard, the integrative power of instrumentation (not only the "Latin" instruments, such as Spanish guitar, claves, bongos, trumpets, and guiro, but also the jazz-based percussion and saxophone) and, above all, gesture and bodily movement. Thus, in *West Side Story,* the opening finger-snap becomes part of a web of gestures that function much as the musical leitmotives do, in similar ways severely limiting the range of possibilities open to the central characters in *West Side Story,* who both move and are moved according to the rhythms of the show's dance styles and music. In coordination with this extended leitmotivic technique, Bernstein's Webern-like manipulations of basic cells may be heard to locate the show on the intractably mean streets of the modern city.

A strong allusive component has also been noted in Bernstein's score; for example, the opening of "Somewhere" recalls both a passage in the tender, other-worldly middle movement of Beethoven's "Emperor" Concerto, and a bass-line late in Tchaikovsky's *Romeo and Juliet,* (underscoring the heavenly response to Friar Laurence's prayers).[23] While both are appropriate for a projection of a "better place" beyond the here and now, the Tchaikovsky reference is at the same time the more obviously appropriate and the more obscure, since his bass-line hardly registers beneath the harp and the soaring violin line above. Yet Bernstein does seem to allude fairly obviously to Tchaikovsky's *Romeo and Juliet* in the primary launching gesture of "Maria" (see ex. 8.1i), which triumphantly resolves the tritone of the show's basic cell in an upward appoggiatura closely resembling the launching gesture of Tchaikovsky's famous love theme; in fact, Bernstein's song, like Tchaikovsky's theme, makes a second ecstatic approach to its "head," this time with a downward appoggiatura (see ex. 8.3; as shown, the downward version produces the "Somewhere" motive in registral transposition):

Example 8.3. (a) Tchaikovsky, Romeo and Juliet Fantasy Overture (two approaches to "love" melody), compared with: (b) Leonard Bernstein and Stephen Sondheim, "Maria" (two approaches to "Maria"), showing relation to: (c) "Somewhere" motive

♩ 8.42
♩ 8.43
♩ 8.44
♩ 8.45
♩ 8.46

Moreover, Bernstein's strategy of audibly relating his conflict and love themes to each other within a process of thematic transformation (see ex. 8.1) may be traced to Tchaikovsky's similar strategy.

The ecstatic opening gesture of "Maria" presents itself as an arrival, as both the inevitable consequence of Tony's earlier "Something's Coming" and a musical derivation that takes shape, motivically, within the mambo number in the dance-set, when the two lovers first see each other. But, just as clearly, their love occupies a world apart from the ongoing strife, and that separation is made explicit from the beginning and at various points in the show (first, of course, within the cha-cha number, when the world around the two lovers seems to disappear). The song itself is strangely embryonic, however assured and optimistic its gestures. Thus, "Maria" traces an incomplete Tin Pan Alley form (AAB-coda, with each of the main phrases only six bars long) that, while based on the tritone cell, resolves that dissonant tritone emphatically after first converting it into an emblem of longing. If the incompleteness of "Maria" as a song tells us how fragile that resolution is, within the larger trajectory of the love story, the following song, "Tonight" (in the balcony scene) produces an apex of optimism in part through the stability of its satisfying AABA melodic structure, in which the subjunctive realm of the flatted sixth degree (G♭ within an overall B♭) is attained at the exact midpoint ("Today, all day I had the feeling / A miracle would happen"; and in a later version, "Today, the minutes seem like hours, / The hours go so slowly").[24] But this comfortably stable structure has a utilitarian function, in that it can support the pre-rumble music that will soon be combined with it, creating a composite that holds the separate worlds in precarious balance within a single combination-song linked by the title word, "Tonight," a combination-song that involves the two gang-leaders, the two lovers, and Maria's confidante Anita (who is also romantically involved with Bernardo, the Shark's leader and Maria's brother). Thus, in the reprise of "Tonight," the gang-related music ("The Jets are gonna have their day / Tonight") combines with the anticipatory love music ("Tonight, tonight / Won't be just any night"), with Anita bridging the wide gap between the two, singing of love (or at least of sex), but to the gang-related music ("Anita's gonna get her kicks / Tonight").

♪ 8.47
♪ 8.48

In the final number within the lovers' trajectory, "Somewhere," tragedy seems inevitable. The song, implicitly a duet ("There's a place for us"), is sung anonymously, offstage, as part of an extended dream sequence that turns into nightmare (a balletic sequence cut for the film version, which converts the number back into a duet). The song follows the formal structure of "Tonight," employing a similar AABA structure and again moving to the flatted sixth degree midway through ("Some day! Somewhere / We'll find a new way of living"), and thereby heightening the verbal contrast between the two (the definite "Tonight" vs. the indefinite "Some day"). The song is built around wave-like repetitions of its basic motive (sometimes in fairly strict canon), overlapping and pushing upward (see ex. 8.1n) until they break against the distant shore at just this moment of release into the flatted sixth region ("Some day!"). This key visionary moment, which projects the resolution of the love story outside the dramatic structure of the show, returns at the end of the song with indeterminate harmony (but not the flatted sixth), and yet again to close the show in a series of three chords on the flatted sixth, but against a contradictory tritone in the bass, left unresolved. By thus re-creating the basic three-note cell within one layered sonority (a gesture recalling the modernist Stravinsky as well as Webern), Bernstein insists on the harsh realities that pervade the show while at the same time reaching aspirationally for something better.

♪ 8.49
♪ 8.50

In only one number in the show do we hear the possibility of reconciliation actually enacted. In "A Boy Like That," Anita bitterly denounces Tony to his lover Maria, after Tony has killed Bernardo (Anita's lover and Maria's brother), and the number proceeds as a heated argument between the two before Maria, almost by sheer force of will, insists on having the final word ("Oh no, Anita, no, / You should know better! / You were in love / Or so you said. / You should know better . . ."). In her arioso conclusion, she repeatedly employs the opening motive of "Somewhere" (see ex. 8.1p above) to state the basic reality of her world: "I love him; I'm his, / And ev'rything he is I am, too. . . . I love him, we're one; / There's nothing to be done." And finally, Anita joins in, to an elaboration of the same motive: "When love comes so strong, / There is no right or wrong, / Your love is your life!"[25] But this reconciliation is brutally cast aside in the following number, euphemistically called the "Taunting Scene"; here, Anita seeks to warn Tony that Chino (whom Bernardo had intended as husband for his sister Maria) is seeking to kill him. When she tries to deliver the message, however, she is nearly gang-raped by the Jets; in bitter rage at her humiliation, she leaves a different message for Tony, that Maria has herself been killed by Chino, and so precipitates Tony's despairing death wish and the tragic denouement.

♫ 8.51
♫ 8.52

What makes "A Boy Like That" effective dramatically, besides Bernstein's contrapuntal skill, is the *difficulty* with which Maria wins the argument. In the world of *West Side Story,* only the difficult is real, and anything that comes easily or seems too secure is automatically suspect. Even the easy confidence of the early "Jet Song" seems much too comfortable

Figure 8.3. Anita and Maria in the 1961 film *West Side Story* (Rita Moreno, sung by Betty Wand, and Natalie Wood, sung by Marni Nixon), singing "A Boy Like That / I Have a Love." In the course of this number, the two briefly reconcile after learning that Maria's lover Tony has killed Bernardo, who is Maria's brother and Anita's lover. (Courtesy of the Academy of Motion Picture Arts and Sciences.)

within its AABA Tin Pan Alley framework. The world of *West Side Story* could not have been created except by artists who placed particular value on difficulty, who deliberately set out to expand the purview of their art in that direction. Central to the enterprise, of course, was Bernstein, caught between high modernism and the popular musical theater, but all the collaborators were fired with a similar zeal to merge the popular with the difficult, to neither pander nor reach beyond Broadway to opera, leaving themselves, on all levels, with no easy answers, and no dramatic, gestural, or musical space within which either a happy ending or a full-blown tragedy might convince. In a curious way, then, the straddling between high and low art that is both the weakness and strength of *West Side Story* well supports its themes, which permit no easily achieved middle ground between the forces at war within it.

Fiddler on the Roof (1964) was the first Broadway musical to run for over three thousand performances (3242) and has played with huge success all over the world. Its central theme might be understood as having more to do with generational conflicts between tradition and change than specifically with race or ethnicity. Certainly its success in Japan and other places without a strong Jewish presence has seemed to confirm the view of its librettist, Joseph Stein, that *Fiddler on the Roof* "isn't a play about Jewish people, it's a play about people who happen to be Jewish."[26] Moreover, its widespread appeal is traceable in part to its treatment of feminist themes of self-determination, a seeming response to the emergent feminism of the 1960s following the comparatively conformist 1950s; similarly, the show resonated with many of the issues attendant on the civil rights movement of the early 1960s (in which many liberal Jews were very active), including racial persecution, diaspora, and intermarriage. But, of course, first and foremost, the show *is* about Jews, however much its story may resonate with other cultures and peoples, and address a variety of wider issues. Among "ethnic musicals" (as Joseph Swain calls this and other shows with a strong ethnic component, such as *Porgy and Bess* and *The King and I*),[27] *Fiddler on the Roof* is unique in having been embraced by Jews as fully their own, occasioning few of the controversies of the sort that have plagued *Porgy and Bess*, or the outrage that *The King and I* has provoked from modern Thailand (see chapter 10). What is most remarkable about *Fiddler on the Roof* is not so much that it played Tokyo with great success (remarkable as that has rightfully seemed), but that it succeeded so well both with American Jews, for whom its songs have achieved the status of Jewish folk-music, and in Israel, where it was widely performed.

In many respects, *Fiddler on the Roof* resembles *Porgy and Bess*, telling its story exclusively from the point of view of its ethnic minority—in this case, Jews in a Russian *shtetl* (a Jewish village)—giving the majority population a small but critical role to play, as oppressors, all-powerful if sometimes sympathetically drawn. Like *Porgy and Bess, Fiddler on the Roof* cast its Jewish minority characters along ethnic lines, if not quite so purely and with not nearly so much difficulty, since Jews had long had a substantial presence on the Broadway stage. And, like *Porgy and Bess, Fiddler on the Roof* creates a distinctive, persuasive, and haunting musical profile for its ethnic minority. But there are important differences between the shows. The characters and events of *Fiddler on the Roof* are not drawn from a verifiably inaccurate Charleston of the recent past; rather, they were drawn from a people and way of life that were systematically erased from existence across the first half of the twentieth century, but which are remembered with nostalgia and deep sorrow. And, however one might measure the relative musical-dramatic accomplishments of Heyward and the Gershwins against those of Jerry Bock, Sheldon Harnick, and Joseph Stein, the creators of *Fiddler* enjoyed two big advantages. They could draw on their own authenticating life experiences, as American Jews born early enough in the century to have been witnesses to the bitter aftermath of World War II and the full discovery of the extent of the Holocaust, in which six million European Jews were systematically murdered. Moreover, they were able to tap successfully into two of the richest veins of nostalgic remembrance of shtetl life: the stories of Sholom Aleichem and the paintings of Marc Chagall. As prominent Israeli author David Grossman movingly recalls, when he learned, growing up, about the Holocaust after having already discovered the world of Sholom Aleichem's books, he came to realize that *this* was the world that the Holocaust destroyed, and these its people.[28] To a large extent, such has been the collective Jewish response to Sholom Aleichem's stories and Marc Chagall's images, and *Fiddler on the Roof* has been widely accepted as an extension of those remembrances. While it is valuable to see wider implications for the show, it has become a central marker of the Jewish experience in the twentieth century.

Sholom Aleichem (literally, "Peace be unto you") was the pen name of Sholem Rabinowitz (1859–1916); in parallel to Mark Twain (Samuel Clemens) in America, his stories re-create in affectionately humorous terms the extraordinary life circumstances of ordinary people, using the vernacular dialect of those people as one of the principal means to achieve a sense of reality and authenticity. For Sholom Aleichem, however, this meant writing in Yiddish, a hybrid language closely related to German (with an admixture of Hebrew and Russian words and idioms) but written with Hebrew characters—a colorful language indeed, but one that had not been used successfully for literary purposes until Sholom Aleichem's older contemporary Mendele Moykher-Sforim ("Mendele the book peddler," the pen name of Sholem Yakov Abramovich, 1836–1917) began to publish his parable-like stories in Yiddish during the 1860s; Sholom Aleichem's own Yiddish writings began to appear in the 1880s. In contrast to Mendele Moykher-Sforim's castigation of the unworldly shtetl Jews who, through lack of education or ambition, failed to make anything of themselves in an age when many of Europe's Jewish intellectuals, artists, and entrepreneurs had risen to prominence,[29] Sholom Aleichem's *shtetl* characters became heroes of survival, and his humor, while often mocking, was also fundamentally sympathetic.

Among the most popular of his writings were his stories of Tevye the Dairyman, whose very name embodied Sholom Aleichem's precariously balanced tone between sympathy and mockery, with which he painted his characters—especially Tevye—as neither heroes nor fools, but somehow both. Thus, "Tevye" (*Tuvya* in Hebrew) means "Goodness of God," carrying an irony that is specifically recalled in *Fiddler on the Roof* when Tevye, in one of his many conversations with God (for the benefit of the audience, of course), asks after learning of a pending pogrom, "I know we are the chosen people, but once in a while couldn't you choose someone else?" In *Fiddler on the Roof,* the particular "goodness" that Tevye has been blessed with includes, besides his poverty and the persecution of his people by the Russian authorities, such indignities as his horse pulling up lame (so that Tevye has to pull his cart himself) and, above all, a houseful of five willful daughters who must be married off (reduced from the seven daughters that Sholom Aleichem's Tevye is "blessed" with, of whom we learn the fates of only these five, each in a separate story). *Tevye's Daughters* became one of the staples in a thriving Yiddish theater in New York City between the two world wars, and thus formed an important part of the specific local background for *Fiddler on the Roof,* since the Yiddish theater, in which many of Sholom Aleichem's characters were brought to dramatic life, helped form the basis for a developing style of Jewish *schtick* (a Yiddish word for comic stage routines) in America, which had in turn often found its way to the Broadway stage long before *Fiddler.*

The other most obvious point of reference for *Fiddler on the Roof* was the work of Marc Chagall (1887–1985, still living during *Fiddler's* run), which inspired both the scenic decor and the title of the musical. Especially relevant were those many paintings depicting rustic and village life, and most especially his series of "fiddler" paintings, the most famous of which is his *Green Violinist* (1923–24), in which the feet of the full-frame fiddler straddle the roofs of two farm buildings.[30] Much of Chagall's work, like the later theatrical traditions associated with Sholom Aleichem, is already richly nostalgic, for he worked mostly abroad (Paris, mainly), drawing heavily on both memory and imagination in his representations of a remembered Russia. In his opening monologue, Tevye explains the specific image recalled by the title of *Fiddler on the Roof*, as a metaphor for life as a Jew in the shtetl, who must try, like the fiddler, "to scratch out a pleasant, simple tune without breaking his neck." But this rather comical and companionable image has a darker side as well, for the fiddler has long served as an emblem of death, often diabolical, a tradition that has many referents in European literature, art, and music (e.g., in the *Freund Hein* movement of Mahler's Fourth Symphony of 1899, and in

Figure 8.4. Marc Chagall's 1908 painting, *The Dead Man (Le Mort)*. In contrast to Chagall's later "fiddler" paintings, some of which are more frequently associated with *Fiddler on the Roof* than this one, *The Dead Man* (or *Death*) engages more substantially with shtetl life, and its fiddler is drawn more nearly to scale. (Oil on canvas, 68.2 × 86 cm. © 2003 Artists Rights Society (ARS), New York / ADAGP, Paris; Photo by Jacques Faujour, CNAC/MNAM/Dist. Réunion des Musées Nationaux / Art Resource, NY; Musée National d'ARt Moderne, Centre Georges Pompidou, Paris, France.)

Stravinsky's *Histoire du Soldat* of 1918).[31] Not surprisingly, the violin is heard prominently in the score of *Fiddler*, often as soloist, and often in combination with other instruments associated with Jewish klezmer traditions, including, most prominently, clarinet, accordion, tambourine, and high-hat percussion (a drum-set with cymbals mounted above, often associated with "boom-chank" style accompaniments). With references to Chagall and evocations of klezmer traditions deepening the nostalgia inherent in Sholom Aleichem's material, *Fiddler on the Roof* fits easily within the tropes of mythologizing nationalism as outlined in chapter 6 (pp. 119–21), contributing to an already extensive mythology of origins for the Jewish people.

While the family saga of *Fiddler* is ostensibly dominated by its male head (Tevye), its key events emasculate him from both within and without. Thus, like his fellow Jews in the shtetl, he has no real power against the Russians, so that, when the latter invite him to dance with them in "To Life," they extend the invitation as if he were a woman.[32] Similarly, in one of the key stories used as a basis for *Fiddler*, "Get Thee Out," the expulsion of the Jews is related directly to the story of his own earlier expulsion of his daughter Chava. Meanwhile, one by one, his daughters usurp his authority to determine their own life courses. If, as seems clear, *Fiddler on the Roof* casts its Jews as feminine in relation to those in the world around them, its young women, in a telling inversion, assert decidedly masculine prerogatives. In this sense, the show projects a cultural transformation from feminine to masculine from within, even as the community is debased and destroyed by the outside world, a plot structure easily correlated with the emergence of the State of Israel in the wake of the Holocaust, and resonant with the fact that, late in the show's original run, Israel's leader was a particularly strong-willed woman (Golda Meir, prime minister from 1969 to 1974).

But the political events that bring each act to a close—the pogrom-like "demonstration" at the wedding celebration of Tzeitel and Motel midway through, and the mass eviction of the Jewish population at the end—serve mainly as the backdrop to one of the central dramas endemic to race-based cultural conflicts: preservation vs. assimilation—a conflict that takes on quite different complexions depending on the degree of oppression experienced from the outside. Thus, in a more benign political environment for Jews (such as that of Western Europe in the first half of the nineteenth century or in twentieth-century America), assimilation, perceived as a merger of cultural strengths, might seem a plausible alternative. In the face of manifest oppression, however, the separatist urge toward preservation will understandably seem to be the only human alternative, for cultural preservation becomes the only viable means of *self*-preservation (in the human sense as opposed to mere animal survival). To some extent, exterior oppression is thereby interiorized and imposed across generations, as this enlarged sense of self-preservation leads parents to insist on an inviolable set of practices and attitudes against the tide of a changing world.[33]

Like the balanced plot structure, which projects an emerging strength in the face of growing oppression, the various denouements of *Fiddler* are a mixture of defeat and hope. The three progressively bold marriages seem bleakly unpromising: Tzeitel's because its fate is tied to a fragile community-based stability, Hodel's because she is in Siberia with the exiled Perchik, victims in a revolution we know will fail (at least in the short run), and Chava's because her love for Fyedka has led her to follow a path of assimilation, in a version of the marriage trope that quite obviously lacks the necessary foundation for success. Yet the political basis of the ending, with its modern echo of the great Diaspora (the scattering of the Jews, beginning after 597 BCE, but especially after the failed revolt against the Romans in 73 CE), projects more hopeful outcomes alongside the most utterly bleak, especially from the perspective of audiences in the 1960s. In the only identified destinations for the evicted Jews, we hear of Yente's plans to go to Jerusalem, and of several others' plans to go to America, both destinations we know will provide havens from the coming storm. But the outcast Chava, who has married the Russian Fyedka, is headed for Cracow, Poland, then a beacon of Jewish learning, but whose Jewish population would be one of the early victims of the Nazi "final solution" to the "Jewish problem." (The latter development was not part of the original stories, in which Chava leaves Fyedka and returns to her birth family, entering exile together with Tevye and Tzeitel; both Golde and Motel are dead by that time).

In drawing most heavily on the stories of the three elder daughters ("Modern Children," "Hodel," and "Chava") and combining and interweaving them with the much later story of the Jews' expulsion ("Get Thee Out"), *Fiddler* narrows its concerns to those of Tevye's immediate family as seen in relation to the Jews' ill treatment by the Russians. But Sholom Aleichem's other Tevye stories also probe the tensions within the Jewish community itself; thus, Schprintze, the fifth daughter, drowns herself after her rich beloved, Aarontchik, accedes to his family's wishes that he forsake her as an unfitting choice, and Beilke, the youngest, marries a rich man with such pretensions that he must deny Tevye the Dairyman as his father-in-law. While these stories are in many ways the most moving and distressing from the series, *Fiddler* has no place for them, since Tevye's immediate family must stand as well for the larger Jewish community. Thus, in *Fiddler*, tensions among the Jews themselves are inconsequential except as a rich subject for humor. Within this framework, the three elder daughters' stories define the range of accommodation acceptable in the face of racial oppression, testing the extent to which sustaining traditions may be compromised without upsetting the delicate balance of the "fiddler." Thus, Tzeitel's choice to marry the poor but hard-working Motel instead of acceding to the arranged marriage with the rich older butcher, Lazar Wolf, provides a model of self-determination and of irrepressibly true love that the other two stories will put to the test. The first test is successful, as Hodel marries a young Marxist revolutionary (Perchik) and follows him into Siberian exile, but the second is not, as Chava's choice of the Russian Fyedka proves too extreme. In the world of *Fiddler*'s Jews, an incipient feminism and even secularization may find acceptance, but not intermarriage.

Fiddler on the Roof opens with "Prologue / Tradition," which establishes the opening condition as a fragile stability in the face of oppression, maintainable only because its constituent elements "know their place," defined in terms of family status, hierarchically arranged: the papas, the mamas, the sons, and the daughters. We might reasonably suspect that this fragile structure will need some adjustment, given how narrowly each group defines its concerns, and how differently in musical terms. Moreover, that the hierarchy is not reflected in Tevye's family is a problem that reduces, on stage, to a matter of numbers: how can Tevye manage, without sons, to maintain his control of so many daughters? Harmonically, the song provides a "Jewish" profile through one of two principal devices that will carry across the show: lowering the second scale degree at key moments, particularly at the approach to the cadence; this device reinforces the parallel endings to the papas' and daughters' verses, each of which expresses a status quo that will later be put to the test:

Papas: And who has the right
       As master of the house   Daughters: Preparing me to marry
       To have the final word at home?   **Whoever papa picks?**

But the payoff for the song (inexplicably left out of the 1971 film, which also curtails and combines the sons' and daughters' verses) stems from the combination-song structure, which will superimpose these four very different perspectives on each other. The result, although opening bravely with a reasonable semblance of contrapuntal propriety, evolves into near chaos: the parts simply don't fit, especially since the papas insist on beginning a bar earlier. Particularly raucous are the crunching dissonances that arise, ironically, when the papas' "Say his daily prayers" combines with the mamas' "A quiet home." Yet this seeming chaos has a larger point to make beyond its surface irony and its slyly affectionate depiction of the perpetually arguing Jew, for it resolves instantly with the key word that justifies everything—"Tradition"—in parallel to the continuation, in which Tevye deliberately provokes an argument ("Horse! Mule!") that is

♩ 8.53

similarly resolved with the word "tradition." In this way, the music embodies the very point of the song.

Tevye's big number, "If I Were a Rich Man" borrows the declamation of the papas in "Tradition" (thus, the title phrase has the same rhythmic profile of "scramble for a living, / Feed a wife and children, / Say his daily prayers") and sets it against a klezmer-like, boom-chank accompaniment, inspiring him at climactic moments to a particularly Jewish dancing style, exuberant with stomping and akimbo arms waving. The song introduces the other principal "Jewish" harmonic device used in the show: alternating major and minor modes, often across melodic repetitions; it also in-

♩ 8.54
♩ 8.55

dulges prominently another Yiddishism, of extended nonsense syllables projecting joy (e.g., "Daidle, deedle, daidle, / Digguh, digguh, deedle, daidle dum"), providing verbal expression when meaningful words fail.

Underlying these specific devices designed to evoke a fully embodied shtetl Jew is, once again, Sholom Aleichem, who provides the inspiration and driving spirit for the song. The song's basic conceit reproduces that of Sholom Aleichem's monologue "If I Were Rothschild," a non-Tevye "story" referring to the famously rich Jewish banker; notably, the Hebrew version of the song as performed in Israel restores that original phrase. But the content and manner of the song ranges far from its titular model, arising instead from the discursive and oblique verbal style of Tevye, which is, again, embodied musically. As shown below, the song begins as if it will follow a conventional AABA structure, but the closing "A" is withheld as Tevye's imaginings become ever more elaborate (four "B" phrases with the third in the major). And, as he repeats the structure, his digressions become even more extreme, reaching a climax with the addition of new material at a slower and more flexible tempo (phrase "C"):

A: "If I were a rich man"	(major-minor, 8 bars)
A: "Wouldn't have to work hard"	(major-minor-major, 8 bars)
B: "I'd build a big tall house"	(minor, 8 bars)
B: "There would be one long staircase"	(minor, 8 bars)
B: "I'd fill my yard with chicks"	(major, 8 bars)
B: "And each loud quack"	(minor, 8 bars)
A: "If I were a rich man"	(major-minor, 8 bars)
A: "Wouldn't have to work hard"	(major-minor-major, 8 bars)
B: "I'd see my wife, my Golde"	(minor, 8 bars)
B: "I see her putting on airs"	(minor, 8 bars)
C: "The most important men in town"	(minor, 8 bars)
B: "And it won't make one bit of diff'rence"	(minor, 8 bars)
B: "If I were rich I'd have the time"	(major, 8 bars)
B: "And I'd discuss the holy books"	(minor, 8 bars)
A: "If I were a rich man"	(major-minor, 8 bars)

A: "Wouldn't have to work hard"   (major-minor-major, 8 bars)
    B: "Lord, Who made the lion and the lamb" (minor, 8 bars)
A: (instrumental)   (major, 4 bars)

The resulting ruminative structure cycles back toward satisfying closure parallel to the way that Tevye's seeming digressions generally prove to be surprisingly pertinent to the matter at hand. Moreover, this turn toward closure begins when "B" comes back in the major ("If I were rich I'd have the time"), a key moment in the song that turns back to the introductory conversation with God, with a wholly characteristic mixture of true piety and calculated bribe (often communicated with a sly glance heavenward after "This would be the sweetest thing of all," as if to be sure God is listening).[34]

♩ 8.56

"Matchmaker," which precedes Tevye's "If I Were a Rich Man," has been criticized as not sounding convincingly Jewish except in its middle section, when Tzeitel impersonates Yente the Matchmaker. Indeed, without this middle section, the music unfolds as a straightforward waltz song in a conventional AABA form. Worse—from this perspective—the song actually became a popular hit, which confirmed for many its cynical pandering to public taste. Yet, the song is easily defended against such attacks. After all, its most obvious point, as a dramatic song, is to confront girlish escapism with the "realities" of the middle section; we might well wonder how this might be done without seeming to pander in its portrayal of the former. Moreover, the song presents the girls' perspective as a dramatic and musical foil to Tevye, which again calls for contrast, and does so with a sense of dynamism lacking in the two songs that frame theirs. Thus, while Tevye sings of tradition and speculates idly about being rich, the girls actually move through three phases: romantic idealizing, more realistic projection, and the beginnings of a sensibility that will support their eventual individual self-actualizations.

♩ 8.57

Probably most important, though, is what the song contributes to the larger trajectory of the first daughter's story, which it initiates, and which will reach its conclusion in another waltz song, "Sunrise, Sunset." The background resonance between these songs resolves girlish romanticism and doubt within one of the most important Jewish traditions, the marriage ceremony, which symbolically combines joy and sadness—and this combination is the central leitmotive of the Tevye stories—in the breaking of the glass at the end, reenacted at the close of the song. For the most part, "Sunrise, Sunset" has less of a specifically Jewish profile in its music than many songs in the show, but manages at the end, with the key concluding words, "Laden with happiness and tears," to create a particularly affecting assonance—a kind of musical rhyme—with "Hatikvah" ("The Hope"; see ex. 8.4), a quintessential Hebrew song, set in a melancholy minor mode, whose text projects the restoration of the state of Israel (and which was, in the event, adopted as Israel's national anthem). In its turn, the bittersweet "Sunrise, Sunset" oddly prefigures two songs of leave-taking in Act II, Hodel's "Far From the Home I Love," oscillating between minor and major, and the dirge-like "Anatevka," with which the show concludes. Like "Sunrise, Sunset," "Anatevka" hints at the melody of "Hatikvah," but to its more "yearning" phrases, recalled in the instrumental conclusion to the first two phrases (see ex. 8.4).

♪ 8.58
♪ 8.59
♪ 8.60

Example 8.4

"Hatikvah" (excerpts)

Jerry Bock and Sheldon Harnick, "Sunrise, Sunset"
(melodic escerpt, transposed)

La - den wth   hap pi ness and   tears.

Jerry Bock and Sheldon Harnick, "Anatevka" (melodic excerpt)

Where else could Sab-bath be so   sweet?   An - a - tev-ka,

"To Life" ("L'Chaim") is the one song in the show that holds the equilibrium between the Russians and the Jews in balance; indeed, it is the only time in the show when the Russians sing and dance, and they are given their own musical profile (including a prominent mandolin, with a sinister edge to it). As already noted, the power imbalance between the groups implicitly casts Tevye and the Jews as "feminine," yet the ensuing dance eventually gives a place to their exuberant music as well. The Russians sing in a mixture of Russian and English, re-creating an effect of imperfect communication even to American audiences; perhaps deliberately, the Russian words ("Za vasha zdarovia . . . nazdrovia") do not include the full sentiment expressed in English ("To your health and may we live together in peace"), wishing the celebrants health but not peace. Musically, the similar structures of the two dances, each of which accelerates through repeating phrases that sequence downward (the Russians' "May you both be favored with the future of your choice" and the Jews' "God would like us to be joyful, / Even when our hearts lie panting on the floor") provide a common ground for the two to coexist. Yet, the music in this regard functions as an analogue of the alcohol that flows freely throughout the scene (it is, after all, a drinking song), facilitating a rapprochement that has no real basis. Thus, it matters both that the union being celebrated is itself the "wrong" one, and that, immediately after the number, Tevye learns of the impending "demonstration," which, as it happens, will disrupt his daughter's actual wedding to Motel. Key to the success of the scene is our sure knowledge that music and dance actually *lie* when they deny the darkness just beyond the light.

♫ 8.61
♫ 8.62

In a series of monologues across the show, Tevye considers each of his daughters' requests for his permission (later, his blessing, and finally, with Chava, his acceptance) to marry as she chooses. With the first two ("Tevye's Monologue" and "Tevye's Rebuttal"), he enacts a musical tug-of-war before he decides to accede to his daughter's request; musically, these each fall precipitously downward through the circle of fifths, modulating to a "weaker" key with each phrase as he weighs his daughter's request, reaching a crux at the recollection of the song "Tradition."[35] The "Chava Sequence," however, takes the form of an elegy to a daughter now lost to him, with no subsequent weighing of pros and cons, but only an abrupt reassertion of "Tradition" at the end. While in the world of *Fiddler*, there can be no question but that this is the decision Tevye must and will make, the judgment of that decision by audiences then and since has been much less certain. From both generational and feminist perspectives, Tevye's rejection of Chava will seem simply wrong, a proof that things have to change, and that the world has to be made safe for the course of true love. But for many Jews—probably most Jews in 1964—his decision will seem correct, for the taboo against mixed marriages was then still strong among Jews, although somewhat weaker now. Even among culturally assimilationist Jews at that time, the prohibition against intermarriage remained strong; for most Jews, intermarriage meant a denial of something essential to their nature. The balance that *Fiddler on the Roof* maintains in its depiction of Tevye's decision, and of its context and consequences, gives its audience room for either approval or disapproval; this is one of its great strengths as a show, and what keeps it from being simply a morality play. In these moments of decision, the audience is witness to events that may be understood as right or wrong, but in any case reflect the real world.

♫ 8.63
♫ 8.64

For Further Consideration

Shuffle Along (1921), *Deep River* (1926), *The Jazz Singer* (film, 1927), *Cabin in the Sky* (1940), *Carmen Jones* (1943), *Annie Get Your Gun* (1946), *South Pacific* (1949), *Flower Drum Song* (1958),

No Strings (1962), *Golden Boy* (1969), *The Wiz* (1975), and *Ragtime* (1996 / 1998)

See Also

Jeffrey Melnick's *A Right to Sing the Blues* offers a contentious account of how race relations have played out in American music (specifically, between African Americans and Jews). Regarding the Harlem Renaissance, see Nathan Irvin Huggins's *Harlem Renaissance* and *Voices from the Harlem Renaissance*, David L. Lewis's *When Harlem Was in Vogue*, and Cary D. Wintz's *Black Culture and the Harlem Renaissance*.

Regarding *Show Boat*, both Geoffrey Block (chapter 2 in *Enchanted Evenings*) and Joseph Swain ("First Maturity" in *The Broadway Musical*) provide extensive discussions of its musical integration, and Ethan Mordden's *Make Believe* offers two useful chapters ("Let's Merge" and "Go Little Boat"). See also Peter Stanfield's discussion of *Show Boat's* treatment of blackface minstrelsy in "From the Vulgar to the Refined"; Miles Kreuger's slightly aging book-length history of the work (*Show Boat: The Story of a Classic American Musical*, 1977); pp. 59–64 in Gerald Mast's *Can't Help Singin'*; chapter 2 in Abe Laufe's *Broadway's Greatest Musicals*; pp. 120–27 in Richard Kislan's *The Musical*; and Will Friedwald's chapter on "Ol' Man River" in *Stardust Melodies*.

Regarding *Porgy and Bess*, chapter 4 of Geoffrey Block's *Enchanted Evenings* addresses many issues raised here; "America's Folk Opera" in Joseph P. Swain's *The Broadway Musical* offers an extensive discussion of its musical integration and generic situation; Hollis Alpert's *The Life and Times of "Porgy and Bess"* provides the most detailed account of the work's history to date; Charles Hamm traces the evolution of "The Theatre Guild Production of *Porgy and Bess*" and its implications for later performances; Wayne Shirley traces the influence of Joseph Schillinger's teaching through close analysis of the music in "'Rotating' *Porgy and Bess*"; and Steven E. Gilbert's *The Music of Gershwin* takes a Schenkerian approach to the show; see also Will Friedwald's chapter on "Summertime" in *Stardust Melodies*. Regarding the various controversies associated with the show, see Richard Crawford's "It Ain't Necessarily Soul: Gershwin's *"Porgy and Bess"* as a Symbol"; David Horn's "Who Loves You Porgy? The Debates Surrounding Gershwin's Musical"; and pp. 106–13 in Philip Furia's *Ira Gershwin; The Art of the Lyricist*.

Regarding *West Side Story*, see chapter 12 of Geoffrey Block's *Enchanted Evenings*; "Tragedy as Musical" in Joseph P. Swain's *The Broadway Musical*; and Jack Gottlieb's "The Music of Leonard Bernstein," for extended treatments with a strong focus on the show's musical sophistication. See also chapter 7 of Arthur Laurents's acerbic memoir *Original Story By*, which begins with an extended discussion of *West Side Story*;

chapter 16 of Scott Miller's *From Assassins to West Side Story*, which offers a director's overview of the show; Stephen Banfield's interesting account of Sondheim's contribution in *Sondheim's Broadway Musicals* (31–38); Elizabeth Wells's provocative "*West Side Story* and the Hispanic"; chapter 26 of Humphrey Burton's *Leonard Bernstein*; pp. 211–21 of Meryle Secrest's *Leonard Bernstein: A Life*; pp. 225–71 of Joan Peyser's *Leonard Bernstein: A Biography*; and chapter 16 of Ethan Mordden's *Coming Up Roses*.

Regarding *Fiddler on the Roof*, see "When Messiah Comes" in Ethan Mordden's *Open A New Window*, and "The Ethnic Musical" in Joseph Swain's *The Broadway Musical* (particularly regarding its musical profile).

Dealing with the Second World War

THE AMERICAN MUSICAL has always played a significant part in helping to define how America sees itself, and this has been especially important in the wake of World War II. Most problematically, in proclaiming itself leader of the free world after the war, America redefined its relationship to Europe, traditionally seen as its "Old World" heritage. Considerable American energy went into the project of rebuilding Europe in the late 1940s and into the 1950s, and of securing as much of it as possible against both the threat of Soviet expansion and the possible reversion to less democratic forms of government. But as the extent of wartime destruction in Europe sank in to American consciousness, and in particular the extent of systematic genocide by the Germans and their collaborators against Jews and other ethnic and racial groups, Americans were faced with trying to understand their relationship not only to *post*–World War II Europe, but also to *pre*–World War II Europe, and especially to the sheer evil—as the Nazis had been widely characterized—that had led to the war and was consummated therein. If this evil were an aberration, as many believed, then Americans needed to understand better the conditions that made it possible in order to protect themselves from it happening again or in America. And, if it were not an aberration, then they had to convince themselves that Americans, conceived to be the spiritual, cultural, and even biological descendants of Europe, had become a fundamentally different people from them.

In adapting the European model of nationalism to their own circumstances (see chapter 6, pp. 119–22), Americans constructed their own national myth of origins, in which a European immigrant population and its descendants tamed a rugged American landscape, conceiving and instituting a cultural and political environment of individual self-determination that officially disregarded ethnicity, religious views, or race as grounds for entitlement. Quite apart from the differences between this conception and American realities, the American nationalist model differed substantially from the European in its fluidity regarding who belonged and who didn't; in America, potentially, *everyone* could belong. If Americans were in general quite proud of this difference—incorporating it into a theory of American exceptionalism, as noted—it nevertheless made their relationship to Europe difficult to define with any precision. Americans conceived their origins as European, claiming Europe's rich cultural heritage as partly theirs, but they at the same time insisted on an essential difference that made direct engagement with that heritage problematic, especially as it became increasingly charged with essentialized notions of national (and racial) difference. World War II made this duality particularly problematic in musical terms, since the richest European musical traditions were perceived to be those of Germany and Italy, precisely our European enemies. (To be sure, the notion that these traditions were the best of European music was largely a matter of education and indoctrination, and much reinforced, ironically, by the many emigré music scholars fleeing Germany, Austria, and Italy who came to America as political refugees in the 1930s and 1940s, each already indoctrinated in the belief that his or her particular tradition was the best.)

The two musicals that we will consider in this chapter address these concerns about America's ties to Europe in both obvious and oblique ways, but from roughly opposite perspectives. That *The Sound of Music* and *Cabaret* were companion pieces of a sort became especially apparent when they were both revived on Broadway in 1998, and it is worth considering here how much the two shows have in common. Both were big hits on Broadway (8 Tonys each for the 1959 *The Sound of Music* and the 1966 *Cabaret*) and became highly successful films a half-dozen years after their openings (5 Oscars and box-office records for the 1965 *The Sound of Music*, and 8 Oscars for the 1972 *Cabaret*). Both have been revived on Broadway, although *Cabaret* has been the more successful (thus, it won 4 more Tonys in 1998). Most important for our purposes, both shows take place in the 1930s in the shadow of critical events on the road to World War II, and each show, in a different way, provides us with a version of Europe that supports our evolving myth of national origin. *The Sound of Music* constructs a pure, good, rural, folk-based, natural, *victimized* European *nation*—the non-Viennese Austria—just before and after the Anschluss (the annexation of Austria by Nazi Germany). *Cabaret* constructs a decadent, bad, urban, unnatural, *victimizing* chaotic piece of Europe that is specifically presented as a *non-nation*: the Berlin cabaret scene, just before Hitler's rise to power. In *The Sound of Music*, we see a latter-day version of who we imagine our true ancestors to have been and, indeed, they emigrate to America at the end. In *Cabaret*, we see the decadent branch of our European heritage, spinning off out of control, potentially seducing us if we're not careful: we see the cabaret star Sally Bowles trapped in this doomed setting, unable to escape its gravitational pull (even though the writer Clifford Bradshaw—Brian Roberts in the film— does escape). For both shows, the movie version heightens this dimension of the original stage version, and we will thus find it useful to consider both film and Broadway versions together.

It is important to remember that both shows place World War II in the context of American concerns, which gives rise to a number of historical distortions and a fair dose of sometimes quite egregious misinformation. This is to some extent inevitable; musically and dramatically, these shows must, as in any entrenched genre, speak the language of their audience: Americans whose experience of Europe had been filtered through a specific set of reference points, and whose "words" for Europe could thus be understood as somewhat monochromatic. Conceived for American audiences, each show had to build its story, characters, and situation around images of Europe that America already had in place. Moreover, their success, both with audiences and in addressing the issues identified here, depends less on their sense of history than on their sense of their audience's *received view* of history, of what they already "know" and of what they are ready to be told. Reflecting the duality outlined above, these shows make two points about America's relationship to Europe, as viewed from an American perspective:

These people are like us, and we can learn from them.
These people are different from us, so we have to be careful.

The Sound of Music (1959) was the final collaboration between Rodgers and Hammerstein, and almost the final collaboration between writers Howard Lindsay and Russel Crouse, who began working together when they took over *Anything Goes* (see chapter 4, pp. 88–98). As a late work by two successful writing teams, the show's underlying sophistication should come as no surprise, even considering the combination of folk-like simplicity, naïveté, and idealism its language and music seek to project, aligned at various points with rural Austria, Christian faith, the Captain's children, politics, and the course of true love. The dramatic crux of the show involves a particularly subtle—and disturbing—version of the marriage trope, made somewhat more explicit in the film version. Whereas in both versions the Anschluss occurs while the Captain and Maria are on their honeymoon, the parallel events are welded together more securely in the film, where, in a particularly eerie application of associational montage, the wedding bells merge directly into the deeper bells announcing the "wedding" of Austria to Germany.[1]

In fact, the device resonates quite strongly with *two* familiar tropes of musical theater. As an example of the marriage trope, it recalls Rodgers and Hammerstein's first collaboration, *Oklahoma!*, when, in lieu of a toast to the new couple, the wedding celebrants immediately launch into the title song, "Oklahoma!," overtly shifting the object of the celebration from the wedding of Laurey and Curly to the projected larger union (see chapter 6, pp. 132–33). In *The Sound of Music*, the dramatic structure is nearly identical, but with one critical difference: Maria, who represents rural Austria and the religious order, marries the Captain, who represents sophisticated, worldly Austria and the military order.[2] But the larger "marriage" in this case—the Anschluss—is between Austria and *Nazi Germany,* with which sophisticated, worldly Austria—that is, Vienna— is seen to have an uneasy alliance. Thus, while the Captain sides with the wholesome, fundamentally good "soul" of Austria—its countryside and the people who live there—Vienna does not follow him, and so Austria is lost. In this contrast between the promise of local resolution and the inexorable force of history, we may see the shadow of, among other traditions, French Grand Opera, where history so often has the dramatic force of inevitable fate, rendering the actions of individuals impotent and often crushing them as they oppose its imperatives. In the case of *The Sound of Music,* we know that Austria cannot be saved from the Nazis, but we also know that the family escapes to America and becomes an international success as the "Trapp Family Singers."

The Sound of Music plays these two familiar tropes off each other, setting up the marriage trope but delivering instead a version of the history-as-fate trope, using Nazi threats to embody the latter. But this is not really a story of the Nazis, nor even, really, of the Anschluss. While the full weight of what the Nazis would do hangs over the film, we see no direct depiction of their ruthless racial persecution and future war-making (much alluded to in *The Story of the Trapp Family Singers*). It's not just that we don't see the Holocaust; we don't see even one Jew who is unmistakably a Jew, and no discussion whatever of this aspect of Nazism. Moreover, the one person who *might* be Jewish (not to mention gay) is Max, the classic practitioner of *Luftgeschäften* ("air-business"),[3] who stands in for those Viennese whose sympathies were aligned properly but who were too "sophisticated"—and thus too weak—to stand up to the Nazis. (That Max cannot actually be Jewish is made much clearer in the stage version, where his complacent acquiescence to the Germans is elaborated more fully.) And the only one who suffers directly at the hands of the Nazis in the film is Captain von Trapp himself, a retired, fabulously rich Naval officer,[4] surely one of the most irrelevant of commodities in a land-locked country. But we are made to feel the victimhood of Austria through him and, implicitly, we are meant to understand his heroic stance and angst in relation to what is about to happen to Europe more generally, with his Austria representing the first victim in Germany's ruinous march into Hell.

But this perspective on Austria's fate, familiar as it is to (and accepted by) most Americans, is at great odds with many historical circumstances. Rural Austria was the remarkably fertile soil that produced not only Hitler himself, but also much of Hitler's grass-roots support; the majority of its population actually favored the Anschluss, and much of their deeply entrenched anti-Semitism survives even today. Yet, compared to almost any scrap of Europe outside of Switzerland, rural Austria—especially Upper Austria and the area in and around Salzburg—suffered the least. Salzburg was neither ravaged by the war nor targeted for postwar retaliation (unlike Vienna, much of which long remained under Russian control). Although it had to endure a decade of foreign occupation, it has managed since then, especially in the wake of *The Sound of Music,* to play the postwar part of "Nazi victim" without having had to go through much of anything in the way of actually being victimized, except as its citizens participated—"unwillingly," of course—in the victimizing. In the European War, rural Austria was in fact the great unvictimized victim.

The Sound of Music balances its historical distortions of Austria within its depiction of the von Trapp family itself. Prior to Maria's arrival, the family is, basically, Fascism *in nuce,* run by an autocratic, militaristic Captain blind to the individual needs of his own children. While the Captain's anti-Nazi politics are made clear enough, his motivations are specifically nationalist, *not* ideological; behaviorally, and even in its fiercely stated nationalism, the image the Captain projects is sufficiently proto-Nazi that the real-life Maria felt compelled to protest that the show's portrayal of a stern tyrant falsified and oversimplified the person she knew to have been much more complex (she was apparently more pleased by the character as rewritten by Ernest Lehman for the screen and realized by Christopher Plummer, although she had been rebuffed in her attempt to have more of a say in his portrayal). But, while we may fairly easily justify this shift of character in dramatic terms, we are faced—as we were with *Oklahoma!* in chapter 6, and will be again with *The King and I* in chapter 10—with the difficult task of explaining its scandalous reversals of historical realities, through which, in this case, *The Sound of Music* manages to sell a scurrilously anti-Semitic Austria as preeminent among Nazi Germany's victims.[5]

A partial explanation lies in what the show seems to be trying to accomplish on behalf of its American audiences half a generation after World War II. In this light, despite its historical travesties, the show, and especially the film version of the show, is paradoxically deeply sensible of history. But it is concerned specifically with history as it would have been understood by its immediate audience, and interprets that history in terms that will both be palatable to that audience and provide a buttress against the disillusionment many Americans then felt about Europe. In this sense, for *The Sound of Music,* it is American history that is at stake, not Austrian, and more specifically America's *nationhood,* which had been undermined both in its sense of a European rootedness and, less obviously then, in the dawning realization of how much the European model of nationalism was directly responsible for the horrors so recently experienced, which were the inevitable result of enforcing an alignment of ethnicity and geography; not only the Holocaust, but also the wider phenomenon known today as "ethnic cleansing" may be counted among its direct results (see chapter 6, pp. 121–22). Yet for Americans of this generation, the European formulation of nationalism continued to wield considerable persuasive force, especially when combined with ideas such as self-determination, or the earlier American formulation of "manifest destiny," which, as argued in chapter 6, lies perilously close to Germany's nefarious "Lebensraum" (see pp. 124–26).

For *The Sound of Music,* the Nazis and the Anschluss provide a specific set of problems to be addressed within this formulation, but the story itself is more centrally about America—about the promise of America, its groundedness, and its role within the postwar era. Remarkably, all this is accomplished with scarcely any direct reference to the United States, although we may note that the von Trapps were at the time of the show already well known in America (although Georg died in 1947), so that their eventual arrival and flourishing here would have been an implicit background for American audiences, and although, as a matter of course, points of especial relevance to an American audience in the von Trapp story would have provided the nucleus of any attempt to mount their story for American audiences. Yet, these three components—America's promise, its groundedness, and its postwar position—are addressed with a precision hard to interpret as happenstance. Thus, for example, *The Sound of Music* places great emphasis on its quietly heroic religious element, so that, at the end of the film, it is only the Catholic church—in reality scarcely a bastion of Nazi resistance—that openly defies the Nazis;[6] this emphasis re-creates an easily recognized semblance of America's historic role as a place of religious freedom, as a place to which, from the beginning, settlers fled to escape religious persecution. It is scarcely surprising, then, to hear the Reverend Mother singing an inspirational "hymn"—"Climb Ev'ry Mountain"—that has much more in common with other inspirational songs from American musicals than with anything Austrian Catholic sensibilities would have been likely to produce. Thus, the song works within an enhanced AABA form, starting with quiet self-possessed confidence, rising heroically in the bridge, returning to the opening phrase on the more assertive level of the dominant, and then repeating the bridge so as to reach an even more ecstatic conclusion in a key a half-step higher. In this way, the melodic and harmonic mountain-climbing of the song is fully managed within the language of inspirational Broadway.

♪ 9.1

Even more important than this resonance with America's past and with its ongoing pride in offering a refuge from tyranny, however, is the huge store America has always placed in its European heritage, and the ways in which *The Sound of Music* addresses this dependence within the context of postwar disillusionment. In painting Austria as a victim of Nazi aggression two decades after the fact, *The Sound of Music* reaffirms the nostalgic mythology that undergirds most nationalist ideologies, including our own: the myth of a rural world, close to nature, that retains the essence of a lost paradise threatened by modern urbanity. This is why *The Sound of Music* portrays Vienna as a place of suspect sophistication, whose worldly ways made them easy prey for the Nazis, even if the reality was quite different. Indeed, *The Sound of Music* comes uncomfortably close, through the figure of Max, to linking sophistication to *both* the Jews and to the spirit of accommodation that facilitated the Anschluss. But the payoff for *The Sound of Music* is an important one, for it thereby also recreates an essentialized, specifically national slice of central Europe as a remnant of America's spiritual past with a similar connection to nature, a slice of Europe ostensibly unimplicated in the perverse strand of nationalist fervor that so nearly destroyed Europe. And we may note in passing that this was a connection Americans were especially ready to affirm after the American occupational forces in western Austria had—seemingly—bonded so successfully with the indigenous population after the war; here, surely, were the "good" Europeans that we so needed to find.[7] And, finally, regarding America's postwar situation, we see in *The Sound of Music* a Europe in need of rescue, a rescue that would be provided in the main by its now-grown-up American progeny, finally ready to take over the family business of running the world.

What the film brings to this enterprise, beyond what is already in the stage show, are an enhanced presence of nature, a Captain more vividly caught between sophistication and innocence, and a new song—"Something Good"—that reaffirms the redemptive value of an authenticating past:

> Perhaps I had a wicked childhood
> Perhaps I had a miserable youth
> But somewhere in my wicked, miserable past
> There must have been a moment of truth . . .
>
> Nothing comes from nothing,
> Nothing ever could.
> So, somewhere in my youth or childhood
> I must have done something good.[8]

While the song is about redemption—referring perhaps to the real-life Maria's own difficult childhood and her youthful contempt for religion—it is also about the relationship between past and present, an assertion of necessary continuity. Thus, it merges, in an intriguing psychological version of the marriage trope, Maria's past and present as something specifically validated as a unified whole by the Captain's loving response to her. Beyond this personal dimension, the song provides an implicit rationale for America's response to Salzburg and its environs after the war: how could a place and people so eminently loveable—and with such music!—come from wickedness? Salzburg thus comes to stand for what Americans might continue to see as the essentially good heart of Europe.

♪ 9.2

The specifically American agenda of *The Sound of Music* was already pervasive in the stage show, however, poignantly embodied in the von Trapp children, future emigrants to America, each then individually poised between innocence and sophistication, an "empty page" that the world is about "to write on." It is above all the children who are at stake in this family's saga, for they not only represent the quintessential family unit that may be preserved in America but will surely be destroyed by totalitarianism, but they also, and more basically, represent the future. They are "tomorrow"—to borrow and invert the language of *Cabaret*—and the show is about whom they will belong to. Thus, the budding romance of the self-important Rolf and the eldest of the Trapp children, Liesl—established in their early duet, "Sixteen Going on Seventeen"—directly parallels and anticipates the main love story, with Rolf showing how easily a youth too eager to grow up might be taken in by the blend of idealism and scoffing sophistication that Nazism seemed to offer, providing as well a foil for the Captain, whose own fascist tendencies are from the beginning held in check by maturity and humor (more so, perhaps, in the film). Implicitly, the relative maturity of the two teenage lovers is reversed from what the song overtly projects, for Liesl at least understands that she still must learn the ways of the world, while Rolf presumes already to know. Accordingly, it is she who is the more sexual, initiating the dance, converting the didactic tone of Rolf's song into a knowing and seductive parody of the innocence he has projected onto her, and then playfully converting the song into a flirtatious waltz (the latter much expanded in the film).

♪ 9.3

We see early on all the risks that the Captain's family must face. Shortly after Maria's arrival, we are shown not only Rolf, the trusted but secretly Nazi boyfriend ready to teach Liesl the ways of the world, but also a trusted but secretly Nazi butler, already betraying the Captain and his sympathies to the soon-to-become authorities. More important, we see that the inner dynamic of the family makes it particularly vulnerable to such exterior threats, for this is a motherless, dysfunctional family in which simple hooliganism could easily evolve into genuine thuggery if left unchecked, whose father is too much the Captain and thus more feared than loved. In terms that will matter most for the show, this is a family that has been denied its inherent musicality, which we understand from the title song to be the conduit to life-sustaining nature.

Maria, of course, represents the key to rescuing the family, and it is remarkable how much the idealized American she is.[9] One of the two new songs added for the film—"I Have Confidence"—specifically addresses her mustering of courage, and, of course, courage was then widely seen to be what the "good" Europe lacked in the 1930s, the courage to stand up to Hitler and Mussolini early on, before it was too late. But she has much more to offer than standing up to the Captain on the children's behalf: she is in touch with nature; she loves freedom too much to accept the life of a nun, despite her devotion; she pays attention to the children and is immediately more mother than governess (which is, after all, a European institution not to be trusted); she is resourceful, able to turn curtains into play clothes; and, of course, she has music, specifically the music that can make you one with nature. As in the nearly contemporaneous *The Music Man*, music solves all the problems in the show, and offers, implicitly, a specifically American salvation. Yet here, that salvation is first of all Austria's, long regarded by Americans as the most musical country in Europe, home to Lehár, the Strausses, Brahms, Schubert, Beethoven, and Salzburg's own Mozart, a locus for two traditions that wielded tremendous influence in America: the prestigious "high art" tradition (Beethoven and Brahms), and the emergent "light classical" world of operetta and waltz (Strauss and Lehár).

In the film, the sophisticated Viennese, Max and the Baroness, simply do not sing, and the songs they sang in the stage show—directly derivative of the sophisticated Viennese operetta tradition—are dropped.[10] As for the Captain, his return to music is more deliberately plotted in the film. As in the stage version, he follows the path charted by Maria by joining first in the title song, which links music to the Austrian landscape, but he then progresses much more quickly into his own realm, with what would have seemed to mid-sixties America the most authentic of musical expressions, the folk song sung to guitar accompaniment. In the stage show, "Edelweiss" is saved for the concert near the end, but in the film he sings it early on, at the request of the children, and it serves to authenticate him much more surely and fundamentally than his growing response to Maria.[11] Especially important here is the white purity of its central image ("Small and white, / Clean and bright"), which symbolically places Austria in the "white" part of continental Europe (traditionally, the German lands and Scandinavia), that part of their European heritage Americans most needed to salvage from the wreckage of World War II; the imagery runs directly parallel to the "empty page" of the children's innocence, projecting a whiteness threatened by the black "spider" of the Nazi swastika.[12] Moreover, the status of "Edelweiss" as a "genuine" folk song is reinforced in a way impossible to re-create onstage, by having the Austrian audience at the folk-music festival join in. While no folk song sounds quite like this—however simple it sounds, its traditional "Tin Pan Alley" form and somewhat unnatural intervals give it away—it does more than just "pass," for it offers in its slow triple-meter lilt a symbolic image of the Austrian countryside—Edelweiss—precious but fragile, set to a compromise between the rural ländler and the sophisticated waltz. Thus, the song is ostensibly a waltz, but in a folklike setting and with an opening upward leap, a gesture directly modeled on the show's official "Ländler." Nor, surely, is this delicate balance between waltz and ländler simply fortuitous; we have earlier heard a reasonably accurate account of the evo-   ♩ 9.6

Figure 9.1. The von Trapp family on stage at the Salzburg Festival singing "Edelweiss," from the 1965 film: Friedrich, Gretl, Brigitta, Maria, Georg, Liesl, Louisa, Marta, and Kurt (Nicholas Hammond, Kym Karath, Angela Cartwright, Julie Andrews, Christopher Plummer, Charmian Carr, Heather Menzies, Debbie Turner, and Duane Chase). In the extended sequence, most of the show's themes come to a head, as it brings into alignment, in musical terms, the family's full "arrival" as a family, their acceptance by the larger group, and their confrontation with what menaces that group (within the context of the show's greatly fictionalized Austria). (Courtesy of the Academy of Motion Picture Arts and Sciences.)

♩ 9.7   lution of these two dances, as the music of the hills—the yodeling in the
♩ 9.8   "The Lonely Goatherd"—becomes the basis for the "Ländler" at the
♩ 9.9   party, where it appears as a kind of trio within the Grand Waltz.

Although Maria is ostensibly of a lower class than the Captain, she enters the house and subsequently the marriage as an equal, and in this, too, the film presages an "American" ideal of classlessness, a cherished American myth of difference from its European parents. Here again, the film trumps the stage show, which had emphasized class-based difference (and the possibility of American redemption) by casting the obviously European Theodore Bikel as the Captain and the quintessential American Mary Martin as Maria.[13] In the film, neither character seems, at first, particularly American, but the casting places both at a comfortable, carefully calculated remove. Plummer's Canadian heritage makes his progression from initial icy reserve to eventual thaw seem almost inevitable, but he is ultimately no match for Julie Andrews's Britishness, which carries an accent and manner—reinforced in her case by an unmatched vocal authority—that have long been invested for most Americans with a particularly elevated Old World sensibility and assumed rectitude.[14]

The film is framed by two remarkable images of nature that merge well with a more specifically American natural grandeur. At the beginning, a series of stunning Alpine images brings us from the sound of forbidding winds to the twittering of birds, and thence to "improvising" flutes and to the horn calls that Rodgers had already written into the verse of the title song, as accompaniment to its opening lines:

My day in the hills has come to an end, I know.
A star has come out to tell me it's time to go.[15]

As the song progresses, it develops a more sophisticated harmonic syntax, producing a chromatic slippage on the first instance of the key word "music" to give that word an added, quasi-mystical charge. Moreover, the song's sense of abundance, raised to a structural level when the "B" phrase repeats within an AABBAC structure (which more conventionally would have been AABA), conveys both a sense of *natural* abundance (through its images) and *God-given* abundance, for it is with the add-on phrases that religion enters in (thus, from the second B, including the phrase just before it: "From a *church* on a breeze . . . Like a lark who is learning to *pray*"; and from the closing phrase: "My heart will be *blessed*"). These added phrases are crucial to a later effect, often cited as the most moving sequence in the show (especially in the film version), and the turning point for the family as a whole: the moment when the Captain first joins his children in song during their reprise of "The Sound of Music." His entrance midway through the song gets an added jolt from his jumping in with the final "A" *before* the repetition of "B" while at the same time

changing the key back to the original D from the children's F. Additionally, his solo across the concluding two phrases has a more satisfying
shape because of the added "C," and his text seems almost magically
transformed to fit the occasion even though it is identical to the earlier
version:

> I go to the hills / When my heart is lonely,
> I know I will hear / What I've heard before.
> My heart will be blessed / With the sound of music   ♪ 9.11
> And I'll sing once more.   ♪ 9.12

If music is thus heard to be grounded in nature and religion—the latter connection reinforced by the juxtaposition of this "nature" music with
a creditable imitation of cathedral music in its first appearance—at the
end of the film we have, with the von Trapp family, completed our course:
we have listened with appropriate attentiveness to the music of nature,
and we have come to understand and occupy a place of musical-natural
communion to which the Nazis have no access, consecrating our arrival
there with the inspirational "Climb Ev'ry Mountain." But what has made
this possible?

Putting aside the immediate drama that has ostensibly taken us to this
place, we have heard the definitive answer to this question in the last song
the family sings. For the second time in the film, the children sing "So
Long, Farewell" to the sophisticated "adult" world, this time joined by
their father and stepmother. Earlier in the film, they sang with wistful
longing for that world, but now in the knowledge that that world is deeply
flawed; indeed, they use their innocence almost in the manner of a shield
against it. Youth, innocence, even naïveté—the quintessential markers of
difference between America and Europe—are thereby shown to be precisely what is needed. In the words of "Something Good," "nothing
comes from nothing"; it is thus the essential goodness of youth, sustained
beyond the innocence of childhood, that must be preserved as the standard of value in the adult world. Not only does *The Sound of Music* imply
that America would, quite appropriately, be the keeper of that particular
flame during the war to come, but it also suggests that America could
scarcely have grown capable of that task had there not been, somewhere
in its "wicked" European "youth or childhood," "Something Good"—
somewhere very much like this fictionalized vision of Austria, and some-
thing powerful enough both to sustain the Euro-American myth and,
eventually, to redeem Europe itself.

    Cabaret (1966) is meant to unsettle. To this end both Hal
Prince (director and producer of the stage version) and Bob Fosse (director of the 1972 film) were individually determined, within their respective

media, to push hard against the perceived boundaries of acceptability without losing their respective audiences. Particularly unsettling about the show is the fact that most things in it can be read in two opposing directions, the result both of specific strategies and of long-standing Broadway conventions that have encouraged double readings, most notably through double entendre and camp. Both of the latter are activated in this case by the sharp emphasis the show places on divergent sexuality; camp, especially, becomes an important lens for understanding the show through the figures of the Emcee (Joel Grey both on Broadway and in the film), who is overtly campy, and Sally Bowles (originally Jill Haworth on Broadway and Liza Minnelli in the film), who comes across as a campy parody (especially Minnelli, whose persona derives from silent film star Louise Brooks, Marlene Dietrich, and her mother, Judy Garland in roughly equal measure, even though she herself—as a character, at least—seems unaware of the fact).[16]

By many accounts, the show originated in an ambitious desire by Hal Prince to revisit the last years of the Weimar Republic era in Germany so as to address issues of political violence during the civil rights movement of the 1960s.[17] Perhaps inevitably, much of the growing sexual license of the 1960s also gets mapped onto the show, with a paradoxical mixture of seeming approval and condemnation that simply cannot be sorted out fully. The narrative fragments of the Englishman Christopher Isherwood, which formed the basis for the show, chronicle his years in Berlin between 1930 and 1933 and were published as *Goodbye to Berlin* just before the outbreak of World War II (Hogarth Press, 1939). The stories had already been used with fair success as the basis for a play (*I Am a Camera,* John van Druten, 1952) that was subsequently made into a film by British director Henry Cornelius (1955); this background of selective adaptation helped Fosse and Jay Presson Allen (who wrote the screenplay for *Cabaret*) to move in a slightly different direction in the film, bringing the focus more directly to bear on the narrator's homosexuality, an aspect of Isherwood's original stories that had until then remained semi-closeted. The reason for this shift was partly historical: by the early 1970s, homosexuality had become a hotter political issue than either civil rights or the 1960s-era sexual revolution, a shift due in part to the three-day Stonewall Rebellion (1969), which began as a routine confrontation between officials and homosexuals at the Stonewall Inn on Christopher Street, New York City, and became the locus for gay activism in major cities across America. Engaging with homosexuality thus allowed Fosse to avoid the fate of the film version of *Hair* later that decade, which almost by default transformed a staged "happening" into a nostalgic retrospective (see chapter 7, p. 162); the matter was especially urgent given that the stage show of *Cabaret* was already in itself, if ambiguously, a nostalgic retrospective.

The element of nostalgia is reinforced by the fact that the musical style for the show is (as it fairly must be) a hybrid, so that, no matter what music might have actually been heard in a Berlin cabaret ca. 1930, what we hear in the show will represent that music through the filters of not only Brecht and Weill, but also American styles ranging from 1920s jazz through 1960s Broadway and Las Vegas. From Brecht and Weill, in particular, comes the slightly askew version of the cabaret style tinged with political commentary, and it is through this dimension that the show becomes in part a prototype for the "concept musical," less about a particular narrative than about establishing perspective. Moreover, it is important to understand the cabaret style developed by Weill with Brecht as itself twice-mediated from American jazz styles. If the latter might be understood to present (in the 1920s) an exuberant sexuality that is at once frank and oblique, the Berlin cabaret appropriation of the style (as arguably also in the later Vegas appropriation) tended already toward a cruder emphasis on sexuality—an emphasis that was magnified in the operatic versions developed by Weill and others (most notably in Ernst Krenek's 1925 *Jonny Spielt Auf,* premiered 1927) to become almost animalistic. What had been a broad wink became a leer. Through the multiple layers of quotation marks placed around this musical language of sexuality, we are encouraged to adopt multiple perspectives on what we hear, enjoying it "straight" while relishing its knowing artificiality. Moreover, to this already layered environment are added the Brechtian commentaries, often heavy-handed (as in Brecht) but layering a measure of insinuation over the broadness of its gestures, so that, in sexual terms, we move from leer to yet another wink, implying a realm of unparalleled sexual perversity and decadence.

What perhaps matters most about all these layers of mediation and meaning is that they both emphasize and hide how much what we are seeing is like America: these people are like us and yet not at all like us, and yet . . . In the original stories, both Isherwood and Sally Bowles were English; for the stage version of *Cabaret,* he (now named Clifford) becomes American, and for the film these roles are flip-flopped, with Minnelli's American Sally playing off a new incarnation of Isherwood as the English Brian.[18] Within a context of allegorical representation, the show chronicles Sally's seduction by German decadence, as witnessed by the young, drifting, would-be author who ultimately escapes seduction; within this structure, the different versions create a broadly scaled "we" (English or English / American) and "them" (German) and play out a variety of marriage tropes. Thus, the English-American "marriage" is undermined by the surrounding German decadence, embodied most explicitly in the film's Maximilian von Heune, who forms alliances with both, while the German-Jewish marriage, pragmatically refused on stage (Fraulein Schneider rejecting the Jewish Herr Schultz), transmutes in the film into the redemp-

tive scenario of the secretly Jewish Fritz, who has been successfully passing as German, fatalistically dooming himself in the pursuit of love by
admitting that he is Jewish to win Natalia. Importantly, all of these relationships seem, like the characters themselves, continually to be something they turn out not to be. Thus, Sally tries unsuccessfully to seduce
the presumed straight Brian, who later puts aside his presumed homosexuality to carry on an affair with her; then, when they each admit to
being Maximilian's lover, a seemingly agreeable menage à trois collapses
when Brian realizes (in a stunning, wordless, three-way embrace) that he
cannot compete for Sally's affection against Maximilian, nor for Maximilian's against Sally.

While the outlines of this cautionary tale seem clear enough, the tendency for its characters and situations to shift without warning makes it
very hard to read in its particulars. Overall, the show seems to suggest
that we should not ignore the turmoil around us or we might end up with
a version of Nazism in America, yet also seems to underscore how foreign
this world is, so that we need not worry overmuch. It seems to suggest
that the Kit Kat Klub (whose initials—the same as the white supremacist
Ku Klux Klan, and with a parallel shift from C to K—implicitly point to
American race problems), and especially the decadent pleasures it offers,
were at once a dangerous distraction and the spiritual cousin to Nazism.[19]
Yet it invites us to enjoy those pleasures and even gives us a fair amount
of permission to do so, since they serve as the vehicle for Brechtian commentary, almost in the manner of political commentary in 1960s America within popular television shows ("That Was the Week That Was,"
1963–65, and "The Smothers Brothers Comedy Hour," 1967–69). Musically, it presents its pastiche, as Sondheim would do in his concept musicals, both as something to enjoy as an instance of a particular genre, and
as something that bodies forth the reasons for distrusting that genre, in
part emblematically (that is, for what it represents), and in part because
it yields its pleasures too easily (see the discussion of *Assassins* in chapter
7, pp. 165–72).

And these are confusions not easily resolved. As argued, it is in the nature of pastiche to present itself doubly in precisely this way. In 1972,
when the film version of *Cabaret* brought new attention to homosexuality as a dimension of decadence, it had to contend with significant friction
between the liberating effect of the emergent post-Stonewall gay mythologies and a long history of scapegoating representation, in which even sympathetically portrayed gays were routinely punished, as object lessons
(they almost always died). Thus, *Cabaret* may implicitly align homosexuality with Nazism, but it also presents Brian (if not Maximilian) with
great sympathy, and he is allowed to escape in the end, even if this might
be construed as a reward for his at least attempting to "go straight." Per-

haps most intriguing is the paradox of escapist entertainment providing a soapbox for fervent, idealistic political suasion. Always, within this combination (whether in the Kit Kat Klub or "The Smothers Brothers"), there is the possibility of taking it all back ("it was all just a joke"). But always, also, if pushed too far, there is a moment of truth, when comedy and escapism abjectly fail in the face of raw political power. And that failure resides equally in both realms; thus, for example, if the real reason that CBS canceled "The Smothers Brothers Comedy Hour" in 1968 was its political content, it is also true that the show became increasingly less funny—and finally less watchable—as it became more engaged with serious issues. In presenting the rise of the Nazis through the lens of the Kit Kat Klub, *Cabaret* seems to say that we cannot afford either to laugh at evil or to confront it, at the same time that the show indulges the temptation to do both. Yet even so, the great failing of the cabaret, and the object lesson of the show, is that it acts out a profound indifference; its ridicule is directed too broadly and its moments of resistance are too readily retracted for the occasional better impulse to make any difference. The sly wink at perversion and the shrug of indifference to the Nazi threat are both attitudes bred by decadence and underlying despair; what redeems Brian / Clifford is, specifically, his *lack* of detachment, even if he tries at first to play that game (i.e., not wanting to know for whom he is working as a smuggler). While it may be true that a world grown decadent gives a place to both his sexual explorations and the Nazis, we are allowed through him to preserve the capacity to distinguish between sexual license and evil.

The opening song, "Willkommen," follows Broadway convention in introducing the audience to the show's setting and community, with the number doubling in this case as an introduction within the cabaret setting, as well. The melodic style and words seem innocuous enough; indeed, for a time in the late 1960s, the song became a staple for schoolchildren, valued for its friendliness and "United Nations" mix of languages. But an insinuating tone is built into the song in various ways. The melody itself dwells a bit too much on dissonant leading-tones; even if they (mostly) resolve, these dissonances are absorbed into the otherwise "normal" harmonic vocabulary to grating effect (boldface indicates a dissonance, bold-italics an unresolved dissonance):

> Will**kom**men, bienvenue, **wel**come!
> Frem*de*, étranger, stranger.
> Glück**lich** zu sehen, . . .

But that grating effect is second nature to the borrowed cabaret style of Brecht and Weill, replete with boom-chank accompaniments, in which the various "chanks" carry a succession of pungent dissonances (see the discussion in chapter 5 of *The Cradle Will Rock,* pp. 114–15). All this, coupled with grotesque staging against a large disorienting mirror, an impish, decidedly seedy Emcee in tuxedo tails and elaborate makeup, and a lineup of equally seedy chorus girls, tells us emphatically not to take anything at face value (even the comedy). From the beginning, the "welcome" is a come-on from the cultural equivalent of a cheap undiscriminating whore, who doesn't care what country you might be from—an attitude, whether welcoming or indifferent, that is set in relief by our knowledge that around 1930 Germans were becoming increasingly obsessed with removing "Fremden" from their midst.

♫ 9.13

The jaded indifference that lies behind the welcoming façade of "Willkommen" is more explicit in the second song of the stage show, originally sung by Lotte Lenya (Kurt Weill's widow, who, along with Marlene Dietrich, was one of the principal points of reference for the 1920s cabaret style, especially for Americans). "So What?," like "No Way to Stop It" in *The Sound of Music* (sung by Max and the Baroness, with the Captain joining in), articulates what many understand to have been key to the Nazis' success: a general cynical indifference among many constituencies that would eventually allow the Third Reich to expand its influence beyond the point of no return. Both songs create a sense of inevitability by evoking obsessive circular motion. Thus, "No Way to Stop It" describes the orbits of satellites, eventually coming around to "I" as the orbital center of the universe. "So What?" uses a standard cabaret type, the jaded waltz, to suggest a different form of egocentric indulgence, again implying circularity (through the waltz idiom itself), the fateful inevitability of cycles, and the tired helplessness of spiritual ennui:

> For the sun will rise and the moon will set
> And you learn to settle for what you get.

That this attitude is meant to carry a substantial part of the weight of responsibility for what is to come is made clear later, when Fraulein Schneider renounces her betrothed Herr Schultz, who is Jewish. Notably, both songs were dropped in the film versions of their respective shows, in *Cabaret* both because the subplot itself was dropped and because, with

♫ 9.14
♫ 9.15

one exception, all the music in the film takes place in the Kit Kat Klub itself.

That exception is "Tomorrow Belongs to Me," which originates in the Kit Kat Klub in the stage version before it later becomes more clearly a Nazi anthem, but is sung only once in the film, by an unnamed youth at a public *Biergarten* (in abysmal lip-synching that may possibly have been deliberate). As he begins to sing (in the film), we are only gradually shown his Nazi uniform when the camera pulls back; as the song's key modulates upward—a traditional device to generate enthusiasm—the song is

Figure 9.2. An unnamed youth sings "Tomorrow Belongs to Me" at an outdoor Berlin cafe in the 1972 film of *Cabaret*. Aside from the Nazi armband, the boy's appearance and demeanor closely resemble those of Friedrich von Trapp at the Salzburg Festival (cf. figure 9.1; Friedrich stands at the far left), a resemblance that extends, as argued here, to the songs they are singing. (Courtesy of the Academy of Motion Picture Arts and Sciences.)

taken up by nearly everyone present, while those who do not sing either leave (Brian, Sally, and Maximilian) or stay behind, trapped and miserable (this is, of course, exactly what happens on a larger scale, historically, when many managed to escape Germany and its rapidly expanding dominions, but many others did not, remaining behind to face a grimly hideous fate).

Stylistically, the song (originally to be sung a capella, that is, without accompaniment) is a Siciliano, a folk dance long associated with the pastorale as a genre, and the lyrics confirm that this grounding in nature is part of a full nationalist trajectory along the lines described in chapter 6 (pp. 119–21). Thus, the natural images are from the beginning as specifically German as possible (stag, forest, linden tree, Rhine) while generically pastorale in their clichéd evocations of meadow and storm (the latter, of course, with metaphoric application to the coming war):

The sun on the meadow is summery warm, / The stag in the forest runs free.
But gather together to greet the storm, / Tomorrow belongs to me.

The branch of the linden is leafy and green, / The Rhine gives its gold to the sea.
But somewhere a glory awaits unseen, / Tomorrow belongs to me.

Oh, fatherland, fatherland show us the sign / Your children have waited to see.
The morning will come when the world is mine. / Tomorrow belongs to me.

The lyric is crude, perhaps deliberately so, but its ingredients are nevertheless carefully assembled, moving into more overt political statements only after the pastoral landscape has been drawn. The reference to the Rhine is already both symbolically and politically charged, since the Rhineland, which looms large in German mythology (hence the oblique reference to Wagner's *Das Rheingold*), was demilitarized after World War I, and would be reclaimed by Hitler as early as 1936. Less subtle is the final verse, which projects a future German domination of the world, albeit through banal clichés. In the song's reprise at the end of the first act (in the stage show), the pastorale Siciliano easily converts into a slow waltz suitable for a German *Biergarten* (its setting in the film) through a change in accompaniment, evoking a type that is stylistically adjacent as well to the folk-like ländler style, as discussed earlier in relation to *The Sound of Music*. Particularly as the song becomes the folk-song basis for community affirmation, one is reminded that the von Trapp family, as depicted in *The Sound of Music*, lies extremely close to the wholesome Germans so often portrayed in Nazi propaganda (it is no coincidence that the actual von Trapp family was sought out by Hitler as window-dressing; see note 1 in this chapter). "Tomorrow Belongs to Me" and "Edelweiss" are thus no less a pair than "So What?" and "No Way to Stop It," as both are seemingly innocuous nationalist folk-anthems in the style of a slow waltz that create paired images of community from which only a very few are excluded. Except that those few are Nazis in *The Sound of Music* and (presumably) Jews in *Cabaret,* and except that we are (presumably) willing to view the Austrians in *The Sound of Music* as victims, there is little to choose between their defiant climactic lines: "The morning will come when the world is mine. / Tomorrow belongs to me" and "Blossom of snow may you bloom and grow / Bloom and grow forever," respectively.   ♩9.16

A number of songs establish the cabaret stage as a place from which to comment on the action outside the cabaret, a device particularly useful for the film version, which can cut more fluidly between the two and which mostly does without song in the "real" world. But the device works well in the stage version, too, as when the music for "Tomorrow Belongs to Me" returns at the beginning of the second act, transmuting from a "kick line" to a goose-stepping Maestoso March. Elsewhere, "Two Ladies" underscores with the overt mockery of burlesque the decadent dimension of the menage à trois that develops among the principal leads, compounding its mockery through the central involvement of the Emcee, who is clearly gay (or at least embodying gay tropes), while at the same time rendering the menage slightly more respectable (at least in the film), since it doesn't involve male homosexuality and plays into traditional heterosexual fantasies.   ♩9.17

More overtly political is "If You Could See Her," which alludes in its final line to anti-Semitism after making a case for the Emcee's attachment to what the libretto describes as a "really rather attractive" female gorilla: "If you could see her through my eyes, / She wouldn't look Jewish at all." Together, these songs underscore the basic thrust of the show, which implicitly argues that the cabaret is both like real life and quite unlike it— thus the prominent distorting mirror in both the stage version and the film—and takes every opportunity to make us squirm a bit when the two come too close together. Finally, in the refrain of the title song, sung by Sally Bowles late in the show, this problematic duality is laid bare: "Life is a cabaret, old chum, / Come to the cabaret." In her sense, the cabaret is both an escape from life and the only place where one can truly live. Implicitly, part of the appeal of the cabaret is that it is a *constructed* reality, seemingly under the control of the actors. But escaping to the cabaret, so as to construct an alternative fantasy world, involves renouncing the capacity to wield constructive control in the outside world, which can then only be criticized, and only at the indulgence of that world. The feeling of control offered within the world of cabaret is in the end illusory. By the end of the show, we have been well prepared to realize this, and to understand both why Sally Bowles has retreated / escaped to that world, and why she is thus doomed.   ♩9.18

Cabaret, the film version of *The Sound of Music,* and *Hair* occupy roughly the same temporal space on the American landscape (1965–67). Moreover, *Cabaret* and *Hair* to a very large extent shared their audience, despite their nearly opposite takes on alternative sexuality: thus, when all is said and done, *Cabaret* functions as a cautionary tale and *Hair* as an endorsement of alternativity. Perhaps this circumstance will seem less odd when we remember that in dramatic terms the parallels between the two shows matter more than their quite different takes on sexual mores. Both shows place sexual license within a context of a projected alternative to a "real world" grown oppressive and dangerous, yet tiptoe around the issue of homosexuality, historically the central marker for sexual deviance. Both shows celebrate their alternative worlds while commenting satirically on the "real world," and in both shows the alternative world ultimately has no defense against the "powers that be." And, perhaps most important, both shows exhibit profound ambivalence about the relative value of the two worlds they project; thus, even the jaded cabaret nurses an occasionally intense flame of defiant idealism, while a sharp edge of cynicism intrudes more than once into the idealistic counterculture projected in *Hair*. Without this ambivalence, neither show would seem quite human—or, at least, quite American, for an ambivalence between reality and fantasy is core to American sensibilities. Inevitably, it is America that is held in the balance in both shows, in the guise of a youthful innocent caught between two worlds.

For Further Consideration

South Pacific (1949), *Candide* (1956), and *The Producers* (1968)

See Also

Regarding *The Sound of Music,* Stacy Wolf offers an intriguing feminist reading of Maria (as performed both by Mary Martin and Julie Andrews) in chapter 5 of *A Problem Like Maria;* chapter 8 of Frederick Nolan's *The Sound of Their Music* provides a wealth of background information; and Richard Dyer's *"The Sound of Music"* (in his *Only Entertainment*) interprets the film version according to the conventions of a "woman's picture". See also pp. 344–54 of Meryle Secrest's *Somewhere for Me,* Peter Kemp's "How Do You Solve a 'Problem' Like Maria von Poppins," and *"The Sound of Music" zwischen Mythos und Marketing* ("'The Sound of Music' between Myth and Marketing").

Regarding *Cabaret,* see Mitchell Morris's provocative and insightful "*Cabaret,* America's *Weimar,* and Mythologies of the Gay Subject," Linda Mizejewski's astute *Divine Decadence: Fascism, Female Spectacle, and the Makings of Sally Bowles,* chapter 2 in Scott Miller's *From "Assassins" to "West Side Story,"* and chapter 9 in Ethan Mordden's *Open a New Window.*

Exoticism   THE AMERICAN MUSICAL has from the beginning traded in exoticism; even *The Black Crook* (1866; see chapter 2, pp. 20–29) presented its European locales as exotic, whereas a large part of the appeal of *The Mikado* (1885), for English and American audiences alike, was its portrayal of exotic difference comingled with the familiar. Ultimately, it is the latter show that set the terms for the East-West dichotomy most typical of exoticism in the American musical, which has tended to rely heavily on Asian subjects; thus, it is with *The Mikado* that we must begin here, even though in important respects it does not fit the paradigm established after World War II.

Exoticism, as a theme, intersects with other categories of musicals, including "ethnic musicals" and the themes explored in chapters 5 through 8, nationalism and ethnicity. An important issue for the categories as we are treating them here is the degree to which *orientalism* is involved, which is to say, the European- and American-based tendency to define themselves as "the West" in relation to an "Other"—most often Eastern, and with few distinctions concerning which particular "Other" is involved (African, Asian, Arabic, Spanish, gypsy, etc.). This lack of differentiation is particularly true of musical representations: "Turkish" music, for example, was a catch-all in the eighteenth century, as was "oriental" music in the late nineteenth and early twentieth. Thus, for the musicals we considered in chapter 8 (race and ethnicity), it mattered most that we could relate the racial interactions directly to situations in America, whereas for this chapter we will be most concerned with musicals that explore the conflicts and interactive possibilities between our culture and another. In general, the pattern for American musicals in recent decades has been to criticize prejudice on both sides, advocate tolerance, and remain smugly entrenched in the notion that, while "West" is better than "East," it can learn to be better. Orientalist tendencies typically involve as well a keen interest in the Other, desiring access to a greater sensuousness, for example, or admiring specific aspects of their traditions; often, belief is strong that we might through the Other reclaim something lost along the way to our own more "advanced" level of civilization or sophistication.[1] Orientalism also reinforces a nationalist tendency for us to define ourselves in part in terms of how we differ from the Others we encounter.

The combination of smug attitudes about the superiority of our own way of life, coupled with the attractions of orientalism, are signs of *colonialist* (or imperialist) attitudes, which typically justify the imposition of our will on other cultures and political systems in terms of entrenched attitudes of superiority (which generally have a racial basis, but may not), but often do so in part out of a love or fascination for what is being subjugated, and an appreciation for its different standards of beauty and value. Such a developed taste for the exotic has long played an important role in music, and specifically on the musical stage. Although ethnomusicology has made it possible for us to understand with greater sophistication, and to preserve with greater accuracy, the various musics of the world, exotic musical tastes have most often been indulged in terms of stereotypes, flavoring a basically Western (that is, European-derived) musical discourse with specific melodic and harmonic devices, styles of song and dance, or instrumentation understood to be representative of a specific exotic source. The two American musicals we will consider here after *The Mikado—The King and I* and *Pacific Overtures*—engage fairly directly with issues of colonialism, taking as their subjects two Asian civilizations, Siam and Japan, that had for centuries successfully resisted European domination but were in the late nineteenth century pressured to open up to the West. The special fascination in both cases has to do with a perceived cultural strength deriving from an unbroken, isolated tradition that governed all aspects of life, and from witnessing the subjection of that tradition to the dynamic of enforced change. While *The King and I* is perhaps the archetype for the kind of musical described here, *Pacific Overtures* tries to overturn the genre by reversing our perspective to that of the Japanese, with intriguing results.

The Mikado; or, The Town of Titipu (1885) is at the same time Gilbert and Sullivan's masterpiece and a deeply problematic work for modern audiences who are more apt than nineteenth-century audiences to be offended by its racial and ethnic stereotypes. Set in a mythocomedic Japan, *The Mikado* flips adroitly between Japanese and English frames of reference, and the mythology of the show itself would have us believe that it is "really" about only one of these, the English. This claim became a basic tenet of *Mikado* reception after it came under official attack in 1907, when the show was temporarily banned so as not to offend a visiting Japanese dignitary (an official action that did not, however, deter the Savoy from performing the show), but it seems no more true than the claim that blackface minstrelsy was "really" about whites. While, certainly, both minstrelsy and *The Mikado* can and do use the cover and personae of racial masks as a protected harbor from which to launch critiques aimed at white, mainstream culture, they are both also deeply invested in representing the culture that their masks purport to evoke, and the ways in which they do this are quite often pointed and negative, even if unintentionally so.

As Michael Beckerman has cogently demonstrated with regard to *The Mikado* and its depiction of the Japanese, and as the 1999 film *Topsy-Turvy* vividly shows to us, authenticity of appearance and manner was critically important to both collaborators.[2] Beckerman's multifaceted argument points out the specific Japanese musical roots of some of the music of *The Mikado* (especially "Miya sama"), the more general use of *faux*-Japanese musical elements in much of the score, the occasional overt use of English musical types (such as the madrigal), and, most intriguingly, the frequent blending of English and Japanese musics, achieved through employing either older European modes, or a pentatonic or "gapped" scale as common ground between older English music and Japanese music. Also figuring into his argument are the characters' "Japanese"-sounding names—which are, like the name of the town itself (Titipu), often thinly disguised baby talk with scatological overtones—and the incorporation of stereotypical behaviors and traits marked as particularly Japanese, such as bowing, walking in a shuffling manner, and, most disturbing, exhibiting a thoroughgoing bloodthirstiness bordering on the macabre.

Nevertheless, it is abundantly clear that neither Gilbert nor Sullivan meant on the whole to disrespect the Japanese. Within the context of late-nineteenth-century England and given the medium of light opera, *The Mikado* is actually quite sympathetic to its subject. Reportedly, a Japanese prince who saw the show in 1907 (despite the official ban) was more amused than offended, however offensive we might today find some of its cardinal elements. Clearly, one of the fascinations for the Japanese in later nineteenth-century England had to do with how very different they seemed to be; both Gilbert and Sullivan were at great pains to present at least the effect of strangeness, and this through as careful a reproduction of Japanese dress, movement, and decorum as the medium of musical comedy permitted. Thus, Gilbert brought in Japanese to demonstrate these behaviors for the cast, and to train them in the use of the fan. Just as clearly, however, of equal fascination for both Gilbert and Sullivan was how much the two cultures had in common despite their obvious differences.

Much in the show draws specific attention to these similarities, many of them deriving from some of the circumstances common to each nation: being set off from the mainland as a group of islands, sustaining an ancient set of traditions, being exaggeratedly proud of its past, and having grandiose notions of its international importance despite its relatively small size. In neither impulse was disrespect a central motivation—in fact, quite the reverse, for it remains true throughout that any barb that may seem to attack Japan is almost automatically directed as well at England. If, for example, the Japanese in *The Mikado* show an unseemly relish for blood—well, then, so were the English bloodthirsty, and they might be more willing to confront this element in their own history and culture through the pervasive double-imaging of *The Mikado*. And if their names embodied all manner of insults (Nanki-Poo, for example, seems to conflate China and Japan in its scatological baby talk; and Pitti-Sing seems to be a clever variant on a banal source of insulting humor, in which "Pretty-Sing" drops its "r" and thereby becomes a perhaps more accurate descriptor), such manipulations are scarcely different from—to choose but one example among many—their naming the Wilde-like poet of *Patience* "Bunthorne," who, indeed, reveals himself to be the archetypal "pain in the ass."[3]

Are we right nevertheless to feel discomfort with *The Mikado*? Of course we are, especially in America, where it resonates all too readily with our own heritage of blackface minstrelsy, with which it overlaps historically—and to which, surely not coincidentally, *The Mikado* twice directly alludes, when "the nigger serenader, and the others of his race" show up on Ko-Ko's "little list" ("As Some Day It May Happen"), and the Mikado himself decrees that women who try artificially to maintain the appearance of youth shall be "blacked like a nigger / With permanent walnut juice" ("From Every Kind of Man"). While "nigger" here does not carry the same charge as it does for Americans today—in England, the epithet referred to the blackface performers themselves—the references have long been routinely covered over, but so crudely that audiences either don't get them at all or understand them for precisely what they meant originally; thus, they are changed, respectively, to the perhaps even more insulting "the banjo serenader, and the others of his race" and the syntactically impaired "painted with vigor / And permanent walnut juice." Moreover, however invested *The Mikado* is in forging a bond between English and Japanese cultures, and however well this might register with audiences (although it seems doubtful that it does so with any reliability, especially in America), the basic strategy of the show sets in sharp relief the cultural background of late-nineteenth-century England, saturated as it was with a smug superiority acquired through a long history of imperialist / colonialist behavior, and within which it simply does not register that the kind of appropriation represented by *The Mikado*, taken in itself, might be grossly insulting.[4]

The special fascination for Japan in both England and America in the second half of the nineteenth century stemmed partly from its long isolation from the rest of the world. Virtually alone among those areas colonized by Western European powers during the two centuries following Columbus's voyages, Japan successfully rid itself of all foreigners and restored as fully as possible its older traditions and ways of life. Between 1639 and 1853, Japan remained closed to outsiders, although some trade was permitted, and although after 1720 foreign books were allowed. In

1853, Commodore Matthew Perry of the United States began to "negotiate" the opening of Japan to foreign trade, although it wasn't until 1868
that this aim was fully accomplished, and then only after the Tokugawa
government, in power for over two centuries, had been overthrown. In response to the growing interest that these events fostered, and also to encourage it, a traditional Japanese village was re-created at Knightsbridge
in 1884, less than two miles from the Savoy Theatre in London, providing the probable inspiration for *The Mikado* (as much as a sword falling
from Gilbert's wall, which is the official legend). Gilbert drew heavily on
that nearby resource, not only for inspiration but also, more directly, borrowing some of its personnel to train his actors and referring comically to
Knightsbridge in the dialogue of *The Mikado,* perhaps by way of homage
(the original program gave official thanks to the "Directors and Native
Inhabitants" of the Knightsbridge installation). In choosing a Japanese
subject, Gilbert was responding directly to the charm of the Knightsbridge
village, which seemed to re-create Japan's traditions and even its curious
sense of removal from the rest of the world, right in the heart of London.
But he was also responding shrewdly to its topicality, as he had so often
in the past; in this way, too, *The Mikado* is "about" the English.

The plot of *The Mikado* details the political machinations in a small
town, Titipu, trying to evade the stringent demands of the Mikado (their
emperor), which serve to bring into close juxtaposition the outwardly incompatible traits of polite decorum and bloodthirstiness, taken to be at
once stereotypically Japanese and—allowing for the comic exaggeration
of topsy-turvydom—English. The conflict hinges on Titipu's failure to execute anyone despite the plentitude of crimes (including flirting) for which
the penalty is death. Nanki-Poo, the son of the Mikado who has been
promised in marriage to the loathsome Katisha, has fled to Titipu in disguise, seeking his beloved Yum-Yum. The second act brings the Mikado
to Titipu; to appease him, Ko-Ko (a former "cheap tailor" recently elevated to Lord High Executioner) and Pooh-Bah (Lord High Everything
Else) present a false coroner's certificate of Nanki-Poo's death, only to discover that Nanki-Poo is none other than the heir apparent. To rescue the
situation, Ko-Ko successfully seduces Katisha, which allows Nanki-Poo
to reemerge with his bride, Yum-Yum.

As Beckerman points out, the overture, which is a typical pot pourri of
tunes from the opera to come, in this case presents precisely those tunes
that are most clearly marked as Japanese, framed by the adapted hymn,
"Miya Sama," and leaves out all those marked as specifically English
(madrigal, glee, etc.). Thus, the show puts its most Japanese musical face
forward first, and makes it easier to notice, if only subliminally, how much
of the rest of the music for the show derives from "Miya Sama." Here,
too, as Beckerman observes, it is Sullivan's apparent reworking of the
hymn tune, giving it a more "Western" profile without sacrificing its "Jap-

anese" character, that permits this kind of integration—although it is also possible, given the nature of the slight differences accruing to Sullivan's version and since it is not clear what his source was for the hymn, that he simply got the hymn slightly wrong, perhaps through an inaccurate or imperfectly heard performance, or through faulty memory. Both the appropriation of the tune and its reworking (or, perhaps, Sullivan's failure to research adequately the precise melodic profile) represent a kind of cultural imperialism—especially since "Miya sama" was of fairly recent vintage, having emerged as a favorite during the overturn of the Tokugawa shogunate and the Meiji restoration (1868).

The process of musical generation can be traced in the opening number ("If you want to know who we are"), which establishes where we are and how that matters, using an all-male chorus singing (mostly) in unison over music that has a distinct and appropriately "characteristic" profile, highly suggestive of choreographed activity. While audiences at the Savoy Theatre would have had the lyrics in front of them—a custom once familiar to opera that has long since fallen away—Sullivan makes it as easy as possible for audiences to hear the words through having the chorus sing in unison, but this also has another aim, as it establishes a "primitive" monophonic texture (as had the opening of the overture) and serves to highlight even more the melodic profile, which follows very clearly the "gapped" pentatonic scale characteristic of "Miya Sama." Even before the voices enter, the swirling, mostly pentatonic unison figures in the orchestra are already bringing into play one of the "Japanese" modes established in the overture, linking it securely to the movement and appearance of the players themselves, as they shuffle and glide in their kimonos and work their fans. The specific notes they sing also link them to the language of the

♫ **10.1**   overture, and specifically "Miya Sama"; in fact, they simply replay, each
♫ **10.2**   in reverse order, the framing gestures of the hymn, as shown in ex. 10.1.

Example 10.1

Arthur Sullivan (derived), "Miya Sama" (melodic excerpt, transposed)

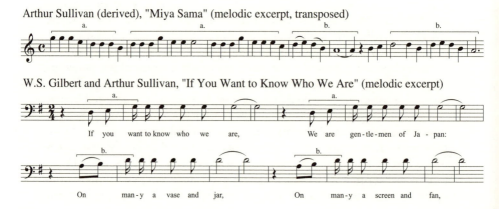

W.S. Gilbert and Arthur Sullivan, "If You Want to Know Who We Are" (melodic excerpt)

Gilbert's lyric for the opening number adroitly guides its choreography:

> If you want to know who we are, We are gentlemen of Japan;
> On many a vase and jar—On many a screen and fan,
>   We figure in lively paint: Our attitude's queer and quaint—
>   You're wrong if you think it ain't, oh!
> If you think we are worked by strings, Like a Japanese marionette,
> You don't understand these things: It is simply Court etiquette.

He is here clearly indicating not only a strangeness of effect, as would be derived in any case through the coaching he arranged courtesy of the Japanese colony at Knightsbridge, but something stereotyped and mechanical, as well. In referring to stylized drawings on "vase and jar" and "screen and fan," and, even more tellingly, in rhyming "Japanese marionette" with "Court etiquette," Gilbert points fairly directly to complex traditions of stylized representation, and a whole host of associations connecting with puppetry in particular, ranging from "pure" entertainment to political satire in practice, and, symbolically, the manipulations of mortals by gods or fate (a theme to be taken up later, most elaborately in the second-act glee, "See How the Fates Their Gifts Allot"). As so often in the show, the number subtly brings together points of contact between the two cultures, both in terms of the "Court etiquette" and the puppetry it seems to imitate.

If the thrust of the first number is to situate the Japanese as different from their English audience, despite these implicit points of contact, the next establishes just as clearly how much they have in common. Nanki-Poo's self-introduction, "A Wandering Minstrel I," frames a brief survey of characteristic songs, all of which might find a home in either England or Japan. The frame itself treats the orchestra as a "big guitar," establishing Nanki-Poo as a singer ostensibly accompanying himself on a plucked string instrument, singing occasional melismas that are suggestive of both "orientalist" music and European traditions of word-painting (as with his "supple" song, and later, "Oh, sorrow!"). If the specific topics are drawn fairly directly from Western traditions, they are all appropriate as well to Japan, moving from a lover's lament, to a comically self-important patriotic march, to a sea chantey (notably, not a hornpipe, which would be more specifically English), to an extension of the "lullaby" reference in the framing music when it returns to close the song.   ♩ 10.3

In the choruses of *The Mikado,* as in most musicals, there is an inherent interchangeability of the singers; what matters for a chorus, after all, is that its members be numerous and individually anonymous. While this egalitarian structure had, in *Pinafore,* its comical side (as when some members clearly did not fully belong, such as Ralph and Dick Deadeye), in *The Mikado* it carries (probably unintended) racist overtones, especially since the players are, in effect, masked (through white makeup and blackened hair) and otherwise made to appear generically Japanese. In the whole show, indeed, only the Mikado himself retains a stable identity within a game of interchangeable pieces; thus, Nanki-Poo is in a disguise that has more presence than his ostensible identity, Ko-Ko is at once a cheap tailor and Lord High Executioner, Pooh-Bah has opportunely assumed a full array of vacated bureaucratic positions, Yum-Yum and her fate are continually bartered over (and, in a traditional comic bit of business in the first act finale, Ko-Ko seems to mistake Pitti-Sing for her), and Katisha slips from the "Daughter-in-Law-Elect" of the Mikado to the wife of the plebeian Ko-Ko. The implications of this structural ploy are potentially disturbing, yet the theme greatly facilitates the reciprocal mapping of Japanese and English even as it is outwardly racially reductive; thus, its kinship to the topsy-turvy accountings of Gilbert and Sullivan's other shows—i.e., the switching of Captain and Ralph in *Pinafore,* or the elevation of the Pirates to noblemen in *Penzance*—reduces the insulting implications of this subtext, particularly for audiences familiar with Gilbert and Sullivan's milieu. From such a standpoint, there is no insult, since the Japanese are simply serving, and fairly transparently, as surrogate English. Nevertheless, it is this context of masked interchangeability that allows Ko-Ko's famous "list" song ("As Some Day It May Happen") to pass as harmless humor, despite its breathtakingly bitter load of bile. Under the double protection of Japanese "whiteface" and comic interchangeability, its barbs can be as sharply pointed as possible, and it has seemed almost a requirement of the song, even in its first performances, to find ways to allude specifically to known cultural and political figures. The music, too, seems to strive for a generic balance, "Japanese" in its repeated, faintly effeminate adaptation of patter rhythms, but thoroughly European in its harmonic and melodic syntax.

♩ **10.4**

With the introduction of the women's chorus, Sullivan again finds inventive ways to affect a Japanese musical profile, and even to add to an already prominent feminine dimension. In music, typically (e.g., in "Turkish" music), representations of the Other reduce to a brutish masculine mode and a seductive feminine mode that often colors as well representations of masculinity. Implicitly, as has been argued by Edward Said and others,[5] Westerners thus tend to feminize the Other in the very act of representing it, a tendency that is here reinforced visually, through the use of kimonos and fans, and through the cultivation of a style of movement that will seem "mincing" to Westerners. In *The Mikado,* we may usefully see three overlapping modes, including the somewhat effeminate "politeness" mode, the more extreme effeminate music of the women (often wrongly described as geishas), and the bloodthirsty tendencies of (especially) the Mikado and Katisha. Most striking here, regarding the second of these, is "Three Little Maids from School Are We," suffused with a musical "giggling" that bubbles throughout, representing their "girlish glee." Even Gilbert's verbal wit seems in this context to be a quasi-musical consequence of girlish energy, as when arithmetic neatness insists on compounding itself with playful misdirection:

> Yum-Yum: **One** little maid is a bride, Yum-Yum—
> Peep-Bo: **Two** little maids in attendance come—
> Pitti-Sing: **Three** little maids is the total sum.
> Together: Three little maids from school!
>
> Yum-Yum: From **three** little maids take **one** away—
> Peep-Bo: **Two** little maids remain, and they—
> Pitti-Sing: **Won't** have to wait very long, they say—
> Together: Three little maids from school!

While the literal subtraction problem in the latter strophe no longer fits neatly into the poetic scheme, Gilbert manages, through the parallel verse-structure and a punning assonance easily emphasized in performance, to create a different, conflicting subtraction problem, oddly transmuting "3 minus 1 equals 2" into an implied "3 minus 2 equals 1," which also neatly reverses the first verse's "One . . . Two . . . Three" structure. Abstractly considered, sound and rhythm here trump mathematical logic in a musical effect set up by Gilbert and deftly realized by Sullivan.   ♩ **10.5**

A slightly different dynamic between lyricist and composer may be traced in the following number, "So Please You, Sir, We Much Regret." As Robert Fink has shown,[6] Sullivan's attention to rhythm (which for him always came first) led him to reject the obvious ways to set Gilbert's lyric, whose iambic tetrameter resembles that of "I think that I shall never see / A poem lovely as a tree" and "Whose woods these are I think I know" (Fink's example), instead running the words together with a concluding explosion that makes no sense *except* as an expression of unheeding girlish enthusiasm—such as is, after all, the subject of the lyric:

> Yum-Yum, Peep-Bo, and Pitti-Sing: So please you Sir, we much **regret**
>   If we have failed in etiquette
>   Towards a man of rank so **high**—
>   We shall know better by and by.

The magic of this solution lies in its balance of "failed etiquette" against the seemingly inadvertent result of girlish carelessness, which gives "high" a precisely appropriate setting. If all of this is ultimately lost in the spectacle of the stuffy Pooh-Bah having to follow the rhythmic declamation—and, often, the dance steps—set down by the girls, we may see Sullivan violating Gilbert's lyric locally to realize more fully his larger conceit.   ♩ **10.6**

Figure 10.1. The "original" "Three Little Maids from School," as re-created in the 1999 film *Topsy-Turvy*, with Cathy Sara (as Sybil Grey playing Peep-Bo), Shirley Henderson (as Leonora Braham playing Yum-Yum), and Dorothy Atkinson (as Jessie Bond playing Pitti-Sing). The film shows, with convincing realism, the careful attention to authenticity—of dress, demeanor, fan use, and even style of walking—that went into this number, a process that involved members of the Knightsbridge Japanese installation serving as models and coaches. (Courtesy of the Academy of Motion Picture Arts and Sciences.)

"I Am So Proud," the ensuing trio for Pooh-Bah, Ko-Ko, and Pish-Tush (a minor noble) is a freely rendered "combination song" of substantial verbal and musical wit, ending in a three-part patter. Gilbert's three-pronged lyric proceeds from extreme difference among the three perspectives in the first verse to full concordance in the third and final verse, and Sullivan rises to the special challenges this structure presents. For the first verse, he sharply etches each perspective before they are combined: Pooh-Bah's ponderous logic begins with a weighty descent and proceeds in lumbering quarter-notes; Ko-Ko's flighty contribution reverses Pooh-Bah's descent and proceeds in "distracted" eighth-notes; while Pish-Tush expresses his lack of concern in a contrasting major mode and a lilting triple meter punctuated with occasional offhand melodic leaps. Notably, the latter contrasts in themselves offer highly sophisticated complications for a combination song, since Pish-Tush's melody must then combine with the minor mode and duple meter of the other two; yet this sophistication is not allowed to call undue attention to itself, as the combination, which presents all three together but with slightly staggered entrances, presents the somewhat generic effect of a contrapuntal glee in which Pish-Tush's starkly contrasting contribution becomes a mere contrapuntal foil for the other two. For the second verse, Sullivan responds directly to Gilbert's lyric by making Ko-Ko's and Pooh-Bah's melodic profiles nearly identical, to be set in relief once again by Pish-Tush's lilting major-mode; this verse ends with only a semblance of combination, setting up the homophonic concluding patter. Overall, the effect of the song is of an argument reaching a consensus, although nothing much is actually settled. ♩ **10.7**

Act II sets off the arrival of the Mikado with its most obviously marked "English" offerings, preceding his entry with the madrigal "Brightly Dawns Our Wedding Day" and glee-like "Here's a How-de-do!" and culminating his initial span on stage with the glee "See How the Fates Their Gifts Allot." In between, "Miya Sama" ushers in the Mikado's entourage, followed by a sequence redolent of Sir Joseph's in *Pinafore*, with the Mikado's authority first being usurped by Katisha, "his daughter-in-law elect" ("From Every Kind of Man") and then reasserted in a solo song that, in this case, barely escaped Gilbert's scissors on opening night. In "A More Humane Mikado," we reach a culmination of the "bloodthirsty" dimension in *The Mikado,* with important echoes in the following number, "The Criminal Cried," and the later "There Is Beauty in the Bellow of the Blast." The sequence as a whole registers as a dramatic highpoint, in part because the refrain to the Mikado's song, "My object all sublime . . . To let the punishment fit the crime" has a recognition quotient nearly equal to *Pinafore*'s "What, never? . . . Hardly ever!" But, putting aside that familiarity, its impact is sufficiently dramatic that its specific content ought to disturb more profoundly than it generally seems to. It is traditional to punctuate the set-up lines "To make, to some extent, / Each evil liver / A running river / Of harmless merriment" (and later musical recurrences) with screams and ghoulish laughter, a combination of suffering and delight (for it is clearly *blood* that runs in this particular river of merriment) that seems barely contained by its own humor and by whatever comfort "we" (as either English or their close relatives) might take in how deftly it projects this blood-mirth onto the Japanese. (All of which serves to cloak a particularly subtle effect devised by Sullivan, with the musical phrase for "My object all sublime" establishing the kinship of Mikado and Nanki-Poo in its near replication of the melodic profile for "A Wandering Minstrel I.") ♩ **10.8**
♩ **10.9**

In any case, most of those who may find lingering discomfort over this number will feel rescued by the less discomfiting comedy that follows, in the equally ghoulish "The Criminal Cried" and "There Is Beauty in the Bellow of the Blast." In the former, we know the execution being described did not actually occur, which allows us to delight easily in Ko-Ko's harmless boastfulness, Pitti-Sing's coquettish smugness, and especially Pooh-Bah's grotesque marriage of polite deference and macabre fascination:

> Now tho' you'd have said that head was dead / (For its owner dead was he),
> It stood on its neck, with a smile well-bred, / And bowed three times to me!—
> It was none of your impudent offhand nods, / But as humble as could be;
> For it clearly knew / The deference due / To a man of pedigree!
> And it's oh, I vow, / This deathly bow / Was a touching sight to see;—
> Though trunkless, yet / It couldn't forget / The deference due to me!

And, in the later "Bellow of the Blast," we easily slip into Ko-Ko's numbed perspective on Katisha's fascination for the scary sublime—after all, both characters have been spectacularly ineffective in realizing their romantic and political designs—and so we relish the contrast between her grotesqueries and the tone of innocent delight with which they conclude ("Sing derry down derry!").

♪10.10
♪10.11

Arguably, the signal achievement of *The Mikado* lies less with its orientalist basis than with the depth of expressivity Sullivan brings to songs that are essentially comic. The sheer loveliness of Yum-Yum's song "The Sun, Whose Rays" is hard to reconcile with Gilbert's arch manipulation of the paired tropes of proud sun and shy moon on the one hand, and the song's Nietzschean assertion of preeminence, held aloft by a subjectively felt sense of self-worth, on the other:

♪ 10.12

> I mean to rule the earth,—/ As he the sky—
> We really know our worth,—/ The sun and I!

Later, Sullivan's mastery of the high style gives Katisha's comic suffering a wholly unexpected dignity, incommensurate with her caricatured persona and the maudlin self-pity of Gilbert's lyric ("Alone and Yet Alive!"). And Ko-Ko's ensuing "Willow, Tit-willow," which can be done as a broadly comic parody, was early discovered to be so beguilingly lyrical that it became almost a special effect of the show, in which we suddenly find the merely comic Ko-Ko capable of a simple, overpowering eloquence, in a song that somehow transmutes Gilbert's pat, clever lyric, with its ridiculously sentimental scenario of a love-struck tom-tit, into a kind of simple, irrefutable truth. In these songs, which anticipate high camp in their expressive disjunctures, we may well see a basic enabling power that Gilbert and Sullivan bequeathed to the American musical, which would later develop its own modes for elevating the ridiculous into the sublime through music.

♪10.13
♪10.14

The King and I (1951) ranks among the great successes
of Rodgers and Hammerstein, winning five Tonys for the original production, five Oscars for the 1956 film, and four more Tonys for the 1996
revival. The cultural division between East and West in *The King and I* is
defined partly by gender, with Anna representing the West and the King
the East; thus, the power relations are reversed on a personal level from
the way they are often understood more broadly within the context of
orientalism, which tends to feminize the Other (cf., for example, *Miss
Saigon*, or the opera *Madama Butterfly*). Yet the gendering here also follows familiar tropes, with the woman representing the softening influence
of civilization on the forceful but primitive male (a dynamic also familiar
from mythologies of the American West; see the discussions of *Oklahoma!* and *Guys and Dolls* in chapter 6, especially pp. 134–36 and 137–
38). Nevertheless, the importance of power relations in the show makes
its representation of the West by a woman alone in an alien cultural environment particularly significant, underscoring that within that culture,
women have no real power and are often treated as little more than slaves.
To this extent, the show also reflects a growing concern in America, especially after World War II, for women's rights.

That the show nevertheless documents a long-standing attitude of unre-
flecting colonialism is clear already from its history as a literary and dramatic property. The show was written as a vehicle for Gertrude Lawrence
(who won a Tony as Anna, but died during the run, in 1952), based on
the successful 1946 film adaptation of Margaret Landon's 1944 novel,
Anna and the King of Siam (*Anna and the King*, dir. John Cromwell, with
Irene Dunne and Rex Harrison), which was in turn based on the less-than-
reliable memoirs of Anna Leonowens from 1870 and 1872. The King
himself was thus originally conceived as a supporting role in the musical;
Rex Harrison, Noel Coward, and Alfred Drake all turned it down, and
when Yul Brynner transformed the part into a career-defining role, he had
to settle originally for a *supporting* actor Tony. (Brynner, who would win
the Oscar for Best Actor in the 1956 film—dir. Walter Lang, screenplay
by Ernest Lehman—played the role, through long runs, revivals, and a
brief television series, over 4600 times.) Significantly, while the film version of the musical implicitly recognized the dramatically central presence
of the King, giving the East at least that much more presence, there were
no Asians among the leads. Moreover, the musical profile is deliberately
not authentic, but trades in generically "oriental" musical devices (see
below), and Jerome Robbins's choreography in a similar way gives the
show a generalized oriental texture through a stylized manner of movement that extends throughout, but is especially clear in the two set pieces,
the processional "The March of the Siamese Children" and the narrated
ballet "The Small House of Uncle Thomas"—all of which was retained
for the film. But the most glaring failure of the show in this regard—and

the reason all versions of the story have been banned in Thailand—is how blatantly wrong it is about Siam's history, and about the character of the King and the historical role he actually played. Thus, as with the other Rodgers and Hammerstein shows we have considered here (*Oklahoma!* and *The Sound of Music*), we must begin by sketching more accurately the historical events *The King and I* purports to dramatize.

Like Japan, Siam evicted Western missionaries early on, so that from 1688 it remained mostly independent of the West. Also like Japan, Siam came under enormous pressure to allow European and American trade in the mid-nineteenth century. The line of rule that is relevant to that era extended back to 1767, when long-time foe Burma conquered Siam and destroyed its capital. Fifteen years later, in 1782, the first King in a new line of succession (Rama I) came to power, moving the capital to Bangkok. King Mongkut (the King in *The King and I*) began his rule in 1851, after spending twenty-six years as a Buddhist monk, traveling the country in poverty while his half-brother ruled. During his seventeen-year rule, King Mongkut worked hard to Westernize Siam, having already taught himself English (working through a Sanskrit / English dictionary because there was then no more direct access); he is widely regarded as a wise ruler who managed to keep European powers at bay (in part by agreeing to trade with them) while moving his reluctant people gradually toward more Western practices. Moreover, besides being a scholar, he was an accomplished scientist, impressing an invited group of European scientists when he predicted a total solar eclipse to the precise second—an event that also led to his early death in 1868, since the viewing occurred in a swamp, where both he and his successor contracted malaria. His son, the future King Chulalongkorn, who recovered from his bout with malaria but was only fifteen at the time of his father's death, began his long rule five years later, serving as King from 1873 to 1910. During his reign, he completed the process of Westernizing the government of Siam, in the early stages of his rule abolishing slavery, establishing a process of legislation, and instituting the rule of law.

As part of King Mongkut's efforts to Westernize without Christian missionaries, he sent in 1862 for the recently widowed English woman Anna Owens (who had begun calling herself Anna Leonowens), then in Singapore, to educate his wives and children; her duties consisted only of teaching English to fewer than a dozen of the King's children, and she had very little contact with the King or other members of the court. In America after the King died, she began the process of romanticizing the exoticism and barbarity of the Siamese court, as well as her role in the ongoing process of Westernizing the country—strategies designed to flatter both herself and her readers—in two sets of memoirs, which Landon's book, the 1946 film, and the musical then pushed farther.[7] Within the musical line of development, especially, the potential of a romantic link between Anna and the King is increasingly developed, but is never made fully explicit in the libretto; significantly, then, the younger Deborah Kerr was chosen to play Anna in the film, to make this dimension more readily believable. In a more subtle way, the dubbing of her voice by Marni Nixon, although less bothersome than her dubbing of Audrey Hepburn in *My Fair Lady* a few years later, detracts from Anna's "presence" and adds to the King's (even if, surely, this was not the intention); moreover, it places the "Broadway" style of her songs, already a deliberate foil to the "oriental" musical idiom of the Siamese numbers, in even higher relief. More important thematically, the show drew much closer to specifically American issues even though (as in *The Sound of Music*) no Americans appear, paralleling the Western film genre in its focus on the civilizing influence of women, and drawing specific parallels between America and Siam on the issue of slavery (America's Civil War was ongoing when Anna arrived in Siam).

Much is made in the show of differing perceptions of gender roles; both East and West profess consternation at the place of women within the other's culture. The fact that England was then governed by Queen Victoria allows Anna in some sense to serve as her stand-in, so that her managerial manner occasions confusion among the King's wives, who call her "Sir." Perhaps in deliberate parallel, America is represented through references to not only "President Lingkong," but also Harriet Beecher Stowe, whose book *Uncle Tom's Cabin* (1852) is requested by Tuptim, and forms the basis for her narrated ballet. The issue of slavery also has two points of reference, overlapping with those for gender roles. *Uncle Toms's Cabin,* of course, is primarily concerned with slavery in America. But the King also speaks fairly often of Moses (in order to dispute the teachings of the Christian Bible), and it was Moses who led the Israelites from slavery in Egypt. In fact, Tuptim's dramatization of "The Small House of Uncle Thomas" conflates events in *Uncle Tom's Cabin* and the Book of Exodus; thus, Buddha creates a miracle—ice—that serves analogously to the parting of the Red Sea, permitting Eliza's escape across the water but dooming Simon Legree, who drowns when the ice melts, like the Egyptian Pharaoh following Moses and the Jews (in the book, it is not Simon Legree who pursues Eliza, nor does her pursuer perish). In a subtle way, too, gender roles and slavery—implicitly two sides of the same coin of inequality—are represented by the performance of the anti-slavery ballet, which is adapted by Tuptim from a book by a woman, and performed entirely by women (who wear masks when they assume male parts).

As suggested, an important issue for the musical, especially from a perspective fifty years later, is racial embodiment. In some ways, one might argue that race is not a central issue in the show (which concerns more centrally issues of gender and slavery), yet the casting of Rita Moreno to play Tuptim in the film registers as racially significant, since her being Puerto Rican would have mattered tremendously in 1956 (just before the stage version of *West Side Story;* she would win an Oscar for her performance as Anita in the film version). Moreover, in a curious inversion of blackface, "The Small House of Uncle Thomas" is performed in whiteface, which serves without apparent irony to underscore the fact that the show uses mainly whites to portray its Asian population, a practice directly analogous to blackface minstrelsy and with similar tendencies toward unnuanced stereotyping.

But, while we today cannot buy into the show's *faux* Siam, the sharp differences it draws between East and West do allow significant general issues to be dealt with in sometimes subtle ways. Especially in and around the ballet sequence, for example, we see the tendency to take a rather narrow perspective on the art and customs of the Other, observing them through filters of our own devising, so that the observer is most particularly affected by what is either most relevant or most strange when observed from that narrow perspective. Thus, Tuptim, in deriving her ballet from Stowe's book, gives more prominence to Eliza's love-driven escape from slavery and the "miracle" of ice (the latter being exotic from a Siamese perspective), than to the main story of Uncle Tom himself. Moreover, having gotten used to the Siamese Court and its harem, we (in the American audience) are ready to see the visiting diplomats in Act II as the harem women do: as cannibals and savages, even if that perception is downplayed in the film, which cuts the song "Western People Funny"— presumably for its stereotyping of the Siamese, even though it offers one of the more scathing indictments of imperialism in the show:

> Western people funny, Western people funny,
> Western people funny, too funny to be true!
> They think they civilize us, / Whenever they advise us
> To learn to make the same mistake / That they are making too!

If the song is meant to amuse us, like the Siamese children's and wives' earlier marveling at Anna's description of snow, it also occurs late enough that our sympathies are wholly with their perspective; perhaps we are meant to realize that *we* also get *them* wrong, which is the point of the first act song: "Getting to Know You" (even if the latter song, originally written for *South Pacific,* was added out of town).

♩ 10.15

Given its mix of good intentions, insights, and blithe indifference to getting things historically right, the show on the whole inevitably patronizes: we are invited to enjoy our superiority, to contemplate as a curiosity a faraway kingdom of harems, slavery, and barbarity, and even to mourn the passing of that culture with the death of its king. To be sure, the show teaches an important object lesson: we are reminded that we in America were at that very historical moment (that is, in the midst of the Civil War) dealing with similar issues. But there is also the lesson of smug insularity: by embodying the main roles through Western actors, by slighting vener-ated historical figures, by making Anna the impetus for reform, the show teaches us to disrespect as childlike a culture and people eminently wor-thy of respect in adult terms—even as it purports, without irony, to teach us the importance of respecting cross-cultural difference. We may note that there were alternatives to this approach, even if commercially prob-lematic; whatever its controversies, Gershwin's *Porgy and Bess* fifteen years earlier had worked hard to create an embodied community of African Americans, and Sondheim's *Pacific Overtures* twenty-five years later would create a beachhead for Asian embodiment on Broadway (without, to be sure, the financial success of *The King and I*). Moreover, Rodgers's music for the show, in creating its images of the Other through generalized "oriental" sounds—e.g., parallel open chords, Asian instru-mentation, and gapped (pentatonic) scales—rather than specifically Sia-mese sources (which he deemed too harsh), foregoes the model of Sulli-van in *The Mikado*, who began, at least, with actual Japanese music.

The show's opening song, "I Whistle a Happy Tune," is a classic inspi-rational number of the child-oriented variety, sung by Anna to her son as they near Bangkok. Displacing the scary chanting of the Siamese oarsmen, the song seems to domesticate tropes of orientalist music by giving great emphasis to its repeated-note motive:

> Whenever **I feel afraid** / I hold my **head erect**
> And whistle **a happy tune,** / So no one will suspect
> I'm afraid.

> While shiver**ing in my shoes** / I strike a **careless pose**
> And whistle **a happy tune** / And no one ever knows
> I'm afraid.

This bringing together of the child-oriented and a primitivist repeated-note motive that will reappear throughout the show as part of its "orien-tal" musical profile serves to reinforce the patronizing attitude already dis-cussed, an attitude compounded soon after in the "March of the Siamese Children," which again uses a repeated-note motive, but more overtly connects its childish component to an orientalist idiom. To be sure, this connection will be problematized in Anna's dealings with the King, for whom patronizing cannot work if she is to wield influence. Nevertheless, the model is set early on: Anna, the Westerner, teaches the childlike Other the ways and superior knowledge of the wiser, more adult West.

♪ 10.16
♪ 10.17

That Anna has something to teach the King, as well as his children and wives, is made clear in the King's soliloquy "Is A Puzzlement," but the song also clarifies that the uncertainty she offers—since learning and presumed certainty do not go together—undermines directly his ability to rule. The song makes of the generational line of the monarchy, when combined with his educational program, a trajectory into increasing uncertainty, for the King is caught between his father's certitude and his son's observance of his own doubt. Here, the repeated-note motive becomes an emblem of resolute truth, but which is routinely undermined by its shifting with each phrase to a different repeated pitch. A similar strategy undermines key arrival pitches that profess to strength and certainty, which are held strongly but then move; as shown, however, when he decides that uncertainty is perhaps better, the arrival note holds:

There are times I almost think / I am not sure of what I absolutely **kno-ow**;
Very often find confusion in conclusion I concluded long **ago-o** . . .

When my father was a king / He was a king who knew exactly what he **kne-ew**,
And his brain was not a thing, / Forever swinging to and fro, fro and **to-oo**.

Shall I, then, / Be like my father and be willfully, unmovable and **stro-ong**?
Or is better to be right? / Or am I right when I believe I may be **wrong**?

As in *Fiddler on the Roof,* the issue comes down to the incompatibility of specifically feminine self-determination with the culturally reinforced expectation of masculine authority. Thus, for example, Tuptim does not win her freedom, but Anna does succeed in changing the way she is treated—at the cost, however, of destroying the old order, of bringing about the King's destruction.

♫ 10.18   The climax of the show is a kind of double-image involving the opposing facets of Western exoticism, which enriches the West only at the expense of destroying the vitality of the fetishized East. In the shadow of the King's imminent destruction—dramatized as his inability to whip Tuptim in Anna's presence—we see the enriching component first as a version of the marriage trope, presented in the powerfully charged "Shall We Dance?" As Scott Miller observes, "the dance becomes a metaphor for monogamy. . . . She is metaphorically teaching him how to be monogamous."[8] Yet he is teaching her something, as well, and it frightens her. He is teaching her in real terms what she now knows only as a faded memory: that dance is also a metaphor for sexuality, and of masculine power over the feminine. Thus, the dance in question is not the feminized waltz, but the more masculine polka, and the sequence of events is carefully managed: the song's lyric innocently proclaims the point of the number by playfully suggesting that "dance" may lead "perchance" to "romance"; she dances for him; they touch (for the first time); they dance together but at a distance; he insists on their dancing as he saw her dance earlier with the Englishman Sir Edward (they had briefly danced a waltz); they dance an exuberantly wild, waltz-like version of the polka (in the film accompanied by an abrupt awareness of the expansive space they are suddenly commanding); they stop, discomfited by what has just transpired, yet not allowed to resolve their feelings since the second part of the double-image (Tuptim's capture) then intrudes, leading to the King's destruction.   ♫ 10.19

Thus, events pull them away from confronting a key but scary premise of the show, that there might be a romance between them—a difficult thing to contemplate both within the context of the show and on the 1951 Broadway stage more generally. Suddenly, with the dance and its aftermath, the King and Anna are adults together; for the first time they rec-

Figure 10.2. Anna (Deborah Kerr) taking dictation from King Mongkut (Yul Brynner) in the 1956 film *The King and I*. The King is writing to President "Lingkong" to support him in his effort to free America's slaves, a gesture that underscores the parallels in their respective situations, as leaders of countries undergoing similarly difficult transitions. (Courtesy of the Academy of Motion Picture Arts and Sciences.)

ognize fully the adulthood of the other, which has been the result of a long process for the King, but a matter of sudden realization for Anna. Part of what makes that point for her is that he has taken her domesticating ditty— "Shall We Dance"—replete with the childish and orientalist repeated-note motive, and converted precisely that motive into an emblem of masculine power and authority.

The possibility of sexual / cultural union here produces a strong, powerful image, sustained through the metaphor of exuberant dance-movement. But it is only an image, and is not sustainable either in the real world of 1950s American sensibilities, when America was just beginning its road to a more genuine multiculturalism, nor in the imaginary world of the "Siamese" court in *The King and I*. But what attenuates possibilities here is not so much those two worlds considered separately, but rather the circumstance that the first of these (1950s America) had not progressed beyond the ready-made fantasyland of picturesque courts and harems in its ability to conceive of the Other. Nor did Americans in 1951 want to do so, for the image was at once too titillating and too comforting to leave behind.

Pacific Overtures (1976) started as a fairly conventional play by John Weidman that treated the "gunboat diplomacy" of nineteenth-century America as it coerced Japan to enter into trade with the West. As detailed earlier in connection with *The Mikado,* Japan had remained closed until 1853, when Commodore Matthew Perry of the United States began to "negotiate" the opening of Japan to foreign trade, setting in motion a chain of events that led to the overthrow of the Tokugawa Shogunate, and the "Meiji Restoration" of 1868, as well as accomplishing Perry's objective of opening up trade with the United States and other foreign powers. Well into the process of mounting the play as Weidman had conceived it, producer-director Hal Prince hit upon the idea of telling the story from Japan's point of view, after seeing Japanese depictions of Commodore Perry with Japanese features and dress. He then brought Stephen Sondheim in (already a frequent collaborator with Prince), who resisted initially because the play seemed more about ideas than characters (the same "Brecht" issue that would arise for him later with *Assassins,* also written by Weidman; see chapter 7, p. 165). The result was a "concept musical" that presents a slice of Japanese history, seemingly from a Japanese perspective (thus using Asian actors and adapting Japanese theatrical modes to the Broadway stage)—opening, with exquisite timing, in January of America's bicentennial year.

The show as reconceived by Prince presented numerous problems, some of them simply practical. Casting was particularly difficult, since Prince insisted that they use only Asians and (until the final number) only men, in line with Japanese Kabuki traditions. But no Asians answered the initial call, forcing them to recruit actors, often with little or no experience, from Asian community theater, through newspaper ads, from California, and even through enlisting the help of the State Department. Broadway, even in 1976, rarely cast Asians for important roles in shows; even when the roles in question were Asian, the custom had always been (and too often still is) to rely on a kind of Asian "blackface," as in *The King and I*. Related expectations also undermined the show's success in New York, for the Asian dimension of the show made it seem like a foreign import, however American its concerns ultimately were.[9] But the cast was committed to the show, and a decision to take it on tour in fall 1976 helped it gain an audience in San Francisco and Los Angeles, where there was a larger Asian population to draw on.

The second act presented problems relating to the integration of theatrical drama and historical narrative, since the two characters who helped center the first-act confrontation around a character-based nucleus, Manjiro and Kayama, could not realistically carry history forward all the way into the Meiji restoration and beyond. Both characters were drawn from history, which was both necessary and limiting. Kayama Yesaemon (Yezaimon), the *daimyo* (governor) of Urago, the harbor where Perry first arrived, was not a particularly important figure, historically, which gave the authors room to manipulate his character within the show's plot while remaining true to "history." Manjiro, on the other hand, was a very prominent figure. Shipwrecked in 1841 at the age of fourteen and rescued six months later by Americans, he became the first Japanese to visit America (the other fishermen who were rescued with him elected to stay in Hawaii). When he returned to Japan ten years later (a few years ahead of Perry's "pacific overtures" of 1853), the Shogunate was at first extremely reluctant to allow him to return, but ultimately came to rely on his training and experience of America in responding to the American trade initiative. Thereafter, for many years, Japan's America was America as Manjiro had experienced it, and he became a central diplomatic and educational force in the newly emergent Japan.

In the show, Manjiro's and Kayama's destinies become intertwined and then diverge in a crossing pattern, so that the Westernized Manjiro becomes a samurai and eventually kills Kayama, whose increasingly appeasing ways have made him a stooge of the West. Yet this is quite a departure from the real-life Manjiro; as Sab Shimono, who created the role of Manjiro, relates,

> I actually met his family in Nagoya, and they're very angry at how he's treated in the show. He came back from America a pacifist and did not believe in the samurai code. But in the play, he becomes a samurai. His story

is so famous in Japan that it would have been like a Japanese playwright writing a play that said George Washington was not the first president of the United States. Yet Manjiro's transformation was a good choice, theatrically.[10]

At some point, the two characters, made very human in Act I, become abstractions, useful as demonstrations of the power of historical events to shape human and cultural destinies and even individual character, but oddly discordant with the aim to honor the Japanese perspective. Also important here (and one of the ways that adhering to the historical record may be important dramatically) is the history-as-fate trope discussed in the previous chapter (see pp. 230–31); since we know what the "endgame" looks like, with Pearl Harbor, World War II, the atomic bombs, and the Japanese industrial renaissance afterwards, we know the general shape of what must happen to the foregrounded characters and their culture. In a sense, the show remains poised irresolutely between a kind of Shakespearean drama, which focuses directly on important historical figures, and French Grand Opera, which foregrounds (like *The Sound of Music*) less important figures whose lives are wrenched apart as cataclysmic historical events play out around them.

To solve the second-act problem, the show's creative team discarded an elaborate sequence that was to detail the industrialization of Japan through puppetry and short sketches, and instead moved directly from the emergence of the Emperor Meiji from his own puppet figure into the final number, "Next," set in the present. The loss of the extended puppet sequence was a defeat of sorts. Not only did they lose the opportunity to enact symbolically Japan's emergence from a Western "puppet state" into a fully autonomous modern nation, which would have directly paralleled on a larger level the Emperor's own emergence from a puppet, but they also lost their best chance to make explicit reference to the atomic bombing of Hiroshima and Nagasaki, which had long been part of the conception. Nevertheless, with the sequence eliminated, Manjiro's assassination of Kayama provided a climax to the personal story late enough to keep the overarching historical dimension fully grounded in the personal, with Manjiro's association with a coalition of militant samurai serving as a direct spur for the emergence of the emperor just before the finale.[11]

Staging and dramatic style were problems analogous in some ways to the musical and poetic problems that composer-lyricist Sondheim would face (which we will consider shortly): how could East and West be combined so as to allow the story to play from both sides, and to project the Westernizing of Japan through enacting a transition of sorts between them? The former set of problems were solved with particular elegance;

in fact, the show's only Tonys—in a year dominated by *A Chorus Line*—
were for Scenic Design (Boris Aronson) and Costumes (Florence Klotz).
As Meryle Secrest describes it, Aronson's sets provided

> a visual indication that a world of "rice paper, origami, kites, bamboo" was
> being shattered. . . . Perry's ship, which moved with "the fragility and del-
> icacy of a paper dragon" . . . came to symbolize what was meant by the
> ironic title ["Pacific Overtures"], gliding toward the audience . . . with its
> fire-eating eyes and menacing, masklike prow.[12]

The dramatic style was an adaptation of *Kabuki* (the most popular Japanese theatrical tradition, with singing and dancing), combined with elements of *Noh* drama (an aristocratic Japanese form of relatively short and
highly stylized narrated drama, featuring expressive masks and fan play)
and *bunraku* (Japanese puppet theater), although, as noted, the latter's
most elaborate sequence was dropped. Kabuki, in some ways the func-
tional equivalent of the American musical, was additionally appropriate
for *Pacific Overtures* because it has tended to absorb aspects of other
musico-dramatic forms, and because it has frequently been used in the
dramatic retelling of historical events (*jidaimono*). Specific Kabuki elements incorporated into *Pacific Overtures* included a runway extending
out over the audience to the back of the theater (*hanamichi*), all-male
casting, a bravura lion's dance (from the ancient *shishimai* tradition), a
Kabuki-derived dance style more generally (for which choreographer Pa-
tricia Birch hired Haruki Fujimoto as a consultant), a somewhat rambling
and episodic plot-line (at least by European dramatic standards), and the
use of a narrator / commentator (reciter) who may assume roles in the
drama as well.

Pacific Overtures uses these and other devices to create a sense of indi-
rectness and ambiguity, or to bring specific moments in the drama into
stylistic relief. Thus, the reciter will sometimes speak (or sob) for the characters, making them mute mimes (figuratively, they become his live pup-
pets). Men playing women's parts or playing multiple men's parts creates
at times an expressive confusion of identity. And the use of bunraku for
the Emperor underscores his role as a figurehead before the 1868 restoration. Particularly disturbing is the triumphal lion's dance, traditionally
used to ward off evil spirits. Since it comes at the end of Act I, after Perry
and his American "barbarians" leave with Japanese land untouched (due
to the subterfuge of laying down mats), we might take it as a Japanese celebration, but as such it is undercut doubly, first because it is generically
unstable (being an Act I finale), and second because the figure dancing is
Commodore Perry, leaving us to wonder who has really triumphed in the
scene we have just watched. The latter ambiguity is set up by the elabo-

rate "silence" about what actually happened in the treaty house, a silence conveyed and sustained through the miraculous "Someone in a Tree" (discussed later).

Sondheim's approach to the music bears some resemblance to Sullivan's with *The Mikado*, although the result is substantially different. Like Sullivan, Sondheim found a useful link between a Japanese sound and something more Western. Sondheim's link is the musical language of the Spanish composer Manuel de Falla, who combined a use of pentatonic (gapped) collections in the conventional sense, often arranged within mildly dissonant four-note vertical sonorities, with a "Phrygian" inflection created through adding half-steps above the tonic and fifth degree, a device which resonates with one of the Japanese modes. The importance of finding some such link may be illustrated by recalling not only Sullivan's fusion of Japanese pentatonicism and English modality, but also Rodgers's merger in *The King and I* of "Siamese" with a child-like "teacher" mode (both involving repeated-note motives). But Sondheim needed more than a link, since he needed to effect a transition from a Japanese sound to one more Western, and the Falla link provided him with this capacity, as well: simply by reversing the orientation of the "Phrygian" component, he could allow the more conventional leading-tones of Western harmony to emerge.[13] More conventionally, but very effectively, the show also uses traditional Japanese instruments (flute and percussion), with traditionally trained Japanese musicians, either in improvised underscoring or, at times, absorbed into the ensemble (or, perhaps, imitated and / or echoed within Jonathan Tunick's instrumentation).

Also falling largely to Sondheim was the task of developing a language that would seem Japanese yet be able to "evolve" toward something more Western. For this, he cultivated a Haiku-like economy and directness of expression, avoiding words with Latin roots. This distinctive and oddly spare use of English he then contrasted with the English spoken by the Americans (and, later, the English, Dutch, Russian, and French), which alternated between two modes. Often, foreigners spoke in what Sondheim would term "translator-ese," analogous to the broken English we routinely hear from foreigners on stage and in films; this not only projects the governing perspective of the Japanese point of view, but also conveys the patronizing manner of the foreigners, who unnecessarily "talk down" to the Japanese. Within songs, on the other hand, the foreigners' lyric style often became stereotypical, so that, for example, the British admiral in "Please Hello" sings an intricately rhymed patter-song. Thus, in parallel to each other and against the latter's more familiar "Broadway pastiche," Sondheim creates two versions of a "reduced" English, one reduced for poetic effect, the other to indicate a more crass sensibility so as to turn the tables on typical American portrayals of foreigners.

Because of the highly developed poetic language of the Japanese, it becomes particularly vivid that Westernizing entails for Japan a significant loss of a valuable human dimension. Additionally and on a larger level, Sondheim attempted to create a Japanese "voice" (or, perhaps, sensibility) both by frequently employing additive constructive principles in devising his lyrics, building them up from small blocks, and by dealing in figurative oppositions between circular (cyclic) and linear (goal-directed) activity and motion, the latter being representative of the West. Sondheim also expressed both of these musically, constructing melodies that emerged in fitful bits so as to keep the small blocks of language audibly separate from each other, and to set the opposition between the circular and the linear, using gradations in rhythmic urgency and a gradual shift to conventional tonal harmonies from more static harmonic modalities. (Ultimately, of course, what makes these devices seem authentic is a mix of their strangeness and naturalness, the latter conveyed through the former being embodied convincingly by an all-Asian cast.)

The opening number, "The Advantages of Floating in the Middle of the Sea," presents a series of circular images (life as ritual) against a primitive background that uses repetitive dissonances redolent of both da Falla and the "primitivist" style of Igor Stravinsky, in particular the hammer-chords near the beginning of the latter's *Rite of Spring* (1913). Sondheim is less extreme than Stravinsky, initially using a four-note pentatonic chord rather than Stravinsky's seven-note polychord within a framing major-seventh, although Sondheim adds intensity through using a six-note chord at climactic moments. Two other vivid points of comparison for this number are "If You Want to Know Who We Are" from *The Mikado* (sung, as here, by an all-male chorus) and "Tradition" from *Fiddler on the Roof*. All three numbers establish a static, tradition-bound atmosphere as a starting position for the drama, and the similarity reminds us of how much *Fiddler on the Roof* engages, like *Pacific Overtures*, with the Westernizing of an oriental culture, even if the shtetl Jews of *Fiddler* would have seemed considerably less remote to a large part of their original Broadway audience. As did Stravinsky, Sondheim uses irregular rhythmic structures to create a highly charged energy that remains nevertheless essentially static, specifically to help convey the ritualistic component of the accompanying activity.

♫ 10.20
♫ 10.21

"Advantages," like its models, is highly schematic, tracing and retracing cycles within cycles. The basic alternation is between sections that describe the relationship between "somewhere" and "here," and sections that describe a particular circular life-ritual (screens, rice, and bows are each given a verse, but the ending makes it clear that the list of cycles to observe is potentially endless, including flowers, moon, gifts, tea, and weaving). Each "somewhere" section describes a cycle of intensification and relaxation, articulated by an initial process of quickening pulse, increasing dissonance, and growing louder, followed by a recession of these energies so as to complete the projected cycle from "here" to "somewhere" and back again to "here":

> In the middle of the world we float / In the middle of the sea.
> The realities remain remote / In the middle of the sea.
>> Kings are burning somewhere, / Wheels are turning somewhere,
>> Trains are being run, / Wars are being won, / Things are being done
>> Somewhere out there, not here.
> Here we paint screens.

For the first two cycles (screens and rice), Sondheim produces a more conventional form of swirling pentatonic orientalism, akin to the opening figures of "If You Want to Know Who We Are" in *The Mikado* or the conventionalized tinkling of *The King and I*. For the third cycle (bows), the music breaks to allow for the introduction of the one-year-old Emperor (a puppet) and the rarely seen Shogun (a curtained palanquin). Besides fulfilling its function as an opening number, establishing context and setting up the drama, "Advantages" also serves as the first half of a comprehensive frame, to which the finale will refer in fairly specific terms.

"Poems" establishes the growing friendship between Kayama and the rescued fisherman Manjiro in an exchange of poems that in some ways resembles haiku. One tradition associated with haiku involves poetic exchanges, in which an opening three-line poem of seventeen syllables (5-7-5) will be answered by a completion in two lines of seven syllables each, which would then be answered by another three-line poem, and so on. In general terms, Sondheim imitates this form in producing additive structures throughout the show, using pithy, epigrammatic verses as building blocks. In this number, he uses as well the idea of trading poems in a cumulative way, but, while paying close attention to syllabic count, he does not adhere to those of the traditional Haiku exchanges. In Sondheim's version of the game, each contribution initially adds a syllable, moving from 4-5-5 to 4-5-6, to 4-7-5, to 4-7-6.[14] Even as the two characters leave this syllabic pattern behind, Manjiro continues to build on the images Kayama uses to describe his wife by applying each of them in its turn to America, cycling through a series of one-word poetic images: rain, haze, moon, wind, song, dawn, leaves, sun. The song has a tragic overtone, which is both imposed from outside—since we know that Kayama's wife has committed suicide in his absence and that America will betray Manjiro's trust—and hinted at from within. Thus, Kayama sings of his lady's tears, her kneeling posture, and her sleeping—all eerily resonant with the suicide we have recently seen enacted—whereas Manjiro describes America as a moon eclipsing "yesterday":

Moon,
I love her like the moon,
Washing yesterday away,
As my lady does,
America.

Musically, as well, the song involves an additive structure, beginning with
a five-note ostinato figure (using all five pitches of the pentatonic) that is
gradually inflected by chromatic pitches and rhythmic complications, first
by the voice, and eventually by added instruments.   ♪ 10.22

"Someone in a Tree," which Sondheim has described as his personal favorite from the show, is the second number to describe a historic event
from multiple points of view. In the first of these, "Four Black Dragons,"
the true nature of that event is clear to us, since the "dragons" (or "volca-
noes") are obviously Perry's ships. But we neither already know nor learn
what happened in the treaty house, the ostensible subject matter of "Someone in a Tree," nor does it really matter (except that we may be assured
that the parties involved have completely different notions about what
happened). Thus, there is a kind of purity to the song, as it is simply about
the act of witnessing, with the witnesses themselves oblivious to what we
are made to understand through the song: that no single perspective provides access to the whole truth. In structural terms, the song gives the con-
structedness of history an almost visceral presence, by demonstrating the
way "history" is pieced together into a narrative from isolated facts; thus,
the song accumulates often insignificant detail as it goes, providing the
semblance of a narrative but without a central thread. The problem of interpretation and mediation is also elaborated as the song unfolds, since
both the boy who watched from the tree and the man that boy grew into
are present, along with a somewhat impatient reciter and another witness
concealed beneath the floorboards of the treaty house.

As in many other numbers in the show (including "Advantages" and
"Poems"), Sondheim manipulates a pentatonic ostinato as a shaping technique, here starting with a four-note chord that intensifies with additional
pitches, breaking into extended moments of relaxation during which the
witnesses sing over a resimplified ostinato. Texturally, Sondheim creates
a variety of interactions among the voices, even apart from how those
voices are layered against the various ostinato figures. Thus, the narrator's impatience registers through his overlapping dialogues with each of
the others, whereas the parallel fifths that develop gradually between the
old man and his younger self, augmented in the final chord to a stack of
fifths sung by all three witnesses, add a strident dimension to the repeti-
tious detail, and highlight the "message" of the song as the witnesses understand it:

It's the fragment, not the day. / It's the pebble, not the stream.
It's the ripple, not the sea, / Not the building but the beam,
Not the garden but the stone, / Not the treaty house,
Someone in a tree.

♩ **10.23**

When the Americans return in Act II, they are followed closely by the English, Dutch, Russians, and French, a chaotic accumulation that is encapsulated within the extended combination song, "Please Hello." Sondheim here deploys his extraordinary ability to re-create the semblance of given song-types, generally termed pastiche. This term is often applied negatively to Sondheim, underscoring his stylistic dependence (and, by implication, his purported lack of originality), and often suggesting as well that the overall result of such dependence is an eclectic hodgepodge of unrelated types and forms (see chapter 7, p. 165). In this case, however, such is to a large extent the point, as each stereotypical genre is captured so definitively that there is no chance whatever of the five combining with any grace. The most distinctive "types" are the first two, an American patriotic march (à la Sousa or *The Music Man*), complete with a relaxed "Trio" episode, and an English patter song (à la Gilbert and Sullivan's patter songs), with an intricate internal rhyme scheme that Sondheim maintains even when the British Admiral cannot be heard through the din of competing types. One of the "lost" verses, for example, runs (with bold-face highlighting the internal rhymes) as follows:

The British **feel** these latest **deal**ings verge on immorality,
The el**ement** of preced**ent** imperils our neutrality.
We're rather **vexed**, your giving e**xtra**territoriality.
We must in**sist** you offer **this** to every nationality!

The remaining three, while distinctive "types," amount to a kind of "shtick," each a highly mannered, stereotypical presentation that reduces the nationality in question to a comic caricature, well within Broadway traditions of representation (even including a complete disregard for historical plausibility, since all are shamelessly anachronistic). Thus, the Dutch Admiral sings a cheeky "wooden-shoe" number and ridicules the Russian and French, the Russian "bear" is moody and distrustful ("Don't touch the coat"), and the French "charmer" is a parody of Maurice Chevalier at his smirking best, a dandy who comes in blowing kisses and then sings a rolling "Ah, Detente!" in a cakewalk (detente being a catchword much in vogue during the 1970s, describing a strategy of mutual tolerance as a means to stabilize Western-Soviet relations). Against the growing chaos, and punctuated by the sound of cannon-fire, the Japanese Lord Abe struggles to maintain order, but only a complete capitulation to the French "Detente," sung by all the admirals in unison, allows the song to reach a satisfying, intricately rhymed conclusion:

Please hello! We must go, / But our intercourse will grow
Through detente, as detente / Brings complete cooperation.
By the way, may we say / We adore your little nation,
And with heavy **cannon** / Wish you **an un-** / Ending please hello!!!   ♪ **10.24**

The particularly intricate referentiality of an Asian actor here turning
the tables simultaneously on *The Mikado* and Broadway, singing a Gilbert
and Sullivan patter song in the Broadway version of a British accent, is
trumped by one of the key numbers in the second act, "Pretty Lady," in
which three "Cockney" sailors (courtesy again of Broadway) mistake a
young woman of good breeding for a geisha. In terms of the plot, the re-
sultant rape is the event that triggers the dénouement: Kayama goes too
far in his appeasement of foreign transgressions, which appeasement leads
Manjiro to assassinate him, which violence leads to the restoration of the
Emperor. Metaphorically, the rape points to the tendency of imperialism
to render cultures subservient, turning its victims into the equivalent of
whores (a theme also explored in the less successful song "Welcome to
Kanagawa"). What makes the situation particularly poignant is that the
British sailors do not intend harm, which suggests that good intentions
are not enough, that the erosion and subjugation of Japanese culture was
the inevitable result of the American's "pacific overtures," however be-
nignly conceived. The music is an elegiac blend of East and West, the latter represented through a sophisticated use of imitative techniques (including augmentation, where the basic motive is sung at half-speed) and
an introductory descending tetrachord (a traditional token of lament), but
given a "Japanese" dimension through the use of parallel open intervals
(fourths and fifths, a common trope of representing "oriental" music with
at least some basis in actual practice). It is specifically the Western dimension, the interweaving of melodic lines into counterpoint, that con-
fuses and disorients the victim, providing a musical analog to the way the
sailors circle around her, blocking her escape. The music is sad and beautiful, even wistful (especially given the sailors' homesickness), yet the
event itself is violent, a powerfully expressive combination redolent of the
"seduction" of Zerlina by the title character in Mozart's *Don Giovanni*
("Là ci darem la mano"), a number so lovely and so familiar that few recognize that it, too, presents rape as seduction, within music that ravishes,
not with violence, but with sheer loveliness.   ♪ **10.25**

"Bowler Hat" and "Next," which frame "Pretty Lady," describe the
process of Westernizing in very specific terms. The former, sung by
Kayama, is particularly admired (Prince singles it out as one of his fa-
vorites) for its concise account of an individual's gradual decline into conformity, a theme Sondheim would return to more elaborately in *Merrily
We Roll Along* (1981). To complete the frame, both around the gentle violence of "Pretty Lady" and for the entire show, "Next" projects a simi-

Figure 10.3. British sailors sing "Pretty Lady" to a young Japanese woman they mistake for a geisha (all played by Asian men), in the original production of *Pacific Overtures*. In one of the most lyrical of operatic "seduction" scenes, the music weaves its web of counterpoint in parallel to the sailors' circling motion around the woman. (© Martha Swope. Used by permission.)

lar trajectory into conformity as aggressively optimistic, a full-frontal embrace of the West's modernity. The music returns to the primitivism of the opening number, "Advantages," with many musical and textual points of reference, but transforms those ingredients into the sound of industrial energy, the sound of Corporate America, News on the March, etc. The endless cycles of "Advantages" become the mindless churning of machinery. Instead of poetry, we get statistics. Instead of tradition we get the pride of survival, of beating the West at its own game, seen as a kind of consolation prize. It is by no means a comfortable moment, however exhilarating. The music lurches, barely in control as it builds up momentum, creating a Western, goal-directed crescendo, but also hinting at the possibility of losing control of the "machinery of progress." It is only here (and in the

Dutch Admiral's passing reference to Nagasaki in "Please Hello") that the disaster of World War II and the atomic bombs is hinted at:

> Kings are burning, / Sift the ashes—/ Next! . . .
>
> Tower tumbles, / Tower rises—/ Next! . . .
>
> First the thunder—/ Just a murmer—/ A little blunder—/ Next! . . .
>
> Never mind a small disaster. / Who's the stronger, who's the faster?
>
> Let the pupil show the master—/ Next! / Next!

While the title word clearly implies in context that we (that is, Japan) should not look back, but only ahead ("Washing yesterday away, / As my lady does, / America"), the aggressive tone of the song seems to be overtly threatening. As Shimono (who played Manjiro) puts it,

> I was never quite comfortable with that last number, "Next!" because it gave a negative ring. It made it sound as if Japan was going to take over (economically), whereas it was just getting better, it was finally coming up in the world. I felt we were attacking the audience, as if to say, "Next! Pearl Harbor is coming again. Next! You better watch it!" I wish the ending had been more of a celebration of the East and West working together.[15]

While optimistic, the tone is also bleak, and upon reflection we cannot help finding it quite sobering.   ♪ **10.26**

The problem of non-Asians—Weidman, Prince, Sondheim—creating a Japanese perspective to be embodied by Asians was similar to what Heyward and the Gershwins faced in trying to create a black perspective in *Porgy and Bess*. Whenever one culture looks at another, especially from so remote a distance, it cannot help essentializing differences, so that often what will barely register for an insider stands out in high relief for an outsider, forming the basis for stylistic imitation. One may imagine, for example, someone unfamiliar with European art music imitating Haydn or Mozart by simplistically setting tunes against simple triads, yet missing completely what someone well acquainted with these composers would identify as central features of their respective styles. Inevitably, imitations thus tend toward the reductive, in ways that firmly entrench the perspective of the imitator, however well meaning. Despite this circumstance, however—and it certainly applies to both *The King and I* and *Pacific Overtures*—the receptive context for *Pacific Overtures* was, overall, not nearly as fraught with mistrust as it was for African Americans and *Porgy and Bess*. Asian Americans have mostly embraced the show for the gestural honor it accords the Asian perspective, and for the simple humanity involved in bringing Asians into the creative process (including the acting!) as the show developed.

How much the show is grounded in Broadway, despite its attempt to project an Asian perspective and to adapt Japanese theatrical traditions, has been made clear by its reception in Japan. Before the original show closed in New York, it was filmed (in a slightly cut version) for broadcast in Japan, where its reception was decidedly mixed. Just as Broadway had found it hard to recruit and make a place for Asian performers and their traditions, few Japanese knew what to make of the show without having a sense for its Broadway context; it was, after all, the first telecast of an American musical in Japan. Yet in 2000 the show was remounted by Amon Miyamoto, in translation, by the New National Theatre in Tokyo with sufficient success that, with Sondheim's endorsement, the production was brought to New York for a limited run in Summer 2002. In reviews, much has been made of the move away from the basic Kabuki approach of the original and toward the more austere and stylized Noh, but what was also striking to critics familiar with both versions was how much was lost in the more obviously Broadway-oriented numbers (i.e., "Welcome to Kanagawa," "Chrysanthemum Tea," and "Please Hello"). Thus, if the new production managed successfully to make the Japanese component more viable, it was at the expense of a significant part of the original rationale, of locating Broadway, and by extension the West, as an intruding Other to be rendered with comic exaggeration.

One may learn from this an important lesson in translation and embodiment, especially regarding the limitations to these activities for achieving full understanding across cultural boundaries. Part of the problem is, to be sure, that the point of exoticism is largely *not* to fully understand the Other, but to keep it usefully at a distance so that its foreign flavor might be savored. Exoticism is not, fundamentally, about honoring what is deemed exotic, but about keeping it in its faraway place to be marveled at. Perhaps the signal achievement of *Pacific Overtures,* beyond its imperfect but nevertheless impressive success in bringing Japanese sensibilities and perspectives more fully to the foreground for American audiences, is that it focuses so much attention on the central importance of the observer's perspective, on the "Someone in a Tree" who can bear only limited witness. Perhaps, also, *Pacific Overtures* has done much to expand the vocabulary of Broadway, so that it has a few more "words" for "Japanese." But there will always be an Exotic that our vocabulary cannot comprehend, simply because we need it in order to know who and where we are. To put it succinctly, we need the Orient to orient ourselves.

For Further Consideration

The Desert Song (1926), *Down Argentine Way* (film, 1940), South *Pacific* (1949), *The Little Mermaid* (film, 1989), *Miss Saigon* (1989), *Aladdin* (film, 1993), *Mulan* (film, 1998)

See Also

Regarding orientalism in general, see Edward Said's *Orientalism*. Regarding orientalist representation in music, see Jonathan Bellman's edited volume, *The Exotic in Western Music* (particularly articles by Bellman, Mary Hunter, Ralph Locke, Michael Pisani, and Richard Taruskin), Ralph Locke's "Reflections on Orientalism in Opera and Musical Theater" (the latter with specific reference to *The King and I*), and "The Orientalist Tradition" in Stephen Banfield's *Sondheim's Broadway Musicals* (249–55). Regarding the general problem of evoking ethnic musical styles, see "The Ethnic Musical" in Joseph Swain's *The Broadway Musical*.

For an astute accounting of *The Mikado*, see chapter 11 of Gayden Wren's *A Most Ingenious Paradox*. Additionally, see Michael Beckerman's discussion of the Japanese component of the show in "The Sword on the Wall: Japanese Elements and their Significance in *The Mikado*," and Robert Fink's eye-opening demonstration of Sullivan's craft in "Rhythm and Text Setting in *The Mikado*."

Regarding *The King and I,* see chapter 1 of Ethan Mordden's *Coming Up Roses*, chapter 3 of Scott Miller's *Deconstructing Harold Hill*, and pp. 199–211 in Frederick Nolan's *The Sound of Their Music*.

Regarding *Pacific Overtures*, Stephen Banfield provides a fascinating set of perspectives in chapter 8 of his *Sondheim's Broadway Musicals;* Mark Eden Horowitz interviews the composer in *Sondheim on Music* (155–64); Meryle Secrest provides a good overview (chaper 14 in *Stephen Sondheim: A Life*), as does Craig Zadan (chapter 20 in *Sondheim and Company*); and Leonard Fleischer's "'More Beautiful Than True'" uses the show as a lens through which to view Sondheim's contribution more generally. See also chapter 6 of Joanne Gordon's *Art Isn't Easy;* pp. 213–20 in Stephen Citron's *Sondheim and Lloyd-Webber;* and Wayman Wong's "Actors Remember *Pacific Overtures*."

Afterword

Other Directions, Other Identities

THE AMERICAN MUSICAL has shown itself to be broadly adaptable, capable of addressing a wide variety of issues and themes, and ranging in its treatment of those themes from the blatantly obvious to the more subtly nuanced. Moreover, the adaptability of the genre extends just as readily to questions of venue and style, and to its capacity to absorb other traditions or to interbreed with them to produce hybrids. Each of these areas of flexibility points to substantial—albeit strategic—limitations in the purview of the present study, which has approached the task of telling the history of the genre through focusing on its treatment of themes relating to how America has been (or how it ought to be) defined as a nation.

The adaptability of the American musical in terms of style and venue has had at least some presence in the foregoing discussions. As I've detailed, the impulse toward *opera* played a large part in the conception of *Porgy and Bess,* and contributed as well to the level of musical sophistication in *West Side Story* and other shows. Because *operetta* played a pivotal and formative role in the early development of the American musical, I have discussed the English variety of operetta (Gilbert and Sullivan) at some length, and indicated the referential potential of its continental cousins. And, in recognition of the potential for *film* to add significantly to the ways in which a musical advances its themes, I considered this dimension as an important secondary focus in my discussions of *The Sound of Music* and *Cabaret.* Clearly, however, each of these three interactive influences warrants a more focused investigation.

Similarly, in exploring such devices as the marriage trope and its close relative, the history-as-fate trope, I have found it most useful to pull focus, so as to consider the larger issues being addressed, zeroing in fairly frequently on the characters, personal crises, and relationships as they are actually presented on stage, but mainly in order to support the framing discussion. Yet the familiarity of these devices, and their useful capacity to give dramatic life to larger-scale political issues, should not obscure a rather obvious fact. Musicals also directly present personal and relational behavior and viewpoints—even if they are "really" about something else—and thus often enough reveal possibilities that echo, extend, and shape our existing attitudes and prejudices about the risks and possibilities of human existence and of connecting with other human beings.

Throughout their history, musicals have provided inspiration to children and adults alike, and have modeled in telling ways the formation and transformation of personal identity, especially regarding such critical and historically volatile areas as gender and sexual roles. And, despite the seemingly ubiquitous presence of the marriage trope in musicals, sometimes—to play off the Freudian *bon mot* that insists that "sometimes, a cigar is just a cigar"—sometimes in musicals, sex is just sex, and a relationship is just a relationship.

American musicals—through their characters, stories, and songs; through the memorable performance of those characters, stories, and songs by charismatic stars; and through the varied ways and degrees to which wider populations merge with those characters, live out their stories, and sing or move to their songs—have given people, in a visceral way, a sense of what it *feels* like to embody whatever alternatives that musicals might offer to their own life circumstances and choices. On a surface level, singing (or, perhaps, lip-synching) the songs from a musical can be empowering, providing a sense of what being a Broadway star might be like. But this kind of reinforcement and projected embodiment reaches much deeper than celebrity identification, engaging on the most fundamental level with what it means to be *human*. On this level, American musicals teach people in powerful ways what and whom to care about, and how to go about caring about them. And they teach these things all the more effectively for giving audiences the opportunity to experience—almost, to taste—what it is like to do so.

If it has not been possible in the present volume to explore these more personal aspects of the American musical as fully as they deserve, a planned companion volume to this one, already well under way, undertakes to do precisely that, following and extending the approaches taken here. Together, these two volumes will provide a set of double perspectives on the musical, the first deeper and the second more immediate. Thus, the present volume deals with historical antecedents to the American musical, while its companion volume will consider later developmental interactions and influences. In terms of themes, the first deals with how musicals frame and embody larger political issues, while the second considers how they provide models on a more personal level. In confining myself in the present volume to questions of American identity-formation, I have thus provided the first half of a historical and thematic frame.

There is an additional threefold payoff to this bifurcated structure. Moving from background to foreground, as I do both within this book and within the larger project, gives a fuller resonance to that foreground than the reverse direction would allow, and avoids the sense—so easy to fall into within a piecemeal treatment of individual shows—that musicals have collectively traced a haphazard trajectory, randomly placing their characters into a bewildering variety of situations, independent of larger considerations. In this respect, it is simply useful to have a sense of what "they all add up to"—and of what is at stake, politically—before considering the characters and their situations more narrowly. Moreover, my two-part framing structure allows me more room, to delineate each theme more fully, to consider each musical more holistically, and to treat more extensively a nontrivial number of individual songs. And, finally, dividing the range of themes between the political and the personal, and considering them within these two groupings, facilitates a parallel bifurcation in their manner of treatment.

From yet another perspective, it is particularly useful to stop at this point because it marks the completion of what has been my central overriding task: to argue a place for a book of this kind. The case I have tried to make is that musicals do matter, and I have endeavored to do so by showing as vividly as possible how they actually make themselves useful and valuable to what is in fact a very large community, including many who do not consider themselves to be particular fans of musicals. Arguably, I might have made that case equally well by considering how musicals have mattered for people in a more universalized sense, as people rather than as Americans. But musicals have rarely had this kind of universalizing ambition; they have tended instead to address audiences of the "here and now," however broadly or narrowly that might be construed. Given this, it has seemed to me most prudent to consider as fully as possible just what that "here and now" has been for the American musical, and just how the genre has interacted with that context. In truth, as I believe I have shown, the American musical has done more than merely *interact* with its local—that is, its American—context. It has played a significant part in *shaping* that context, as well, by addressing both the ideals of America and its realities, and helping us deal with the frequent disparity between them. Sometimes this has meant that musicals have led us to ignore those discrepancies in favor of more palatable images. Certainly the survival of the genre has depended on reaching audiences who have more often sought comfort and diversion than a chance to reevaluate their place in the world. Yet the practitioners of the American musical have time and again proven that commercial success and presenting a challenge to audiences are not mutually exclusive potentialities. Time and again, they have proven the American musical to be one of the most effective venues for cultural negotiation and renegotiation. And—considering that Americans have traditionally taken especial pride in their ability to adapt to a changing world—what could be more American than that?

APPENDIX A

Art and Commerce

The Business of Making Musicals

AMERICAN MUSICALS, like most forms of popular culture, may be understood as a contested intersection of art and commerce. This juncture has often been viewed as necessarily antagonistic, and many argue that, in musicals as with other forms of popular culture, art has little chance to survive as such when it becomes too enmeshed with commerce. Yet an argument from the other perspective, that the only valuable art is one that holds itself accountable to a substantial audience—and in modern America, that can only mean art that is to some extent market-driven—is eminently feasible, and has many adherents. Moreover, both positions routinely face counterarguments based on circumstances that are hard to put aside, as when self-indulgent "Artists" produce work that has no relevance for anyone beyond themselves, or when budgetary concerns necessitate a lowering of artistic standards. But in managing such a continuum between artistic and market-driven concerns, which may indeed come into conflict in a venture that incurs such large expenses and such a high risk of failure, only the open market has had any real success. Private patronage still exists, of course, but few "angels" who back a Broadway show want to see their money wasted, and this source of funding has mostly devolved into a species of venture capitalism. Governmental patronage has been even more problematic, for it will sooner or later be accountable not only to the marketplace on at least some level, but also to shifts of ideological orientation among constituencies and power brokers. In any case, no show survives playing to empty houses for long, however richly funded it might be; to be successful, a musical must have a public.

The "tried and true" method for managing the "Art vs. Commerce" conflict involves a fundamental division of labor between those who manage a show and those who make it a show worth managing. Importantly, this division is both sharply defined and fluid in implementation, for each function within the governing hierarchy of a musical must have both autonomy and accountability in some degree, and often has to manage a shifting balance between the two. Bernard Rosenberg and Ernest Harburg have usefully divided the various roles that typify the business structure of American musicals into "administrative" roles and "nonadministrative" roles, roughly denoting those that take place "behind the scenes" and those whose performances are directly witnessed by an audience, respectively. But it is important to remember that these roles are also somewhat fluid in implementation, and that there may be other useful ways to conceptualize them. What follows here is a summary of these roles as delineated by Rosenberg and Harburg, beginning with the "administrative" roles.[1]

The person in charge of the *business* of mounting the musical is the *producer,* who hires and fires, and will sometimes impose decisions about content (from above, as it were). The person who generally maintains creative control of the show is the *director.* Both the producer and director can have *assistants,* who work as go-betweens for the various people involved (and also as buffers, thus helping as well to enforce the relative autonomy of each function; this might be especially important in those cases when the same person directs and produces). To mount a musical, three properties must be either in existence or in development. The first of these, written by a *playwright,* is the *book,* a highly specialized artifact that resembles a normal play in most respects, but will lead up to a somewhat larger number of internal climaxes—without, however, providing those climaxes, which will be embodied musically. Thus, each show also needs *music* and a set of *lyrics,* to be provided by a *composer* and *lyricist* generally working in collaboration (and who are sometimes one and the same person; book and lyrics are also sometimes written by a single person). Owing to time constraints and the specialized training that has evolved for Broadway, the composer generally does not produce a *full score;* the latter will instead be produced by an *arranger* and / or *orchestrator,* whose job it is to ensure that each song will sound the way it should, adapting as necessary to the specific singers' strengths and weaknesses, instrumentation constraints, microphone use and placement, and performing space. The *choreographer,* who stages the musical numbers, has more or less importance depending on what type of show is being mounted—although the importance of this function has grown over time, in part because significant creative personalities have emerged in this realm. The *musical director* is responsible for rehearsing the musical numbers and otherwise shaping the musical experience of the show; this function is often combined with that of the *conductor,* who directs the actual performance from the orchestra pit (and is thus the only "administrative" role who might be seen as such during the performance).

The "nonadministrative" roles reduce mainly to what we perceive to be the actual show. This category includes first of all the *musicians* in the orchestra, who will normally introduce much of the show's music in an overture and will be heard intermittently throughout; because of successful unionization efforts in the early decades of the twentieth century, their number has long been fixed, as a minimum. Most obviously and centrally, though, this category includes the onstage performers: the *actors* and *singers* who take leading roles, members of the *chorus* who will sing in various groupings, the *dancers* (who may or may not also be members of the chorus), and, very occasionally, instrumentalists who might be asked to appear on stage; in theory, any of these categories might overlap. As for those responsible for designing the *costumes* and *sets*, setting and executing the *lighting* cues, and managing the *sound* levels (especially important in later years, after miking became standard and instruments became louder)—because these contributions are a palpable part of the "show" and very directly a part of the audience's experience, they too may be considered within this general category.

Finally, the *audience* itself plays a major part as a collaborator (although, to be sure, they generally must pay for that privilege), a function that has long been an institutionalized part of how shows develop. Mainly, this function occurs during out-of-town tryouts, held traditionally in New Haven, Connecticut, or in one of the trio immortalized in Cole Porter's "Another op'nin', another show": "Philly, Boston, or Baltimo'" (*Kiss Me, Kate*, 1948). Here, many substantial changes might occur in a show, prompted by audience response, and it is the rare show that is not transformed, however slightly, between this earlier opening and its official opening on Broadway. But even during the course of a show's Broadway run, it might change, even substantially, in response to feedback from audience and critics. But here we are moving from describing a (non-paid) role within a business hierarchy, to describing the final stage of a larger creative process, and it is useful, again, to borrow from Rosenberg and Harburg, who liken this larger process to the *stages of development* in the formation of a church. As they describe these stages, a musical begins life as a *concept* (stage one), which can come from any number of sources, becomes a *cult* (stage two) when there is a strong cadre of individuals who believe strongly that the musical can and should be made, a *sect* (stage three) when money is raised and creative and administrative hierarchies develop, and a *church* (stage four) as these hierarchies grow more rigid and controlled, most often along the lines outlined above. It is during this later phase, when there is a lot at stake for everyone involved, that marketability becomes both testable and of central concern; hence the out-of-town tryout and the formative contribution from the audience.

APPENDIX B

Additional Resources

IN THIS APPENDIX, I provide supplementary material for each of the musicals covered separately in the main text, including, when possible, a plot summary (unless I have provided a summary in the text, in which case I provide a page-number reference), a list of songs (in almost all cases according to the original production), and a list of available source materials, including recordings, films or videotapes, the book (if published), and musical scores. I have not tried to be comprehensive in these lists, confining myself to what is readily available and/or particularly interesting. Corresponding soundtrack recordings are not listed separately if the film version of a show is given. The items listed here are not repeated in the main bibliography.

Chapter Two

The Black Crook (1866)
Book: Charles Barras
Lyrics: unknown
Music: Thomas Baker and others

Plot: Rodolphe, a poor artist, is in love with Amina, who is betrothed to the corrupt Count Wolfenstein. Wolfenstein imprisons Rodolphe, but Hertzog (the "Black Crook," an alchemist trading in black magic) helps him escape and promises him gold. Hertzog, however, is planning to sacrifice Rodolphe to prolong his own life, as part of his Faustian pact with Zamiel, an evil devil-like figure. On the way to rendezvous in the "Serpent's Glen," Zamiel's lair, Rodolphe saves a white dove, who is in reality Stalacta, Queen of the Golden Realm. In gratitude, Stalacta and her band of Amazons rescue him, and reward him with both the promised gold and his beloved Amina in a climactic "transformation scene" in an underground grotto.

Books
[Barras, Charles]. *The Black Crook, A Most Wonderful History*. Philadelphia: Barclay, 1866 (published form of the original play).
Morley, Christopher. *Rudolph and Amina; or The Black Crook*. New York: John Day, 1930 (a version of the play in the form of a novel).

Musical Scores
"You Naughty, Naughty Men." In *Show Songs, from "The Black Crook" to "The Red Mill": Original Sheet Music for 60 Songs from 50 Shows, 1866–1906*. Ed. Stanley Appelbaum. New York: Dover, 1974.

"The Black Crook Songster / A Collection of Choice, Jolly and Happy Songs, Now Published for the First Time / including 'You Naughty Men!' as sung at Niblo's with great applause by the late Millie Cavendish." New York: R. M. De Witt, 1867.

Various individual numbers published as sheet music, including:

The Black Crook Galop. Arr. Thomas Baker. William A. Pond, 1866.

The Black Crook Lancers. (No composer or arranger given.) H. B. Dodworth, 1867.

The Black Crook Waltz. Arr. Thomas Baker. William A. Pond, 1866.

The Black Crook Waltzes. Arr. Joseph Noll. H. B. Dodworth, 1867.

March of the Amazons. Arr. Emil Stigler. H. B. Dodworth, 1866.

H.M.S. Pinafore; or, The Lass That Loved a Sailor (1878)
Book and Lyrics: W. S. Gilbert
Music: Arthur Sullivan

Plot: see pp. 39–40.

Songs

We Sail the Ocean Blue
I'm Called Little Buttercup
But Tell Me Who's the Youth
The Nightingale / A Maiden Fair to See
My Gallant Crew
Sir, You Are Sad
Sorry Her Lot
Over the Bright Blue Sea / Sir Joseph's Barge Is Seen
Gaily Tripping
I Am the Monarch of the Seas
When I Was a Lad
For I Hold That on the Seas
A British Tar
Refrain, Audacious Tar
Can I Survive This Overbearing? / Messmates, Ahoy!
First Act Finale: Oh Joy, Oh Rapture Unforeseen
Fair Moon, to Thee I Sing
Things Are Seldom What They Seem
The Hours Creep on Apace
Never Mind the Why and Wherefore
Kind Captain, I've Important Information
Carefully on Tiptoe Stealing
Pretty Daughter of Mine
He Is an Englishman!
Farewell, My Own!
A Many Years Ago
Oh Joy, Oh Rapture Unforeseen

Recordings

W. S. Gilbert and Arthur Sullivan. *H.M.S. Pinafore* and *Trial by Jury.* New York: Arabesque Recordings Z8052–2, 1986 (reissue from the 1927 and 1930 D'Oyly Carte Opera Company recordings, Victor HMV 100 with Malcolm Sargent conducting and Henry Lytton as Sir Joseph; includes the only extant recording of Sir Arthur Sullivan, from 1888).

W. S. Gilbert and Arthur Sullivan. *H.M.S. Pinafore; or, The Lass That Loved a Sailor.* Decca LK-4002/3, 1949 (D'Oyly Carte Opera Company recording, with Isidore Godfrey conducting and Martyn Green as Sir Joseph).

W. S. Gilbert and Arthur Sullivan. *H.M.S. Pinafore; or, The Lass That Loved a Sailor.* New York: Angel ANG.35718, 1958 (Pro Arte Orchestra and Glyndebourne Festival Chorus, with Malcolm Sargent conducting).

W. S. Gilbert and Arthur Sullivan. *H.M.S. Pinafore; or, The Lass That Loved a Sailor.* London: London A 4234, 1960 (D'Oyly Carte Opera Company recording, A 4234 London, with Isidore Godfrey conducting and John Reed as Sir Joseph).

W. S. Gilbert and Arthur Sullivan. *H.M.S. Pinafore; or, The Lass That Loved a Sailor.* MCA MCAD 2–11012, 1987 (New Sadler's Wells Opera, Simon Phipps conducting, based on the "complete authentic score").

W. S. Gilbert and Arthur Sullivan. *H.M.S. Pinafore; or, The Lass That Loved a Sailor.* Telarc CD-80374, 1994 (Welsh National Opera, Charles Mackerras conducting).

W. S. Gilbert and Arthur Sullivan. *H.M.S. Pinafore; or, The Lass That Loved a Sailor.* TER CD TER2 1259, 2000 (New D'Oyly Carte Company recording; highly regarded).

Arthur Sullivan and Mark Savage (adapted from W. S. Gilbert). *Pinafore!* Hollywood: Belva BVR 002, 2002 (clever adaptation staged at the Celebration Theatre in Hollywood in 2001: The Pinafore, Flagship of the New Gay Navy, is docked in Palm Springs. Ralph, renamed here Dick Dockstrap, is the only straight sailor on board, in love with Captain's "daughter" Josephine, unaware that "she" is in drag. Resolution comes when Ralph and the Captain reverse roles and sexual orientations, freeing the latter to marry Bitter Butterball).

Films and Video Recordings

H.M.S. Pinafore; or, The Lass That Loved a Sailor. 1973. D'Oyly Carte Opera Company (made for television).

H.M.S. Pinafore; or, The Lass That Loved a Sailor. 1998. Stratford Festival (1981 performance by the Ontario, Canada group).

H.M.S. Pinafore; or, The Lass That Loved a Sailor. Concord, Mass.: Opera World PIN10V, 1982 (made for television).

H.M.S. Pinafore; or, The Lass That Loved a Sailor. Essgee Entertainment, 1997. Essgee (Simon Gallaher) Entertainment (extravagantly mounted, freely adapted, generally preferred over their production of *The Mikado*).

Books

W. S. Gilbert. *Plays & Poems of W. S. Gilbert.* Preface by Deems Taylor. New York: Random House, 1932 (contains the Bab Ballads, on which some of the operettas—including *Pinafore*—were based, with drawings by Gilbert).

W. S. Gilbert. *The First Night Gilbert and Sullivan, Containing Complete Librettos of the Fourteen Operas, Exactly as Presented at their Premiere Performances; Together with Facsims. of the Firstnight Programmes.* Edited by Reginald Allen. Foreword by Bridget D'Oyly Carte. New York: Heritage Press, 1958.

W. S. Gilbert. *The Complete Gilbert and Sullivan: Librettos from all Fourteen Operettas.* Preface by Deems Taylor. New York: Black Dog & Leventhal, 1960.

W. S. Gilbert. *The Complete Annotated Gilbert and Sullivan.* Edited by Ian Bradley. Oxford: Oxford University Press, 1996.

Musical Scores

W. S. Gilbert and Arthur Sullivan. *H.M.S. Pinafore; or, The Lass That Loved a Sailor.* Piano reduction by Ephraim Hammett Jones. Mineola, N.Y.: Dover, 2002 (vocal score).

W. S. Gilbert and Arthur Sullivan. *H.M.S. Pinafore; or, The Lass That Loved a Sailor.* "Authenic version edited by Bryceson Treharne." New York: G. Schirmer, 2002 (vocal score with dialog).

W. S. Gilbert and Arthur Sullivan. *H.M.S. Pinafore in Full Score.* Edited by Carl Simpson and Ephraim Hammet Jones. Dover, 2002 (full score).

Chapter Four

> *Anything Goes* (1934)
> Book: Howard Lindsay and Russel Crouse, after Guy Bolton and P. G. Wodehouse
> Music and Lyrics: Cole Porter

Plot: Billy Crocker sees off nightclub singer Reno Sweeney (still in love with Billy), who is sailing on the *American,* a luxury liner bound from New York to England. Billy decides to stow away when he discovers that his ex-fiancée, Hope Harcourt, is also aboard, now engaged to Sir Evelyn Oakleigh under pressure from her family (her father's business is in trouble). To escape capture, Billy teams up with Moon Face Martin (Public Enemy No. 13), who is disguised as Reverend Moon; Billy and Moon Face later assume other disguises, as well. In the end, the Harcourt family business is sold, enabling Billy and Hope to wed; Reno falls for Sir Evelyn; and Moon Face is removed from the "most-wanted" list by presidential decree.

Songs

> I Get a Kick Out of You
> Bon Voyage
> All Through the Night
> There'll Always Be a Lady Fair (Sailor's Chantey)
> Where Are the Men?
> You're the Top
> Anything Goes
> Act One Finale (You're the Top)

Public Enemy Number One
Blow, Gabriel, Blow
Be Like the Bluebird
Buddie, Beware
The Gypsy in Me
Finale
Dropped: "There's No Cure Like Travel"; "Kate the Great"; "Waltz Down
the Aisle"

Recordings

Cole Porter. *Anything Goes.* Washington, D.C.: Smithsonian Collection (RCA
Special Products) DPM 1–0284, 1977 (historic performances from the 1934
Broadway cast and 1935 London casts, including vocals by Ethel Merman, and
several songs from the show sung by Cole Porter).

Cole Porter. *Anything Goes.* Sony: B0000024VD, 1990 (reissue of 1962 Off-
Broadway Cast, Epic XSB 57297–57298).

Cole Porter. *Anything Goes: The New Broadway Cast Recording.* New York:
RCA Victor 7769–2-RC, 1988.

Cole Porter. *Anything Goes: First Recording of the Original 1934 Version.* Hayes
Middlesex, England: EMI Records CDC 7 49848 2, 1989.

Films and Video Recordings

Anything Goes. 1936. Dir. Lewis Milestone. Bing Crosby, Ethel Merman, Ida
Lupino, Charles Ruggles, Arthur Treacher, Grace Bradley.

Anything Goes. 1956. Dir. Robert Lewis. Bing Crosby, Mitzi Gaynor, Donald
O'Connor, Jeanmarie, Phil Harris, Kurt Kazner (mostly inadequate adaptation,
with a very different story).

Musical Scores

Cole Porter. *Anything Goes.* London: Chappell and New York: Harms, 1936
(vocal score).

Cole Porter. *Anything Goes; Vocal Selections.* Revival edition. New York: Warner
Bros. Publications, 1988 (vocal score).

Cole Porter. *Anything Goes; Vocal Selections.* New York: Warner Bros. Publications, 1983 (vocal score).

Chapter Five

Little Johnny Jones (1904)
Music, Book, and Lyrics: George M. Cohan

Plot: American jockey Johnny Jones (George M. Cohan) goes to London to ride
in the Derby, and is approached by Anthony Anstey (played by Cohan's father) to
throw the race. He refuses, but is accused anyway when he loses, in part because
Anstey has accused him of other crimes, so that the crowd turns against him. He
stays in England to clear his name; vindication comes when a rocket is fired from
the ship, which is a prearranged signal that Anstey has confessed to attempting to

frame Johnny. All is not well, however, as we learn that Anstey has kidnapped Johnny's betrothed Goldie Gates, and Johnny follows them to San Francisco's Chinatown, where he rescues her.

Songs

The Cecil of London Town
They're All My Friends
Mamselle Fauchett
Captain of the Ten Day Boat
'Op In Me 'Ansom Cab
Nesting In a New York Tree
The Yankee Doodle Boy
Off to the Derby
Girls from the USA
Sailors of the St. Hurrah
Goodbye Flo
So Long Sing Song
Good Old California
A Girl I Know
Give My Regards to Broadway
March of the Frisco Chinks
Life's a Funny Proposition, After All (*later replacement:* "I'm Mighty Glad I'm Living and That's All")
Songs not on original list but performed in the show: "Foong Toong Fee"; "If Mr. Boston Lawson Has His Way"

Recordings

George M. Cohan. *Yankee Doodle Dandy.* New York: Olympic Records 7111, 1977 or before (includes recordings of Cohan singing "Life's a Funny Proposition After All," "Give My Regards to Broadway," and "I'm Mighty Glad I'm Living and That's All).

George M. Cohan. *George M!* New York: Columbia KOS-3200, 1969 (original cast recording of 1968 Broadway show, with Joel Grey as Cohan).

Carousel of American Music; The Fabled 24 September 1940 San Francisco Concerts. Berkeley: Music & Arts Programs of America, 1997 (includes recordings of Cohan performing "Give My Regards to Broadway" and "The Yankee Doodle Boy").

Music from the New York stage, Volume 1: 1890–1908. Sussex, England: Pearl GEMM CDS 9050–2, 1993 (includes recordings of Cohan performing "Life's a Funny Proposition, After All" and "I'm Mighty Glad I'm Living and That's All").

Films and Video Recordings

Little Johnny Jones. 1983. Goodspeed Opera House (not available commercially).
Yankee Doodle Dandy. 1942. Dir. Michael Curtiz. James Cagney, Walter Huston (includes a staging of two numbers from *Little Johnny Jones:* Cagney, singing

and dancing in Cohan's manner, performs "The Yankee Doodle Boy" and "Give
My Regards to Broadway").

George M! 1972. Joel Grey (television, not currently available).

Musical Scores
George M. Cohan. *Gems from* Little Johnny Jones. New York: F.A. Mills, 1904
(vocal score).

The Cradle Will Rock (1938)
Music, Book, and Lyrics: Marc Blitzstein

Plot: Moll, a prostitute, is arrested when she refuses a police officer. At the Steeltown Night Court, she meets Harry Druggist, arrested for vagrancy, and the Liberty Committee, respected citizens who are stooges of Mister Mister, mistakenly
arrested for being at a pro-union rally that they were supposed to disrupt. In the
course of the evening, we learn how each of these and others—Reverend Salvation, Editor Daily, Dr. Specialist, President Prexy and Professors Mamie, Trixie,
and Scoot (the latter four from College University), Mrs. Mister's artist protégés
Dauber and Yasha—have become prostitutes, selling out to Mister Mister. We also
learn of the trivial pursuits of the latter's children, Junior and Sister. Later in the
evening, Larry Foreman, a union agitator, is brought into night court (for inciting
to riot), and Mister Mister arrives to try (unsuccessfully) to buy him off. From offstage, we hear that the pro-union initiative has won the day.

Songs
Moll's Song
Moll and Gent
I'll Show You Guys
Soliticin'
Oh What a Filthy Night Court
Hard Times—The Sermon
Croon Spoon
The Freedom of the Press
Let's Do Something
Honolulu
Summer Weather
Love Duet (Gus and Sadie)
Don't Let Me Keep You
Ask Us Again
Art for Art's Sake
The Nickel under Your Foot
Which of You Guys? / Leaflets
The Cradle Will Rock
Joe Worker
Finale

Recordings

Marc Blitzstein Discussing "The Cradle Will Rock," "No for an Answer," and "Regina." New Rochelle: Spoken Arts SA 717, 1956.

Marc Blitzstein. *The Cradle Will Rock.* Composers Recordings CRI SD 266, 1972 (reissue of 1964 Theater Four production, MGM SE 4289–2OC, 1965).

Marc Blitzstein. *The Cradle Will Rock. Original 1985 Cast Recording.* Jay Records: CDJAY2 1300, 1985 (directed by John Houseman, with Patti LuPone, includes a verbal account by John Houseman of the first production).

Marc Blitzstein. *The Cradle Will Rock.* The Blank Theatre Company B00001WRSI, 1994 (Los Angeles cast).

Films and Video Recordings

Cradle Will Rock. 1999. Dir. Tim Robbins. Hank Azaria, Ruben Blades, John Cusack, Joan Cusack, Cary Elwes, Angus MacFayden, Bill Murray, Susan Sarandon, John Turturro, Cherry Jones, Vanessa Redgrave, Emily Watson (interweaves the story of the first production of the show with the story of Diego Rivera's 1933 mural for Rockefeller).

Books

Marc Blitzstein. *The Cradle Will Rock.* New York: Tams-Witmark Music Library, 1937 (typescript).

Marc Blitzstein. *The Cradle Will Rock.* New York: Random House, 1938.

Orson Welles. *The Cradle Will Rock; An Original Screenplay.* Santa Barbara: Santa Teresa Press, 1994 (the basis for an incomplete 1984 movie project).

Musical Scores

Marc Blitzstein. *The Cradle Will Rock.* New York: Chappell, 1938 (vocal score).

Chapter Six

Oklahoma! (1943)
Book: Oscar Hammerstein II (after Lynn Riggs)
Lyrics: Oscar Hammerstein II
Music: Richard Rodgers

Plot: Curly, a cowboy in love with Laurey, niece of farmer Aunt Eller, comes calling, but is rebuffed by Laurey, who, in a fit of pique, decides to go to the box social with brutish farmhand Jud Fry, who is obsessed with her. Meanwhile, a comic love triangle develops around Ado Annie, Will Parker (just back from Kansas City), and a Persian peddler. Act I closes with Laurey's dream ballet, in which Jud disrupts her wedding with Curly, knocking him unconscious. At the box social, Curly outbids Jud for Laurey's box supper (by putting up his saddle and gun), which leads directly to marriage plans. During the shivoree, just after their wedding, Jud reappears and falls dead on his knife while fighting with Curly. Curly is acquitted, and Will and Ado Annie are reconciled.

Songs

Oh, What a Beautiful Mornin'
The Surrey with the Fringe on Top

Kansas City
I Cain't Say No
Many a New Day
It's a Scandal! It's an Outrage!
People Will Say We're in Love
Pore Jud Is Daid
Lonely Room
Out of My Dreams
The Farmer and the Cowman
All er Nothin'
Oklahoma
Finale

Recordings
Oscar Hammerstein II and Richard Rodgers. *Oklahoma!* Polygram Records B00004T9TF, 2000 (original 1943 cast, with added tracks).
Oscar Hammerstein II and Richard Rodgers. *Oklahoma!* RCA Red Seal CBL1–3572. 1980 (1979 Broadway cast).
Oscar Hammerstein II and Richard Rodgers. *Oklahoma!* Relativity: B00002EPLJ, 1999 (1998 Royal National Theatre production, London).

Films and Video Recordings
Oklahoma! 1955. Dir. Fred Zinnemann. Gordon MacRae, Shirley Jones, Gloria Grahame, Rod Steiger.
Oklahoma! 1999. Dir. Trevor Nunn. Hugh Jackman, Maureen Lipman, Josefina Gabrielle, Shuler Hensley (production of the Royal National Theatre production filmed for TV; American DVD release 2003).

Books
Lynn Riggs. *Green Grow the Lilacs.* New York and Los Angeles: S. French, 1931 (original play that *Oklahoma!* was based on).
Oscar Hammerstein II and Richard Rodgers. *Oklahoma!* New York: Williamson Music, 1943.

Musical Scores
Oscar Hammerstein II and Richard Rodgers. *Oklahoma!* New York: Williamson Music, 1943.

Guys and Dolls (1950)
Book: Joe Swerling and Abe Burrows
Music and Lyrics: Frank Loesser

Plot: The opening scene ("Runyonland") introduces the everyday inhabitants of Times Square; among these are tourists, police, con artists, tinhorn gamblers (including Nicely Nicely Johnson) and the Save-a-Soul Mission band (including Sergeant Sarah Brown). Nicely Nicely and his cohorts work for Nathan Detroit, whose "Oldest Established Permanent Floating Crap Game in New York" is in danger of lapsing if he cannot come up with $1000 to secure a safe location. In desperation, Detroit bets high-roller Sky Masterson $1000 that the latter cannot take a "doll" of his choosing to Havana, then chooses Sarah Brown. Sky visits Sarah at the mission, and gives her his marker: if she will agree to come with him to Havana, he will deliver at least a dozen sinners to her upcoming prayer meeting, thereby saving the mission from having to close for lack of business. Meanwhile, Nathan is under pressure from all sides: from Lieutenant Brannigan of the New York Police Department, from out-of-town gamblers looking for action, and from his fiancée of fourteen years, Adelaide, lead singer at the Hot Box nightclub, who has developed a chronic cold due to Nathan's endless postponements of their wedding.

In Havana, unwittingly under the influence of alcohol, Sarah falls in love with Sky, but is disillusioned to find later that the mission has been the site of Detroit's crap game, believing that Sky has used her. The next evening, Sky arrives at Nathan's crap game, which is now being held in a sewer, and bets each gambler there $1000 against his soul: if Sky wins, they must all attend the prayer meeting. All is resolved when the gamblers' attendance impresses the mission's visiting General Abernathy: Sarah marries Sky, and Detroit, finally on the verge of marrying Adelaide, suddenly acquires her chronic case of the sneezes.

Songs

Runyonland Music
Fugue for Tinhorns
Follow the Fold
The Oldest Established
I'll Know
A Bushel and a Peck
Adelaide's Lament
Guys and Dolls
Havana
If I Were a Bell
My Time of Day
I've Never Been in Love Before
Take Back Your Mink
More I Cannot Wish You
The Crapshooters' Dance
Luck Be a Lady
Sue Me
Sit Down, You're Rockin' the Boat
Marry the Man Today
Finale

Recordings

Frank Loesser. *Guys and Dolls*. Decca DL 9023, 1953 (original cast recording).
Frank Loesser. *Guys and Dolls*. Motown M6 876S1, 1976 (all-black cast).
Frank Loesser. *Guys and Dolls*. EMI 7243 8 56204 2 3, 1982 (original National Theatre cast).

Frank Loesser. *Guys and Dolls. BMG/RCA VICTOR 9027 61317 2, 9027 61317 4,* 1992 (revival cast, with Nathan Lane).

Frank Loesser. *Guys and Dolls.* Jay Records CDJAY2 1294, 1996 (London studio recording, "first complete recording"; includes "Traveling Light," cut before the Broadway opening, complete Havana music, and songs added for the film version).

Films and Video Recordings
Guys and Dolls. 1955. Dir. Joseph L. Mankiewicz. Frank Sinatra, Vivian Blaine, Marlon Brando, Jean Simmons, Stubby Kaye.

Guys and Dolls: Off the Record. BMG LM-569, M-569, 1992 (video of the 1992 revival cast recording).

Books
Damon Runyon. *Guys and Dolls.* New York: Frederick A. Stokes, 1931 (original short stories).

Frank Loesser, Jo Swerling, and Abe Burrows. *Guys and Dolls: A Musical Fable of Broadway.* 1951 (typescript).

Frank Loesser, Jo Swerling, and Abe Burrows. *The Guys and Dolls Book.* London: Methuen, 1982.

Musical Score
Frank Loesser. *Guys and Dolls.* New York: Frank Music, 1953 (vocal score).

The Music Man (1957)
Music, Book, and Lyrics: Meredith Willson

Plot: July 4, 1912: Salesmen on a train entering Iowa discuss an unusual con artist who sells band instruments and uniforms to a town and promises to organize a boy's band, then absconds with the proceeds. Charlie Cowell, an anvil salesman and the main source for this story, is on his trail, but thinks Harold Hill, the "music man," is too smart to try Iowa. As the train is about to leave River City, Hill disembarks, revealing who he is to the astounded salesmen. Hill gets a frosty reception in River City until he stirs up the townspeople against the perils of a new pool table, then offers to solve their "trouble" with a boy's band. On all sides, he averts possible difficulties through musical deflection. He organizes the members of a bickering school board, who demand to see his credentials, into a barbershop quartet. The mayor's wife Eulalie is to head a ladies' dance group. More difficult is Marian Paroo, a librarian who gives piano lessons and lives, under a cloud of unfounded suspicion regarding her relationship with the deceased "Miser Madison" (the town's philanthropist), with her widowed mother and lisping younger brother Winthrop. Marian sees through Hill, and is about to expose him, when she sees how Hill has coaxed Winthrop out of his shell. As she then becomes involved, playing piano for the ladies' dance group, she also comes out of her shell.

Hill, torn between needing to leave town before he is caught and his growing love for Marian, is stunned to discover that she has known all along that he is a fraud, but believes in him anyway. Meanwhile, Cowell has returned, and the town is out looking for Hill. In the climactic scene, Marian convinces the townspeople that all the excitement and civic pride Hill had promised has actually been realized. The town is wavering, when suddenly the band appears in uniform, and under Hill's reluctant leadership performs Beethoven's Minuet in G, which they have rehearsed using Hill's spurious "think system." Bad as the performance is, it nevertheless saves the day, and the town responds with warm enthusiasm.

Songs

Rock Island
Iowa Stubborn
Ya Got Trouble
Piano Lesson / If You Don't Mind My Saying So
Goodnight, My Someone
(Columbia, the Gem Of The Ocean)
Ya Got Trouble (Reprise)
Seventy-Six Trombones
Sincere
The Sadder but Wiser Girl
Pick-A-Little, Talk-A-Little / Goodnight Ladies
Marian the Librarian
My White Knight
The Wells Fargo Wagon
(Eulalie's Ballet)
It's You
Shipoopi
Lida Rose / Will I Ever Tell You?
Gary, Indiana
Till There Was You
Goodnight, My Someone / Seventy-Six Trombones
(Beethoven's Minuet in G)
Finale

Recordings
Meredith Willson. *The Music Man*. Capitol CDP WAO 990, 1958 (original cast recording).
Meredith Willson. *The Music Man*. EMI CSD 1361, 1961 (original London cast).
Meredith Willson. *The Music Man*. *The New Broadway Cast Recording*. Atlantic Records 92915–2, 2000.

Films and Video Recordings
The Music Man. 1962. Dir. Morton DaCosta. Robert Preston, Shirley Jones, Buddy Hackett, Hermione Gingold, Paul Ford, Ronny Howard, Pert Kelton.
The Music Man. 2003. Dir. Jeff Blecker. Matthew Broderick, Kristin Chenoweth, Victor Garber, Debra Monk (filmed for television).

Book
Meredith Willson. *The Music Man*. New York: G.P. Putnam, 1958.

Musical Score
Meredith Willson. *The Music Man*. New York: Frank Music, 1957 (vocal score).

Chapter Seven
Hair (1967–68)
Book and Lyrics: Gerome Ragni and James Rado
Music: Galt MacDermot

Plot: Episodic exploration of the counterculture centered around George Berger, with his friend Claude Hooper Bukowski appearing as a sympathetic outsider who does not go along with everything. Others in the "Tribe" include Sheila, an NYU protestor; Crissy, a lost-soul flower child; Woof, a long-haired goofball of uncertain sexual orientation; Hud, a "black pride" advocate; and Jeannie, an acid-head hippie. At the end of the first act—the "Be-In" that famously involves nudity and drug use—all but Claude burn their draft cards. In the end, Claude is drafted and sent to Vietnam; the final number is centered around his uniformed corpse.

Songs
Aquarius
Donna
Hashish
Sodomy
Colored Spade
Manchester England
I'm Black
Ain't Got No
I Believe In Love
Air
Initials
I Got Life
Going Down
Hair
My Conviction
Easy to Be Hard
Don't Put It Down
Frank Mills
Be-In
Where Do I Go?
Electric Blues
Black Boys
White Boys
Walking in Space
Abie Baby
Three-Five-Zero-Zero
What a Piece of Work Is Man
Good Morning Starshine
The Bed
The Flesh Failures (Let the Sunshine In)

Recordings

Gerome Ragni, James Rado, and Galt MacDermot. *Hair.* RCA LSO1143,1967 (original off-Broadway cast).

Gerome Ragni, James Rado, and Galt MacDermot. *Hair.* RCA LOC/LSO-1150, 1968 (original Broadway cast).

Gerome Ragni, James Rado, and Galt MacDermot. *Haare.* Polydor 249 266, 1968 (German cast).

Gerome Ragni, James Rado, and Galt MacDermot. *Hair.* Orfeon LP-JM-53, 1968 (Mexican cast).

Gerome Ragni, James Rado, and Galt MacDermot. *Hair.* Sonet SLP-70, 1968 (Swedish cast).

Gerome Ragni, James Rado, and Galt MacDermot. *Hair.* Spin SEL-933544, 1969 (Australian cast).

Gerome Ragni, James Rado, and Galt MacDermot. *Hair.* Fermata FB 265, 1969 (Brazilian cast).

Gerome Ragni, James Rado, and Galt MacDermot. *Hair.* Atco SD7002, 1969 (London cast).

Gerome Ragni, James Rado, and Galt MacDermot. *Hair.* Koch 34276, 1995 (Broadway Musical Company, European tour).

Hit Covers

The Age of Aquarius. The Fifth Dimension. Buddha / BMG, 2000 (reissue of 1969 album release with extra tracks).

Billboard Top Rock 'n' Roll Hits, 1969. Santa Monica: Rhino R2 70630, 1993 (includes "Aquarius / Let the Sunshine In" by the Fifth Dimension, "Hair" by the Cowsills, and "Good Morning Starshine" by Oliver).

Suitable for Framing. Three Dog Night. ABC Dunhill DS-50058, 1969 (album includes "Easy to Be Hard").

Films and Video Recording

Hair. Dir. Milos Forman. Treat Williams, John Savage, Beverly D'Angelo, Annie Golden, Dorsey Wright, Don Dacus, Cheryl Barnes, Ren Woods.

Book

Gerome Ragni, James Rado, and Galt MacDermot. *Hair; the American Tribal Love-Rock Musical.* New York: Pocket Books, 1969.

Musical Scores

Gerome Ragni, James Rado, and Galt MacDermot. *Hair.* New York and London: United Artists Music, 1968 (vocal score).

Gerome Ragni, James Rado, and Galt MacDermot. *Hair.* Los Angeles : United Artists Music, 1979 (vocal score).

Assassins (1991)
Book: John Weidman
Music and Lyrics: Stephen Sondheim

Plot: A shooting-gallery proprietor distributes guns to would-be assassins, including Leon Czolgosz (William McKinley), John Hinckley (attempted Ronald Reagan), Charles Guiteau (James Garfield), Giuseppe Zangara (attempted Franklin D. Roosevelt), Samuel Byck (attempted Richard Nixon), Lynette "Squeaky" Fromme (attempted Gerald Ford), Sara Jane Moore (attempted Ford), and John Wilkes Booth (Abraham Lincoln). The story unfolds in episodes, with a balladeer singing the stories of successful assassins Booth, Czolgosz, and Guiteau. In other episodes, Booth persuades Zangara to try to kill Roosevelt; bystanders explain how they saved Roosevelt; Emma Goldman talks to Czolgosz; Moore and Fromme discover mutual interests; Czolgosz, Booth, Guiteau, and Moore sing a paean to guns; Hinckley and Fromme hook up as worshipful admirers of Jodie Foster and Charles Manson, respectively; and Sam Byck prepares tape recordings for Nixon and Leonard Bernstein. The assassins and would-be assassins come together ("Another National Anthem") and dispose of the balladeer; then, with Booth taking the lead, they persuade Lee Harvey Oswald to assassinate John F. Kennedy.

Songs

Something Just Broke (added for the 1992 London production)
Everybody's Got the Right
The Ballad of Booth
How I Saved Roosevelt
Gun Song
The Ballad of Czolgosz
Unworthy of Your Love
The Ballad of Guiteau
Another National Anthem
November 22, 1963 (School Book Depository)
Finale (Everybody's Got the Right)

Recording

Stephen Sondheim. *Assassins*. RCA Victor 60737–2-RC, 1991 (original cast recording).

Book

John Weidman and Stephen Sondheim. *Assassins*. New York: Theatre Communications Group, 1991.

Musical Scores

Stephen Sondheim. *Assassins*. Secaucus, N.J.: Warner Bros. Publications, 1992 (vocal score).
Stephen Sondheim. *Something Just Broke*. Secaucus, N.J.: Warner Bros. Publications, 1993 (vocal score of song added for the London production).

Chapter Eight

Show Boat (1927)
Book and Lyrics: Oscar Hammerstein II
Music: Jerome Kern

Plot: Early 1880s: Cap'n Andy of the show boat "Cotton Blossom" arrives in town. His leading man Steve, married to star Julia Verne, fights a local man out of jealousy, who then notifies the authorities that Julie is part black. Meanwhile, Cap'n Andy's daughter Magnolia, aching to be on stage, falls for gambler Gaylord Ravenal, and confides in Joe, a black worker, and Julie, who teaches her "Can't Help Lovin' Dat Man." Queenie, overhearing the latter, recognizes it as a "colored" song. When Julie is accused of being black by the local authorities, Steve drinks some of her blood to avoid being arrested for miscegenation (mixed marriage), since he can then claim to have "Negro blood" in him. When they both have to leave the show, Magnolia and Gaylord take their places and soon marry. Act II opens at the Chicago Fair (1893), and will eventually move, a decade later, to the Trocadero, after Gaylord leaves Magnolia and she is trying to reignite her career in Chicago. Unknown to Magnolia, Julie is singing at the Trocadero, but is on the verge of losing her job if she continues to be unable to perform from excessive drinking. Julie pretends to be unable to sing to give Magnolia a chance, thus sacrificing what is left of her career. Many years later, with Magnolia a long-established star and her daughter grown up, Gaylord returns and a new show boat is launched.

Songs

Cotton Blossom
Cap'n Andy's Ballyhoo
Where's the Mate for Me
Make Believe
Ol' Man River
Can't Help Lovin' Dat Man
Life Upon the Wicked Stage
Till Good Luck Comes My Way
Mis'ry's Comin' Aroun'
I Might Fall Back on You
Queenie's Ballyhoo
Villain Dance
You Are Love
At the Fair
Why Do I Love You?
In Dahomey
Bill
Apache Dance
Goodbye, My Lady Love (period song by Joseph E. Howard, 1904)
After the Ball (period song by Charles K. Harris, 1893)
Hey, Feller!
Finale

Recordings

Jerome Kern and Oscar Hammerstein II. *Show Boat*. CBS 155, 1932 (1932 cast recording).
Jerome Kern and Oscar Hammerstein II. *Show Boat*. Sony Broadway SK53330, 1993 (1946 Broadway revival).

Jerome Kern and Oscar Hammerstein II. *Show Boat*. Sony SK/ST 61877, 2002 (1962 studio recording with Barbara Cook and William Warfield; includes some original cast performances from 1928: "Bill" by Helen Morgan and "Can't Help Lovin' Dat Man" by Tess Gardella).

Jerome Kern and Oscar Hammerstein II. *Show Boat*. RCA LSO 1126, 1966 (1966 Lincoln Center cast, including Barbara Cook and William Warfield).

Jerome Kern and Oscar Hammerstein II. *Show Boat*. Angel 7777498472, 1988 (studio recording directed by John McGlinn, with Frederica von Stade and Teresa Stratas).

Jerome Kern and Oscar Hammerstein II. *Show Boat*. EMI CDS 7 49111 2, 1988 (first full recording of 1927 version).

Jerome Kern and Oscar Hammerstein II. *Show Boat*. TER Classics CDTER2 1199, 1993 (first full recording of 1946 published version).

Jerome Kern and Oscar Hammerstein II. *Show Boat*. LivEnt Music RSPD 257, 1994 (Toronto revival cast recording).

Films and Video Recordings
Show Boat. 1929. Dir. Harry A. Pollard (part silent, part sung).
Show Boat. 1936. Dir. James Whale. Irene Dunne, Paul Robeson, Hattie McDaniel, Helen Morgan, Charles Winninger, Allan Jones.
Show Boat. 1951. Dir. George Sidney. Kathryn Grayson, Howard Keel, Ava Gardner, Joe E. Brown, Marge Champion, Gower Champion, William Warfield (generally disliked version).
Show Boat. 1989. Dir. Robert Johanson. Eddie Bracken, Rebecca Baxter, Richard White, P. L. Brown (generally admired version).

Books
Edna Ferber. *Show Boat*. Garden City, N.Y.: Doubleday, 1926.
Jerome Kern and Oscar Hammerstein II. *Show Boat*. London: Chappell, 1928.

Musical Score
Jerome Kern and Oscar Hammerstein II. *Show Boat*. London: Chappell and New York: T. B. Harms Music Co., 1928 (vocal score).

Porgy and Bess (1935)
Libretto: Dubose Heyward and Ira Gershwin
Music: George Gershwin

Plot: see p. 194

Songs
Introduction and Jasbo Brown Blues
Summertime
A Woman Is a Sometime Thing
Here Come de Honey Man
Oh, Little Stars
Gone, Gone, Gone
Overflow

My Man's Gone Now
Leavin' for the Promise' Lan'
It Take a Long Pull to Get There
I Got Plenty o' Nuttin'
The Buzzard Song
Bess, You Is My Woman Now
Oh, I Can't Sit Down
I Ain't Got No Shame
It Ain't Necessarily So
What You Want Wid Bess?
Oh, Doctor Jesus
Strawberry Woman / Honey Man / Crab Man
I Loves You, Porgy
Oh, Doctor Jesus (Hurricane Scene)
Oh, Dere's Somebody Knockin'
A Red-Headed Woman
Clara, Clara
There's a Boat Dat's Leavin' Soon for New York
Good Mornin', Sistuh!
Oh, Bess, Oh, Where's My Bess
Oh, Lawd, I'm on My Way

Recordings

George Gershwin, DuBose Heyward, and Ira Gershwin. *Porgy and Bess*. Columbia OSL 162, 1951 (studio recording with Lawrence Winters).

George Gershwin, DuBose Heyward, and Ira Gershwin. *Porgy and Bess*. RCA LSC 2679, 1963 (studio cast; selections, with Leontyne Price, William Warfield, McHenry Boatright, and John Bubbles).

George Gershwin, DuBose Heyward, and Ira Gershwin. *Porgy and Bess*. London OSA-13116, 1976 (studio cast conducted by Lorin Maazel, with Willard White, Leona Mitchess, McHenry Boatright, Florence Quivar, and Barbara Hendricks).

George Gershwin, DuBose Heyward, and Ira Gershwin. *Porgy and Bess*. RCA ARL 3-2109, 1977 (Houston Opera production, conducted by John DeMain, with Clamma Dale, Donnie Ray Albert, and Larry Marshall).

George Gershwin, DuBose Heyward, and Ira Gershwin. *Porgy and Bess*. EMI/Angel CDCC-49568, 1986 (Glyndebourne Festival Opera production, conducted by Simon Rattle, with Cynthia Haymon, Willard White, and Damon Evans).

Films and Video Recordings

Porgy and Bess. 1959. Dir. Otto Preminger and Rouben Mamoulian. Sidney Portier (sung by Robert McFerrin), Dorothy Dandridge, Sammy Davis, Jr., Pearl Bailey, Brock Peters, Leslie Scott, Diahann Carroll.

Porgy and Bess. 1993. Dir. Trevor Nunn. Willard White, Cynthia Haymon, Gregg Baker, Cynthia Clarey, Paula Ingram (sung by Harolyn Blackwell), Damon Evans (first filmed version of the complete opera; for television).

Porgy and Bess. 2002. Dir. Tazewell Thompson. Marquita Lister, Alvy Powell, Timoth Robert Blevins, Dwayne Clark (slightly cut opera version; for television).

Books

DuBose Heyward. *Porgy,* New York: George H. Doran, 1925.
Dubose and Dorothy Heyward. *Porgy; A Play in Four Acts.* New York: Doubleday, Doran, 1928.
(Libretto available with 1976, 1977, and 1986 recordings listed earlier.)

Musical Scores

George Gershwin, DuBose Heyward, and Ira Gershwin. *Porgy and Bess.* New York: Random House, 1935 (vocal score).
George Gershwin, DuBose Heyward, and Ira Gershwin. *Porgy and Bess.* New York: Gershwin Pub., 1935.

West Side Story **(1957)**
Book: Arthur Laurents
Lyrics: Stephen Sondheim
Music: Leonard Bernstein

Plot: On New York City's West Side, two rival youth gangs vie for territory. The "American" gang, the Jets, are led by Riff, and the Puerto Rican newcomers, the Sharks, are led by Bernardo. At a dance in neutral territory, Riff's friend and former Jet Tony meets and falls in love with Bernardo's sister Maria, just arrived from Puerto Rico and intended for Chino. Maria and Tony "wed" in a mock ceremony, while the others prepare for a showdown between the gangs. At the "Rumble," a reluctant Tony tries to intervene, but succeeds only in allowing Bernardo to kill Riff; enraged, Tony retaliates by killing Bernardo (Maria's brother). Forgiving Tony, Maria convinces Anita (Bernardo's lover and Maria's confidante) to renounce her bitter hatred and help her by arranging a rendezvous with Tony, but when Anita tries to do so, the Jets "taunt" (nearly rape) her. Humiliated, she leaves a different message: Maria is dead. In despair, Tony, knowing Chino is gunning for him, makes himself an easy target. Enraged and grief-stricken when Tony is killed, Maria enforces an uneasy truce between the gangs.

Songs

Prologue
Jet Song
Something's Coming
The Dance at the Gym
Maria
Tonight
America
Cool
One Hand One Heart
Tonight (Quintet)

The Rumble
I Feel Pretty
Somewhere
Gee Officer Krupke
A Boy Like That / I Have a Love
Taunting Scene
Finale (Somewhere)

Recordings

Leonard Bernstein and Stephen Sondheim. *West Side Story*. Columbia OL 5230, 1957 (original cast recording).

Leonard Bernstein and Stephen Sondheim. *West Side Story*. Deutsche Grammophon R 215404, 1985 (studio performance conducted by Bernstein, with Kiri Te Kanawa, José Carreras, Tatiana Troyanos, Kurt Ollmann, and Marilyn Horne).

Leonard Bernstein and Stephen Sondheim. *West Side Story*. Jay Records CDJAY2 1261, 1993 (first complete recording, conducted by John Owen Edwards, with Paul Manuel, Caroline O'Conner, Tinuke Olafimihan, Nicholas Warnford, and Sally Burgess).

(A large number of recordings are available in other languages, as well.)

Films and Video Recordings

West Side Story. 1961. Dir. Robert Wise. Natalie Wood (sung by Marni Nixon), Richard Beymer (sung by Jim Bryant), Rita Moreno (sung by Betty Wand), Russ Tamblyn , and George Chakiris.

Leonard Bernstein: The Making of West Side Story. Deutsche Gramophon DVD 073 017–9, 2002 (television documentary of the 1985 studio recording; see above).

Books

Arthur Laurents, Stephen Sondheim, and Leonard Bernstein. *West Side Story*. New York: Random House, 1958.

William Shakespeare, Arthur Laurents, Stephen Sondheim, and Leonard Bernstein. *Romeo and Juliet / West Side Story*. New York: Dell, 1965.

Musical Scores

Leonard Bernstein and Stephen Sondheim. *West Side Story*. New York: G. Schirmer,1959 (vocal score).

Leonard Bernstein and Stephen Sondheim. *West Side Story*. New York: Boosey & Hawkes, 1959 (vocal score).

Leonard Bernstein and Stephen Sondheim. *West Side Story*. Orchestrations by Leonard Bernstein with Sid Ramin and Irwin Kostal. New York: Jalni Publications and Boosey & Hawkes, 1994 (full score).

Fiddler on the Roof (1964)
Book: Joseph Stein
Lyrics: Sheldon Harnick
Music: Jerry Bock

Plot: In the Jewish shtetl of Anatevka in Russia, 1905, the dairyman Tevye, his wife Golde, and their five daughters live precariously, sustained by ancient Jewish traditions. One by one, his daughters test those traditions. Tzeitel, whose marriage to the widower Lazar Wolfe has already been arranged, asks permission to marry the poor tailor Motel instead. Tevye accedes, convincing Golde by recounting a "dream" in which Lazar's first wife and Tzeitel's namesake return from the dead to warn them not to go through with the arranged marriage. Act I ends with Tzeitel's marriage to Motel, which is broken up by a pogrom supervised by the Russian authorities. In Act II, Tevye's second daughter Hodel asks Tevye's blessing (rather than permission) to marry the revolutionary Perchik, who has been serving as the girls' tutor. Tevye gives them his blessing, but Perchik is arrested and sent to Siberia, and Hodel follows him. The third test of tradition, however, is too severe for Tevye, and he renounces his third daughter Chava after she marries the Russian Fyedka before a priest. Disaster then befalls the community, as the Russian constable announces that the Jews must leave Anatevka in three days. As the family is leaving, Chava reappears with Fyedka to announce that they are leaving, too, even though they are not being forced to. The story ends with only a hint of possible reconciliation between Chava and her estranged family.

Songs

> Prologue / Tradition
> Matchmaker
> If I Were a Rich Man
> Sabbath Prayer
> To Life (L'Chaim)
> Tevye's Monologue (The Pledge)
> Miracles of Miracles
> The Dream
> Sunrise, Sunset
> Wedding Dances
> Now I Have Everything
> Tevye's Rebuttal
> Do You Love Me?
> The Rumor
> Far from the Home I Love
> Chava Sequence
> Anatevka
> Finale

Recordings

Jerry Bock and Sheldon Harnick. *Fiddler on the Roof.* RCA Victor LOC-1093, 1964 (original cast recording).

Jerry Bock and Sheldon Harnick. *Fiddler on the Roof.* Columbia OS 3050, 1965 (original Israeli cast recording, sung in Yiddish).

Jerry Bock and Sheldon Harnick. *Fiddler on the Roof.* NMC Music Ltd. GOLD 20520–2, 1965 (original Israeli cast recording, sung in Hebrew).

Jerry Bock and Sheldon Harnick. *Fiddler on the Roof.* Columbia Broadway Masterworks SK 89546, 2001 (original London cast, 1967).

Film and Video Recording

Fiddler on the Roof. 1971. Norman Jewison. Topol, Norma Crane, Rosalind Harris, Leonard Frey, Molly Picon, Paul Mann, Michele Marsh, Neva Small, Paul Michael Glaser, Ray Lovelock.

Books

Sholem Aleichem. *Tevye's Daughters; Collected Stories of Sholem Aleichem.* Translated by Frances Butwin. New York: Crown, 1949.

Joseph Stein and Sheldon Harnick. *Fiddler on the Roof.* New York: Crown, 1964.

Musical Score

Jerry Bock and Sheldon Harnick. *Fiddler on the Roof.* New York : Sunbeam Music, 1964 (vocal score).

Chapter Nine

> *The Sound of Music* (1959)
> Book: Howard Lindsay and Russel Crouse
> Lyrics: Oscar Hammerstein II
> Music: Richard Rodgers

Plot: In 1938 Salzburg, just before the Anschluss, Maria, a postulant at the Abbey, is sent by the Reverend Mother to be a governess at the nearby estate of Captain Georg von Trapp, where she wins over the seven difficult children and councils the eldest, Liesl, regarding her clandestine romance with Rolf. While the Captain is away in Vienna, Maria teaches the children to sing (music had been forbidden since their mother died). On the Captain's return with his betrothed (the Baroness von Schroeder) and friend Max, he is initially angry at the children's apparent lack of discipline, but is then astonished at how well they sing, and soon joins them. At a dress ball in honor of their guests, Maria dances a ländler with the Captain, and they both begin to realize they are falling in love. In panic, she returns to the Abbey, but the Reverend Mother insists she return and face whatever might come. Seeing the Captain and Maria's love for each other, the Baroness retires gracefully, but Max remains in the hopes of entering the children in the Salzburg Music Festival, even though he and the Captain have quarreled about politics. The Anschluss comes while the Captain and Maria are on their honeymoon, and with it comes the demand that Georg assume command of a submarine base. Unable to become part of the Third Reich, the Captain joins his family in competing at the festival, but only as a ruse; they win the highest prize, but make their escape during the award ceremony.

Songs

Preludium / Morning Hymn / Alleluia
The Sound of Music
Maria
My Favorite Things
Do-Re-Mi
Sixteen Going on Seventeen
The Lonely Goatherd

How Can Love Survive?
The Sound of Music (with children and Captain)
Grand Waltz / Ländler / Fox-Trot
So Long, Farewell
Climb Ev'ry Mountain
No Way to Stop It
An Ordinary Couple
Processional
Canticle (Confitemini Domino)
Edelweiss
So Long, Farewell (with Captain and Maria)
Finale: Climb Ev'ry Mountain

Recordings
Richard Rodgers and Oscar Hammerstein II. *The Sound of Music*. Columbia KOL 5450, 1959 (original Broadway recording).
Richard Rodgers and Oscar Hammerstein II. *Members of the Trapp Family Singers Sing and Play the Songs from Rodgers and Hammerstein's* The Sound of Music. RCA Victor LSP-2277, 1960.
Richard Rodgers and Oscar Hammerstein II. *The Sound of Music*. EMI Angel 52656, 1961 (original London cast).
Richard Rodgers and Oscar Hammerstein II. *The Sound of Music*. RCA Victor 63207, 1998 (original Broadway revival cast).

Films and Video Recordings
The Sound of Music. 1965. Dir. Robert Wise. Julie Andrews, Christopher Plummer (sung by Bill Lee), Peggy Wood (sung by Margery McKay), Richard Haydn, Eleanor Parker, Charmian Carr, Nicholas Hammond, Heather Menzies, Duane Chase, Angela Cartwright, Debbie Turner, and Kym Karath.

Books
Maria Augusta Trapp. *The Story of the Trapp Family Singers*. Philadelphia and New York: J. B. Lippincott, 1949.
Howard Lindsay, Russel Crouse, and Oscar Hammerstein II. *The Sound of Music*. New York: Random House, 1960.

Musical Score
Richard Rodgers and Oscar Hammerstein II. *The Sound of Music*. New York: Williamson Music, 1959 (vocal score).

Cabaret (1966)
Book: Joe Masteroff
Lyrics: Fred Ebb
Music: John Kander

Plot: A young American writer, Clifford Bradshaw, arrives in 1929 Berlin to gather material for a novel, taking up residence at Fraulein Schneider's rooming house, and frequenting the Kit Kat Klub cabaret, where he becomes enamored of Sally

Bowles, a young English star, who moves in with him when she is thrown out of her place. Sally becomes pregnant and Cliff gets involved with smuggling, inadvertently aiding the Nazis. Meanwhile, Fraulein Schneider backs out of her engagement with Herr Schultz, fearing consequences because he is Jewish. Throughout, the Kit Kat Klub, led by its decadent Emcee, provides biting commentary on everything that happens: sexual license ("Two Ladies"), illicit income ("Sitting Pretty"), the growing Nazi threat (a goose-stepping version of "Tomorrow Belongs to Me"), and the inconvenience of Jewish connections ("If You Could See Her"). Cliff is determined to take Sally to America, but she elects to have an abortion and remain in Berlin; in the end he leaves without her.

Songs

Wilkommen
So What?
The Telephone Song
Don't Tell Mama
Perfectly Marvelous
Two Ladies
It Couldn't Please Me More
Tomorrow Belongs to Me
Why Should I Wake Up?
Sitting Pretty (the Money Song)
Married
Meeskite
If You Could See Her
What Would You Do?
Sally's Revolt
Cabaret
Finale

Recordings

John Kander and Fred Ebb. *Cabaret*. Columbia Broadway Masterworks SK 60533, 1998 (1966 original cast, with additional material).
John Kander and Fred Ebb. *Cabaret*. RCA Victor 09026–63173–2, 1998 (Revival Broadway cast recording).

Films and Video Recordings

I Am a Camera. 1955. Dir. Henry Cornelius. Julie Harris, Laurence Harvey, Shelley Winters, Ron Randell, Patrick McGoohan.
Cabaret. 1972. Dir. Bob Fosse. Liza Minnelli, Michael York, Joel Grey, Helmut Griem, Fritz Wepper, Marisa Berenson.

Books

Christopher Isherwood. *The Berlin Stories. The Last of Mr. Norris. Goodbye to Berlin*. New York: J. Laughlin, 1954 (original stories from the 1930s).
John Van Druten. *I Am a Camera*. New York: Random House, 1952 (earlier play version).

Joe Masteroff and Fred Ebb. *Harold Prince's Cabaret*. New York: Random House, 1967.

Musical Scores

John Kander and Fred Ebb. *Vocal Selections from Cabaret*. New York: Sunbeam Music, 1966 (vocal score).

John Kander and Fred Ebb. *Cabaret*. New York: Sunbeam Music, 1968 (vocal score).

John Kander and Fred Ebb. *The Complete* Cabaret *Collection*. Milwaukee, Wis.: Hal Leonard, 1999 (1966 Broadway production).

Chapter Ten

The Mikado; or, The Town of Titipu (1885)
Book and Lyrics: W. S. Gilbert
Music: Arthur Sullivan

Plot: see p. 253

Songs

If You Want to Know Who We Are
Gentlemen, I Pray You Tell Me
A Wandering Minstrel I
Our Great Mikado, Virtuous Man
Young Man, Despair
And Have I Journeyed for a Month
Behold the Lord High Executioner
Taken From the County Jail
As Some Day It May Happen (the list song)
Comes a Train of Little Ladies
Three Little Maids from School Are We
So Please You, Sir, We Much Regret
Were You Not to Ko-Ko Plighted
I Am So Proud
Act I Finale: With Aspect Stern / The Threatened Cloud / Your Revels Cease / Oh Fool, That Fleest / Away, Nor Prosecute Your Quest / For He's Going to Marry Yum-Yum / The Hour of Gladness / Ye Torrents Roar
Braid the Raven Hair
The Sun, Whose Rays
Brightly Dawns Our Wedding Day
Here's a How-de-do!
Miya Sama
From Every Kind of Man
A More Humane Mikado
The Criminal Cried
See How the Fates Their Gifts Allot
The Flowers That Bloom in the Spring
Alone, and Yet Alive! / Hearts Do Not Break / Oh, Living I!

On a Tree by a River (Tit-Willow)
There Is Beauty in the Bellow of the Blast
Finale: For He's Gone and Married Yum-Yum / The Threatened Cloud

Recordings

W. S. Gilbert and Arthur Sullivan. *The Mikado; or, The Town of Titipu.* Pearl GEM 137/8 (acclaimed 1926 D'Oyly Carte recording, audio quality problematic).

W. S. Gilbert and Arthur Sullivan. *The Mikado; or, The Town of Titipu.* Sounds on CD VGS 245 (1936 D'Oyly Carte recording, the first with Martyn Green).

W. S. Gilbert and Arthur Sullivan. *The Mikado; or, The Town of Titipu.* Decca 4010–1 (1950 D'Oyly Carte recording, the standard issue from the Martyn Green years).

W. S. Gilbert and Arthur Sullivan. *The Mikado; or, The Town of Titipu.* EMI CDS7 47773–2, 1956 (studio version: Pro Arte Orchestra, Glyndebourne Festival Chorus, conducted by Malcolm Sargent; the first recording to challenge the D'Oyly Carte monopoly).

W. S. Gilbert and Arthur Sullivan. *The Mikado; or, The Town of Titipu.* London A-4231, 1957 (a favorite of the D'Oyly Carte series, with Donald Adams, Thomas Round, Peter Pratt, Kenneth Sandford, Jean Hindmarsh, Beryl Dixon, and Ann Drummond-Grant).

W. S. Gilbert and Arthur Sullivan. *The Mikado; or, The Town of Titipu.* Sony S2K-58889, 1990 (first recording from the New D'Oyly Carte Opera Company).

W. S. Gilbert and Arthur Sullivan. *The Mikado; or, The Town of Titipu.* Telarc CD-80284, 1992 (mix of opera and D'Oyly Carte veterans Donald Adams and Richard Stuart, conducted by Charles Mackerras, Orchestra and Chorus of the Welsh National Opera).

Films and Video Recordings

The Mikado; or, The Town of Titipu. 1939. Dir. Victor Schertzinger. Martyn Green, Kenny Baker, Sydney Granville, John Barclay, Jean Colin, Constance Willis, Gregory Stroud, the D'Oyly Carte Chorus (DVD release 1998, Image Entertainment ID4529JFDVD; oddly reworked plot and manner of presentation).

The Mikado; or, The Town of Titipu. British Home Entertainment BHE00IV, 1966. D'Oyly Carte Opera Company.

The Mikado; or, The Town of Titipu. Opera World MIK10V, 1982. Dir. Michael Geliot and Rodney Greenberg. Clive Revill, Anne Collins, Kate Flowers, John Stewart, Stafford Dean, William Conrad, Cynthia Buchan, Fiona Dobie, Gordon Sandison (made for television).

The Mikado; or, The Town of Titipu. Acorn Media, 1982. Dir. Norman Campbell. Stratford Festival (well mounted).

The Mikado; or, The Town of Titipu. ABC Video, 1988. Elizabethan Sydney Orchestra, Australian Opera Chorus (opera version).

The Mikado (1939). Warner Home Video, 1989. Jonathan Miller: English National Opera. Erik Idle, Bonaventura Bottone, Richard Angas, Richard van Allan, Mark Richardson, Lesley Garret, Ethna Robinson, Susan Bullock, and

Felicity Palmer (updated from 1880s Japan to 1930s England and set in an art deco seaside resort; made for television).

The Mikado; or, The Town of Titipu. Polygram 0864643, 1992. New D'Oyly Carte Players, Chorus, and Orchestra (lightly regarded).

The Mikado; or, The Town of Titipu. Essgee Entertainment, 1995. Essgee (Simon Gallaher) Entertainment (extravagantly mounted, freely adapted).

Topsy-Turvy. 1999. Dir. Mike Leigh. Jim Broadbent, Alan Corduner, Timothy Spall, Lesley Manville, Ron Cook, Wendy Nottingham, Kevin McKidd, Shirley Henderson, Dorothy Atkinson, Martin Savage (the "back story" of *The Mikado,* wonderfully wrought).

The Mikado; or, The Town of Titipu. Carl Rosa CRV001, 2001 (uses award-winning costumes and sets from *Topsy-Turvy).*

Books

W. S. Gilbert. *Plays & Poems of W. S. Gilbert.* Preface by Deems Taylor. New York: Random House, 1932 (contains the *Bab Ballads).*

W. S. Gilbert. *The First Night Gilbert and Sullivan, Containing Complete Librettos of the Fourteen Operas, Exactly as Presented at their Premiere Performances; Together with Facsims. of the First Night Programmes.* Edited by Reginald Allen. Foreword by Bridget D'Oyly Carte. New York: Heritage Press, 1958.

W. S. Gilbert. *The Complete Gilbert and Sullivan; Librettos from all Fourteen Operettas.* Preface by Deems Taylor. New York: Black Dog and Leventhal, 1960.

W. S. Gilbert. *The Complete Annotated Gilbert and Sullivan.* Edited by Ian Bradley. Oxford: Oxford University Press, 1996.

Musical Scores

W. S. Gilbert and Arthur Sullivan. *The Mikado; or, The Town of Titipu.* London: Chappell and New York: W. A. Pond, 1885 (vocal score).

W. S. Gilbert and Arthur Sullivan. *The Mikado; or, The Town of Titipu.* Farnborough Hants., England: Gregg International, 1968 (full score).

W. S. Gilbert and Arthur Sullivan. *The Mikado; or, The Town of Titipu.* Mineola, N.Y.: Dover, 1999 (full score).

W. S. Gilbert and Arthur Sullivan. *The Mikado; or, The Town of Titipu.* Mineola, N.Y.: Dover, 2000 (vocal score).

W. S. Gilbert and Arthur Sullivan. *The Mikado; or, The Town of Titipu.* New York: G. Schirmer, 2002 (vocal score, with dialog).

The King and I (1951)
Book and Lyrics: Oscar Hammerstein II
Music: Richard Rodgers

Plot: An English widow, Anna Leonowens, arrives in Bangkok, 1862, with her son, to tutor the wives and young children of King Mongkut. Anna is disappointed that she is not given a separate residence as agreed. The young Burmese Tuptim, secretly in love with Lun Tha, is offered to the King as a slave; Anna offers the young woman sympathy and reading material, including Harriet Beecher Stowe's

Uncle Tom's Cabin. The King and his court grapple with the uncertainties that come with education. Meanwhile, visitors from England are due to arrive to determine whether Siam should be made a protectorate or allowed to remain independent; convincing them that the King is not a "barbarian" will be the crux. As entertainment at the Western-style banquet, Tuptim presents a ballet version of *Uncle Tom's Cabin,* stressing the escape of the slave Eliza. The banquet is a success, and in exhilaration afterward, the King asks that Anna teach him to dance as he had seen her dance with one of the Englishmen. In the midst of their dance, the slave Tuptim is brought in; she has been captured trying to escape with Lun Tha (who has died in the attempt). The King commands that she be whipped, but Anna intercedes, which (apparently) precipitates the King's terminal illness. Although Anna is set to leave, the King and her pupils implore her to stay, and she agrees.

Songs

I Whistle a Happy Tune
My Lord and Master
The March of the Siamese Children
Hello, Young Lovers
(Happy Land / Home Sweet Home / There's No Place Like Home)
A Puzzlement
School Song
Getting to Know You
We Kiss in a Shadow
Shall I Tell You What I Think of You?
Something Wonderful
Western People Funny
I Have Dreamed
"The Small House of Uncle Thomas"
Song of the King
Shall We Dance?
Finale

Recordings

Richard Rodgers and Oscar Hammerstein II. *The King and I.* MCA Classics MCAD-10049, 1990 (original 1951 Broadway cast recording).

Richard Rodgers and Oscar Hammerstein II. *The King and I.* Columbia Masterworks 8040, 1964 (studio recording with Barbara Cook and Theodore Bikel).

Richard Rodgers and Oscar Hammerstein II. *The King and I.* RCA Victor LSO 1092, 1964 (Music Theater of Lincoln Center cast recording, with Risë Stevens and Darren McGavin.)

Richard Rodgers and Oscar Hammerstein II. *The King and I.* RCA Victor RCD1–2610, 1977 (revival cast recording with Constance Towers and Yul Brynner).

Richard Rodgers and Oscar Hammerstein II. *The King and I.* Philips 438 007–2, 1992 (Hollywood studio cast recording, with Julie Andrews and Ben Kingsley).

Richard Rodgers and Oscar Hammerstein II. *The King and I.* TER 1214, 1994 ("first complete recording" by London studio cast).

Richard Rodgers and Oscar Hammerstein II. *The King and I*. Varèse 5763, 1996 (Broadway revival cast recording, with Donna Murphy and Lou Diamond Philips).

Films and Video Recordings

Anna and the King. 1946. Dir. John Cromwell. Irene Dunne, Rex Harrison, Linda Darnell, and Lee J. Cobb.

The King and I. 1956. Dir. Walter Lang. Yul Brynner, Deborah Kerr (sung by Marni Nixon), Rita Moreno (sung by Leona Gordon), Carlos Rivas (sung by Reuben Fuentes), Martin Benson, Terry Saunders, Rex Thompson, and Patrick Adiarte.

The King and I. 1999. Dir. Richard Rich. Voices of Miranda Richardson, Christiane Noll, Martin Vidnovic, and Ian Richardson (animated version, much altered).

Anna and the King. 1999. Dir. Andy Tennant. Jodie Foster and Chow Yun-Fat.

Books

Anna Leonowens. *The Romance of the Harem*. Edited by Susan Morgan. Charlottesville, Va: University Press of Virginia, 1991 (memoir of 1872).

Anna Leonowens. *Siamese Harem Life*. London: A. Barker, 1952 (memoir of 1872).

Anna Leonowens. *The English Governess at the Siamese Court; Being Recollections of Six Years in the Royal Palace at Bangkok*. New York: Roy Publishers, 1954 (memoir of 1870).

Margaret Landon. *Anna and the King of Siam*. New York: John Day, 1944.

Oscar Hammerstein II. *The King and I*. New York: Random House, 1951.

Musical Score

Richard Rodgers and Oscar Hammerstein II. *The King and I*. New York: Williamson Music, 1951.

Pacific Overtures (1976)
Book: John Weidman and Hugh Wheeler
Music and Lyrics: Stephen Sondheim

Plot: Manjiro, a Japanese fisherman rescued many years before, returns to Japan in 1853 from the United States. He becomes a useful friend to Kayama Yasaemon, governor of Uraga, when Commodore Perry's four ships arrive there to open up Japan for trading with the West. The Japanese response is evasive: Kayama's wife commits suicide, and the Shogun takes to his bed, where he is poisoned by his mother. Kayama and Manjiro outwit the Americans by covering the ground with mats so that they can conclude their treaty without the Americans "setting foot" on sacred Japanese soil. As the new Shogun (Lord Abe) discovers, however, the American visit is the first of many, since other countries, too, want to open up trade with Japan. As the process of Westernizing continues across the second half of Act II, Manjiro becomes more traditional and even becomes a samurai, but Kayama becomes increasingly Western and accommodating. The climax for this part of the story occurs when three British sailors mistake a young woman for a geisha, and are killed by a swordsman; shortly after that, Manjiro kills Kayama as well, and the puppet Emperor seizes power from the Shogun, determined to modernize Japan. The final number, "Next," condenses over a century of Japanese history, including World War II and the ensuing industrial renaissance of Japan.

Songs
The Advantages of Floating in the Middle of the Sea
There Is No Other Way
Four Black Dragons
Chrysanthemum Tea
Poems
Welcome To Kanagawa
Someone in a Tree
Please Hello
A Bowler Hat
Pretty Lady
Next

Recordings
Stephen Sondheim. *Pacific Overtures*. RCA Victor RCD1–4407, 1976 (original Broadway cast recording).
Stephen Sondheim. *Pacific Overtures*. TER 2 1152, 1987 (English National Opera cast recording).

Film and Video Recording
Pacific Overtures. 1976 (the original Broadway staging, filmed for Japanese television, may be screened on request at the Museum of Television and Radio, New York and Beverly Hills).

Books
John Weidman, Stephen Sondheim, and Hugh Wheeler. *Pacific Overtures*. New York: Dodd, Mead, 1977.
John Weidman, Stephen Sondheim, and Hugh Wheeler. *Pacific Overtures*. New York: Theatre Communications Group, 1991.

Musical Score
Stephen Sondheim. *Pacific Overtures*. New York: Revelation Music, 1977 (vocal score).

NOTES

Chapter One
Contexts and Strategies

1. I am following here the convention of using the term "American," in both its adjectival and noun forms, to refer specifically to the United States, in full awareness that the term slights the rest of the Americas—Canada, Mexico, Central America, and South America—by exclusion. There is, however, no widely recognized alternative, and there are many common combinations—such as "American musical"—that could scarcely be avoided here.

2. D. A. Miller gives a passionately wise and wryly witty account of gay involvement in the American musical in his *Place for Us [Essay on the Broadway Musical]* (Cambridge, Mass., and London: Harvard University Press, 1998. Regarding the presence of gays and camp in musicals generally, see Richard Dyer's "It's Being so Camp as Keeps Us Going" in *Only Entertainment* (London and New York: Routledge, 1992), Chuck Kleinhans's "Taking Out the Trash: Camp and the Politics of Parody" in The Politics and Poetics of Camp, ed. Moe Meyer (London and New York: Routledge, 1994), and Mark Steyn's "The Fags," in *Broadway Babies Say Goodnight: Musicals Then and Now* (New York: Routledge, 1999).

3. As Rick Altman puts it (in boldface!) in *The American Film Musical* (Bloomington and Indianapolis: Indiana University Press, 1987), "The marriage which resolves the primary (sexual) dichotomy also mediates between two terms of the secondary (thematic) opposition" (p. 50).

4. Spike Lee's powerful presentation is, however, only a part of the truth regarding minstrelsy; see W. T. Lhamon, Jr.'s *Raising Cain: Blackface Performance from Jim Crow to Hip Hop* (Cambridge Mass., and London: Harvard University Press, 1998) for a more balanced view of its representational dynamic. Regarding the persistence of blackface, see Michael Rogin's *Blackface, White Noise: Jewish Immigrants in the Hollywood Melting Pot* (Berkeley, Los Angeles, and London: University of California Press, 1996).

5. "Transformation scenes," most often staged at climactic moments in a show, amounted to a kind of "tableau vivant" (living picture) in which the setting and / or the characters would magically shift their appearance, an effect managed by some combination of stage machinery, lighting, scrims, doubles, and, perhaps, a cloaking vapor. Most famous from the nineteenth century was the transformation scene in *The Black Crook* (see chapter 2, pp. 20–29). Both *Into the Woods* (1987) and *Beauty and the Beast* (1994) include latter-day examples of transformation scenes, when, respectively, the witch transforms into a beautiful woman and the beast back into a prince.

6. See appendix B for a listing of the principal available material along these lines for the shows discussed in this book.

7. Readers of this book also have recourse to a website that provides audio clips of illustrative musical examples, musical notation when useful, and additional pictures; see the "Explanatory Note about Audio Examples" on page xiii.

Chapter Two
Nineteenth-Century European Roots: Models and Topics

1. Weber's "Wolf's Glen" would be evoked prominently a decade later, as well, in the preparation of the "philtre" in Gilbert and Sullivan's *The Sorcerer* (1876), a scene that the 1999 film *Topsy-Turvy* attempts to re-create.

2. *Mark Twain's Travels with Mr. Brown,* collected and ed. Franklin Walker and G. Ezra Dane (New York: Knopf, 1940), 85–86.

3. Quoted in Gintautiene, "The Black Crook: Ballet in the Gilded Age" (Ph.D. diss., New York University, 1984), 96.

4. Quoted in ibid., 97.

5. See ibid., 95–97.

6. *Mark Twain's Travels with Mr. Brown,* 85.

7. Ibid. See also Gintautiene, "The Black Crook," 82.

8. Quoted in Gintautiene, "The Black Crook," 99.

9. For this conjecture we have at least circumstantial evidence, derived from sheet music published in 1866 and 1867. Most of this music—e.g., "The Black Crook Waltz" (William A. Pond, 1866), "March of the Amazons" (H. B. Dodworth, 1866), and "The Black Crook Waltzes" (H. B. Dodworth, 1867)—lists no composer, but only an arranger (Thomas Baker, Emil Stigler, and Joseph Noll, respectively). Even more suggestive is the credit listing for "The Black Crook Galop" (William A. Pond, 1866): "Arr. by Thomas Baker, Composer of the Black Crook Music"—an odd circumlocution that would seem to indicate that Baker was *not* the actual composer even as it attempts to convey the impression that he was. But the clincher is the more forthright declaration in the heading of "The Black Crook Lancers" (H. B. Dodworth, 1867): "Adapted by permission of Sigr. David Costa [original choreographer for *The Black Crook*] from Melodies composed by European Authors, as performed in *The Black Crook.*"

10. At an earlier stage in Hervé's career, he joined the Odéon Theater just after it had mounted a different balletic version of *La Biche au Bois* (1845); mistakenly, many accounts of the *The Black Crook* cite this earlier production as the source for the projected mounting of *La Biche au Bois* in New York. The 1845 version was an early member of a string of successful fairy-tale adaptations for the Parisian ballet stage; perhaps coincidentally, the Odéon had earlier also mounted adaptations of Weber's *Singspiele*, including *Der Freischütz* (as *Robin des Bois*) in 1824.

11. The song was such a success that a collection of song lyrics was published almost immediately under the rubric "The Black Crook Songster / A Collection of Choice, Jolly and Happy Songs, Now Published for the First Time / including 'You naughty men!' as sung at Niblo's with great applause by the late Millie Cavendish"—which included, however, no other songs from the show.

12. All quotations from lyrics in this book are as given in the sources listed in appendix B, unless otherwise indicated.

13. The most obvious symptom of this decline is the Savoy Theatre's having to close its doors between 1982 and 1988.

14. As quoted in Robert Fink, "Rhythm and Text Setting in *The Mikado*," *Nineteenth-Century Music* 14 (1990–91): 37.

15. Quoted in Arthur Jacobs, *Arthur Sullivan: A Victorian Musician*, 2nd ed. (Portland, Ore.: Amadeus, 1992), 69.

16. The *Bounty* was mutinied in 1789, and all but one of its captured mutineers hanged in 1792. Among the many artifacts spawned by the mutiny is a 1985 London musical (*Mutiny!*—book, lyrics, and music by Richard Crane and David Essex); less than twenty years earlier, *The Smothers Comedy Brothers Hour* used *Mutiny on the Bounty* as the subject for a parody of musical-comedy conventions.

17. The deliberateness of the allusion to Wilde was subsequently underscored by Carte's sponsoring Wilde on his highly successful tour of America in early 1882 to set the stage for the American production of *Patience* (at that time Wilde had published little and was not well-known in America).

18. Alexander Graham Bell's first telephone patent is dated February 14, 1876; the device was workable by March 10 ("Mr. Watson, come here, I want you.") and on display, along with the newly improved typewriter, when the Centennial Exposition in Philadelphia opened on May 10, 1876. The reference in *Pinafore* occurs late in the second act, when Ralph Rackstraw is being taken to the ship's "dungeon": "He'll hear no tone / Of the maiden he loves so well! / No telephone / Communicates with his cell!"

19. To English audiences of the time, the figure of Sir Joseph was a clear parody of William Henry (W. H.) Smith, a stationer and bookseller turned politician, whose business ventures continue to thrive today. Smith was appointed First Lord of the Admiralty in 1877, and, soon after *Pinafore* opened in 1878, acquired the nickname of "Pinafore Smith."

20. The affected nature of the madrigal as a type is already evident in Gilbert's text: "The Nightingale / Sighed for the moon's bright ray, / And told his tale / In his own melodious way! / He sang 'Ah, well-a-day!'" In the version of this show mounted as *Pinafore!* in West Hollywood (2001), in which Ralph (renamed Dick Dockstrap) is supposedly the only *non*-gay member of the crew, the rest of the crew hear this song as a dead give-away, echoing his last line with a skeptical "He *says* that he's not gay!" (See Fig. 1.1, p. 7.) ♫ 2.8

21. Yara Sellin has written perceptibly about the gendered roles in *Pinafore*, and of how they relate to a nationalist context, in "'Equality Is Out of the Question': Constructions of Class and English Identity in *H.M.S. Pinafore*" (unpublished paper read at the Annual Meeting of the American Musicological Society, Columbus, Ohio, October–November 2002).

Chapter Three
Early American Developments; Minstrelsy, Extravaganza, Pantomime, Burlesque, Vaudeville

1. Regarding the American vogue for Wagner during this period, see Joseph Horowitz's *Wagner Nights*.

2. The term "ballad opera" refers to a short-lived eighteenth-century English genre based not on ballads but on a mix of dialogue and songs, the latter usually based on existing tunes. The most famous of these was John Gay's "The Beggar's Opera" (1728), which was the basis for Kurt Weill's and Bertolt Brecht's *Dreigroschenoper* exactly two centuries later (discussed in connection with *The Cradle Will Rock* in chapter 5; see p. 114). The genre had mostly disappeared by the time of the American Revolution.

3. In this brief summary of American developments, I have relied on a variety of sources that treat these subjects at greater length; see the list at the end of this chapter.

4. See chapters 1–2 of W. T. Lhamon, Jr.'s *Raising Cain* regarding pre–1843 blackface in America.

5. Regarding the evolution of the barbershop quartet as a type, see Gage Averill's *Four Parts, No Waiting: A Social History of American Barbershop Harmony* (Oxford and New York: Oxford University Press, 2003).

6. See Noel Ignatiev's *How the Irish Became White* (New York: Routledge) for an extended general discussion of this dynamic; see especially p. 42.

7. For an extensive consideration of how and why music became aligned with the feminine, especially in the nineteenth century, see Richard Leppert, *The Sight of Sound: Music, Representation, and the History of the Body* (Berkeley, Los Angeles, and London: University of California Press, 1993), especially chapters 4–8 (pp. 62–211).

8. See William J. Mahar's *Behind the Burnt Cork Mask: Early Blackface Minstrelsy and Antebellum American Popular Culture* (Urbana: University of Illinois Press, 1999) for a carefully researched refutation of such claims.

9. Edwin Christy, stepfather to fellow blackface performer George Christy, founded the much-imitated Christy Minstrels in 1846, after performing in blackface for some four years before that date. The term "Christy's Minstrels" became to some extent generic (especially in England), as many competing companies used the name. So respected was the Christy name that Stephen Foster allowed "Old Folks at Home" to be published as Christy's, presumably so as to boost sales.

10. For a somewhat different view of how this dynamic played out, see Lawrence W. Levine's *Highbrow / Lowbrow: The Emergence of Cultural Hierarchy in America* (Cambridge, Mass., and London: Harvard University Press, 1988). Regarding the emergence and appeal of "low culture" more generally, see Herbert Gans's *Popular Culture and High Culture* (New York: Basic, 1974); see also Joan Shelley Rubin's *The Making of Middlebrow Culture* (Chapel Hill: University of North Carolina Press, 1992).

11. Rosenfeld, who published his song under the name of "F. Belasco," one of his many pseudonyms, derived his dance postlude from a familiar marching tune. Earlier texts sung to the tune included "Hey, Betty Martin, Tiptoe Fine" (War of 1812) and "Johnny, Get Your Gun" (Civil War). Presumably, Rosenfeld included the dance as an homage to the latter, which provided the inspiration for the "hook" in his song. It seems likely that Sullivan would have known that the tune was not original with Rosenfeld, but he probably did not know of its earlier, pre-minstrelsy provenance. In 1917, George M. Cohan again quoted the familiar tune and its Civil War text, newly elaborated, to head the verse of "Over There":

"Johnnie get your gun, get your gun, get your gun, / Take it on the run, on the run, on the run" (later elaborated, in the second verse, as "Johnnie get your gun, get your gun, get your gun, / Johnnie show the Hun, you're a son-of-a-gun"). For Rosenfeld's setting and further information, see Richard Jackson, *Popular Songs of Nineteenth-Century America* (New York: Dover, 1976), 97–101 and 272–73. ♪ **3.3**

Chapter Four
American Song through Tin Pan Alley

1. Although the designation I use of a "classic" period (or "golden age") of Tin Pan Alley for the 1920s and '30s has wide currency and is based on the continuity—and some would say, perfection—of a practice, it is arguably inaccurate in a technical sense. Among various discussions of Tin Pan Alley and what exactly the term designates, see particularly Charles Hamm's "The Music of Tin Pan Alley," chapter 13 in his seminal *Music in the New World* (New York: Norton, 1983), which has provided a solid foundation for much of the following, allowing me to bring my focus more quickly to individual songs.

2. In "Early Minstrel Show Music, 1843–1852," Robert Winans elaborates more fully on how this music would have sounded in the nineteenth century, see pp. 71–97 in *Musical Theatre in America: Papers and Proceedings of the Conference on the Musical Theatre in America*, ed. Glenn Loney (Westport, Conn., and London: Greenwood, 1981).

3. This bittersweet cadential type heightens the dissonance just before the arrival by sustaining the "escape tone" (a major third above the tonic) briefly but longingly against the seventh of the dominant harmony, a major seventh below the escape tone. While this sentimentalizing cadence type comes across today as something of a mannerism in Foster's music, it was a common enough device in his time.

4. Hamm, *Music in the New World*, 339.

5. See Charles Hamm, "The Music of Tin Pan Alley" (in *Music in the New World*); see also his "Dvořák in America: Nationalism, Racism, and National Race," in his *Putting Popular Music in Its Place* (Cambridge: Cambridge University Press, 1995). Interestingly, Hamm has also argued against placing too strong an emphasis on the African American roots of the Tin Pan Alley style. Thus, at the end of his chapter on the first generation of Tin Pan Alley in *Yesterdays: Popular Song in America* (New York and London: Norton, 1983), his summation reads, "Tin Pan Alley did not draw on traditional music—it created traditional music" ("'After the Ball'; or, The Birth of Tin Pan Alley," pp. 284–325 in *Yesterdays*), 325. He later elaborates this point further: "I question the role of 'negro' music in the formation of the song styles of Stephen Foster and of the first generation of Tin Pan Alley writers. Similarly, I believe that only several quite superficial aspects of 'negro' music were skimmed off by songwriters of the 1910's, '20s, and '30s. . . . It does the history of music by black musicians no lasting good to insist on interpretations that are historically unsound, and it may also obscure the profound effect that black music had on American song in the mid-1950s and afterward" (358).

6. For a cogent analysis of the forces that worked toward such musical assimilations, see "Out of Many, One? Western European Ethnicity," in Jon Finson's *The Voices That Are Gone: Themes in Nineteenth-Century American Popular Song* (New York and Oxford: Oxford University Press, 1994), 270–314.

7. As Finson puts it (*The Voices That Are Gone,* 72), Americans purchased "nearly two million copies of sheet music for the song in about two years, an order of magnitude larger than publishers in the sixties or seventies enjoyed over the period of many years"; see also "After the Ball" in Hamm's *Yesterdays,* 285, and David Cockrell's "Nineteenth-Century Popular Music," pp. 158–85 in *The Cambridge History of American Music,* ed. David Nicholls (Cambridge and New York: Cambridge University Press, 1998), 164.

8. See Finson, *The Voices That Are Gone,* 153–54.

9. Regarding the early history of recording and its association with popular music, see chapters 1–3 in William Howland Kenney's *Recorded Music in American Life: The Phonograph and Popular Memory, 1890–1945* (New York and Oxford: Oxford University Press, 1999); see also Andre Millard's *America on Record: A History of Recorded Sound* (Cambridge: Cambridge University Press, 1995), and Michael Chanan's *Repeated Takes: A Short History of Recording and Its Effects on Music* (London: Verso, 1995).

10. An "original" recording of the song (from 1902), by noted minstrel singer Arthur Collins, is easily available on *American Pop: An Audio History. From Minstrel to Mojo: On Record 1893–1946,* vol. 1 (3 of 9 CDs) (Toronto: West Hill Audio Archives, 1997–98).

11. Regarding the growing importance of radio, see Susan Douglas's *Inventing American Broadcasting, 1899–1922* (Baltimore: Johns Hopkins University Press, 1987); J. Fred MacDonald's *Don't Touch That Dial: Radio Programming in American Life from 1920 to 1960* (Chicago: Nelson Hall, 1979); Daniel J. Czitrom's *Media and the American Mind from Morse to McLuhan* (Chapel Hill: University of North Carolina Press, 1982); and chapter 12 in Russell Sanjek's *Pennies from Heaven: The American Popular Music Business in the Twentieth Century* (New York: Da Capo Press, 1996).

12. See Hamm, *Music in the New World,* for a fuller description of the evolution of the verse-chorus structure, especially pp. 254–55 (regarding the nineteenth-century version), 355–61 (regarding the increasing emphasis on the chorus), and 367 and 369–70 (regarding its interaction with jazz performing styles).

13. For another discussion of "Always," see Philip Furia, *Irving Berlin: A Life in Song* (New York: Schirmer, 1998), 115–18.

14. See Will Friedwald, *Stardust Melodies: A Biography of Twelve of America's Most Popular Songs* (New York: Pantheon, 2002), 184–85.

15. Dvořák's decision to base his symphony on a blend of European, Indianist, and African-American idioms was controversial in its time. Intriguingly, William Grant Still, who attached great significance to his own racial blend (African, European, American Indian), may have been intending his allusions to draw attention to the similarly blended styles of Dvořák and Gershwin; indeed, the passage he quotes from the former is from the most Indianist of its movements, and *Girl Crazy,* largely set in the American West, includes a scene in which a "sheriff" (a

former New York City cabbie) tries to talk to the local Indians in Yiddish. Still, however, was embarrassed to be accused of "stealing" from Gershwin, and intimated that the "theft" might well have been the other way around, since his own use of similar figures was likely known to Gershwin; his incorporation of the lick into his symphony, which he began to compose two weeks after *Girl Crazy* opened, may thus have been a way for him to reclaim what was his (if so, this incident is but one of many instances when white composers have been accused of stealing ideas from blacks). For an extended discussion of this matter, see Catherine Parsons Smith's *William Grant Still: A Study in Contradictions* (Berkeley and Los Angeles: University of California Press, 2000) 114–15 and 136–44. Still was apparently not asked about the Dvořák allusion, which seems to have passed unnoticed until now.

16. See Will Friedwald, "I Got Rhythm" (pp. 180–210 in *Stardust Melodies*), for an extended discussion of the song's durability as a jazz standard.

17. See Will Friedwald, "My Funny Valentine" (pp. 348–73 in *Stardust Melodies*, 355–56.

18. An additional bittersweet poignancy accrues to this song if we imagine, with Will Friedwald, that Hart is obliquely referencing his own lack of physical beauty and diminutive stature (*Stardust Melodies*, 358). This kind of ambivalent "taking back" of apparent sincerities on the one hand, or suddenly reversing apparent mockery on the other, was a particular specialty of Hart; see Philip Furia's excellent discussion in *The Poets of Tin Pan Alley: A History of America's Great Lyricists* (New York and Oxford: Oxford University Press, 1990), 95–125.

19. We will not here consider the "standard" version that was created for the 1962 revival, which instituted—and institutionalized—many changes to the original.

20. While the reference to cocaine passed Broadway standards, it had to be dropped for radio and for both the 1936 and 1956 film versions of the show as well. Substitutes have included "perfumes of Spain" and (later) "bop-type refrain."

21. See Alec Wilder, *American Popular Song: The Great Innovators, 1900–1950*, ed. James T. Maher (New York and Oxford: Oxford University Press, 1990), 237–38. For a somewhat different interpretation of the triplets in this song, see Geoffrey Block, *Enchanted Evenings: The Broadway Musical from Show Boat to Sondheim* (New York and Oxford: Oxford University Press, 1997), 55–56.

22. The original lyric here—"I shouldn't care for those nights in the air / That the fair Mrs. Lindbergh goes through"—had to be changed in the wake of the 1932 kidnaping and murder of the Lindbergh's child.

23. This alternate lyric has also been credited to Porter himself, and so Robert Kimball includes it in *The Complete Lyrics of Cole Porter*, ed. Robert Kimball (New York: Knopf, 1983), 120–21 (although he doubts the attribution; see p. 119).

24. Cf. Mark Steyn's discussion of this device in *Broadway Babies Say Goodnight*, 233.

25. Thus, "trim my lamp" could refer to the prostitute's red lamp, from which the "red-light district" acquires its name, and "good by night" is clearly designed to work both sides of the "reform" fence.

Chapter Five
Whose (Who's) America?

1. There were, of course, many sets of lyrics accruing over the years to this song, whose origins were obscure and which seemed endlessly capable of modification according to the occasion. This is the main version that eventually "stuck" to the tune. "Macaroni" apparently builds on an existing British term of disparagement for the Italian "dandy" with a taste for fancy dress, so that the lyric indirectly calls the colonialist an *imitation* Italian fop, whose pretenses to fashion are so ridiculous that a feather in his cap might count as "dressing up."

2. For a general discussion of the treatment of the Irish in late nineteenth-century America, see Ignatiev, *How the Irish Became White.*

3. As quoted in Stephen M. Vallillo, "George M. Cohan's *Little Johnny Jones*" (pp. 233–43 in *Musical Theatre in America*), 236.

4. For a consideration of other forces at work in this quest, especially those demarcating the purview of the high-culture end of musical theater in the first half of the twentieth century, see Paul DiMaggio's "Cultural Boundaries and Structural Change: The Extension of the High Culture Model to Theater, Opera, and the Dance, 1900–1940" in *Cultivating Differences: Symbolic Boundaries and the Making of Inequality,* ed. Michèle Lamont and Marcel Fournier (Chicago and London: University of Chicago Press, 1992), 21–57.

5. The 1999 film *Cradle Will Rock* (dir. Tim Robbins) provides a reasonably accurate account of the genesis of *The Cradle Will Rock,* along with the attendant political issues. The film interweaves a thematically related story (Diego Rivera's 1933 mural for Rockefeller, destroyed by the latter because Rivera refused to edit out a portrait of Lenin)—which was not, however, contemporaneous with the musical.

6. Intriguingly, while Blitzstein borrows from the cabaret style of Weill, itself based partly on a filtered jazz-idiom, he does not in any obvious way use American jazz-based styles, not even to critique them. The kinds of fusions that Gershwin and Still carried out, incorporating jazz into "classical" venues (discussed in chapter 4; see pp. 83–85), seem not even to be on Blitzstein's radar screen here, perhaps because their underlying romantic sensibilities were so foreign to his own project. (Copland, who tried his hand at using jazz idioms in the 1920s, moved mostly in another direction during his populist phase in the 1930s and '40s.)

Chapter Six
American Mythologies

1. The term "ethnic cleansing" came into wide usage after the breakup of Yugoslavia in the early 1990s, which led to ethnic-based brutality, slaughter, and forced relocations, especially in Kosovo. But this kind of activity was scarcely new. Throughout the twentieth century in Europe, from Magyarization in pre–World War I Hungary through the Nazi era and the post–World War II period, there were countless examples of brutally enforced relocations, mass murder, or (in some cases) forced assimilation, so as to create and enforce an alliance between political units and the ethnicity of their populations.

2. An excellent and concise account of European nationalism may be found in Ernest Gellner's *Nationalism* (London: Weidenfeld and Nicolson, 1997).

3. See Hamm, "Dvořák in America" (pp. 344–53 in *Putting Popular Music in its Place*).

4. Dvořák was notorious for endorsing the status quo regarding the largest of America's disenfranchised groups, its women, whom he claimed in widely publicized interviews to be the intellectual inferiors of men and therefore incapable of the creative intellectual endeavor of composing music. Amy Beach's *Gaelic* Symphony (1896, three years after Dvořák's *New World*)—the first symphony by a woman performed in America—may thus be seen to champion the other two of these groups struggling for a mainstream political acceptance: explicitly the Irish, and implicitly women.

5. For a particularly useful delineation of Schiller's theories as applied to composing music, see Thomas K. Nelson, "The Fantasy of Absolute Music" (Ph.D. diss., University of Minnesota, 1998), 164–205.

6. For a somewhat different account of the themes in *Oklahoma!* (including nature as the source of music, and the rhythms of life as the source for dance), see Rick Altman's *The American Film Musical* (Bloomington and Indianapolis: Indiana University Press, 1987), 306–14.

7. In the film version made more than a decade later, a single high note accompanies Curly at the beginning of the song.

8. Regarding Rodgers and Hammerstein's manipulation of the thirty-two-bar form, see Gerald Mast, *Can't Help Singin': The American Musical on Stage and Screen* Woodstock, N.Y.: Overlook, 1987), 205–7; Mast likens the longer of these structures to arias. Regarding Rodgers's use of the form up to and including *Oklahoma!*, see Graham Wood, "The Development of Song Forms in the Broadway and Hollywood Musicals of Richard Rodgers" (Ph.D. diss., University of Minnesota, 2000), especially pp. 74–163 (regarding general features) and 233–39 (regarding *Oklahoma!*; he discusses "Oh What a Beautiful Mornin'," 238–39). Regarding the evolution of verse-chorus forms in Tin Pan Alley songs more generally, see Hamm, *Yesterdays*, 358–61.

9. Not only does Curly refuse to see the willow in its traditional role as an emblem of mourning, but he also approves of the busy *breeze*, which will of course do a fair amount of mischief in the 1930s; as discussed later, the song "Oklahoma" will pursue this oblique connection even more vigorously.

10. Phyliss Cole Braunlich, *Haunted by Home: The Life and Letters of Lynn Riggs* (Norman: University of Oklahoma Press, 1988), 71–72; also quoted in Craig S. Womack's "Lynn Riggs as Code Talker: Toward a Queer Oklahomo Theory and the Radicalization of Native American Studies," pp. 271–303 in his *Red on Red: Native American Literary Separatism* (Minneapolis and London: University of Minnesota Press, 1999), 274), as part of an exploration of how Riggs's homosexuality might have mattered in his work.

11. In the play, Curly's scene with Jud is Scene 3, but becomes Scene 2 in the musical—whose first scene, however, is greatly extended, containing seven songs.

12. Lynn Riggs, *Green Grow the Lilacs* (New York and Los Angeles: S. French, 1931), Scene 6.

13. For a somewhat different view of *Oklahoma!*'s engagement with race, see

Andrea Most's "'We Know We Belong to the Land': Jews and the American Musical Theater" (Ph.D. diss., Brandeis University, 2001).

14. As transcribed from the film version, with Marlon Brando playing Sky. Runyon's original reads:

> Son, you are now going out into the wide, wide world to make your own way, and it is a very good thing to do, as there are no opportunities for you in this burg. I am only sorry that I am not able to bank-roll you to a very large start, but not having any potatoes to give you, I am now going to stake you to some very valuable advice, which I personally collect in my years of experience around and about, and I hope and trust you will always bear this advice in mind.
>
> Son, no matter how far you travel, or how smart you get, always remember this: Some day, somewhere, a guy is going to come to you and show you a nice brand-new deck of cards on which the seal is never broken, and this guy is going to offer to bet you that the jack of spades will jump out of this deck and squirt cider in your ear. But son, do not bet him, for as sure as you do you are going to get an ear full of cider. (*A Treasury of Damon Runyon,* ed. Clark Kinnaird [New York: Modern Library, 1958], 3–4)

15. Prohibition lasted, roughly, from 1919, when the Volstead Act provided the means for enforcing the Eighteenth Amendment to the Constitution, prohibiting the "manufacture, sale, or transportation of intoxicating liquors" in the United States, to 1933, when it was repealed through the Twenty-First Amendment, returning the regulation of alcohol to the individual states.

16. See Gage Averill, *Four Parts, No Waiting: A Social History of American Barbershop Harmony* (Oxford and New York: Oxford University Press, 2003) for an extensive and well-reasoned account of the various intermixings that produced, largely in retrospect, the American barbershop "tradition," whose true history Averill characterizes as "hybrid and miscegenated" (11).

17. In Scriabin's whole-tone version of the dominant-seventh chord, the fifth of the chord is raised a half-step; thus, above G, the chord would include B, D♯, and F. This manipulation should not be confused with Scriabin's infamous "Mystic" chord, which stacks perfect fourths atop a French augmented-sixth chord (the latter also a subset of the whole-tone collection, obtainable by shifting the fifth in a dominant-seventh chord down a half-step instead of up).

18. As Willson himself explains it, he had actually written the two songs before he realized they could be used to create a bond of sorts between the characters: "I didn't think it was the right time to tell him that I had also used the same melody ["Seventy-Six Trombones"] as a three-four ballad. Particularly when I didn't know what to do with it yet. Although I was getting an idea. . . . Maybe it would be interesting if [Marian and Harold] could subtly convey to the audience this [loneliness] they had in common by separate renderings of the same song—a march for him, a ballad waltz for her" (Meredith Willson, *"But He Doesn't Know the Territory"* [New York: Putnam, 1959], 37–38). Another musical link between Marian and Harold was to have been forged by uniting their skewed views of each other in a combination song, to serve as part of the Act I finale ("My White Knight" and "The Sadder but Wiser Girl," which were written to go together in counterpoint; ibid., 64–65).

19. What is easy to miss in "Sincere," in part because of the pacing, is the saucy point of it all, which is the man's desire not to be sent home "early" (that is, before sex): "Tell me, what can be fair in farewell dear, while one single star shines above?" The line recalls Marian's earlier scene with Amaryllis, when the first star of the evening, the "wishing" star, betokens romantic possibilities.

Chapter Seven
Counter-mythologies

1. For more detailed information about this complex era, see Robert Walser, "The Rock and Roll Era," pp. 345–87 in *The Cambridge History of American Music.*

2. While a great many successful Broadway shows have not been star-driven, their marketing has long tended to emphasize this dimension, although (since the key element is name recognition) the "stars" in question might well be members of the creative team. In any case, it is against a presumption of conventionality, as much as a reality, that *Hair* rebelled.

3. Thus, on the quoted list, the first two are hallucinogenic drugs, the third is a motor-oil additive, the fourth and sixth are New York subway lines, and the fifth is a grocery store chain.

4. John Weidman, Sondheim's collaborator, as quoted and paraphrased by Meryle Secrest, *Stephen Sondheim: A Life* (New York: Knopf, 1998), 362.

5. Frank Rich, *The New York Times,* January 28, 1991, as quoted by Secrest, *Stephen Sondheim,* 363.

6. In the case of *Dreigroschenoper,* this claim of automatic sympathy is of course much truer for Lucy and Jenny, who are plainly victims, than for the scoundrels Macheath and Peachum. To the extent that the social dynamic of *Dreigroschenoper* resembles that of *Assassins,* it is through the shared victimhood of Macheath's women and the title characters of the latter; from this perspective, Macheath, Peachum, and Tiger Brown represent various components of the false promises of the established order and are not, in the sense I mean, disenfranchised. On a more basic level, and on the reverse side of the sympathy coin, *Dreigroschenoper* offers a biting critique of capitalism, so that any perceived assonance between it and *Assassins* will reinforce the belief that the latter is meant as a similarly conceived critique of the United States.

7. Quoted in Secrest, *Stephen Sondheim,* 362–63.

8. Virtually every account of Sondheim's music makes note of his uncanny knack for pastiche (or, more negatively, his unhealthy dependence on pastiche). His most cited work in this regard is *Follies* (1971); for recent discussions pertaining to this aspect of *Assassins,* see Lovensheimer, "Sondheim and the Musical of the Outsider," pp. 181–96 in *The Cambridge Companion to the Musical,* ed. William A. Everett and Paul R. Laird (Cambridge and New York: Cambridge University Press, 2002), 185–87; and Steven Swayne, "'It Started Out Like a Song': Sondheim's *Assassins* and the Power of Popular Music," in his "Hearing Sondheim's Voices" (Ph.D. diss., University of California, Berkeley, 1999), 115–58. For a discussion of Sondheim as a modernist, see Geoffrey Block, who compares

Sondheim to Schoenberg in "Happily Ever After *West Side Story* with Sondheim," pp. 274–93 in his *Enchanted Evenings*. For an exploration of Sondheim's reputation as "difficult," see "The Genius" in Mark Steyn's *Broadway Babies Say Goodnight.*

9. "Something Just Broke," added as an alternative opening number in revival, provides a more palatable perspective for audiences to identify with before they are introduced to that of the assassins in the carnival-based "Opening." "Something Just Broke" overlaps reactions of the assassins' uncounted victims among the larger population of Americans, referencing the assassinations of Lincoln, Garfield, and McKinley.

10. "Hail to the Chief" was used for this purpose since the early nineteenth century, but the march-song was not adopted as an official presidential anthem until 1954 (coincidentally, the same year that the "Pledge of Allegiance" took its now current form). Ironically, given its appearance here, the tune was originally a show-tune, gaining initial prominence as part of a musical version of Sir Walter Scott's *The Lady of the Lake* (1811), which achieved some popularity in both London and New York. It was transformed into an early version of "Hail to the Chief" in 1815 for a (posthumous) celebration of George Washington's birthday. James Sanderson is generally credited with the melody, and Albert Gamse the lyric, although it appears to have been an adaptation rather than his original tune even in the original show, and enjoyed popularity as a march and with several different sets of lyrics throughout the first half of the nineteenth century.

11. In a 1997 interview, however, Sondheim discounts the significance of the shifting meter because it is counterbalanced by the strong, regular pulse of the banjo chords; see Mark Eden Horowitz, *Sondheim on Music: Minor Details and Major Decisions* (Lanham, Md., and Oxford: Scarecrow, 2003), 33.

12. "El Capitan" (1895) was from one of Sousa's more successful operettas, of the same name; thus, both it and "Hail to the Chief" had their origins on the musical stage. The other principal Sousa march evoked in "How I Saved Roosevelt" is the Washington Post March (1889), which functions similarly in the second act of *Show Boat,* as part of a suite of preexistent musical numbers quoted to evoke a specific American past. The most striking recollection here is given to Zangara, borrowing from a transitional passage in Sousa's march: "You think I am left? / No left, no right, no anything!"

13. Midway through Act II of *Into the Woods,* the community of characters in the story sacrifices the somewhat annoying but reassuring narrator in an attempt to appease the giantess. This leaves them on their own to work out their lives, but in dramatic terms the more important effect is that the events we witness are suddenly unmediated, which pulls us without warning into an alarming sense of immediacy and danger.

14. Personal communication with Rose Rosengard Subotnik, June 24, 2003.

15. Irving Wardle, *The Independent,* November 1, 1992, cited in Secrest, *Stephen Sondheim,* 366.

16. Quoted in André Bishop, "Preface" to *Assassins* by John Weidman and Stephen Sondheim (New York: Theatre Communications Group, 1991), xi.

Chapter Eight
Race and Ethnicity

1. Hollywood films continued for some years to indulge a taste for blackface. It was a trademark of some stars, such as Al Jolson (best known today for his blackface numbers in *The Jazz Singer,* 1927) and Eddie Cantor; the latter, for example, appeared on Broadway doing a blackface medley as late as 1941 (*Banjo Eyes*) and continued to appear in blackface roles throughout the 1940s (e.g., in *If You Knew Susie,* 1948). More mainstream stars appearing on screen in blackface during this period included Fred Astaire (*Swing Time,* 1936), Irene Dunne (*Show Boat,* 1936; see pp. 192–93), Judy Garland alone (*Everybody Sing,* 1938) and with Mickey Rooney (*Babes on Broadway,* 1941), Bing Crosby and Marjorie Reynolds (*Holiday Inn,* 1942), and Betty Grable (*The Dolly Sisters,* 1945).

2. See, along with more specialized writings, John Graziano, "Images of African Americans: African-American Musical Theatre, *Show Boat* and *Porgy and Bess*," in *The Cambridge Companion to the Musical,* 63–76; and Thomas Riis, *Just Before Jazz: Black Musical Theater in New York, 1890–1915* (Washington, D.C.: Smithsonian Institution Press, 1989), and *More Than Just Minstrel Shows: The Rise of Black Musical Theatre at the Turn of the Century* (Brooklyn: Institute for Studies in American Music, 1992).

3. *West Side Story* did win two Tony Awards: Oliver Smith for Scenic Design and Jerome Robbins for Choreography.

4. See Joseph Swain, *The Broadway Musical: A Critical and Musical Survey,* 2nd ed. (Lanham, Md., and Oxford: Scarecrow, 2002), 40.

5. Thus, the American composer Charles Ives alludes to "Deep River" at the beginning of "Tom Sails Away," an obliquely anti-war song that refers also to George M. Cohan's "Over There" and to Taps. For more information on "Deep River," see Wayne D. Shirley's "The Coming of Deep River," *American Music* 4 (1997): 493–534.

6. The version of this spiritual that probably would have been best known in the 1920s was the 1917 arrangement by Harry T. Burleigh, especially as sung by Burleigh's student Paul Robeson. Burleigh himself studied with Dvořák in the 1890s.

7. Cf. Hamm's arguments in "Genre, Performance, and Ideology in the Early Songs of Irving Berlin," in *Putting Popular Music in Its Place,* 370–80.

8. Cf. Allen Forte's discussion of this tune in *The American Popular Ballad of the Golden Era, 1924–1950* (Princeton: Princeton University Press, 1995), 55–59.

9. Beginning with *The Jazz Singer,* it became common practice for films to show the performer blacking up, in part so that audiences would know who the performer was; other examples of this practice include Fred Astaire in *Swing Time,* and Judy Garland and Mickey Rooney in *Babes on Broadway.* Regarding this particular scene, see also Peter Stanfield's "From the Vulgar to the Refined: American Vernacular and Blackface Minstrelsy in *Showboat,*" pp. 147–56 in *Musicals: Hollywood and Beyond,* ed. Bill Marshall and Robynn Stilwell (Exeter, England, and Portland, Ore.: Intellect, 2000), 150.

10. Contrary to what *Show Boat* indicates, the Dahomey exhibit at the Chicago Fair was constructed by the Fon, a people from Dahomey, and so was fairly authentic. On the other hand, the exhibit did much to convince whites that blacks were essentially a savage people, further reinforcing existing stereotypes. Dahomey, an African kingdom in what is now Benin, was once feared for its military might; it was a major exporter of slaves during the height of the slave trade, and was also the source of Voodoo practices (Vodou) in the West Indies and South America. The name of the musical number in *Show Boat,* "In Dahomey," was an homage to a landmark musical from 1903, by Will Marion Cook (music), with Paul Lawrence Dunbar and Alex Roger (lyrics; much rewritten in the course of the show), based on an idea by George Walker, who acted in it with fellow vaudevillian Bert Williams. *In Dahomey* was the first major musical with an all-black cast to enjoy a long Broadway run; notably, its representation of life in Dahomey was exactly the kind of projection that *Show Boat* implies took place in Chicago a decade earlier. For a discussion of these and related representations, see Graziano, "Images of African Americans," 63–71.

11. Despite the oddity of this interpolation—as Ethan Mordden put's it, "Why didn't the authors write their own 'After the Ball'?" (in *Make Believe: The Broadway Musical in the 1920s* [New York and Oxford: University of Oxford Press, 1997] 214)—the song helps remind us of *Show Boat*'s basis in a familiar American reality.

12. For a somewhat contrasting view, see Ethan Mordden's discussion of Julie's role, in *Make Believe,* as "*Show Boat*'s principal player" (pp. 208–10, 208. See also Stanfield's "From the Vulgar to the Refined."

13. Regarding the nature of the collaboration, see Philip Furia's *Ira Gershwin: The Art of the Lyricist* (New York and Oxford: University of Oxford Press, 1996), 106–13. Furia claims that "the number of songs for which George set Heyward's poetry to music constitute fewer than a third of the opera" (108). Even if this were true, however, Ira worked strenuously to preserve the spirit and language of Heyward's material, and to extend and polish it as necessary; the nature of the collaboration was such that it lends itself more to description—which Furia does quite well—than to quantification.

14. See Richard Crawford, "It Ain't Necessarily Soul: Gershwin's *Porgy and Bess* as a Symbol," pp. 17–38 in *Yearbook of Inter-American Musical Research* (1972), and David Horn, "Who Loves You Porgy? The Debates Surrounding Gershwin's Musical," pp. 109–26 in *Approaches to the American Musical,* ed. Robert Lawson Peebles (Exeter: University of Exeter Press, 1996).

15. More specifically, the seven-note chord includes A, B♭, C, C♯ (D♭), E♭, E, and G.

16. For a good discussion of Gershwin's association of themes with characters in *Porgy and Bess,* and of how he manipulates and interweaves them in coordination with the dramatic action, see Block, "*Porgy and Bess*: Broadway Opera" (pp. 60–84 in *Enchanted Evenings*) 75–84. Despite striking similarities, in an important sense Gershwin's approach is directly opposed to Wagner's, in that he infuses his recitative with tunefulness, whereas Wagner aspired to make every moment, and every melodic gesture, appropriately dramatic.

17. Regarding Schillinger, see Warren Brodsky's "Joseph Schillinger (1895–

1943): Music Science Promethean," *American Music* 21 (2003): 45–73. Wayne Shirley's "'Rotating' *Porgy and Bess*" is an intriguing attempt to trace Schillinger's method in Gershwin's music for *Porgy and Bess;* see pp. 21–34 in *The Gershwin Style: New Looks at the Music of George Gershwin,* ed. Wayne Schneider (New York and Oxford: Oxford University Press, 1999).

18. See Geoffrey Block, *"Porgy and Bess"* (pp. 60–84 in *Enchanted Evenings*), 79–80.

19. This pattern of assimilationist attitudes among immigrants to America was a recurring feature in American popular song dating from the nineteenth century; see Finson, *The Voices That Are Gone,* 284–314.

20. Regarding Bernstein's use of the huapango, seis and other Hispanic idioms, see Elizabeth Wells's "*West Side Story* and the Hispanic," in *Echo* 2, no. 1 (2000).

21. For an extended consideration of the Latin American influence on music of the United States, see John Storm Roberts's *The Latin Tinge: The Impact of Latin America Music on the United States,* 2nd ed. (New York and Oxford: Oxford University Press, 1994).

22. See, for example, Jack Gottlieb, "The Music of Leonard Bernstein: A Study of Melodic Manipulations" (D.M.A. diss., University of Illinois, 1964); Swain, "Tragedy as Musical" (pp. 221–64 in *The Broadway Musical*); and Block, "*West Side Story:* The Very Model of a Major Musical" (pp. 245–73 in *Enchanted Evenings*).

23. See Block, "*West Side Story*" (pp. 245–73 in *Enchanted Evenings*), 252–54.

24. I am indebted to Stuart DeOcampo, in an as-yet unpublished work, for his development of this notion of a musical subjunctive. For related discussions of the ♭ VI, see Susan McClary, "Pitches, Expression, Ideology: An Exercise in Mediation" *Enclitic* 7 (1983): 76–86; and Nelson, "The Fantasy of Absolute Music."

25. Ralph Locke discusses this moment of reconciliation within the context of orientalism, as part of his consideration of Saint-Saëns's *Samson et Dalila;* see his "Constructing the Oriental 'Other': Saint-Saëns's *Samson et Dalila,*" *Cambridge Opera Journal* 3 (1991): 300–301.

26. As quoted in Swain, "The Ethnic Musical" (pp. 247–74 in *The Broadway Musical*), 247.

27. See ibid. Swain's discussion is particularly useful in identifying the musical techniques employed to evoke, through the idioms of Broadway, particular ethnicities—as, for example, the instrumentation and modal inflections discussed later in relation to *Fiddler on the Roof.*

28. David Grossman, speaking at the Skirball Cultural Center, Los Angeles, California, February 20, 2001.

29. Part of Mendele Moykher-Sforim's project, and a primary reason for him to write in Yiddish, was to make shtetl Jews aware of both the narrowness of their world and the possibilities open to them beyond its confines.

30. This is a close variant of his 1920 *Music,* painted for the Moscow Jewish State Theater when he briefly served as artistic director, and an only slightly more distant variant of his 1912–13 *The Fiddler;* his *Blue Violinist* similarly shows a large fiddler atop buildings, but seated.

31. Occasionally, in Chagall, this dimension seems explicit, as in *The Dead*

Man (1908), where a fiddler plays from a rooftop at a funeral, but the figure in this early masterwork may also be interpreted more simply, as providing mournful music suitable for the occasion. There is also some evidence that the association of Jewish death and the fiddle carries over into anti-Semitic texts, as with the Grimm story of the Jew in the thorn bush (in which the Jew cannot stop dancing while the fiddle is being played), alluded to during the serenade of Beckmesser in Richard Wagner's *Der Meistersinger* (remembering also that Beckmesser is a figure often understood in terms of Wagner's anti-Semitism); see Barry Millington, "Nuremberg Trial: Is There Anti-Semitism in *Die Meistersinger?*" *Cambridge Opera Journal* 3 (1991): 258–59.

32. While this characterization holds according to the conventions of Broadway, it may also represent a redirected challenge by the Russian after Tevye inadvertently bumps into him, as part of a culture of male dancing. From this perspective, dancing represents a potential meeting ground between the two cultures, since male dancing was common to both, perhaps even acknowledging a similarity in male-dominated traditions that would soon be threatened, by revolution more widely, and by Tevye's daughters within the family dynamic of the show. Nevertheless, the unequal power relations between the two groups are palpable throughout the scene.

33. A third alternative for Jews historically, not always possible and often ruled out of hand, was to assimilate outwardly but preserve traditions privately (e.g., as with many Jews during the Spanish Inquisition).

34. The general approach to form here resembles that of Rodgers and Hammerstein in songs such as "The Farmer and the Cowman" in Oklahoma! (see chapter 6, pp. 130–32) or "Soliloquy" in Carousel (1947); on the development of these forms, see Mast, *Can't Help Singin'*, 201–18.

35. The first of these monologues fully resolves only in a subsequent song, "The Dream," in which Tevye deftly substitutes the authority of older generations (Tzeitel's grandmother and Lazar Wolf's first wife Fruma Sara) to trump the closely related authority of tradition, and thereby convinces his wife that Tzeitel should marry Motel.

Chapter Nine
Dealing with the Second World War

1. The juxtaposition of wedding and Anschluss is wholly an invention of the show, since the actual marriage took place in 1927, more than a decade before the Anschluss. Other fairly obvious differences between Maria Augusta Trapp's 1949 *The Story of the Trapp Family Singers* and *The Sound of Music* include a wholesale (and wholly understandable) renaming of the children and a recasting of the family's manner of leaving Austria. The family, already well known as a singing group, was confronted with a barrage of "opportunities" to serve the Reich just after the Anschluss (March 11, 1938); Maria, it should also be noted, was at that time pregnant after two miscarriages in a row, refusing abortion even though the pregnancy threatened her own life (she would later give birth in America). Georg was offered command of a submarine base (which he came close to accepting);

the oldest son, a newly minted doctor, was offered a prominent position on the medical team of a prestigious Viennese hospital (there were then, suddenly, many such openings, recently held by Jews); and the entire family was invited to sing as part of the birthday celebration of Adolf Hitler. Rather than face the consequences of refusing these honors, they went "mountain climbing" in Northern Italy (a day before the borders closed, by their account), collected a small navy pension owed Georg by the Italian government, to use for travel funds, and, leaving their home behind, set off for London and—after obtaining the necessary visas and additional funds from an American promoter—America.

2. In an excellent essay, Richard Dyer identifies this and other features of the film as resonant with many features of the "woman's picture." Dyer offers many other insights into the film, including some taken up here (e.g., regarding the alliance of music, religion, and nature in *The Sound of Music,* and the importance of folk music to its "romantic nationalism"). See *"The Sound of Music"* in his *Only Entertainment,* 45–59.

3. Successful Jews were frequently accused of *Luftgeschäften,* whether through trading in capital (money-lending or banking) or other activities such as making arrangements or acting as a middleman. Historically, the high proportion of Jews in such professions stemmed in large part from restrictions that made it difficult or impossible for them to conduct other kinds of business.

4. In fact, the bulk of the family's fortune was lost in 1935, when Georg transferred his money from Lloyd's of London to an Austrian bank in a show of patriotic loyalty, only to see that bank fail immediately thereafter, an event that both directly and indirectly helped launch the family's singing career well in advance of the Anschluss.

5. Intriguingly, neither Austrians nor Germans responded well to the film. The reasons for the former not liking *The Sound of Music* (however well it advances their claims of Nazi victimhood) seem to have much less to do with its lack of historical accuracy, than with the north-German accents that were used to dub the film for Austrian distribution, the laughable sense of geography that proposes an escape across the border near Salzburg (which would have landed them squarely in Germany), and the incessant demands from tourists ever since for them to sing their national anthem, "Edelweiss"—which was, of course, a faux folk-song written for the show.

6. And even here, the Catholic church is represented by women—the nuns— not the usual church authorities.

7. In general terms, the response of Americans to Austrians was quite positive (especially among those willing to believe individual Austrians' claims of wartime innocence), but Austrians, as might be expected, were quite often much more resentful of the occupying forces than they let on. Thus, in an extensive online exchange among those who remember the occupation years (from either side), a Salzburg native now living in Canada writes, "It was ugly. We hated it and we hated the Americans. We'd do anything to hurt them. . . . On the weekends we'd go to the bars where American soldiers and their Austrian girl friends hung out and we'd ask their girls to dance and when they refused we'd say something nasty and pick a fight" (http://www.image-at.com/salzburg/feedb96.htm). Even apart from resentment over the Americans' very presence (a daily reminder of Austrian

defeat) and their easier access to many Austrian women (thousands of whom would emigrate to America under the provisions of the War Brides Act), Austrians had much to complain about. As the introductory text for the website recounts, "the victors' passion for 'souvenirs'—watches, fountain pens, German medals and insignias—sometimes . . . turned into outright plunder. . . . [Austrian women who consorted with Americans were] frequently reviled with insulting names such as 'chocolate girls' and 'Yank brides' . . . Almost 2,000 illegitimate children of the occupation were born between 1945 and 1955 in the province of Salzburg alone" ("'Liberators and the Liberated' / 'Occupiers and the Occupied' / The Encounter of the People of Austria with US Soldiers after World War II / An Austrian-American Dialogue," http://www.image-at.com/salzburg).

8. This lyric was contributed by Rodgers himself, since Hammerstein died in 1960, long before plans for the film were underway.

9. See Stacy Wolf's *A Problem Like Maria: Gender and Sexuality in the American Musical* (Ann Arbor: University of Michigan Press, 2002), for related claims regarding the "American" orientation of Maria, and of the film more generally. As Wolf claims in the preface and argues passim, "Julie Andrews . . . may be British in origin and speech, but she has come to represent the all-American girl" (xi).

10. Stacy Wolf argues that the removal of these songs—"How Can Love Survive" and "There's No Way to Stop It"—depoliticizes the show and makes it more about personal relationships (*A Problem Like Maria,* 218–21 and 226–27). One might as easily argue the opposite, however, since these songs actually personalize the political dimension of the show and serve to distract from a broader understanding of its political themes, narrowing the focus to issues of personal courage and accommodation.

♩9.4

11. "Edelweiss," a mountain flower symbolic also of Bavaria (and thus, of Hitler's Berchtesgaden), had a number of specific symbolic associations during the years of the Nazi Reich, ranging from youthful resisters and dropouts ("Edelweiss pirates") to the code word for an important phase of Hitler's Russian campaign, and, later, to the illegal maintenance of Nazi troops after the war, rumored to be protecting Hitler, who had by some accounts not died in his Berlin bunker. The flower remains the symbol of elite mountain troops in Germany, and has figured often in songs; thus, in the words of one song from 1933, "Adolf Hitlers Lieblingsblume ist das schlichte Edelweiß" ("Adolf Hitler's favorite flower is the simple edelweiss"). The latter may be heard in the 1973 documentary *The World At War, Vol. 1: A New Germany, 1933–39,* directed by Hugh Raggett (London: Thames Television, 1980) (VHS release New York: HBO Video 1063).

♩9.5

12. See Stacy Wolf, *A Problem Like Maria,* 223–24, for a related discussion of the show's "whiteness."

13. Bikel is, in fact, Jewish and Zionist; born in Vienna, he moved to Palestine in the 1930s.

14. Inevitably, Julie Andrews's performance as Maria merged for audiences with her performance in *Mary Poppins,* released a year earlier; see Peter Kemp's "How Do You Solve a 'Problem' Like Maria von Poppins?" (pp. 55–61 in *Musicals: Hollywood and Beyond*). We may add, to the parallels Kemp lays out, a shared "Madonna" trope: both roles assign the name of the Madonna, Mary/

Maria, to a (presumed) virgin who assumes the role of a surrogate mother. Kemp identifies, as part of Andrews's vocal persona, "a perfectly pitched, superbly articulated vocal instrument ideal for the lyric-dependent songs of stage and movie musicals," and differentiates her performance from the "egocentric appropriation" typical of other female singers in American musicals (60).

15. Perhaps deliberately, the harmony for the horn-calls shifts chromatically with the last three words, "time to go," at this point replicating precisely the notes and two-part harmonies that open Beethoven's *Les Adieux* Sonata (*Das Lebewohl*), with its similar use of horn-call figures, or "horn fifths," to signify departure.   ♫ 9.10

16. I am indebted to Mitchell Morris for much of my reading of *Cabaret*'s camp dimension, and with the show's engagement with sexuality generally; see his "*Cabaret*, America's Weimar, and Mythologies of the Gay Subject" (*American Music* 22(2004): 145–57); for an extended study that addresses similar issues, see Linda Mizejewski, *Divine Decadence: Fascism, Female Spectacle, and the Makings of Sally Bowles* (Princeton: Princeton University Press, 1992). Louise Brooks (1906–85) was an American silent film star who appeared in a brief series of European films between 1929 and 1930, most notoriously as Lulu (a prostitute) in *Der Büchse der Pandora* (*Pandora's Box*, G. W. Pabst, 1929, based, like Berg's unfinished 1935 opera *Lulu*, on Frank Wedekind's *Lulu* plays). Consigned to virtual exile by the Hollywood studio system in the 1930s, Brooks gradually became an icon of feminist defiance and reemerged as a writer on film from the 1950s on; her trademark pageboy hairstyle was virtually copied for Minnelli's Sally Bowles. Dietrich (1901–92), a Berlin native, starred as a nightclub singer who ruins the life of a professor in *The Blue Angel* (Josef von Sternberg, 1930); shortly thereafter, Dietrich followed Sternberg to America, where she remained throughout her life an icon of scandalous sexuality, famous for her occasional appearances in men's clothing (e.g., in Sternberg's 1930 *Morocco*); her affairs with both men and women were widely gossiped about. Regarding Minnelli's apparent channeling of her mother's persona, Mitchell Morris writes, "Minnelli's hyperexpressive performance, developed, according to her, in collaboration with Fosse, creates a sense of her own mother's idiosyncrasies even as it evokes silent film acting. As important is the quality of extreme neediness she repeatedly conveys. . . . We may easily understand her exaggerations as the façade of security that gives away the secret of the longing it pretends to conceal. . . . Playing Judy in this way not only helped Minnelli win the Oscar for Best Actress, it also marked her ascent to the status of gay diva. A crucial aspect of such a role has always been artifice: the most enduring gay divas have always tended towards intensely mannered modes of self-presentation" (151–52).

17. The original time frame for the show was 1929–30, but this was moved up for the film to 1931, placing its events closer to when Adolf Hitler became Chancellor in early 1933. The race riots in America spread from Harlem (New York City, summer 1964) to Watts (Los Angeles, summer 1965), and to Cleveland and Chicago (summer 1966), in an era framed by the assassinations of black leaders Malcolm X (February 1965) and Martin Luther King, Jr. (April 1968).

18. Perhaps by design, the lyric in "Cabaret" (Sally's big number in Act II) permits the casting of either an English or an American Sally, since there is a Chelsea

in both countries (two in America, one near Boston and the other a neighborhood in Manhattan).

19. There was some historical basis for this claim, since before the Nazi purge in 1934, beginning with the "Night of Long Knives," homosexuals were sufficiently prominent in the party that they became a political liability.

Chapter Ten
Exoticism

1. The standard text on this subject is Edward Said, *Orientalism* (New York: Vintage, 1994).

2. See Michael Beckerman, "The Sword on the Wall: Japanese Elements and Their Significance in *The Mikado*," *The Musical Quarterly* 73 (1989): 303–19. Of principal concern in Mike Leigh's *Topsy-Turvy* is how tenuous the larger enterprise of the Savoy operas was by this point, fraught with mistrust on both sides, with Gilbert sensitive to any perceived slight to the value of his own contribution, and Sullivan concerned that his continued collaboration with Gilbert constituted a cheapening of his art. What *Topsy-Turvy* shows with particular effectiveness is the wide disparity between the muddled lives of those who created and performed in *The Mikado*, and the near-legendary perfection of the work itself. The film thereby makes clear the place and importance of each individual contribution— Gilbert's tenacious and meticulous care for "authenticity" of appearance and action (in part to set in relief his pointed manipulations of both the English language and English cultural tropes), Sullivan's warm enthusiasm and ease of responsive musical invention, England's position as a smug perpetrator of cultural imperialism (which is seen to be an important shared background of not only the three main parties, but also the cast), the costume designer's ability to balance "authenticity" against the expected standard of feminine display, the quirks of a stock company of individual singer-actors whose strengths and proven assets had to be both preserved and modified to accommodate the new show, while their foibles and potentially disastrous weaknesses were held in check, etc. But the film also believably places the calm managerial style of Richard D'Oyly Carte squarely at the center of it all, as the principal enabling and stabilizing force. It was Carte— a patient, astute impresario / entrepeneur / businessman and visionary—who brought Gilbert and Sullivan together and managed to keep them together (for a time, at least), and who in 1881 established the Savoy Theatre so as to provide their collaborative work a suitable home.

3. Oscar Wilde would be even more outrageous in *The Importance of Being Earnest* (premiered 1895, just before Wilde's ruinous trial), when Algernon confesses to being a "Bunburyist," referring fairly crudely to the physical act of sodomy, should anyone care to notice.

4. This attitude of self-satisfied obliviousness is subtly rendered, in *Topsy-Turvy*, through casual conversation between two of the English players—held symbolically over a lunch of oysters that will later make them violently ill—about the slaughter of the celebrated English General Charles Gordon by al-Mahdi and his rebel force to end the siege of Khartoum in late January 1885. They scarcely

blink when their companion, a Scotsman, gently reminds them of English atrocities on the Isle of Skye just three years earlier during the so-called Crofters' War—which seem, however, not to have taken place as he describes them.

5. See Said, *Orientalism*.

6. See Fink, "Rhythm and Text Setting in *The Mikado*."

7. For example, the episode in which the King cannot punish Tuptim in Anna's presence—just after "Shall We Dance" (the two scenes, taken together, mark the climactic point of their relationship)—seems to derive from a scene of public punishment described in Anna Leonowens's memoirs, but which was probably fabricated by her.

8. Scott Miller, "The King and I," pp. 37–51 in *Deconstructing Harold Hill: An Insider's Guide to Musical Theatre*, (Portsmouth, N.H.: Heinemann, 2000).

9. In Prince's words, the theater billboards made the show look like "a limited engagement of a Japanese show" (quoted in Secrest, *Stephen Sondheim*, 282).

10. As quoted in Wayman Wong, "Actors Remember *Pacific Overtures*," *The Sondheim Review* 4, no. 4 (spring, 1998): 23.

11. In an off-Broadway revival in 1984 directed by Fran Soeder, Weidman and Sondheim returned once again to the show, giving slightly more emphasis to the personal story and toning down the brashness of the Kabuki style. This version, performed in a smaller, more intimate theater, ran for fewer performances than the original; nevertheless, many felt it to be an improvement, and it became the licensed version of the show.

12. Secrest, *Stephen Sondheim*, 280; her quotations are from Howard Kissel writing in *Horizon*, October 1981. The punning title "Pacific Overtures" comes from a passage in Perry's journal, read aloud in the course of the show, in which he makes clear that he means to back up America's "peaceful" overtures with overwhelming force, if necessary.

13. For an extensive, more technically grounded discussion of these musical devices, see Stephen Banfield, "*Pacific Overtures*," chapter 8 of his *Sondheim's Broadway Musicals* (Ann Arbor: University of Michigan Press, 1993).

14. See Stephen Banfield, "*Pacific Overtures*," in *Sondheim's Broadway Musicals*, 266–68, for a discussion of Sondheim's manipulation of syllable-counts in "Poems."

15. As quoted in Wong, "Actors Remember *Pacific Overtures*," 23.

Appendix A
Art and Commerce: The Business of Making Musicals

1. While this account is based largely on Bernard Rosenberg and Ernest Harburg (*The Broadway Musical; Collaboration in Commerce and Art* [New York and London: New York University Press, 1993] 71–175), there are of course many other treatments, from a variety of perspectives. Ethan Mordden provides an engaging account of how each creative role developed historically, in *Broadway Babies: The People Who Made the American Musical* (New York: Oxford University Press, 1983). Richard Kislan focuses on the products and contribution of those creative parties in chapters 10–14 of *The Musical: A Look at the American*

Musical Theater, rev. exp. ed. (New York and London: Applause, 1995). Lehman Engel builds his consideration of individual musicals around such considerations in *The American Musical Theater: A Consideration* (New York: Macmillan, 1967). (Martin Gottfried manages to accomplish much the same task in *Broadway Musicals* [New York: Harry N. Abrams, 1979], but it's sometimes hard to notice against the backdrop of a truly gorgeous panoply of pictures.) Mark Steyn's *Broadway Babies Say Goodnight* assembles the ingredients differently, but with provocative insight. For an insightful account of a deeper, thematic parallel between the American musical and American business, see Carey Wall's "There's No Business Like Show Business: A Speculative Reading of the Broadway Musical," pp. 24–43 in *Approaches to the American Musical.*

BIBLIOGRAPHY

American Pop: An Audio History. From Minstrel to Mojo: On Record, 1893–1946, vol. 1 (3 of 9 CDs total). Toronto: West Hill Audio Archives, 1997–98.

Alpert, Hollis. *The Life and Times of* Porgy and Bess: *The Story of an American Classic*. New York: Knopf, 1990.

Altman, Rick. *The American Film Musical*. Bloomington and Indianapolis: Indiana University Press, 1987.

Austin, William W. *"Susanna," "Jeanie," and "The Old Folks at Home": The Songs of Stephen C. Foster from His Time to Ours*. 2nd ed. Urbana and Chicago: University of Illinois Press, 1989.

Averill, Gage. *Four Parts, No Waiting: A Social History of American Barbershop Harmony*. Oxford and New York: Oxford University Press, 2003.

Banfield, Stephen. *Sondheim's Broadway Musicals*. Ann Arbor: University of Michigan Press, 1993.

Baur, Steven. "Let Me Make the Ballads of a Nation and I Care Not Who Makes Its Laws: Music, Culture, and Social Politics in the United States, c. 1860–1890." Ph.D. diss., University of California, Los Angeles, 2001.

Baxter, Carol G. "The Federal Theatre Project's Musical Productions." Pp. 381–88 in *Musical Theatre in America; Papers and Proceedings of the Conference on the Musical theatre in America*. Edited by Glenn Loney. Westport, Conn. and London: Greenwood Press, 1981.

Beckerman, Michael. "The Sword on the Wall: Japanese Elements and their Significance in *The Mikado*." *The Musical Quarterly* 73 (1989): 303–19.

Bellman, Jonathan, ed. *The Exotic in Western Music*. Boston: Northeastern University, 1998.

Bennett, Robert Russell. *"The Broadway Sound": The Autobiography and Selected Essays of Robert Russell Bennett*. Edited by George J. Ferencz. Rochester, N.Y.: University of Rochester Press, 1999.

Bishop, André. "Preface" to *Assassins*, by John Weidman and Stephen Sondheim. New York: Theatre Communications Group, 1991.

Block, Geoffrey. *Enchanted Evenings: The Broadway Musical from* Show Boat *to* Sondheim. New York and Oxford: Oxford University Press, 1997.

———. *Richard Rodgers*. New Haven and London: Yale University Press, 2003.

———. *The Richard Rodgers Reader*. Oxford and New York: Oxford University Press, 2002.

Bordman, Gerald. *American Musical Theatre; A Chronicle*. New York: Oxford University Press, 1986.

———. *American Operetta from* H.M.S. Pinafore *to* Sweeney Todd. New York and Oxford: Oxford University Press, 1981.

Braunlich, Phyliss Cole. *Haunted by Home: The Life and Letters of Lynn Riggs*. Norman: University of Oklahoma Press, 1988.

Brodsky, Warren. "Joseph Schillinger (1895–1943): Music Science Promethean." *American Music* 21 (2003): 45–73.

Burton, Humphrey. *Leonard Bernstein*. New York: Doubleday, 1994.

Chanan, Michael. *Repeated Takes: A Short History of Recording and Its Effects on Music*. London: Verso, 1995.

Citron, Stephen. *Sondheim and Lloyd-Webber: The New Musical*. Oxford and New York: Oxford University Press, 2001.

Clutter, Timothy. "Alone: The 'Outsider' in Sondheim's Works." *The Sondheim Review* 6, no. 3 (Winter 2000): 26–29.

Cockrell, David. *Demons of Disorder: Early Blackface Minstrels and Their World*. Cambridge: Cambridge University Press, 1997.

_____. "Nineteenth-Century Popular Music." Pp. 158–85 in *The Cambridge History of American Music*. Edited by David Nicholls. Cambridge and New York: Cambridge University Press, 1998.

Crawford, Richard. "It Ain't Necessarily Soul: Gershwin's *Porgy and Bess* as a Symbol." Pp. 17–38 in *Yearbook of Inter-American Musical Research* (1972).

Czitrom, Daniel J. *Media and the American Mind from Morse to McLuhan*. Chapel Hill: University of North Carolina Press, 1982.

DiMaggio, Paul. "Cultural Boundaries and Structural Change: The Extension of the High Culture Model to Theater, Opera, and the Dance, 1900–1940." Pp. 21–57 in *Cultivating Differences: Symbolic Boundaries and the Making of Inequality*. Edited by Michèle Lamont and Marcel Fournier. Chicago and London: University of Chicago Press, 1992.

Douglas, Susan. *Inventing American Broadcasting, 1899–1922*. Baltimore: Johns Hopkins University Press, 1987.

Dyer, Richard. *Only Entertainment*. London and New York: Routledge, 1992.

Engel, Lehman. *The American Musical Theater: A Consideration*. New York: Macmillan, 1967.

Everett, William A., and Paul R. Laird, eds. *The Cambridge Companion to the Musical*. Cambridge and New York: Cambridge University Press, 2002.

Ewen, David. *Complete Book of the American Musical Theater*. New York: Henry Holt, 1959.

Fink, Robert. "Rhythm and Text Setting in *The Mikado*." *Nineteenth-Century Music* 14 (1990–91): 31–47.

Finson, Jon W. *The Voices That Are Gone: Themes in Nineteenth-Century American Popular Song*. New York and Oxford: Oxford University Press, 1994.

Fleischer, Leonard. "'More Beautiful Than True' or 'Never Mind a Small Disaster': The Art of Illusion in *Pacific Overtures*." Pp. 107–24 in *Stephen Sondheim; A Casebook*. Edited by Joanne Gordon. New York and London: Garland, 1997.

Forte, Allen. *The American Popular Ballad of the Golden Era, 1924–1950*. Princeton: Princeton University Press, 1995.

_____. *Listening to Classic American Popular Songs*. New Haven and London: Yale University Press, 2001.

Friedwald, Will. *Stardust Melodies: A Biography of Twelve of America's Most Popular Songs*. New York: Pantheon, 2002.

Furia, Philip. *Ira Gershwin: The Art of the Lyricist*. New York and Oxford: Oxford University Press, 1996.

_____. *Irving Berlin: A Life in Song*. New York: Schirmer, 1998.

_____. *The Poets of Tin Pan Alley; A History of America's Great Lyricists*. New York and Oxford: Oxford University Press, 1990.

Gans, Herbert. *Popular Culture and High Culture*. New York: Basic, 1974.

Gänzl, Kurt. *The Musical; A Concise History*. Boston: Northeastern University Press, 1997.

Gellner, Ernest. *Nationalism*. London: Weidenfeld and Nicolson, 1997.

Gilbert, Steven E. *The Music of Gershwin*. New Haven: Yale University Press, 1995.

Gintautiene, Kristina. "The Black Crook: Ballet in the Gilded Age (1866–1876)." Ph.D. diss., New York University, 1984.

Gordon, Eric A. *Mark the Music: The Life and Work of Marc Blitzstein*. New York: St. Martin's Press, 1989.

Gordon, Joanne. *Art Isn't Easy; The Achievement of Stephen Sondheim*. Carbondale and Edwardsville: Southern Illinois University Press, 1990.

_____, ed. *Stephen Sondheim; A Casebook*. New York and London: Garland, 1997.

Gottlieb, Jack. "The Music of Leonard Bernstein: A Study of Melodic Manipulations." D.M.A. diss., University of Illinois, 1964.

Gottlieb, Robert, and Robert Kimball. *Reading Lyrics*. New York: Pantheon, 2000.

Gottfried, Martin. *Broadway Musicals*. New York: Harry N. Abrams, 1979.

_____. *More Broadway Musicals: Since 1980*. New York: Harry N. Abrams, 1991.

Graziano, John. "Images of African Americans: African-American Musical Theatre, *Show Boat* and *Porgy and Bess*." Pp. 63–76 in *The Cambridge Companion to the Musical,* edited by William A. Everett and Paul R. Laird. Cambridge and New York: Cambridge University Press, 2002.

Green, Stanley. *Broadway Musicals Show by Show*. Milwaukee: Hal Leonard, 1985.

_____. *Ring Bells! Sing Songs! Broadway Musicals of the 1930's*. New Rochelle, N.Y.: Arlington House, 1971.

_____. *The World of Musical Comedy; The Story of the American Musical Stage as Told Through the Careers of its Foremost Composers and Lyricists*. New York: Ziff-Davis, 1962.

Hamm, Charles. *Music in the New World*. New York: Norton, 1983.

_____. *Putting Popular Music in Its Place*. Cambridge: Cambridge University Press, 1995.

_____. "The Theatre Guild Production of *Porgy and Bess. The Journal of the American Musicological Society* 40 (1987): 495–532.

_____. *Yesterdays: Popular Song in America*. New York and London: Norton, 1983.

Hirsch, Foster. *Harold Prince and the American Musical Theatre*. Cambridge and New York: Cambridge University Press, 1989.

Horn, Barbara Lee. *The Age of* Hair; *Evolution and Impact of Broadway's First Rock Musical*. New York, Westport, Conn., and London: Greenwood Press, 1991.

Horn, David. "Who Loves You Porgy? The Debates Surrounding Gershwin's Musical." Pp. 109–26 in *Approaches to the American Musical*. Edited by Robert Lawson-Peebles. Exeter: University of Exeter Press, 1996.

Horowitz, Joseph. *Wagner Nights; An American History*. Berkeley, Los Angeles, and London: University of California Press, 1994.

Horowitz, Mark Eden. *Sondheim on Music: Minor Details and Major Decisions*. Lanham, Md. and Oxford: Scarecrow, 2003.

Huggins, Nathan Irvin. *Harlem Renaissance*. London, Oxford, and New York: Oxford University Press, 1971.

_____. *Voices from the Harlem Renaissance*. London, Oxford, and New York: Oxford University Press, 1976.

Ignatiev, Noel. *How the Irish Became White*. New York: Routledge, 1995.

Jackson, Richard. *Popular Songs of Nineteenth-Century America*. New York: Dover, 1976.

Jacobs, Arthur. *Arthur Sullivan: A Victorian Musician*. 2nd ed. Portland, Ore.: Amadeus, 1992.

Jasen, David A. *Tin Pan Alley; The Composers, the Songs, the Performers and Their Times*. New York: Donald I. Fine, 1988.

Jenkins, Jennifer R. "'Say It with Firecrackers': Defining the 'War Musical' of the 1940s." *American Music* 19 (2001): 315–39.

Kammerhofer-Aggermann, Ulrike, and Alexander G. Keul, eds. *"The Sound of Music" zwischen Mythos und Marketing*. Salzburg: Salzburger Landesinstitut für Volkskunde, 2000.

Kanter, Kenneth Aaron. *The Jews of Tin Pan Alley: The Jewish Contribution to American Popular Music, 1830–1940*. New York: Ktav, and Cincinnati: American Jewish Archives, 1982.

Kemp, Peter. "How Do You Solve a 'Problem' Like Maria von Poppins?" Pp. 55–61 in *Musicals: Hollywood and Beyond*. Edited by Bill Marshall and Robynn Stilwell. Exeter, England, and Portland, Ore.: Intellect, 2000.

Kenney, William Howland. *Recorded Music in American Life: The Phonograph and Popular Memory, 1890–1945*. New York and Oxford: Oxford University Press, 1999.

Kislan, Richard. *The Musical: A Look at the American Musical Theater*. Rev. exp. ed. New York and London: Applause, 1995.

Kleinhans, Chuck. "Taking Out the Trash: Camp and the Politics of Parody." Pp. 182–201 in *The Politics and Poetics of Camp*, edited by Moe Meyer. London and New York: Routledge, 1994.

Kreuger, Miles. *Show Boat: The Story of a Classic American Muscial*. New York and Oxford: Oxford University Press, 1977.

Lamb, Andrew. *150 Years of Popular Musical Theatre*. New Haven and London: Yale University Press, 2000.

Laufe, Abe. *Broadway's Greatest Musicals*. Rev. ed. New York: Funk and Wagnalls, 1977.

Laurents, Arthur. *Original Story By: A Memoir of Broadway and Hollywood*. New York: Knopf, 2000.

Lawson-Peebles, Robert, ed. *Approaches to the American Musical*. Exeter: University of Exeter Press, 1996.

Leppert, Richard. *The Sight of Sound: Music, Representation, and the History of the Body*. Berkeley, Los Angeles, and London: University of California Press, 1993.

Lerner, Alan Jay. *The Musical Theatre: A Celebration*. New York, St. Louis, San Francisco, Hamburg, and Mexico: McGraw-Hill, 1986.

Levine, Lawrence W. *Highbrow / Lowbrow: The Emergence of Cultural Hierarchy in Amercia*. Cambridge, Mass. and London: Harvard University Press, 1988.

Lewis, David L. *When Harlem Was in Vogue*. New York: Vintage, 1982.

Lhamon, Jr., W. T. *Raising Cain: Blackface Performance from Jim Crow to Hip Hop*. Cambridge, Mass. and London: Harvard University Press, 1998.

Locke, Ralph. "Constructing the Oriental 'Other': Saint-Saëns's *Samson et Dalila*." *Cambridge Opera Journal* 3 (1991): 261–302.

———. "Cutthroats and Casbah Dancers, Muezzins and Timeless Sands: Musical Images of the Middle East." *Nineteenth-Century Music* 22 (1998): 20–53 (and pp. 104–36 in *The Exotic in Western Music*, edited by Jonathan Bellman. Boston: Northeastern University, 1998).

———. "Reflections on Orientalism in Opera and Musical Theater." *The Opera Quarterly* 10 (1993): 48–64.

Loney, Glenn, ed. *Musical Theatre in America; Papers and Proceedings of the Conference on the Musical Theatre in America*. Westport, Conn. and London: Greenwood Press, 1981.

Lott, Eric. *Love and Theft: Blackface Minstrelsy and the American Working Class*. New York and Oxford: Oxford University Press, 1993.

Lovensheimer, Jim. "Stephen Sondheim and the Musical of the Outsider." Pp. 181–96 in *The Cambridge Companion to the Musical*, edited by William A. Everett and Paul R. Laird. Cambridge and New York: Cambridge University Press, 2002.

MacDonald, J. Fred. *Don't Touch That Dial: Radio Programming in American Life from 1920 to 1960*. Chicago: Nelson-Hall, 1979.

Mahar, William J. *Behind the Burnt Cork Mask: Early Blackface Minstrelsy and Antebellum American Popular Culture*. Urbana: University of Illinois Press, 1999.

Marshall, Bill, and Robynn Stilwell, eds. *Musicals: Hollywood and Beyond*. Exeter and Portland: Intellect Books, 2000.

Mast, Gerald. *Can't Help Singin': The American Musical on Stage and Screen*. Woodstock, N.Y.: Overlook, 1987.

Mates, Julian. *America's Musical Stage; Two Hundred Years of Musical Theatre*. Westport, Conn., and London: Greenwood, 1985.

McClary, Susan. "Pitches, Expression, Ideology: An Exercise in Mediation." *Enclitic* 7 (1983): 76–86.

Melnick, Jeffrey. *A Right to Sing the Blues; African Americans, Jews, and American Popular Song*. Cambridge, Mass., and London: Harvard University, 1999.

Millard, Andre. *America on Record: A History of Recorded Sound*. Cambridge: Cambridge University Press, 1995.

Miller, D. A. *Place for Us [Essay on the Broadway Musical]*. Cambridge, Mass., and London: Harvard University Press, 1998.

Miller, Scott. "*Assassins* and the Concept Musical." Pp. 187–204 in *Stephen Sondheim; A Casebook,* edited by Joanne Gordon. New York and London: Garland, 1997.

———. *Deconstructing Harold Hill: An Insider's Guide to Musical Theatre.* Portsmouth, N.H.: Heinemann, 2000.

———. *From "Assassins" to "West Side Story"; The Director's Guide to Musical Theatre.* Portsmouth, N.H.: Heinemann, 1996.

———. *Rebels with Applause: Broadway's Groundbreaking Musicals.* Portsmouth, N.H.: Heinemann, 2001.

Millington, Barry. "Nuremberg Trial: Is There Anti-Semitism in *Die Meistersinger?*" *Cambridge Opera Journal* 3 (1991): 247–60.

Mizejewski, Linda. *Divine Decadence: Fascism, Female Spectacle, and the Makings of Sally Bowles.* Princeton: Princeton University Press, 1992.

Mordden, Ethan. *Beautiful Mornin': The Broadway Musical in the 1940s.* New York and Oxford: Oxford University Press, 1999.

———. *Better Foot Forward; The History of the American Musical Theatre.* New York: Grossman, 1976.

———. *Broadway Babies: The People Who Made the American Musical.* New York: Oxford University Press, 1983.

———. *Coming Up Roses: The Broadway Musical in the 1950s.* New York and Oxford: Oxford University Press, 1998.

———. *Make Believe; The Broadway Musical in the 1920s.* New York and Oxford: Oxford University Press, 1997.

———. *Open a New Window: The Broadway Musical in the 1960s.* New York and Oxford: Oxford University Press, 2001.

Morris, Mitchell. "*Cabaret,* America's Weimar, and Mythologies of the Gay Subject." *American Music* 22(2004): 145–57.

Most, Andrea. "'We Know We Belong to the Land': Jews and the American Musical Theater." Ph.D. diss., Brandeis University, 2001.

Nelson, Thomas K. "The Fantasy of Absolute Music." Ph.D. diss., University of Minnesota, 1998.

Nicholls, David, ed. *The Cambridge History of American Music.* Cambridge and New York: Cambridge University Press, 1998.

Nolan, Frederick. *The Sound of Their Music; The Story of Rodgers and Hammerstein.* New York: Applause Theatre and Cinema Books, 2002.

Ostrow, Stuart. *A Producer's Broadway Journey.* Westport, Conn., and London: Praeger, 1999.

Peyser, Joan. *Leonard Bernstein: A Biography.* New York: Beech Tree, 1987.

Porter, Cole. *The Complete Lyrics of Cole Porter.* Edited by Robert Kimball. New York: Knopf, 1983.

Preston, Katherine A. "American Musical Theatre Before the Twentieth Century." Pp. 3–28 in *The Cambridge Companion to the Musical,* edited by William A. Everett and Paul R. Laird. Cambridge and New York: Cambridge University Press, 2002.

Riggs, Lynn. *Green Grow the Lilacs.* New York and Los Angeles: S. French, 1931.

Riis, Thomas L. *Just Before Jazz: Black Musical Theater in New York, 1890–1915.* Washington, D. C.: Smithsonian Institution Press, 1989.

_____. *More Than Just Minstrel Shows: The Rise of Black Musical Theatre at the Turn of the Century.* Brooklyn: Institute for Studies in American Music, 1992.

_____, ed. *The Music and Scripts of "In Dahomey."* Madison: A-R Editions, 1996.

Riis, Thomas L., and Ann Sears, with William A. Everett. "The Successors of Rodgers and Hammerstein from the 1940s to the 1960s." Pp. 120–36 in *The Cambridge Companion to the Musical.* Edited by William A. Everett and Paul R. Laird. Cambridge and New York: Cambridge University Press, 2002.

Roberts, John Storm. *The Latin Tinge: The Impact of Latin American Music on the United States.* 2nd ed. New York and Oxford: Oxford University Press, 1999.

Robbins, Tim. Cradle Will Rock: *The Movie and the Moment.* New York: New-market, 2000.

Rogin, Michael. *Blackface, White Noise: Jewish Immigrants in the Hollywood Melting Pot.* Berkeley, Los Angeles, and London: University of California Press, 1996.

_____. "New Deal Blackface." Pp. 175–82 in *Hollywood Musicals: The Film Reader.* Edited by Steven Cohan. London and New York: Routledge, 2002.

Rosenberg, Bernard, and Ernest Harburg. *The Broadway Musical: Collaboration in Commerce and Art.* New York and London: New York University Press, 1993.

Rubin, Joan Shelley. *The Making of Middlebrow Culture.* Chapel Hill: University of North Carolina Press, 1992.

Runyon, Damon. *A Treasury of Damon Runyon.* Edited by Clark Kinnaird. New York: Modern Library, 1958.

Said, Edward. *Orientalism.* New York: Vintage, 1994 (originally published New York: Pantheon, 1978).

Sanjek, Russell. *Pennies from Heaven: The American Popular Music Business in the Twentieth Century.* Updated by David Sanjek. New York: Da Capo Press, 1996 (originally published 1988).

Sears, Ann. "The Coming of the Musical Play." Pp. 120–36 in *The Cambridge Companion to the Musical,* edited by William A. Everett and Paul R. Laird. Cambridge and New York: Cambridge University Press, 2002.

Secrest, Meryle. *Leonard Bernstein: A Life.* New York: Alfred A. Knopf, 1994.

_____. *Somewhere for Me: A Biography of Richard Rodgers.* New York: Knopf, 2001.

_____. *Stephen Sondheim: A Life.* New York: Knopf, 1998.

Sellin, Yara. "'Equality Is Out of the Question': Constructions of Class and English Identity in *H.M.S. Pinafore.*" Unpublished paper read at the Annual Meeting of the American Musicological Society, Columbus, Ohio, October–November 2002.

Shirley, Wayne D. "The Coming of Deep River." *American Music* 4 (1997): 493–534.

_____. "'Rotating' *Porgy and Bess.*" Pp. 21–34 in *The Gershwin Style: New Looks at the Music of George Gershwin,* edited by Wayne Schneider. New York and Oxford: Oxford University Press, 1999.

Smith, Catherine Parsons. *William Grant Still: A Study in Contradictions.* Berkeley and Los Angeles: University of California Press, 2000.

Smith, Cecil, and Glenn Litton. *Musical Comedy in America.* New York: Theatre Arts Books, 1950 and 1981.

Stanfield, Peter. "From the Vulgar to the Refined: American Vernacular and Blackface Minstrelsy in *Showboat.*" Pp. 147–56 in *Musicals: Hollywood and Beyond.* Edited by Bill Marshall and Robynn Stilwell. Exeter, England, and Portland, Ore.: Intellect, 2000.

Steyn, Mark. *Broadway Babies Say Goodnight: Musicals Then and Now.* New York: Routledge, 1999.

Swain, Joseph P. *The Broadway Musical; A Critical and Musical Survey.* 2nd ed. Lanham, Md., and Oxford: Scarecrow, 2002.

Swayne, Steven. "Hearing Sondheim's Voices." Ph.D. diss. University of California, Berkeley, 1999.

Taruskin, Richard. "Nationalism." Pp. 689–706 in *The New Grove Dictionary of Music and Musicians,* vol. 17. Edited by Stanley Sadie and John Tyrrell. London: Macmillan, 2001.

Tawa, Nicholas E. *The Way to Tin Pan Alley: American Popular Song, 1866–1910.* New York: Schirmer, and London: Collier Macmillan, 1990.

Toll, Robert C. *Blacking Up: The Minstrel Show in Nineteenth-Century America.* London, Oxford, and New York: Oxford University Press, 1974.

Twain, Mark. *Mark Twain's Travels with Mr. Brown,* collected and edited by Franklin Walker and G. Ezra Dane, New York: Knopf, 1940.

Vallillo, Stephen M. "George M. Cohan's *Little Johnny Jones.*" Pp. 233–43 in *Musical Theatre in America: Papers and Proceedings of the Conference on the Musical Theatre in America,* edited by Glenn Loney. Westport, Conn., and London: Greenwood, 1981.

Wall, Carey. "There's No Business Like Show Business: A Speculative Reading of the Broadway Musical." Pp. 24–43 in *Approaches to the American Musical.* Edited by Robert Lawson-Peebles. Exeter: University of Exeter Press, 1996.

Walser, Robert. "The Rock and Roll Era." Pp. 345-87 in *The Cambridge History of American Music,* edited by David Nicholls. Cambridge: Cambridge University Press, 1998.

Warfield, Scott. "From *Hair* to *Rent:* Is 'Rock' a Four-Letter Word on Broadway?" Pp. 231–45 in *The Cambridge Companion to the Musical,* edited by William A. Everett and Paul R. Laird. Cambridge and New York: Cambridge University Press, 2002.

Wells, Elizabeth. "*West Side Story* and the Hispanic." *Echo: A Music-Centered Journal* 2, no. 1 (Spring 2000). Online at www.echo.ucla.edu.

Wilder, Alec. *American Popular Song: The Great Innovators, 1900–1950.* Edited by James T. Maher. New York and Oxford: Oxford University Press, 1990 (originally published in 1972).

Wilk, Max. *OK! The Story of* Oklahoma! New York: Grove, 1993.

Willson, Meredith. *"But He Doesn't Know the Territory."* New York: Putnam, 1959.

Winans, Robert B. "Early Minstrel Show Music, 1843–1852." Pp. 71–97 in *Musical Theatre in America: Papers and Proceedings of the Conference on the Mu-*

sical Theatre in America, edited by Glenn Loney. Westport, Conn., and London: Greenwood, 1981.

Wintz, Cary D. *Black Culture and the Harlem Renaissance.* Houston, Tex.: Rice University Press, 1988.

Wolf, Stacy. *A Problem Like Maria: Gender and Sexuality in the American Musical.* Ann Arbor: University of Michigan Press, 2002.

Woll, Allen L. *Black Musical Theatre: From* Coontown *to* Dreamgirls. Baton Rouge: Louisiana State University Press, 1989.

Womack, Craig S. *Red on Red: Native American Literary Separatism.* Minneapolis and London: University of Minnesota Press, 1999.

Wong, Wayman. "Actors Remember *Pacific Overtures.*" *The Sondheim Review* 4, no. 4 (Spring 1998): 23.

Wood, Graham. "The Development of Song Forms in the Broadway and Hollywood Musicals of Richard Rodgers." Ph.D. diss., University of Minnesota, 2000.

The World at War, Vol. 1: A New Germany 1933–39. Documentary directed by Hugh Raggett. London: Thames Television, 1980 (VHS release New York: HBO Video 1063).

Wren, Gayden. *A Most Ingenious Paradox; The Art of Gilbert and Sullivan.* Oxford: Oxford University Press, 2001.

Zadan, Craig. *Sondheim & Co.* 2nd ed. (greatly expanded from the 1974 edition). New York: Harper & Row, 1986.

INDEX